Debating Regime Legitimacy in Contemporary China

This comprehensive volume is a three-part study of whether the Chinese political system has maintained a significant degree of regime legitimacy in the context of rising domestic discontent, in particular the popular protests against socio-economic inequality and environment degradation. Part I presents the scholarly debate on the theoretical refinement and empirical measurement of regime legitimacy in contemporary China. Part II focuses on the challenges to regime legitimacy of the increasingly widespread popular protests and civil activism. Part III examines the regime's responses to these challenges, including coercive repression, adaptation and economic performance. This book finds that while repression can hardly stop popular protests – and often backfires – economic performance legitimacy is increasingly difficult to be maintained. The only way out is the adaptation to the changing domestic and international environment. The chapters in this collection were originally published in *Journal of Contemporary China*.

Suisheng Zhao is a Professor and the Director of the Center for China–US Cooperation at Josef Korbel School of International Studies, University of Denver, USA, and the Founding Editor of *Journal of Contemporary China*.

Debating Regime Legitimacy in Contemporary China

Popular Protests and Regime Performances

Edited by

Suisheng Zhao

Routledge
Taylor & Francis Group
LONDON AND NEW YORK

First published 2017 by Routledge

2 Park Square, Milton Park, Abingdon, Oxfordshire OX14 4RN
52 Vanderbilt Avenue, New York, NY 10017

Routledge is an imprint of the Taylor & Francis Group, an informa business

First issued in paperback 2018

British Library Cataloguing in Publication Data
A catalogue record for this book is available from the British Library

ISBN 13: 978-1-138-28961-1 (hbk)
ISBN 13: 978-0-367-13931-5 (pbk)

Typeset in Times
by diacriTech, Chennai

Publisher's Note
The publisher accepts responsibility for any inconsistencies that may have arisen during the conversion of this book from journal articles to book chapters, namely the possible inclusion of journal terminology.

Contents

Citation Information

The following chapters were originally published in the *Journal of Contemporary China*. When citing this material, please use the original issue numbers, date of publication and page numbering for each article, as follows:

Chapter 1

How Do You Solve a Problem Like Legitimacy? Contributing to a new research agenda
Peter Sandby-Thomas
Journal of Contemporary China, volume 23, issue 88 (2014) pp. 575–592

Chapter 2

Political Legitimacy in Contemporary China Revisited: theoretical refinement and empirical operationalization
Gunter Schubert
Journal of Contemporary China, volume 23, issue 88 (2014) pp. 593–611

Chapter 3

The Debate on Regime Legitimacy in China: bridging the wide gulf between Western and Chinese scholarship
Jinghan Zeng
Journal of Contemporary China, volume 23, issue 88 (2014) pp. 612–635

Chapter 4

Political Process and Widespread Protests in China: the 2010 labor protest
Ray Ou Yang
Journal of Contemporary China, volume 24, issue 91 (2015) pp. 21–42

Chapter 5

Disorganized Popular Contention and Local Institutional Building in China: a case study in Guangdong
Feng Chen and Yi Kang
Journal of Contemporary China, volume 25, issue 100 (2016) pp. 596–612

Chapter 6

Pollution, Institutions and Street Protests in Urban China
Yang Zhong and Wonjae Hwang
Journal of Contemporary China, volume 25, issue 98 (2016) pp. 216–232

Chapter 7

Pushing the Envelope for Representation and Participation: the case of home-owner activism in Beijing
Yousun Chung
Journal of Contemporary China, volume 24, issue 91 (2015) pp. 1–20

Chapter 8

Requests for Environmental Information Disclosure in China: an understanding from legal mobilization and citizen activism
Xinhong Wang
Journal of Contemporary China, volume 25, issue 98 (2016) pp. 233–247

Chapter 9

Grand Mediation and Legitimacy Enhancement in Contemporary China—the Guang'an model
Jieren Hu and Lingjian Zeng
Journal of Contemporary China, volume 24, issue 91 (2015) pp. 43–63

Chapter 10

Performance Legitimacy, State Autonomy and China's Economic Miracle
Hongxing Yang and Dingxin Zhao
Journal of Contemporary China, volume 24, issue 91 (2015) pp. 64–82

Chapter 11

The Sichuan Earthquake and the Heavenly Mandate: legitimizing Chinese rule through disaster discourse
Florian Schneider and Yih-jye Hwang
Journal of Contemporary China, volume 23, issue 88 (2014) pp. 636–656

Chapter 12

Repression Backfires: tactical radicalization and protest spectacle in rural China
Kevin J. O'Brien and Yanhua Deng
Journal of Contemporary China, volume 24, issue 93 (2015) pp. 457–470

Chapter 13

Patrolling Harmony: pre-emptive authoritarianism and the preservation of stability in W County
Xiaojun Yan
Journal of Contemporary China, volume 25, issue 99 (2016) pp. 406–421

Notes on Contributors

Feng Chen is a Professor of Government and International Studies at Hong Kong Baptist University, China. He has published articles in *The China Quarterly*, *The China Journal* and *Modern China*.

Yousun Chung is an Assistant Research Fellow in the Institute of Political Science at Academia Sinica, Taiwan. Her current research focuses on the relationship between local governance, state–society relations, social policy and the transitional political economy of contemporary China.

Yanhua Deng is a Professor at the School of Public Administration, Southwestern University of Finance and Economics, China.

Jieren Hu is an Associate Professor in the Law School/Intellectual Property Institute at Tongji University, China, and a Research Fellow at the Institute for Civil Society Development at Zhejiang University, China.

Wonjae Hwang is an Associate Professor in the Department of Political Science at the University of Tennessee, USA. His research interests focus on globalization, compensation politics and Korean politics.

Yih-jye Hwang is an Assistant Professor of International Politics at Leiden University College the Hague, Leiden University, the Netherlands.

Yi Kang is an Assistant Professor of Government and International Studies at Hong Kong Baptist University, China. Her research relates to the politics of non-democratic systems and post-disaster management.

Kevin J. O'Brien is the Alann P. Bedford Professor of Asian Studies, a Professor of Political Science and the Director of the Institute of East Asian Studies at the University of California, Berkeley, USA.

Peter Sandby-Thomas is currently a Visiting Lecturer in Political Science at the University of Massachusetts Dartmouth, USA.

Florian Schneider, PhD, is a Lecturer for the Politics of Modern China at the Leiden University Institute of Area Studies, the Netherlands. His research interests include questions of governance, political communication and public administration in the PRC, Taiwan and Hong Kong.

Gunter Schubert, PhD, is a Chair Professor of Greater China Studies at the Institute of Chinese and Korean Studies, Tübingen University, Germany. He is also the Director of the European Research Center on Contemporary Taiwan (ERCCT) at this university.

Xinhong Wang is a Researcher affiliated to the Centre for East Asian Studies at the University of Turku, Finland.

Xiaojun Yan is an Associate Professor in Politics and Public Administration at the University of Hong Kong, China. He is a comparative political scientist with special expertise in the politics of China.

Hongxing Yang is an Assistant Professor in the School of Public Economics & Administration at Shanghai University of Finance and Economics, China. His research interests include economic sociology, political sociology, organizational sociology and population studies.

Ray Ou Yang is currently a PhD candidate in political science at the University of Iowa, USA. He majors in comparative politics and international relations.

Jinghan Zeng is a Lecturer at Royal Holloway, University of London, UK. His research lies in the field of Chinese politics with more specific interests in the study of China's authoritarian politics, political communication, political economy and foreign policy. He is the author of *The Chinese Communist Party's Capacity to Rule: Ideology, Legitimacy and Party Cohesion* (2015). His academic papers have appeared in *Journal of Contemporary China*, *International Affairs*, *JCMS: Journal of Common Market Studies* and *Contemporary Politics,* among others.

Lingjian Zeng is an Associate Professor in the Applied Law School at Southwest University of Political Science and Law, China.

Dingxin Zhao is a Professor of Sociology at the University of Chicago, USA, and a Qianren Professor at Zhejiang University, China. His research interests cover political sociology, historical sociology and sociological methodology.

Suisheng Zhao is a Professor and Director of the Center for China–US Cooperation at Josef Korbel School of International Studies, University of Denver, USA, and the Founding Editor of *Journal of Contemporary China.*

Yang Zhong is a Changjiang Scholar at the School of International and Public Affairs of Shanghai Jiao Tong University, China, and a Professor in the Department of Political Science at the University of Tennessee, USA.

How Do You Solve a Problem Like Legitimacy? Contributing to a new research agenda

PETER SANDBY-THOMAS

Previously in this journal, Gunter Schubert's article, entitled 'One-party rule and the question of legitimacy in contemporary China', called for the setting up of a new research agenda to analyze the legitimacy of the Chinese Communist Party (CCP). While making a valuable contribution to the study of the CCP's legitimacy, Schubert's emphasis on the empirical measurement of this concept gives rise to a number of conceptual and theoretical issues. As a consequence, this article seeks to contribute to the research agenda by addressing these issues. In so doing, it suggests that a shift away from a narrow empirically-measured focus on legitimacy towards a broader conceptually-driven concern with legitimation would allow for a more inclusive agenda within the China studies community and lead to a more complete understanding of why the CCP remains in power.

Introduction

The problem of legitimacy has puzzled social scientists for many years. Indeed, Zelditch traces this back to the fifth century BCE and concludes that legitimacy is 'one of the oldest problems in the history of social thought'.[1] Yet, despite this, legitimacy continues to be operationalized in the study of politics. The reason for this may lie in the fact that, of the many concepts available, legitimacy offers the best possibility of providing a coherent, multi-faceted and multi-dimensional explanation for why regimes maintain or lose power. In light of this, it is perhaps not surprising that, with the prospect of the Chinese Communist Party (CCP) losing power appearing to be low, there has been a rise in the number of scholars in the China

1. Morris Zelditch, 'Processes of legitimation: recent developments and new directions', *Social Psychology Quarterly* 64(1), (2001), p. 4.

studies field deploying the concept.[2] And yet, Holbig and Gilley make the point that '[s]cholars ... approach the question of legitimacy in contemporary China with much trepidation. They not only want to avoid a teleology of inevitable democratization, but also seek to avoid the equal and opposite teleology of an inevitable authoritarian durability'.[3] It is against this backdrop that, previously in this journal, Gunter Schubert proposed a research agenda for the collaborative study of legitimacy which offers the possibility of avoiding the pitfalls identified by Holbig and Gilley.[4] This research agenda is valuable, not only in putting forward a method for the 'systemic exploration' of legitimacy at the micro-political level but also in articulating a broader approach to conceptualizing the CCP's legitimacy.[5] That said, this article contends that there are a number of important conceptual and methodological issues within this research agenda concerning the way in which its claims are substantiated. The intention of this article, therefore, is to address these issues and, in so doing, contribute to the ongoing development of this agenda. It will begin by highlighting the areas in which Schubert's article makes a significant contribution before identifying and addressing the issues raised by the research agenda. The final part of the article will suggest that the research agenda would benefit from moving beyond a narrow empirically-measured focus on legitimacy towards a broader conceptually-driven concern with legitimation and, to that end, will briefly present my own research on the Party's legitimating use of the stability discourse since 1989.

Asking the right questions: contributions

Schubert's article makes three principal contributions to the study of the CCP's legitimacy. The first one is to take 'Western *academe*' to task for the widely-held view that the end of its rule is inevitable.[6] Indeed, amongst scholars focusing on the political durability of the CCP, the main difference of opinion centers only on how long the Party will remain in power, with some making specific predictions about when 'regime change' will take place while others insist only that such change will eventually happen. For Schubert, the effect of such thinking has been to produce research in which the political, economic and social successes of the reform period have been discounted in favor of highlighting the problems and potential challenges

2. Examples include, but are not limited to: Cheng Chen, 'Institutional legitimacy of an authoritarian state: China in the mirror of Eastern Europe', *Problems of Post-Communism* 52(4), (2005), pp. 3–13; Peter Hays Gries and Stanley Rosen, eds, *State and Society in 21st-Century China: Crisis, Contention and Legitimation* (London: RoutledgeCurzon, 2004); Thomas Heberer and Gunter Schubert, eds, *Regime Legitimacy in Contemporary China: Institutional Change and Stability* (London: Routledge, 2009); Heike Holbig, *Ideological Reform and Political Legitimacy in China: Challenges in the Post-Jiang Era*, GIGA Working Papers No. 18, (March 2006), pp. 1–36; C. S. Bryan Ho, 'Re-conceptualizing "legitimacy" for studying electoral politics in rural China', *Journal of Chinese Political Science*, (12 February 2011), pp. 1–21; André Laliberté and Marc Lanteigne, eds, *The Chinese Party-State in the 21st Century: Adaptation and the Reinvention of Legitimacy* (London and New York: Routledge, 2007).

3. Heike Holbig and Bruce Gilley, 'Reclaiming legitimacy in China', *Politics & Policy* 38(3), (2010), p. 414.

4. Gunter Schubert, 'One-party rule and the question of legitimacy in contemporary China: preliminary thoughts on setting up a new research agenda', *Journal of Contemporary China* 17(54), (2008), pp. 191–204.

5. In terms of the broader approach to conceptualizing the CCP's legitimacy, it is less that Schubert's article is the only work to do so and more that it explicitly addresses the question of legitimacy in relation to the wider China studies field. Indeed, as Schubert acknowledges in the article, one of the aims of the article is to 'trigger' debate within the field.

6. *Ibid.*, pp. 191–192.

to the reform. While agreeing with the thrust of this argument, it must also be acknowledged that the Chinese political system is fragile. Indeed, the concept of legitimacy helps to bring this fragility into sharp relief by offering the possibility of analytically distinguishing between the legitimacy of the political system and the regime.[7] The extent to which this distinction can be made is dependent upon the extent to which power has been institutionalized, with a political system in which power has been institutionalized being viewed as more stable. In the case of the People's Republic of China (PRC), the entwining of the system's legitimacy with that of the Party means that power has not been fully institutionalized and so results in a less stable system.[8] Indeed, though the effect of this entwining has been to raise the costs of challenging the Party's power, it has also increased the likelihood of systemic change in the event of a successful challenge.

However, acknowledging the fragility of the PRC's political system does not mean that the CCP necessarily lacks legitimacy. Indeed, amongst scholars who have been predicting regime change, there has often been a failure to explain why the CCP has managed to remain in power since 1989. Rather, the predictions of imminent collapse in the aftermath of the 1989 demonstrations have given way to claims of 'resilience' and 'delay' to account for the regime's continued hold on power. Such explanations, however, still presuppose the inevitability of change and, as such, do not acknowledge the possibility of the CCP generating legitimacy over the course of the reform process.[9] Acknowledging such a possibility is the second principal contribution of Schubert's article. Indeed, this possibility constitutes its central argument, namely that 'the Chinese political system is able to generate significant degrees of regime legitimacy by adapting rather successfully to a changing domestic and international environment'.[10] The level of popular support recorded in a wide array of public opinion surveys alone adds weight to this argument. Summarizing the results, Kennedy states that '[a]ll surveys examining public opinion toward the CCP conducted since the early 1990s show that over 70 percent of respondents support the central government and the party'.[11] Even the widespread number of protests taking place at the local level each year does not directly diminish the findings of these surveys, with much research indicating these protests are mostly confined to specific localized grievances.[12] That said, the use of such evidence to support Schubert's

7. Leslie Holmes, *The End of Communist Power: Anti-Corruption Campaigns and Legitimation Crisis* (Cambridge, MA: Polity Press, 1993), p. 25. Johnson draws a similar observation, albeit using the concept of 'power deflation', when asserting that authoritarian regimes are more vulnerable than democratic regimes because of their increased reliance on coercion. For more, see Chalmers Johnson, *Revolutionary Change* (Stanford, CA: Stanford University Press, 1982), pp. 29–33.

8. Moves towards the partial institutionalization of power have taken place in recent years, most notably with leadership transition. However, this institutionalization has been largely confined to the elite level and still falls short of the separation of Party and State (*dang zheng fankai*) envisioned in Zhao Ziyang's 13th Party Congress Work Report.

9. Indeed, there are grounds to suggest that this lack of acknowledgement is rooted in ideology, i.e. the notion that no non-democratic system can be legitimate. However, if one accepts that all democratic systems are not equally legitimate, then it follows that all non-democratic systems are not equally illegitimate and so the corollary must be that non-democratic systems can acquire legitimacy.

10. Schubert, 'One-party rule and the question of legitimacy in contemporary China', p. 193.

11. John James Kennedy, 'Maintaining popular support for the Chinese Communist Party: the influence of education and the state-controlled media', *Political Studies* 57, (2009), p. 517.

12. Vivienne Shue, 'Legitimacy crisis in China?', in Gries and Rosen, eds, *State and Society in 21st-Century China*, p. 29.

hypothesis draws attention to the need for the definition of legitimacy being deployed to be made explicit. Indeed, despite its common usage, it is possible to identify three emergent strands within the academic literature on legitimacy.[13]

The first strand takes a normative view of legitimacy in which particular regimes are assessed against a set of prescriptive criteria, such as the protection of individual human rights and levels of civic participation. In this, the position of the analyst is privileged by determining legitimacy in terms of what it ought to be.[14] The second strand that can be identified takes an analytical view of legitimacy in which particular regimes are assessed using measurements of popular support, such as public opinion surveys.[15] In this, the views of people are privileged by determining legitimacy in terms of what it is. The final strand within the academic literature is a blending of the first two strands, so that legitimacy constitutes a mixture of what it is and what it ought to be.[16] Of the three strands, Schubert's research agenda seems intended to fall within the second strand. However, it is the first strand that is the most commonly accepted and applied understanding of legitimacy and, as such, many analysts find the second strand, with its exclusive reliance on the beliefs of people, to be problematic. This viewpoint is encapsulated by Schaar, who reasons that

> [i]f a people hold the belief that the existing institutions are 'appropriate' or 'morally proper', then those institutions are legitimate ... [hence] the investigator can examine nothing outside popular opinion to decide whether a given regime, institution or command is legitimate or illegitimate.[17]

For many analysts, this point is particularly relevant when assessing the legitimacy of the CCP, given the Party's continued control over the flow of information and use of coercive force. As such, the notion of the CCP generating legitimacy is rejected on moral/normative grounds. Indeed, Schubert appears to acknowledge this possibility when suggesting that '[e]ven if such a regime type [a rather strong and enduring "party-state democracy"] runs counter to our beliefs, the "legitimacy hypothesis" could at least be useful in a counterfactual sense'.[18] However, I would go beyond Schubert in suggesting that normative and analytical approaches towards legitimacy are ontologically distinct and, despite using the same term, are intended to research different phenomena. Consequently, research that adopts an analytical approach towards legitimacy should not be discounted on account of morally uncomfortable

13. Rodney Barker, *Legitimating Identities: The Self-Presentations of Rulers and Subjects* (Cambridge: Cambridge University Press, 2001), pp. 8–10.

14. See, for example: Jean-Marc Coicaud, *Legitimacy and Politics: A Contribution to the Study of Political Right and Political Responsibility* (Cambridge: Cambridge University Press, 2002); William Connolly, ed., *Legitimacy and the State* (New York: New York University Press, 1984); John Kane, *The Politics of Moral Capital* (Cambridge: Cambridge University Press, 2001).

15. See, for example: John A. Booth and Mitchell A. Seligson, *The Legitimacy Puzzle in Latin America: Political Support and Democracy in Eight Nations* (Cambridge: Cambridge University Press, 2009); Bruce Gilley, *The Right to Rule: How States Win and Lose Legitimacy* (New York: Columbia University Press, 2009).

16. A prominent example is David Beetham, *The Legitimation of Power* (Basingstoke: Macmillan, 1991). This work will be addressed more directly later in this article.

17. John H. Schaar, *Legitimacy in the Modern State* (New Brunswick, NJ: Transaction, 1981), pp. 20–21.

18. Schubert, 'One-party rule and the question of legitimacy in contemporary China', p. 193.

outcomes but rather be pursued by scholars who intend to better explain why the CCP remains in power.[19]

The third major contribution made by Schubert's article is to conduct research on the legitimizing effects of political reform at the micro-political level. The significance of this contribution is that it helps to move the debate on the CCP's legitimacy beyond the oft-cited 'economic performance + nationalism − communism' formula. This formula is not incorrect *per se*; rather, it does not fully capture the complexity of the CCP's legitimacy. Moreover, the link between each element in this formula and the legitimacy of the CCP is more complex than commonly acknowledged. On the notion of economic performance, while it is widely agreed that the consistently high growth rates have benefited the regime, the relationship between such growth and regime legitimacy is unclear. As Zhong points out, 'economic growth in and by itself does not directly contribute to political stability … [i]n fact, it has been argued that economic development and modernization lead to political instability'.[20] Given the uneven nature of economic development in China thus far, both geographically and amongst different sections of society, the expectation would be for more instability to have occurred than there has been to date. For some, this lack of instability provides evidence for the legitimizing effect of nationalism. Again, while the extensive propagation of 'patriotic education' in the post-Tiananmen period can be said to have promoted political loyalty to the state, the 1990s also witnessed the emergence of a *popular* nationalism that has contested the government's *official* nationalism. Indeed, Gries and Rosen go so far as to suggest that the Party's 'legitimacy now depends on meeting the expectations of nationalists'.[21] As for the communist ideology, while largely derided for its lack of legitimizing force, the Party's continued investment in and promulgation of communism suggests that, though it may not resonate amongst the wider populace, it still plays a role in intra-Party legitimization. Consequently, acknowledging the explanatory shortcomings of the Party's legitimacy 'formula' suggests that it is necessary to interrogate further sources of CCP legitimacy in the reform period.

Getting the right answers: issues

Having highlighted its principal contributions, this article will now outline the main issues arising from the research agenda on legitimacy proposed in Schubert's article. To that end, three key issues have been identified. These issues are largely focused on the conceptual implications arising from the methodological approach used to assess the CCP's legitimacy. In this, the intention is not to call into question the quality of

19. Barker makes the point that 'an unlegitimated state is a contradiction in terms, whatever further judgements may be made about the political character and moral status of the regime'. As such, undertaking an analysis of the ways in which the CCP attempts to legitimate its regime is a valid piece of social scientific inquiry. See Barker, *Legitimating Identities*, p. 20.

20. Yang Zhong, 'Legitimacy crisis and legitimation in China', *Journal of Contemporary Asia* 26(2), (1996), p. 202.

21. Peter Hay Gries and Stanley Rosen, 'Introduction', in Gries and Rosen, eds, *State and Society in 21st-Century China*, p. 24.

Schubert's research; rather, it is to draw attention to the way in which claims about the CCP's legitimacy are substantiated.

The first issue concerns the micro-political approach towards the measurement of legitimacy. Although the value of the more commonly-used method of macro-quantitative surveys is acknowledged, Schubert's article suggests that the micro-political approach is 'the most promising trajectory to understand political legitimacy in contemporary China'.[22] This suggestion is premised on its potential to capture an 'on the ground' view of legitimacy often missed by higher-level surveys. In particular, Schubert's article suggests that this approach would be more sensitive to measuring legitimacy at the local level in areas such as governance reform (*zhengzhi tizhi gaige*), where central government policies have been adapted and/or replaced by bottom-up initiatives. However, though this approach would undoubtedly provide valuable information about political arrangements at the local level, it suffers from the problem of scale, in that a micro-level method is being deployed to measure the macro-level concept of legitimacy. Schubert's article appears to be aware of this issue, albeit indirectly, and the suggestion that legitimacy constitutes 'the net sum of ... "partial legitimacies" ... generated in different spaces, as well as at different administrative layers and by different personal relationships within the Chinese political system' can be construed as offering a conceptual solution.[23] However, such 'aggregation' rests on the presupposition that power is evenly distributed, both vertically and horizontally, throughout the Chinese political system. This is because no distinction is made between these 'partial legitimacies' in terms of their effect on overall regime legitimacy. The corollary is that, for example, legitimacy measured at the village level is equally weighted with that concerning the policies of the central government.

By contrast, I would contend that certain actors within the political system hold disproportional power and, by extension, can affect the legitimacy of the regime to a greater or lesser extent. Moreover, in acknowledging this point, the need to disaggregate society into strategic groups for the purpose of operationalizing legitimacy becomes apparent. Indeed, Weber's conceptualization of legitimacy disaggregates society into three principal groups: chiefs, staffs and masses. Applying this to the People's Republic of China, three comparable groupings can be identified, with the 'chiefs' being equivalent to the group of cadres at the rank of county magistrate or division chief and above,[24] the 'staffs' referring to those in the national bureaucracy below the level of county magistrate and division chief, and the 'masses' being made up of the broader population-at-large. The effect of this disaggregation is to highlight the relational dimension of legitimacy by drawing attention to links between each of the groupings. In Weber's schema, three separate but interdependent relationships are identified: elites–cadres; elites–masses; and cadres–masses. Furthermore, these relationships are hierarchically ordered in terms of their effect on overall regime legitimacy, with elite–cadres regarded as the most important,

22. Schubert, 'One-party rule and the question of legitimacy in contemporary China', p. 203.
23. *Ibid.*, p. 194.
24. For more detail on these groups, see Andrew G. Walder, 'The Party elite and China's trajectory of change', in Kjeld Erik Brødsgaard and Zheng Yongnian, eds, *The Chinese Communist Party in a New Era: Renewal and Reform* (London: Routledge, 2006), p. 19.

followed by elite–masses and, finally, cadres–masses. Indeed, in relation to China, Walder goes so far as to suggest that

> [t]he political elite of 500,000 cannot rule the country unless it can retain the obedience of 40 million state cadres ... and if the elite maintains the discipline of state bureaucrats and the allegiance of party members, it can withstand challenges from other groups in society, even in periods of economic hardship and social upheaval.[25]

In terms of legitimacy, Walder is effectively stating that the views of the masses are less important, if not irrelevant, to the regime's maintenance of power.[26] The example of the 1989 demonstrations would appear to support this position, in so far as, despite the millions of people protesting across the nation, the political elite were able to maintain the discipline and loyalty of party members in sufficient numbers to withstand the challenge.

In addition to the vertical disaggregation of society, the 1989 demonstrations highlight a facet of relational legitimacy not identified by Weber, namely the horizontal disaggregation of society. More specifically, during 1989, it was the loss of legitimacy within the leadership elite that, arguably, played a decisive role in bringing the regime to the brink of collapse. For Alagappa, this form of 'intra-elite' legitimacy is important because

> [f]rom the ruler's viewpoint, legitimacy is not just a stratagem to secure more effective control or perpetuate themselves in office. Self-justification in moral terms is crucial for most rulers. They need to believe they are serving the national interest or a moral cause even if it necessitates a 'noble lie'.[27]

Indeed, in his analysis of the Soviet Union collapse, Holmes identifies the leadership's loss of belief in itself as one of the main factors, specifically the moment when the United States announced its Strategic Defense Initiative.[28] By contrast, in China in 1989, though some of the leadership disagreed with the use of military force in suppressing the demonstrations, a sufficient number of significant members, including Deng Xiaoping, believed that this was an appropriate course of action to ensure that a regime collapse would be avoided.

With regard to Schubert's article, the need for disaggregation is explicitly acknowledged when he states that 'it is ... necessary to disaggregate the Chinese political system (or state) and look at ... different spatial, administrative and personal levels in order to assess the Communist regime's overall legitimacy'.[29] Despite this, however, only two relationships are identified for analytical investigation: elites–masses and cadres–masses. While accepting that it is extremely

25. *Ibid.*, p. 21.

26. This view is supported by, amongst others, Di Palma, who, when considering communist regimes in Eastern Europe, commented that '[w]hen legitimation comes from the top, the decisive operative relationship is not that between rulers and people, but that between rulers and Weber's administrative staff—in communist parlance, the *cadres*'. See Giuseppe Di Palma, 'Legitimation from the top to civil society: politico-cultural change in Eastern Europe', *World Politics* 44(1), (October 1991), p. 57.

27. Muthiah Alagappa, 'Introduction', in Muthiah Alagappa, ed., *Political Legitimacy in Southeast Asia: The Quest for Moral Authority* (Stanford, CA: Stanford University Press, 1995), p. 4.

28. Holmes, *The End of Communist Power*, p. 30.

29. Schubert, 'One-party rule and the question of legitimacy in contemporary China', p. 194.

difficult to obtain detailed and reliable data on the elites, it nevertheless raises the question as to whether the research agenda is actually measuring overall regime legitimacy as opposed to a partial variant thereof. A further issue arising from the disaggregation of legitimacy in the research agenda concerns how legitimacy captured 'on the ground' affects the overall legitimacy of the regime. Indeed, when discussing the rising numbers of peasant protests, Schubert suggests that 'conflict at the local level does not necessarily translate into overall regime delegitimization'; yet, when discussing effective local governance, Schubert suggests that, by virtue of a 'bridging effect', '[g]ains in legitimacy here may translate into overall regime legitimacy'.[30] Consequently, on the one hand, negative material action is dismissed on the grounds of (alleged?) intention whilst, on the other hand, positive intention is privileged in the absence of material action. While accepting that these two viewpoints are not necessarily contradictory and indeed can coexist, it is clear that a fuller conceptualization of legitimacy which can account for these outcomes needs to be elaborated.[31]

Having identified the level(s) at which legitimacy is measured, the second issue is concerned with the method used to measure this legitimacy. Schubert's article proposes that Easton's approach to regime legitimacy offers 'the most sophisticated approach to the "legitimacy conundrum" because it encourages a multi-dimensional research program for the empirical investigation of people's ideas and opinions in different contexts'.[32] Indeed, this approach has been adopted by other scholars examining the legitimacy of the CCP, most prominently Chen Jie,[33] and is notable for its conceptual elaboration of measuring 'supportive attitudes' within a political system.[34]

While agreeing with Schubert that Easton's approach constitutes a sophisticated attempt to measure the legitimacy of a regime, there are a number of areas of concern. Firstly, Easton's approach was developed for operationalization in a democratic political system and, as such, is focused on measuring the level of support amongst the wider population. As noted above, the role played by the masses in the Chinese

30. *Ibid.*, p. 198.

31. An example is provided by the CCP itself. According to Holbig and Gilley, the CCP views legitimacy not as a single value variable that provides a measurement of legitimacy independent of context but rather as a set of variables that are viewed in terms of Bayesian probability. Moreover, material action is privileged in the belief that it can set off 'a cascade of preference shifts' which could threaten the political system. More broadly, the CCP approach seems to view legitimacy in terms of systemic survival while Schubert's article appears to view it in terms of systemic approval. Again, though not mutually exclusive, these approaches do point at differences in emphasis and further suggest the need for clarity over how the concept of legitimacy is defined when undertaking a research project. See Holbig and Gilley, 'Reclaiming legitimacy in China', p. 398.

32. Schubert, 'One-party rule and the question of legitimacy in contemporary China', p. 194.

33. Examples of Chen's work include: Chen Jie, 'Popular support for the political regime in China: intensity and sources', *Asia Special Report* 104, (August 2002), pp. 11–16; Chen Jie, *Popular Political Support in Urban China* (Stanford, CA: Stanford University Press, 2004); Chen Jie, 'Sociopolitical attitudes of the masses and leaders in the Chinese village: attitude congruence and constraint', *Journal of Contemporary China* 14(44), (August 2005), pp. 445–464.

34. According to Easton, supportive attitudes can be identified when '[w]e can say that *A* supports *B* either when *A* acts on behalf of *B* or when he orients himself favorably toward *B*. *B* may be a person or a group; it may be a goal, idea, or institution'. In this, supportive attitudes are equated with political support on behalf of the public and are directed towards three groups—the regime, the authorities and the political community, with the regime being the most important. See David Easton, *A Systems Analysis of Political Life* (New York: Wiley, 1965), p. 278.

political system is not as significant in determining the overall legitimacy of the regime. Though Schubert's article does suggest the need to also measure the attitudes of cadres,[35] it is unclear how Easton's method can be successfully operationalized to measure the attitudes of other significant actors within the political system. Following on from this, Easton's conceptualization of supportive attitudes involves distinguishing between the regime, the authorities and the political community. Again, as noted above, this distinction is difficult to make in a system where the CCP, the government and the civil service are so closely entwined and where a fully independent and autonomous civil society is not permitted. Though this issue is not directly addressed in Schubert's article, the distinction made between the central and local state elsewhere in the article does offer a possible solution. A further area of concern is the relationship between diffuse and specific support that makes up supportive attitudes.[36] The key distinction between these two forms of support is temporal, yet this aspect of the relationship is neither clearly conceptualized nor explicitly acknowledged. Indeed, while diffuse support is held to build over a longer period of time than specific support, it is not clear when or, indeed, how specific support can be transformed into diffuse support. This lack of conceptualization raises the question of whether diffuse and specific support can be meaningfully captured at the empirical level.[37] This question is significant because capturing these differing levels of support constitutes the basis on which Easton's approach claims to measure legitimacy. Consequently, providing a convincing answer is necessary if Easton's approach is to demonstrate that it can measure legitimacy rather than simply offering a more elaborate examination of popular opinion.

The final issue concerns the scope of the legitimacy being measured. With the lack of nationwide democratic elections, Schubert's article suggests that it is necessary to develop an alternative way of measuring legitimacy. To that end, 'zones' of legitimacy-building within the Chinese political system are identified. Moreover, the identification of these zones corresponds to the dimensions of ideology, structure and personal authority that make up Easton's concept of legitimacy. Within the dimension of ideology, these 'zones' are concerned with ideological change that have reshaped state–society relations, for example, the 'Three Represents' and 'Harmonious Society' concepts. Within the dimension of structure, these zones relate to, for example, the implementation of the 'socialist rule of law', including efforts to increase cadre transparency and protection of citizen rights, and governance reform, such as initiatives to enhance 'intra-party' democracy and the quality of cadre

35. Schubert, 'One-party rule and the question of legitimacy in contemporary China', p. 203.

36. According to Easton, diffuse support is comprised of two dimensions of 'belief in legitimacy' and trust, which correspond to a person's belief that the existence and actions of the government are in accordance with their ethical and moral principles regarding the political. In this, diffuse support is built over a long time period through exposure to continuous socializations as well as repeated judgments on a government's performance. As such, once diffuse support has formed, it tends to hold firm and remain stable, and is subject only to gradual change. By contrast, specific support refers to a person's satisfaction with the policies and performance of the government and so is both short-term and prone to volatility, usually in response to the perceived benefits and costs of specific policies. Hence, Easton's composite concept of political support consists of both belief and opinion, albeit with diffuse support being held as the more dominant variable. For more, see David Easton, 'A re-assessment of the concept of political support', *British Journal of Political Science* 5(4), (October 1975), pp. 437–452.

37. Gerhard Loewenberg, 'The influence of parliamentary behavior on regime stability: some conceptual clarifications', *Comparative Politics* 3, (1971), p. 184.

recruitment. Within the dimension of personal authority, these zones refer to the quality of people's relationship with the local state, including local elections as well as the evaluation of cadres' performance.

While not disagreeing with those listed in Schubert's article, both the process by which these zones are identified and the criteria on which they have been included are unclear.[38] In turn, it is unclear why possible areas of enquiry are not included as zones of legitimacy. For example, within the dimension of ideology, only the Party concepts of the 'Three Represents' and 'Harmonious Society' are identified as worthy of empirical investigation. While it is important to investigate the legitimizing effect of these concepts, I would argue that they constitute a 'formal' type of ideology that is supplemented and, arguably surpassed, by an 'informal' type of ideology. Whereas this formal ideology is narrowly concerned with the Party doctrine and is as much, if not more so, intended for CCP members as public consumption, the informal ideology is broadly concerned with the justification of the CCP rule and is intended for all levels of society. Indeed, the economic reorientation of Chinese society over the past 30 years provides a clear example in which the Party's formal ideology of 'reform and opening up' has been supplemented by an informal ideology of 'market liberalism' propagated in different media formats.[39] Other possible areas of enquiry include the legitimizing impact of events and international sources of legitimacy.[40] Indeed, the conceptualization of legitimacy put forward in Schubert's article appears to be not only exclusively concerned with domestic sources of legitimacy but also with the official line of the Chinese Communist Party. That said, it is not that such a conceptualization is necessarily incorrect but rather that it does appear to be unnecessarily limited and, as such, again suggests that the research agenda does not capture the totality of the CCP's legitimacy.[41]

Asking different questions: solutions

The previous section identified concerns with the scale, scope and method used by Schubert's research agenda to capture the legitimacy of the CCP. However, as stated elsewhere, raising these concerns is not intended to question the quality of the

38. The significance of this point is highlighted by Zeng's analysis of Chinese scholars' writing which, amongst other things, highlights the multiplicity of understandings of legitimacy both between and within the Western and Chinese scholarly communities. For more, see Jinghan Zeng, 'The debate on regime legitimacy in China: bridging the wide gulf between Western and Chinese scholarship', *Journal of Contemporary China* 23(88), (2014), doi: 10.1080/10670564.2013.861141.

39. Anne-Marie Brady, 'Mass persuasion as a means of legitimation and China's popular authoritarianism', *American Behavioral Scientist* 53, (2009), p. 448.

40. Indeed, Schneider and Hwang's article in this volume provides an excellent example of the former, in this instance the Sichuan earthquake in 2008. For more, see Florian Schneider and Yih-jye Hwang, 'The Sichuan earthquake and the heavenly mandate: legitimizing Chinese rule through disaster discourse', *Journal of Contemporary China* 23(88) (2014), doi: 10.1080/10670564.2013.861145. For an example of the latter, see Heike Holbig, 'International dimensions of legitimacy: reflections on Western theories and the Chinese experience', *Journal of Chinese Political Science*, (12 February 2011), pp. 1–21.

41. Schubert's response to these points, along with an updated and revised approach to the issue of legitimacy, can be read in the following article of this volume. See Gunter Schubert, 'Political legitimacy in contemporary China revisited: theoretical refinement and empirical operationalization', *Journal of Contemporary China* 23(88) (2014), doi: 10.1080/10670564.2013.861139.

research being undertaken; rather, it is to suggest that legitimacy does not constitute the most appropriate conceptual framework in which to present such research. More specifically, it is the difficulty in operationalizing the concept that is problematic. Schubert does acknowledge such difficulty when stating that 'research on legitimacy poses serious methodological pitfalls, not to mention considerable practical problems'.[42] However, the proposed 'on the ground' approach does not convincingly overcome such pitfalls because it cannot capture the totality of the CCP's legitimacy. That said, Schubert's own research seems less concerned with measuring the legitimacy of the CCP *per se* than with measuring the effect of certain policies, particularly governance reforms, on the legitimacy of the CCP. In light of this, this article suggests that legitimation, rather than legitimacy, would offer a better conceptual framework. Although the two concepts are often used interchangeably, a distinction can be made and, in that regard, I follow Bourricaud in viewing legitimacy as a static property external to a political system and legitimation as a dynamic process essential for a political system.[43] Indeed, for Barker, legitimation should be viewed as an 'active, contested political process ... [and] since it is an activity, it involves creation, modification, innovation, and transformation'.[44] By conceptually shifting from legitimacy to legitimation, Schubert's research agenda would be disencumbered from the difficulties of operationalizing the former concept. Such a shift would not invalidate Schubert's existing empirical research; rather, it would change the basis of the claims being made about it. Consequently, governance reforms would no longer be measured in terms of the CCP's overall legitimacy but rather analyzed as part of the regime's variegated attempts at legitimation. As such, legitimacy's claims of causality and certainty are replaced by legitimation's acknowledgement of complexity and contingency. And though this may appear to lack 'scientific' rigor, I believe that the conceptual framework of legitimation offers the possibility of capturing more fully the governance of Chinese society.

The first reason for this is actorial perspectivity, in that legitimation's concern with the process of justifying power opens up areas of inquiry beyond legitimacy's narrow focus on measuring power as a property. Indeed, where legitimacy, in only measuring the views and attitudes held by the populace, privileges the perspective of the individual recipient in determining the rightfulness of a regime, legitimation acknowledges the multiplicity of actors involved in the political process and, in so doing, allows for the perspectives of both the producer and recipients of justifying claims to be taken into account. Indeed, as Luckman points out, 'legitimation is making sense of power ... to those who exercise power; to those who are subject to the exercise of power; or to both'.[45] Moreover, as noted above, within the Chinese political system, it is less clear that the views of the populace are as decisive as those within the party structure in maintaining the regime's power. As such, this suggests

42. Schubert, 'One-party rule and the question of legitimacy in contemporary China', p. 200.

43. François Bourricaud, 'Legitimacy and legitimization', *Current Sociology* 35(2), (1987), p. 57. Bourricaud actually uses the term 'legitimization' in place of legitimation. However, both terms are similar in so far as they focus on the process of acquiring legitimacy.

44. Barker, *Legitimating Identities*, p. 28.

45. Thomas Luckman, 'Comments on legitimation', *Current Sociology* 35(2), (1987), pp. 109–117.

that it is necessary to pay greater attention to the regime's production of legitimating claims. To that end, Barker introduces the concept of identity when arguing that '[l]egitimation is important to rulers for the cultivation of their own identification, quite apart from any conventionally instrumental function it may have'.[46] Rothschild concurs when suggesting that '[d]iscussions of legitimacy and legitimation risk irrelevancy if they overlook this crucial dimension of a ruling elite's sense of its legitimacy and focus exclusively on the other dimension of the public's or the masses' perceptions of that elite's legitimacy'.[47] In addition, Freudenburg and Alario make the point that attention should focus not only on what is produced but also on what is *not* produced. This form of 'non-legitimation' can be detected in the lack of and/or diversion away from issues that may challenge and undermine a regime's legitimation claims.[48] Taken together, employing a legitimation approach can provide a more complete account of the CCP's (non)legitimating strategies as well as explain why particular views and attitudes of the CCP may be held.

The second reason is methodological plurality. As indicated above, the two main approaches to legitimacy involve public opinion surveys and the studies of legitimate beliefs and (non)compliant behavior. As Hurrelmann *et al.* note in the case of the former, due to their inherent limitations, they 'ultimately fail to determine whether revealed attitudes are truly grounded in judgements about the legitimacy of a political system'.[49] In the case of the latter, there are similar limitations, in that it is difficult to meaningfully establish the linkages between conventional behavior and legitimacy beliefs. In light of these methodological issues, and given the need to pay greater attention to the production of legitimation claims, the importance of communication has been identified by a number of scholars. Hurrelmann *et al.* pay attention to legitimation's '(re)production, contestation and transformation' across different media discourses,[50] while Beetham, in particular, also makes conceptual space for the role played by ideology in the legitimation of a regime.[51] Beyond this inclusion of a communicative dimension, however, legitimation's broader, conceptually-driven concern with the justification of power does not impose the restrictions on the use of particular methods that is the case with the empirical study of legitimacy. Indeed, if one accepts the proposition that wherever power is exercised, there exists a need to justify this power, then it also follows that the boundaries of the political must be extended, both vertically and horizontally, beyond one group's view on the form and function of government. In light of this, legitimation is more likely to yield greater methodological innovation for the purpose of accessing less commonly researched areas of inquiry.

Alongside methodological plurality, legitimation also benefits from theoretical openness. This openness is reflected in the theoretical framework, the strategic-

46. Barker, *Legitimating Identities*, p. 137.

47. Joseph Rothschild, 'Observations on political legitimacy in contemporary Europe', *Political Science Quarterly* 92(3), (1977), p. 491.

48. William R. Freudenburg and Margarita Alario, 'Weapons of mass distraction: magicianship, misdirection, and the dark side of legitimation', *Sociological Forum* 22(2), (June 2007), p. 147.

49. Achim Hurrelmann *et al.*, 'Why the democratic nation-state is still legitimate: a study of media discourses', *European Journal of Political Research* 48, (2009), pp. 485–486.

50. *Ibid.*, p. 486.

51. Beetham, *The Legitimation of Power*, pp. 12–18.

relational approach, adopted in my own research.[52] This approach is concerned with the interaction between structure, agency and ideas[53] and, though not specific to legitimation, it allows for the concept to provide greater explanatory depth. This notion of openness also relates to the collaborative aspect of conducting research on the power of the CCP. Given that one of the stated aims of Schubert's article is to form a research agenda, I contend that the lack of theoretical and methodological prescriptiveness with legitimation offers greater prospect for cross-disciplinary collaboration. Indeed, whereas legitimacy is something akin to a closed concept, legitimation can be regarded as more 'open-source', in that it provides a common conceptual language for researchers from a numbers of fields across the social sciences to communicate their findings on the authority of the party-state.

A final reason for adopting the conceptual framework of legitimation is that it fixes attention on the question of why the CCP has remained in power. Though legitimacy can be deployed to address this question, Barker makes the general point that '[e]nquiries as to whether or not a regime is legitimate too easily conclude with a judgement which has either no explanatory future, or no descriptive content'.[54] In the case of China, most empirical approaches attempt to measure how much the CCP has, with the result that much, if not all, of the research is more concerned with predicting the future direction of the Party rather than explaining its current predicament.[55] Given the difficulties of forecasting in more open and transparent political systems,[56] the China studies' field and, indeed, the social sciences in general would be better served by addressing the question of why the CCP has remained in power. It is the conceptual framework of legitimation that brings this question back into focus.

In order to demonstrate how legitimation can be deployed to address this question, the final part of this article will (briefly) present my own research on the CCP's discourse of stability in the post-Tiananmen period.[57] The identification of stability as a source of regime legitimation was first proposed by Shue, who suggested that the CCP no longer derived its legitimacy from its 'technical capacity' to deliver economic growth but from its 'political capacity' to create a stable environment in which economic development can take place.[58] This stable environment is, according to Shue, dependent on the Party's capacity to fulfill the transcendental truths of 'Truth, Benevolence and Glory'. While the validity of such a claim is difficult to prove, Shue's work suggests the need for analytical investigation into the Party's successful creation of a stable environment. More recently, Weatherley has also

52. Peter Sandby-Thomas, *Legitimating the CCP since Tiananmen: A Critical Analysis of the Stability Discourse* (Abingdon and New York: Routledge, 2010).

53. For more on this approach, see Colin Hay, *Political Analysis* (Basingstoke: Palgrave Macmillan, 2002); Bob Jessop, *State Power* (Cambridge, MA: Polity Press, 2007).

54. Barker, *Legitimating Identities*, p. 23.

55. As noted earlier, Chen Jie attempted to measure the political support for the regime from 1995 to 1999. The central finding—that the legitimacy of the CCP had declined during this period—supported Chen's conclusion that this decline would likely continue into the future, has clearly not been realized and highlights the difficulties of both generalizing contextual data and in using such data to make predictions about the future of the regime. For more, see Chen, *Popular Political Support in Urban China*.

56. Philip E. Tetlock, *Expert Political Judgment: How Good Is It? How Can We Know?* (Princeton, NJ: Princeton University Press, 2006).

57. Sandby-Thomas, *Legitimating the CCP since Tiananmen*.

58. Shue, 'Legitimacy crisis in China?'.

identified stability as a source of legitimacy and, eschewing Shue's transcendentalist turn, views stability as a supplement to the Party's reliance on economic performance and nationalism. However, his brief treatment reinforces the need for more research on this topic so as to develop a fuller understanding of the CCP's use of stability in legitimating its rule in the post-Tiananmen period.

In terms of deploying the concept of legitimation, my research sought to move beyond Weber's commonly-used 'modes of legitimation' approach,[59] for though it is useful in describing how a regime maintains its authority, Weber's concept is necessarily limited in explaining why a regime maintains its authority. This is because it does not provide space in which to conceptualize why people believe in the identified modes of legitimation. Indeed, Weber's conceptualization suggests that regimes which act in accordance with norms and rules (that it has established) will continue to be legitimate. As such, this conceptualization is overly structuralist and, though the inclusion of the *Lebenswelt* concepts of belief, meaning and intention suggest a role for agency, it is effectively reduced to that of material circumstances.[60] Criticism of Weber is widespread and, indeed, Beetham suggests that much of the difficulty in operationalizing the concept in the social sciences can be traced back to his foundational definition. By way of solution, Beetham puts forward a more dynamic and multi-dimensional version that attempts to overcome Weber's structural bias. To that end, he proposes three universal and objective criteria against which a regime can be judged.[61] However, in 'solving' this issue, Beetham's model creates a number of new problems. Chief among these is his model's emphasis on the conferment of a regime's legitimacy by the subordinate, which in the case of communist political systems are identified as the masses, as it fails to acknowledge the role played by endogenous legitimation. Indeed, Beetham goes so far as to assert that this form of legitimation is 'chiefly of consequence for the members of the state apparatus, or the political elite, and has little relevance for the population as a whole'.[62] However, given that subordinate consent is largely centered on acts of compliance and resistance, Beetham's model appears to confuse the exercise of power with its efficacy. In this, the suggestion is that the exercise of power can be analytically separated from legitimation. By contrast, I would argue that legitimation is an essential pre-condition for the exercise of power, at the very least by those who decide to exercise it. As Bourdieu points out, '[n]o power can be satisfied with

59. This approach identified three 'ideal type' modes: legal-rational; charismatic; and traditional. In contemporary applications, analysts have employed additional modes, such as those of ideology and 'eudaemonism'.

60. Robert Grafstein, 'The failure of Weber's conception of legitimacy: its causes and implications', *The Journal of Politics* 43(2), (1981), p. 457.

61. These criteria are: *conformity of rules*—the extent to which a regime's power conforms to established rules; *justifiability of rules*—the extent to which these rules are justified in terms of shared beliefs; and *legitimation expressed through consent*—the extent to which there is evidence of consent expressed by those who are subordinate. More specifically, Beetham views these criteria as interrelated, so that the illegitimacy only occurs when all three of the criteria are not maintained. For more, see Beetham, *The Legitimation of Power*, chs 1 and 2.

62. *Ibid*., p. 33. Interestingly, Beetham does appear to acknowledge the role of endogenous legitimation at the systemic level when stating that '[l]ike any other political body exercising jurisdiction, international institutions require justification in terms of the purposes or ends they serve, which cannot be met by other means, in this case by nation states themselves, or at the individual state level. A continuing ability to meet these purposes, therefore, would seem to be an important condition for the legitimacy of their authority'. See David Beetham and Christopher Lord, *Political Legitimation and the European Union* (London: Longman, 1998), p. 12.

existing just as power, that is, as brute force, entirely devoid of justification—in a word, arbitrary—and it must thus justify its existence'.[63] Applying this to political leaders, Kailitz makes the further point that

> [t]he justification of power is usually not merely window-dressing by rulers. To be a pillar of the stability and effectiveness of a political regime, the legitimation of the political regime must be credible. To make a credible claim, the rulers should believe in their legitimization.[64]

A final point is that while the formal model put forward by Beetham offers a useful heuristic device for assessing the legitimacy of a regime, it appears more concerned with establishing how legitimate a regime is rather than explaining why a regime is legitimate. In light of this, I opted to reconceptualize legitimation so as to allow for fuller consideration of why people believe what they believe. Of particular interest was providing the space in which to consider the role played by ideas in the maintenance of a regime's authority. To that end, the concept of legitimation was situated, as noted above, within the strategic-relational approach and the role played by ideas analyzed in terms of different discourses.

In terms of specifically analyzing the CCP's use of the stability discourse to legitimate its authority, my research focused on the media as the site of enquiry. Although there are other discursive sites that may more directly reflect the views of the leadership, such as speeches, the media was selected because of the legitimating role that it performs within the Chinese political system, both in reflecting the views of the leadership and in disseminating these views to other groups within society. More specifically, the *People's Daily* was selected as the source of enquiry. While Central People's Radio (CPR) and, especially, China Central Television (CCTV) reach a substantially higher number of people and the stories produced by Xinhua are picked up by newspapers across China, and despite the steep decline in the circulation figures for 'hard copies' in recent year,[65] the position of the *People's Daily* as the 'organ' of the CCP Central Committee and its direct link to the Party's Propaganda Department mean that it still plays an influential role in 'setting the tone' (*ding diaozi*) of the official discourse.[66] Within the *People's Daily*, the analysis was carried out on editorials (*shelun*) and commentaries (*pinglun*) on account of both their authority as well as their style.[67] In addition, within the time period in which the research was conducted (1989–2010), three specific instances were identified for analysis: the 'Beijing Spring' in 1989, the 'anti-*Falun Gong*' campaign in 1999 and the 'anti-Japan' demonstrations in 2005. These events were selected on the basis that

63. Pierre Bourdieu, *The State Nobility: Elite Schools in the Field of Power*, translated by Lauretta Clough (Cambridge, MA: Polity Press, 1996), p. 265.

64. Steffen Kailitz, 'Classifying political regimes revisited: legitimation and durability', *Democratization* 20(1), (2013), p. 41.

65. David Shambaugh, 'China's propaganda system: institutions, processes and efficacy', *The China Journal* 57, (January 2007), p. 56.

66. Guoguang Wu, 'Command communication: the politics of editorial formulation in the *People's Daily*', *The China Quarterly* 137, (March 1994), p. 195.

67. In terms of authority, they were considered to most directly represent the views of the Party leadership while, in terms of style, these types of articles, unlike news reports, are more explicitly argumentative in justifying particular viewpoints and so more useful for the purpose of the research.

they constituted exceptional instances in which the stability discourse was used to legitimate the CCP's authority. Furthermore, in each of these three instances, the challenge to the Party's power was different and, as such, carrying out an analysis of how the stability discourse was used in each of these instances would lead to a more complete understanding of the discourse.

The method used to analyze the selected articles for each event was the discourse-historical approach. This method was developed by Wodak and the 'Vienna School' and is associated with the broader school of critical discourse analysis (CDA).[68] In this approach, discourse is viewed as a form of social practice that both constitutes and is constituted by other social practices, with the distinction between the discursive and the non-discursive viewed as analytical and so not demonstrated solely through empirical analysis of texts. In terms of analyzing texts, my research followed the proposed four-step approach laid out in the discourse-historical method by, firstly analyzing the main themes (or topics) of the selected texts. The second step was to analyze the discursive strategies employed in the selected texts, while the third step focused on the linguistic means featured in the texts. The final step in the textual analysis was to highlight 'context-dependent linguistic realizations'.

The resulting analysis found that the use of stability was relatively consistent during the post-Tiananmen period. In this, stability was presented in a nominalized form that served to 'mystify' its definition and thus enabled it to be 'discursively flexible'. From there, stability was discursively constructed as a positive value that served to legitimate, often indirectly, the authority of the CCP, and, as a negative value that worked to delegitimate the 'other', be that the demonstrators in 1989, *Falun Gong* demonstrators in 1999 or the 'anti-Japan' demonstrators in 2005. In this positive and negative construction of stability, the same argumentation strategies were employed. For the positive construction, the direct link between maintaining stability and preserving the power of the CCP was obscured in favor of presenting stability as an issue of national interest. This link, which was initially established through the headline, worked to frame each challenge to the government in terms of its future consequences. In this, the space was opened up to put forward the CCP's vision of the future and, in so doing, close off competing alternatives.

This vision of China's future was reinforced by the construction of stability's negative value. Although the identification of the 'other' changed in each of the three events, the argumentation differed only in explicitness. In the cases of the military suppression in 1989 and the 'anti-*Falun Gong*' campaign in 1999, the government's actions necessitated the explicit negative presentation of the other while, in the cases of the pre-military suppression period and the 'anti-Japan' demonstrations in 2005, this negative presentation was achieved through implicature. Nevertheless, the arguments were effectively the reverse of those used in the positive construction of stability, in that the intention of the negative other, sometimes in collaboration with foreign states, was to 'destroy' China's stability which would, in turn, lead to the collapse of the CCP and so bring about a future state of 'chaos' similar to those experienced during periods of upheaval from China's modern history.

68. For more on this approach, see Ruth Wodak, 'The discourse-historical approach', in Ruth Wodak and Michael Meyer, eds, *Methods of Critical Discourse Analysis* (London: Sage, 2001), pp. 87–121.

In terms of legitimation, my research found that the CCP's use of the stability discourse throughout the post-Tiananmen period has relied on 'consequentialist' arguments to persuade members of Chinese society to support its authority. In this, China's undetermined future has been imagined in terms of 'good' and 'bad' consequences and, in so doing, appealed to people's fear and self-interest. Using Zhong's classification of 'positive' and 'negative' legitimation, however, it is possible to suggest that such arguments constitute a form of 'negative' legitimation, in that they avoid finding 'appropriate solutions to solve emerging economic, political and social problems'.[69] Consequently, while the stability discourse may well continue to sustain the regime in the short- to medium-term, there remains a question over whether it can continue to do so over the longer-term. Indeed, given that the stability discourse has remained largely the same in the pre- and post-Tiananmen periods, my research suggests that its legitimatory effectiveness has been due, in large part, to the political context after 1989 'favoring' this discourse. Drawing on the framework of the strategic-relational approach, I suggest that the events in 1989 constituted a *strategic* moment in the formation of the stability discourse in which the CCP's hegemonic interpretation of these events, as well as the subsequent collapse of communist regimes, has shaped the favorable political context for the reception of the stability discourse. As such, accepting this view suggests that, at some future point, the political context may no longer favor this discourse and so it will lose its effectiveness in legitimating the CCP's authority. Indeed, the increasingly numerous demonstrations that have been taking place at the local level across China expose the limits of this discourse in instances where grievances are specific rather than systemic. Furthermore, these instances highlight a possible area of future research which, by focusing on the reception of the stability discourse, would contribute to our understanding of the Party's legitimation at the micro-political level.

Conclusion

The aim of this article has been to broadly consider the utility of deploying the concept of legitimacy to explain the continued rule of the CCP. To that end, it has specifically focused on the research agenda put forward by Schubert in the pages of this journal. As stated above, Schubert is not the only scholar in the field making use of this concept; however, by virtue of his research agenda, he has attempted to initiate a welcome and much-needed debate on researching the legitimacy of the CCP. Moreover, this agenda makes a number of valuable contributions, not least by drawing attention to the pervasive view within Western academia discounting the longer-term survival of the CCP. While this view may well turn out to be correct, its effect has been to produce research focusing more on the problems than the successes of the regime's rule. By contrast, Schubert's research agenda focuses more on the successes and, through the concept of legitimacy, proposes a framework in which these successes can be viewed in terms of sustaining the Party's rule. In addition, the agenda's commitment to consider the legitimizing effects of reforms at the micro-political level helps to move the debate on the Party's legitimacy beyond, and

69. Zhong, 'Legitimacy crisis and legitimation in China', pp. 217–218.

below, the commonly cited macro-level 'economic performance + nationalism – communism' explanation.

However, this article has also sought to highlight a number of important issues with Schubert's research agenda. These issues are largely concerned with the conceptual implications of the proposed methodological approach and, as such, are intended to draw attention to the difficulty in substantiating claims about the legitimacy of the CCP. The first issue to be highlighted was that of scale, in that the proposed measurement of legitimacy at the micro-political level appears to privilege the views of the populace over those of other, possibly more, important actors within the political system. Beyond this, there is also uncertainty over how the views of the populace would directly impact the overall legitimacy of the regime. The second issue concerned the method being used to measure legitimacy, in that the 'systems analysis' approach advocated by Schubert appears to be conceptually flawed. In addition to being developed for use in a democratic context, it is unclear that the approach's distinction between legitimacy and support, which rests on temporality, can be meaningfully captured at the level of the empirical and so raises the question of whether this method actually measures legitimacy or a more elaborate form of popular support. The final issue to be highlighted concerned the scope of the research agenda, in particular the deployment of legitimacy 'zones'. In addition to the apparent ontological inconsistency between analytically distinguishing between these zones and attempting to empirically measure them, there is a lack of clarity over the process of identifying these zones. Furthermore, not only is the exclusion of particular zones, such as events and international sources of legitimacy, puzzling but such identification indicates the deployment of a normative definition of legitimacy and so raises the question of whether what is being measured actually constitutes legitimacy.

The cumulative effect of these issues is to question whether the concept of legitimacy proposed in Schubert's research agenda can be successfully operationalized to capture the totality of the CCP's legitimacy. And though it may well be possible to reconceptualize legitimacy so that it overcomes the issues raised in this article, the fact that legitimacy has not been convincingly operationalized by scholars, despite numerous attempts, suggests that this is unlikely. As a consequence, this article has proposed solving the problem of legitimacy by shifting towards the concept of legitimation. With regard to Schubert's research agenda, it would no longer be encumbered by the difficulties of operationalizing the concept of legitimacy. Furthermore, such a shift would not invalidate its existing empirical research; rather, the basis of the claims being made about it would change. With regard to the broader China studies' field, the conceptual framework of legitimation, through its greater theoretical and methodological flexibility, holds out the possibility of a common language in which researchers from a number of different fields across the social sciences can communicate their findings on the authority of the party-state. In this, legitimation, rather than legitimacy, offers the prospect of better explaining why the CCP has managed to remain in power.

Political Legitimacy in Contemporary China Revisited: theoretical refinement and empirical operationalization

GUNTER SCHUBERT

In the first part of this article the author comments on Peter Sandby-Thomas' contribution and critically assesses his suggestion to focus on 'legitimation' instead of 'legitimacy' when investigating the Chinese political system. In the second part, the author, in an effort to refine his analytical model to study legitimacy presented in an earlier article published in this journal, argues for combining Eastonian systems analysis and policy analysis, particularly at the local level of the Chinese state. The systematic accumulation of knowledge on local policy implementation with regard to procedure, output effectiveness and public responses, undertaken from an Eastonian perspective, provides China scholars with a fruitful approach to the study of legitimacy even if some methodological pitfalls remain.

Introduction

Peter Sandby-Thomas has critically assessed my article on 'One-party rule and the question of legitimacy in contemporary China', published in the *Journal of Contemporary China* in 2008.[1] At the time, I considered my thoughts to be very preliminary in nature and expressed my hopes for more scholarly debate on the topic.[2] I therefore wholeheartedly welcome the rigorous criticism to which the piece

1. Gunter Schubert, 'One-party rule and the question of legitimacy in contemporary China: preliminary thoughts on setting up a new research agenda', *Journal of Contemporary China* 17(54), (2008), pp. 191–204. The two other contributions in the special section are good examples of how this new research agenda could be pursued. See Jinghan Zeng, 'The debate on regime legitimacy in China: Bridging the wide gulf between Western and Chinese Scholarship', *Journal of Contemporary China* 23(88), (2014), doi: 10.1080/10670564.2013.861141; Florian Schneider and Yih-jye Hwang, 'The Sichuan earthquake and the heavenly mandate: legitimizing Chinese rule through disaster discourse', *Journal of Contemporary China* 23(88), (2014), doi: 10.1080/10670564.2013.861145.

2. In early July 2010, the Fudan Institute for Advanced Study in Social Sciences held a conference at Fudan University, Shanghai, on 'Legitimacy and Governance' that brought together Chinese and Western scholars to discuss the state and conditions of regime legitimacy in contemporary China. A collection of papers was later published as a special issue of the *Journal of Chinese Political Science* 16(2), (2011). An edited volume also appeared in the same year: Deng Zhenglai and Sujian Guo, eds, *Reviving Legitimacy* (Lexington, MA: Lanham, 2011). All chapters in the latter publication deal with methodological and theoretical issues concerning the concept of legitimacy and its applicability to the Chinese context, making it a very valuable contribution to the new research agenda for which I have argued in recent years.

has been subjected in this special section.[3] A new research agenda requires a good deal of methodological deliberation on how to research legitimacy (or legitimation), and Sandby-Thomas has made a useful contribution in this direction.

On the following pages, I will first respond to some of the issues Sandby-Thomas has raised concerning the relationship between legitimacy and legitimation, and his subsequent suggestion to abandon the 'soft' concept of legitimacy to focus instead on legitimation. I will then delineate an alternative framework of analysis in line with my original proposal to investigate *legitimacy*, even if it does involve certain methodological pitfalls which are hard to avoid. Although it may be easier to employ the concept of legitimation to gain insights into the state of the Chinese political system (or other political systems), I argue that this approach has its limits, too, as it cannot fully supplant our efforts to come to terms with legitimacy, which still remains an important issue.

Between legitimacy and legitimation

As Sandby-Thomas correctly notes, my 2008 article starts out with a simple hypothesis, i.e. 'the Chinese political system is able to generate significant degrees of regime legitimacy by adapting rather successfully to a changing domestic and international environment'.[4] Legitimacy, as I understand it, indeed pertains to the second strand, or 'analytical view' that Sandby-Thomas identifies within the academic literature, as it focuses on what people actually regard to be a legitimate order and takes these views seriously. Many years of fieldwork in different parts of China have convinced me that villagers and urbanites have a strong commonsense understanding of what is happening in their environment. Moreover, the party's control over information and its potential to use coercive force do little to bolster its popular image when it fails to deliver on the ground. Schaar's argument,[5] also cited by Sandby-Thomas, that adopting an analytical perspective towards legitimacy limits researchers to mere investigations of public opinion is misleading, as the local populace is often very well aware of both policy outcomes and official strategies to manipulate public opinion and does not take party statements at face value. As in many places, day-to-day politics is unspectacular in the local state and people know their rulers well. In present-day China, therefore, public opinion regarding local cadres and governments is indeed a strong and quite reliable indicator of regime and system legitimacy that needs to be taken seriously by China scholars.[6]

3. Peter Sandby-Thomas, 'How do you solve a problem like legitimacy?: contributing to a new research agenda', *Journal of Contemporary China* 23(88), (2014), doi: 10.1080/10670564.2013.861138.

4. Schubert, 'One-party rule and the question of legitimacy in contemporary China', p. 193.

5. John H. Schaar, *Legitimacy in the Modern State* (New Brunswick, NJ: Transaction, 1981), pp. 20–21.

6. Critical voices have repeatedly raised the question of whether researchers can reliably capture public opinion at all, given the control of local governments and cadres and the associated restrictions on doing fieldwork in China. It has also been suggested that scholars' efforts to secure long-term access to the field have compromised their objectivity. This has been most clearly argued by Carsten Holz in a provocative article published some years ago. See Carsten A. Holz, 'Have China scholars all been bought?', *Far Eastern Economic Review* 170(3), (2007), pp. 36–40. To what extent I myself may have been 'bought' is for others to judge. Trying to be as critical and self-reflective as possible when conducting fieldwork, I hold that qualitative data gathered in the Chinese local state are reliable, because, simply put, people do say what they think—a result of a pluralizing society and a state apparatus that is increasingly doomed to be service-oriented and law-abiding—or face the danger of public dissatisfaction and unrest, resulting in social instability and, consequently, endangering cadre careers.

Sandby-Thomas acknowledges this himself by saying that the analytical approach should not be dismissed 'on account of morally uncomfortable outcomes but rather be pursued by scholars who intend to better explain why the CCP remains in power'. From my standpoint, taking public opinion seriously always includes normative issues, as people are not only rational individuals but also moral agents who judge their political leaders based on normative categories and beliefs.[7]

The central question is indeed how claims about the CCP's legitimacy can be substantiated. This is the juncture at which Sandby-Thomas starts to take issue with my approach. He disputes the suggestion that micro-level analyses of the policy process can be related to macro-level assumptions about system legitimacy—mostly because this presupposes an even distribution of power, both vertically and horizontally, throughout the Chinese political system. 'Partial legitimacies' cannot simply be summated to calculate the overall degree of system legitimacy. This is true. The author then proposes a 'disaggregation' of Chinese politics by examining three kinds of relations, based on a Weberian typology, that are critical for generating legitimacy in the political system: elites–cadres, elites–masses and cadres–masses. Interestingly, Sandby-Thomas explicitly situates his 'chiefs' and 'staff' (elites and cadres) in the county and township bureaucracies, neatly supporting my stance in a number of publications that the legitimacy of the Chinese political system materializes most clearly where policies are implemented 'on the ground', or where 'the state meets the people'. In other words: at county level and below. As I have argued in a recent article co-authored by Thomas Heberer, county and township cadres constitute a 'strategic group' that is critical for effective policy implementation. This group is faced with an increasingly demanding populace.[8] As a matter of fact, elite–mass and cadre–mass relations are as critical to system legitimacy as elite–cadre relations, and if 'partial legitimacies' must be weighted, then the lowest administrative levels of the Chinese political system should be assigned the highest factors.[9]

7. David Beetham's approach to legitimacy conforms to this view with his notion of *normative justifiability* of the rightful source of authority. Ultimately, it is the people who decide what is justifiable in normative terms, not authorities. However, Beetham urges social scientists to make both a critical and emphatic assessment of normative justifiability with regard to a specific historical and socio-political context, and not to rely on public opinion, or the 'belief in legitimacy', on the part of the populace. See David Beetham, *The Legitimation of Power* (Houndsmills: MacMillan, 1991).

8. The relationship between county and township cadres roughly corresponds with what Sandby-Thomas defines as elite–cadre relations and what he claims to miss in my 2008 piece. However, if this comparison stands, elite–cadre relations have long been a part of my analytical focus. See Gunter Schubert and Anna L. Ahlers, 'County and township cadres as a strategic group: "building a new socialist countryside" in three provinces', *China Journal* 67, (2012), pp. 67–86; Thomas Heberer and Gunter Schubert, 'County and township cadres as a strategic group. A new approach to political agency in China's local state', *Journal of Chinese Political Science* 17(3), (2012), pp. 221–249.

9. I think the 1989 demonstrations do not serve as a good example to prove how meaningless the masses are for system legitimacy. First of all, Walder's arguments, which Sandby-Thomas refers to, address the maintenance of power, not legitimacy. Second, legitimacy under 'crisis' conditions varies considerably from legitimacy in a 'politics as usual' state. In the former case, the regime's capacity to survive depends foremost on the effectiveness of its coercive apparatus and not on 'specific' or 'diffuse support'—in Easton's terminology—on the part of the populace.

Ascertaining overall system legitimacy by aggregating 'partial legitimacies' still remains problematic,[10] and Sandby-Thomas aptly exposes the methodological pitfalls that come with David Easton's theoretical undertaking. Easton's approach, which emphasizes the people's belief in legitimacy and their (specific and diffuse) support of a political system, does face a number of problems, even more so when applied to authoritarian China. As explained above, I would contest Sandby-Thomas' claim that 'the role played by the masses in the Chinese political system' can be largely dismissed when it comes to determining overall system legitimacy. And I certainly believe that the attitudes of (local) elites and cadres are just as critical in this regard. However, the exact measurement of specific and, more so, diffuse support remains a problem. To some extent, these concerns can be addressed by systematic and long-term empirical data on people's and cadres' attitudes as collected, for instance, by the World Value Survey and East Asia Barometer. However, as I will argue below, this quantitative approach must be complemented by a qualitative counterpart in order to be more telling and lay to rest a number of remaining concerns related to the reliability of quantitative data. This would also satisfy the widely held conviction among scholars that only a combination of quantitative and qualitative methods lets us really close in on 'reality'.

Finally, Sandby-Thomas is not satisfied with the logic behind my 'zones of legitimacy', and with good reason. This classification was in fact more commonsensical than systematic. My approach involved defining areas which I believed to be relevant for system legitimacy in China. That's why I would and did label these zones 'potential'. My typology was conceived as an open-ended 'toolbox' for explorations of legitimacy along the lines of Easton's three sources of legitimacy, i.e. ideology, structure and personal authority. In that sense, it is certainly 'unnecessarily limited' and open for refinement.

Having exposed the problems of an approach that measures *legitimacy*, Sandby-Thomas suggests abandoning this endeavor in favor of a conceptual framework that prioritizes *legitimation* as a conceptual framework for system (or regime) legitimacy in China. Legitimation, he argues, would allow us to grasp the process dynamics of a political system more fully. Most importantly, it would also do away with the problem of measuring of *legitimacy*. In addition, it would change the claims made about the political system, because 'governance reforms would no longer be measured in terms of the CCP's overall legitimacy but rather analyzed as part of the regime's variegated attempts at legitimation'. Legitimation is concerned with 'the process of justifying power', as the author writes, and where

> legitimacy's narrow focus on measuring (...) the views and attitudes held by the populace, privileges the perspective of the individual recipient in determining the rightfulness of a regime, legitimation acknowledges the multiplicity of actors involved in

10. By analytically privileging the policy process in the local state, I certainly do not claim that local governance matter-of-factly contributes to the production of all system legitimacy, as much as I do not claim that local conflict does not contribute to delegitimization, which is, of course, possible. 'Bridging effects' can impact system legitimacy, positively or negatively. I would argue, however, that governance and policy implementation in 'day-to-day' local Chinese politics ultimately add to, rather than detract from, the legitimacy of the political system.

> the political process and (...) allows for the perspectives of both the producer and recipients of justifying claims to be taken into account.

I take no issue with paying 'greater attention to the regime's production of legitimating claims' and to the ruling elite's sense of its own legitimacy as a 'crucial dimension' of overall system legitimacy. I would hold, however, that *legitimation* adopts a different analytical angle than *legitimacy.* It therefore produces different insights into the reality of a political system and demonstrates limitations when it comes to approaching system (or regime) legitimacy, which still remains an important topic.

To begin with, legitimation is an art of justifying, i.e. maintaining power—a point that Sandby-Thomas highlights himself. Although it depends on shared beliefs as to a just political order or proper rules on the part of the people, as highlighted in Beetham's approach, it is the authorities who steer the process of legitimation. Sandby-Thomas points out that 'the social sciences in general would be better served by addressing the question of why the CCP has remained in power' instead of focusing on how legitimate one-party rule in China is. He argues his point foremost with respect to a bigger scope of methodological and theoretical variety when studying legitimation. However, this is quite a different research agenda from exploring the legitimacy of CCP rule, even if one subscribes to the view that 'wherever power is exercised, there exists a need to justify this power', i.e. justified power is legitimate. So, if Sandby-Thomas implicitly contends that his analytical preference for legitimation at least indirectly reflects the degree of system legitimacy, which I think he does, then we have to carefully look at how he explains 'why people believe in the identified modes of legitimation', and how he puts his approach to empirical testing.[11]

At this point, Beetham comes in, or more correctly, Sandby-Thomas' interpretation of Beetham's approach. I do understand the author's criticism of that model as too elite-focused, running the risk of delegating legitimation to an intra-elite discourse on strategies to secure public support which may become detached from the 'masses'. Lest it merely claims to be legitimate, while forcefully silencing dissent when opportune or necessary, legitimate power needs feedback from the people. As a matter of fact, Beetham says little on how the link between legitimation and public consent can be *empirically* tested, which ultimately makes this model as problematic in methodological terms as Easton's approach to legitimacy. Aware of this issue, Sandby-Thomas wants to make an alternative attempt 'to reconceptualize legitimation so as to allow for fuller consideration of why people believe what they believe'. But does he succeed in establishing this empirical link through his reconceptualization? As valuable as I find the 'strategic-relational approach' that Sandby-Thomas applies to the CCP's 'stability discourse' by subjecting articles from the *People's Daily* to rigorous discursive analysis, it is hard to see for me how that relates to the public mindset. What makes the author so certain that the findings from his analysis reflect the shared beliefs of those who are addressed? There may be good

11. Note here that Sandby-Thomas explicitly criticizes the Weberian approach as 'structuralist' and thus inadequate in terms of the agency of those who are addressed by legitimation strategies.

reasons for the CCP regime to nurture and push forward a stability discourse, but it is difficult to grasp the extent to which this corresponds with what the people think and want. How far are we from mere indoctrination here—which would certainly not be the kind of successful legitimation that Sandby-Thomas (or Beetham, for that matter) has in mind?

In the end, the link between legitimation and public consent is not established empirically, but by contextual inference. For instance, the author argues that 1989

> constituted a strategic moment in the formation of the stability discourse in which the CCP's hegemonic interpretation of these events, as well as the subsequent collapse of communist regimes, has shaped the favorable political context for the reception of the stability discourse.

This may be a plausible assumption, but it is not (and cannot be) empirically tested. I fully understand that Sandby-Thomas does not endeavor to resolve the methodological problem of measuring people's opinions and perceptions in his approach to legitimation, which is, so he claims, more promising as a conceptual trajectory to make sense of system (or regime) legitimacy. However, an investigation of legitimation—whether following Beetham or taking his arguments a step further—cannot sidestep the necessity of dealing with the empirical problem of showing what is justifiable, and not only what is claimed to be justified![12]

And it is this point, based on my understanding of the final section of Sandby-Thomas' valuable contribution, that gets lost. It escapes me how the identification of 'the main themes (or topics) of the selected texts', the analysis of 'discursive strategies' and 'linguistic means' employed in theses texts, and, finally, 'context-dependent linguistic realizations', which expose a 'stability discourse' to legitimate CCP rule, can really tell us more about Chinese system legitimacy than an empirical assessment—methodologically problematic as it may be—of the people's 'beliefs'. To put it differently: to what extent is stability a value in Chinese society that is shared by the people and hence justifies the official claim to one-party rule? Along the same lines, the author's assumption that 'at some future point, the political context may no longer favor this discourse and so it will lose its effectiveness in legitimating the CCP's authority' may be correct—but again, what is the empirical basis for this assumption?[13]

To sum up, Sandby-Thomas is right to point out the deficits of my 'preliminary thoughts on setting up a new research agenda' proposed in 2008, which emphasized a micro-political approach to the study of systemic legitimacy. My approach focused,

---

12. The weak, and equally strong, point in Beetham's approach to legitimacy is his argument for a context-specific interpretation on the part of the researcher to assess if the chosen strategy of legitimation corresponds to justifiable rules and norms in a given society. This is for the researcher to judge by taking into account and assessing 'shared beliefs, regulated according to understood conventions and confirmed through the expression of consent' in a given society. However, Beetham reveals little on how this assessment should be conducted and actually seems more to appeal to the researcher's historical knowledge and cultural empathy than to empirical investigation to come to the right conclusions. See Beetham, *The Legitimation of Power*, p. 31.

13. As a matter of fact, Sandby-Thomas is very close to Beetham here, as he makes an informed statement on the social justifiability of stability. Interestingly, he then suggests that the 'reception of the stability discourse' at the micro-level is necessary to 'contribute to our understanding of the Party's legitimation', thus explicitly pointing at the necessity to empirically verify informed statements that have been gathered (exclusively) based on textual analysis and historical context.

rather restrictively, on public responses to local policy implementation as the most important means of assessing legitimacy, and exposed some arbitrariness concerning the identification of 'zones of legitimacy' within the Chinese political system. As a consequence, the author suggests dispensing with legitimacy as an analytical concept, because 'though it may well be possible to reconceptualize legitimacy (...), the fact that legitimacy has not been convincingly operationalized by scholars, despite numerous attempts, suggests that this is unlikely'. Alternatively, Sandby-Thomas recommends turning to legitimation as a concept that has 'greater theoretical and methodological flexibility' and can hence be more easily operationalized. Although I agree with this practical point, I believe that investigating legitimation produces quite different results from researching legitimacy and does not necessarily tell us more about 'why the CCP has managed to remain in power' than rigorous attempts to come to terms with the tricky measurement of legitimacy.

In the rest of this article I will, hopefully, undertake a more systematic attempt than in my 2008 piece to make Easton's approach accessible to empirical testing, hence maintaining my earlier claim that his model, combined with an identification of 'zones of legitimacy building' throughout the political system, is helpful for an assessment of system legitimacy in contemporary China. For this purpose, Easton's model must be complemented by other conceptual approaches allowing for empirical testing. I will argue that a valuable pathway to solving the 'legitimacy conundrum' is the successive accumulation of knowledge on local policy implementation processes that, actually, exposes all the relationships that Sandby-Thomas has identified as critical to researching legitimacy, and makes them practical objects of scholarly investigation: elite–masses, cadre–masses and elite–cadres. My further reflections will, I am afraid, not do away with most of Sandby-Thomas' concerns, but they should help to make a stronger argument for adhering to the concept of legitimacy instead of abandoning it in favor of legitimation.

Eastonian systems theory revisited[14]

As I noted back in 2008, I still consider David Easton's political systems theory a useful starting point to tackle the 'legitimacy conundrum'. For Easton, a political system is identified 'as a set of interactions, abstracted from the totality of social behaviour, through which values are authoritatively allocated for a society'.[15] It is conceptualized as an open and adaptive system which interacts dynamically with society. The political system is constantly exposed to *stimuli* from its environment and must react to those which may become dangerous to its survival. Hence, if the political system manages to constantly process these stimuli so that the authoritative allocation of values and 'relative frequency of compliance with them'[16] on the part of society is maintained, it will remain stable; if it fails to do so, it will break down. More precisely, in order to survive, the political system must successfully transform

14. The following sections are based on an earlier article co-written by Anna L. Ahlers and Gunter Schubert, '"Adaptive authoritarianism" in contemporary China: identifying zones of legitimacy building', in Deng Zhenglai and Sujian Guo, eds, *Reviving Legitimacy*, pp. 61–81.

15. David Easton, *A Systems Analysis of Political Life*, 2nd edn (New York: Wiley, 1967), p. 57.

16. *Ibid.*, p. 24.

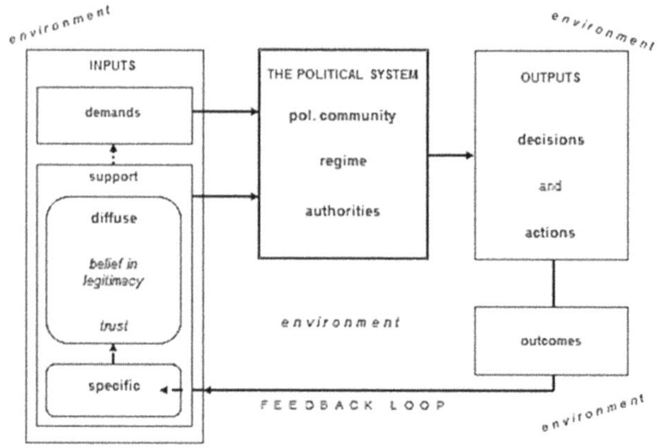

Figure 1. The Eastonian model. *Source*: Ahlers and Schubert, '"Adaptive authoritarianism" in contemporary China', p. 66.

inputs into *outputs*, which flow into the system as *demands* and *support* on the part of the populace (see Figure 1). These outputs (which are translated into specific *outcomes*, i.e. policies) must be positively assessed by the members of society, producing new support and new demands that are then channeled back into the political system. If this *feedback loop*[17] is interrupted so that output or outcomes do not produce support, the system becomes dysfunctional and will eventually collapse.[18]

I still stand behind my working hypothesis that the Chinese political system is endowed with enough problem-solving savvy 'to cope with stress'[19] from its environment and, in the process, generate a critical degree of political stability to perpetuate itself. Hence, a positive feedback loop exists between output (outcomes) and support: the Chinese people are, in *grosso modo*, content with the performance of their political system. Moreover, they also consent to its underlying values, institutions and authorities. Hence, the Chinese political system not only enjoys *specific*, i.e. performance-related support,[20] but also sufficient *diffuse* support, i.e. 'favorable attitudes or good will that helps members to accept or tolerate outputs to which they are opposed or the effect of which they see as damaging to their wants'.[21] Hence, the Chinese political system is considered to be legitimate by most members

17. The feedback loop 'consists of the production of outputs by the authorities, a response to these on the part of the members of society, the communication of information about this response to the authorities and finally, possible succeeding actions on the part of the authorities. By this means, a new round of outputs, response, information feedback and reaction on the part of the authorities is set in motion and is part of a continuous, never-ending flow' (*Ibid.*, pp. 28–29).

18. This model has often been criticized as tautological (and even apologetic), because any system may be called stable and legitimate, that is, capable of persisting, as long as it continues to operate. However, I believe that the tautology can be avoided by an empirical operationalization of the model along the lines explained below.

19. *Ibid.*, p. 29.

20. Specific support, according to Easton, 'is directed towards the political authorities and authoritative institutions. It assumes that members have sufficient political awareness to be able to associate satisfaction and dissatisfaction with the perceived behaviour of these authorities, whether the behaviour is in the form of identifiable actions or some attributed general performance' (David Easton), 'A reassessment of the concept of political support', *British Journal of Political Science* 9, (1975), p. 439.

21. Easton, *A Systems Theory of Political Life*, p. 273.

Table 1. Sources and objects of legitimacy in Easton's political systems theory

	Objects of legitimacy	
Sources of legitimacy	Regime	(Political) Authorities
Ideology	*Ideological legitimacy*	
	Moral convictions about the validity of the regime	Moral convictions about the validity of incumbents of authority
Structure	*Structural legitimacy*	
	Independent belief in validity of the structure (institutions) and norms of the political order	Overflow from belief in structure to the incumbent of the authority roles
Personal qualities	*Personal legitimacy*	
	Overflow from belief in the validity of the incumbents of authority roles to the authority roles (structure and norms of regimes) themselves	Independent belief in validity of authorities because of their personal qualities

Source: Easton, *A Systems Theory of Political Life*, p. 287.

of society. I argue that the functional circle of the Eastonian model, including the measurement of support, can be empirically tested and does not need to remain in the realm of abstract causality. However, this requires a further refinement of the analytical framework to be applied.[22]

Legitimacy (i.e. the belief therein) in the Eastonian model is accorded to the political regime (i.e. the political structure) and the political authorities (i.e. political office holders). It is one of two dimensions of diffuse support (the other being trust) and derives

> from the conviction on the part of the member that it is right and proper for him to accept and obey the authorities and to abide by the requirements of the regime. It reflects the fact that in some vague or explicit way he sees these objects as conforming to his own moral principles, his own sense of what is right and proper in the political sphere,[23]

and 'no other source of support can assure such ready acceptance of the outputs'[24] of a political system than the belief in a regime's legitimacy. The *sources of legitimacy*, according to Easton, are to be found in *ideology*, *structure* and *personal authority* (see Table 1).[25] However, Easton does not provide us with any tools to measure legitimacy empirically—a problem that will be addressed below.

22. Keep in mind that I do not postulate that the Chinese political system *is* legitimate. I only claim that it makes sense to propose such a hypothesis in order to test the modified Eastonian model.
23. *Ibid.*, p. 278.
24. *Ibid.*, p. 310.
25. *Ibid.*, ch. 19. Though Easton retains Weber's notion of a *belief in legitimacy*, he criticizes Weber's approach as overly simplistic (as David Beetham does), especially concerning his legal-rational ideal type of legitimate authority (*legitime Herrschaft*) (pp. 301–302).

David Beetham,[26] in his critique of Max Weber's conception of legitimacy, and implicitly of Easton's as well, rejects the accentuation of *belief* and argues for a multidimensional approach to (political) legitimacy that focuses on the *conformity of rules* (or *legal validity*), the *justifiability of rules in terms of shared beliefs* and *legitimation through expressed consent*,[27] with all three elements interrelated and providing 'the subordinate with moral grounds for compliance or cooperation with the powerful'.[28]

At the same time, legitimacy is bound to the expression of consent, i.e. political action. As Beetham argues,

> specific actions (...) are important because they *confer* legitimacy on the powerful, not because they provide evidence of the people's beliefs. They confer legitimacy because they constitute public expressions by the subordinate of their consent to the power relationship and their position within it; of their voluntary agreement to the limitation of their freedom by the requirements of a superior.[29]

Hence, actions, as expressed consent, are the only measurable manifestation of the subordinate's consent to political authority.[30] Beetham's approach, which is explicitly proposed to the social scientist, requires the researcher assessing the significance of the *rule of law* in a given regime to investigate the visible scope of 'expressed consent' and—the most tricky part—to verify to what extent political claims of power and authority can be justified in terms of values and norms as 'shared beliefs' in a given society.[31]

Although Beetham rejects the Weberian tradition of conceptualizing legitimacy, while Easton certainly upholds this tradition, I think that his approach can actually help us to clarify and sharpen the Eastonian concept of legitimacy in theoretical terms and, to some extent, empirically as well: it is not individual beliefs that count, but the way in which support (or rejection) of political decisions becomes visible through action. Moreover, *belief in legitimacy* must be assessed against the background of historical traditions and events that have shaped the moral foundations of and value orientations

26. Beetham, *The Legitimation of Power*; see also David Beetham, 'Max Weber and the legitimacy of the modern state', *Analyse und Kritik* 13(1), (1991), pp. 34–45; and David Beetham, 'Political legitimacy', in Kate Nash and Allan Scott, eds, *The Blackwell Companion to Political Sociology* (Oxford: Blackwell Publishers, 2001), pp. 107–116.

27. 'For power to be fully legitimate, then, three conditions are required: its conformity to established rules, the justifiability of the rules by reference to shared beliefs; the express consent of the subordinate, or of the most significant among them, to the particular relations of power' (Beetham, *The Legitimation of Power*, p. 19).

28. *Ibid.*, p. 16.

29. *Ibid.*, p. 91.

30. Such actions may materialize in electoral participation or 'taking part in consultations or negotiations with the powerful, either about aspects of policy or about the terms on which a particular service is rendered, which culminate in agreement'. But also 'swearing an oath of allegiance' or 'public acclamation' confer legitimacy through expressed consent. See *Ibid.*, pp. 92–94.

31. Beetham requires the researcher, or China scholar in our case, to conduct a 'systematic comparison between different forms of legitimacy appropriate to different historical types of social and political system' and to assess 'the degree of legitimacy-in-context of a given power relationship, as a necessary element in explaining the behavior of those involved in it'. As he notes further, 'this is the immanent judgement or assessment of the social scientist, as opposed to the normative philosopher's assessment of a power relationship against independent, external standards or criteria'. Thus the social scientist must be historically informed and equipped with sufficient cultural knowledge and empathy to engage in a hermeneutical undertaking to identify the norms and values in a society which are relevant for legitimizing power relationships. See *Ibid.*, pp. 22–23.

within a given society. This, of course, is an interpretive exercise based on historically (culturally) informed expertise and argumentative plausibility. However, Eastonian theory, even if complemented by Beetham's three-dimensional approach to legitimacy, still needs some additional fine-tuning to make it fit for empirical testing.

Integrating policy analysis

Eastonian systems analysis provides us with a useful terminology and an 'analytical logic' to investigate a political system's different modes of operation. However, with regard to the question of how legitimacy is generated, it remains too abstract for empirical analysis. As argued above, Beetham's approach is more specific, as it clarifies how 'belief in legitimacy' should be conceptually and empirically tackled to become analytically meaningful. This particularly relates to the dimension of 'expressed consent'. However, the 'justifiability of norms and values as shared beliefs' remains a problematic dimension, as it gives social scientists considerable leeway to interpret past and present based on their own understanding of a society's history, culture and politics. As I have emphasized above, a recourse to *legitimation* as a more promising trajectory for understanding the nature of society's shared beliefs has its limitations as well, most notably because it takes a top-down perspective and can only indirectly infer the extent to which official legitimation strategies reflect normative values in a society. At this point, I argue that social scientists should address the 'belief in legitimacy' conundrum by applying a micro-political approach to empirical reality. My main argument is that the legitimacy of the Chinese political system depends on how the people perceive and evaluate the quality of local policy making and implementation. It is particularly at the local level, where the state (i.e. its authorities) directly faces the people, that 'specific' and 'diffuse' support for a political system are engendered, individual and collective 'beliefs' are created and remolded, and consent to the authorities is most often 'expressed'. This is where policy analysis comes in.

Policy making follows a cycle that consists of five consecutive phases: problem definition, agenda setting, policy formulation, implementation and evaluation.[32] Functionally, these can be directly related to the operating mode of the Eastonian model: the processing of inputs corresponds to the phases of problem definition and agenda setting. Output can be understood as the product of policy formulation; outcomes represent the implementation of results (that vary). Finally, the feedback loop can be likened to policy evaluation, which may or may not bring about support (see Figure 2).[33] Linking Eastonian systems analysis and policy analysis is plausible because the survival

32. However, the number of phases that are addressed varies in the relevant literature. See, e.g. Volker Schneider and Frank Janning, *Politikfeldanalyse. Akteure, Diskurse und Netzwerke in der öffentlichen Politik* [*Policy Analysis. Actors, Discourses and Networks in Public Policy*] (Wiesbaden: VS-Verlag, 2006); Frank Fischer, Gerald J. Miller and Mara S. Sidney, eds, *Handbook of Public Policy Analysis: Theory, Politics and Methods* (London: CRC Press Taylor & Francis, 2007); Michael J. Hill and Christopher Ham, *The Policy Process in the Modern State* (London: Prentice Hall/Harvester Wheatsheaf, 1997).

33. Easton's feedback loop requires that the 'members of society', that is, the people, assign support. Therefore, policy evaluation must ensure that the policy makers take into account the people's concerns, lest they become detached from reality and thus fail to generate support. In the Chinese case, as in most authoritarian systems, direct citizen participation in the making and assessment of policies is restricted or even non-existent. This means that policy evaluation, if aimed at sustaining the feedback loop, must factor in public opinion in different ways (see below).

of a political system—for instance the Chinese system—can best be understood by highlighting its capacity to identify, define and successfully implement system-relevant policies, that is, policies that are decisive for the generation of legitimacy.

Policy analysis alone is not very revealing with regard to the driving forces of the policy process, nor can it explain why the different phases take the specific paths that we observe. To put it differently: a systems analysis based on the Eastonian model and the concurrent tracing of policy cycles can tell us a great deal about a political system's functional dynamics, but both lack explanatory power as to why outcomes develop as they do—and to what effect in terms of legitimacy building. For that matter, we should look more closely at the political actors who shape the policy process at the local level, most notably local officials,[34] because the stability and legitimacy of the Chinese political system ultimately depends strongly on local state dynamics as well as the evaluation of policy outcomes on the ground.[35]

In tracing the policy cycle, we address the strategies which local cadres apply in order to adjust and implement policies handed down from the central state and their more immediate superiors at the provincial and prefectural levels. At the same time, we factor in the changing institutional environment in which these actors pursue their agendas, such as formal modes of political participation and resistance (e.g. village elections, consultation mechanisms, petitioning), cadre evaluations, the legal order (anti-corruption legislation) and the fiscal system, as well as informal institutions including information and knowledge (on, for example, central laws and upper level guidelines, government programs), public opinion and certain cultural norms (clientelistic reciprocity, clan affiliation, etc.). Hence, assessing the legitimacy of the Chinese political system builds on a systematic empirical analysis of local policy processes in which local governments respond to public demands that have been identified by the central state and translated into policy prescriptions that local governments must eventually adjust to circumstances on the ground and implement. How effectively these policies are implemented in terms of local policy blueprints, and how they are evaluated by the local populace, are important references to assess the legitimacy of the local authorities and, arguably, the political system as a whole.

Zones of legitimacy building

The analytical framework which has been sketched out above applies to all administrative tiers, though it is particularly concerned with the county, township and village levels. It starts by tracing policy initiatives which the central state has identified as highly relevant for the long-term stability of the Chinese political system. In the recent past, relevant policies have targeted the fiscal system, social welfare, labor relations, environmental protection, land management, agricultural development, rural–urban integration and urban community building. The researcher

34. Although *peasants*, *migrants*, *private entrepreneurs* and *social activists* are also potential actors to be investigated in this context, they usually pale in comparison to county, township and village cadres when it comes to local policy implementation. For an elaboration of this argument see Heberer and Schubert, 'County and township cadres as a strategic group'.

35. From an Eastonian perspective, local cadres represent the *political authorities* (or *authority figures*), and their *personal qualities*, which are important sources and objects of legitimacy.

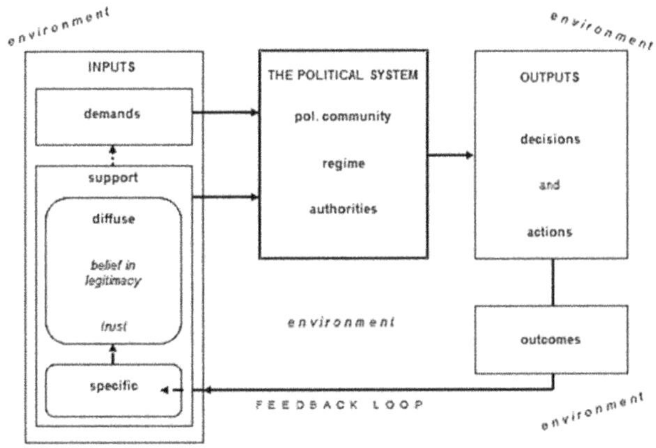

Figure 3. Identifying zones of legitimacy building in the Eastonian model. *Source*: Ahlers and Schubert, '"Adaptive authoritarianism" in contemporary China', p. 73.

begins by reconstructing political agenda setting at the national level, followed by the successive concretization of central guidelines at lower administrative tiers. Then he or she looks at how effectively they are implemented and evaluated, both in terms of internal target assessment and public responses. While policies are framed at the central level, they are adapted to local conditions by city and, most notably, county governments further down in the administrative hierarchy. Projecting the policy cycle onto the operational mode of an Eastonian political system, we can distinguish between three zones of (potential) legitimacy building (see Figure 3). As the 'production sites' for outputs and outcomes, it is in these zones where system performance, arguably, is transformed into legitimacy.

(1) Output zone

In this zone, policy reforms and institutional innovations are formulated and transformed into outputs. It covers the stages of problem definition, agenda setting and policy formulation, conducted at the central (national) level of government. The structural imperatives of system adaptability and legitimate authority require a political system to identify policies that are relevant for solving critical problems which the system faces. To assess this *relevancy*, the following research questions should be asked:

- Which problems are identified by the political system? How does the system respond to input and stress from its environment?
- How much importance is attached to a problem identified by the system, i.e. where does the problem range on the political agenda?
- What decisions are made to tackle the problem? What kind of policy is formulated? Which targets are set, and who is addressed?
- How is this policy justified ideologically?

Hence, in this zone we pinpoint the political system's capability to formulate policies that respond to problems which are critical for its survival. Our hypothesis is that for the time being, the central authorities in China are able to identify the most pressing problems and come up with reasonable solutions, the latter of which are informed by rational and strategic macro planning. More recent examples of relevant agenda-setting are the rural tax and fee reform initiated in the early 2000s, a new comprehensive approach to rural development under the label of 'Constructing a New Socialist Countryside' (officially launched in 2006), and the promotion of rural–urban integration thereafter. The ideological framing of those policies, as most prominently undertaken by the concept of a *Harmonious Society* in the Hu Jintao era (2002–2012), might seem only loosely related at first sight, but should not be underestimated as a tool for legitimation.[36] Even though local cadres often fail to properly implement policy guidelines passed down from the central state, the latter can still retain its legitimacy. As a matter of fact, the center is often believed to have good intentions by the majority of the populace.[37] This belief is reinforced by the official ideological discourse, e.g. the promotion of a *Harmonious Society*, which evokes the image of a 'caring state' that shows strong consideration for the people's lot and does its best to remedy their grievances.[38]

(2) Implementation zone

This is the zone in which outputs materialize and are transformed into outcomes, and the locus of action where adaptive reforms are implemented and contextualized, i.e. locally embedded and legitimized. In this zone, empirical investigation centers on local cadres, their institutional environment and their interaction with 'the people'.[39] To assess a policy's *embeddedness* at the local level, the following questions should be asked:

- How has a policy been implemented, i.e. how have local governments and cadres interpreted and adjusted policy guidelines issued from above?
- How does the (institutional) environment of local cadres impact local policy adaptation?

36. See, for example, Ann Mary Brady, 'Mass persuasion as a means of legitimation and China's popular authoritarianism', *American Behavioral Scientist* 53(3), (November 2009), pp. 434–457.

37. An often cited article for this argument is Lianjiang Li, 'Political trust in rural China', *Modern China* 30(2), (2004), pp. 228–258.

38. The construction of a *Socialist Harmonious Society* (*shehui zhuyi hexie shehui*) is targeted for completion by 2020. It was inscribed in the CPC's constitution in 2007 and has since then been regarded as Hu Jintao's special contribution to the party's ideological evolution. Together with the *Scientific Concept of Development* (*kexue fazhan guan*), it arguably marks a qualitative innovation in the existing paradigm of development, adding a more socially balanced vision of prosperity, as well as including aspects such as sustainability and the importance of protecting and preserving natural resources and the environment.

39. At this point, the researcher has to deal with the interplay between agency and structure and make a decision as to the theoretical approach to be applied. Policy analysis, for its part, does not provide a theory of agency or institutions. One option would be an approach pertaining to 'bounded rationality' or the 'new institutionalism'. See, e.g. Guy B. Peters, *Institutional Theory in Political Science. The 'New Institutionalism'* (London: Continuum, 1999); Fritz W. Scharpf, *Games Real Actors Play: Actor-Centered Institutionalism in Policy Research* (Boulder, CO: Westview Press, 1997). For strategic group analysis, which integrates components of Bourdieu's social theory, including social fields, capital formation and 'habitus', see Heberer and Schubert, 'County and township cadres as a strategic group'.

- What strategies and programs are formulated to respond (and make use) of specific local conditions?
- To what extent do the people participate in the implementation process, e.g. by voting, deliberation or consultation?
- What specific outcomes does the policy yield?

In this zone, the process of local policy implementation is traced and the role of the local cadre bureaucracy in this process investigated. Outcomes are analyzed on the basis of both quantitative and qualitative data. One guiding hypothesis with respect to generating legitimacy is that the more locally embedded a policy is, the more it will be supported—irrespective of whether the outcomes are optimal in terms of invested resources and 'objective' (external) benchmarks. Moreover, local authorities should enjoy legitimacy if they are inclined to be responsive, accountable and committed to procedural and distributive fairness.[40]

(3) Evaluation zone

This zone relates to the evaluation of policy outcomes. The political authorities at the local level might enjoy legitimacy because of the positive results of policy implementation in the perception of the populace. *Acceptance* of a policy, which is also based on a policy's relevancy and embeddedness, is measured by assessing public responses to policy outcomes, on the one hand, and performance evaluation (*kaohe*), an intra-party mechanism institutionalized by the political authorities themselves, on the other. Both are essential feedback mechanisms for the political system. The following questions are addressed at this stage of the analysis:

- How does the populace respond to local policy implementation (both in terms of overt consent or resistance)?
- How do the political authorities assess the success or failure of their policies?

Measuring legitimacy building by assessing a policy's acceptance is by no means a simple task. From the perspective of the political system, the political authorities must gather all possible information on an implemented policy (*feedback*) in order to correct it (if necessary) and thus maintain the system's stability. At this point, a thorough investigation of the different performance or target evaluation systems that feature so prominently in China's state and party organization is both useful and necessary. This means determining whether pre-defined targets or benchmarks for a policy have been checked against reported performance data, and to what extent target evaluation has positively influenced the quality of policy implementation. Even though the effects of the *kaohe* on local policy implementation are contested

40. Local cadres may not only be regarded as political authorities, but also as 'relevant members' of society in David Easton's terms. Although they are critical for the central state (the political system) as political agents, they are also suppliers of legitimacy in the sense that they believe that the political order they help to maintain is just. They have a *sense of legitimacy* directed at higher-level authorities or the political regime *per se*, which is an important prerequisite for their compliance in implementing policy. In my own fieldwork, I found that mid-level and lower-ranking local cadres often feel a strong moral commitment to implement policy measures which they thought to be ethically coherent and morally just, and they frequently linked this attitude to their individual histories, as many of them were brought up in the area where they now work.

by many observers,[41] as indicators are often negotiated and results whitewashed, internal policy evaluation is indeed a rather efficient mechanism for the political authorities to ensure effective local policy implementation. Regular cadre and target reviews are combined with career advancement and financial incentives (or penalties) to produce reliable, or at least approximate, information on the success or failure of a policy initiative. Studying this internal feedback mechanism and its impact on local governance reveals much of the Chinese political system's capability to learn from mistakes and adapt to changing demands from the environment, which is of paramount importance for its legitimacy. However, it is problematic to assert an immediate link between the (positive) results of internal performance evaluation and the legitimacy of local authorities without taking public responses into account.[42]

Public responses may range from emphatic affirmation to open resistance. There is much uncertainty concerning the extent to which overt (or express) consent (e.g. taking part in village elections, debating policy decisions in village representative assemblies or other formal and informal settings of policy deliberation now so common in many cities, counties and townships throughout China) does in fact reflect public support for the political authorities. It is certainly problematic to claim a positive link between grassroots participation *per se* and regime legitimacy, although the former is an important indicator for the success of legitimation strategies, as Sandby-Thomas (and Beetham) correctly notes.[43] Also, conducting qualitative interviews based on small *N* samples poses the problem of data robustness. These problems can only be effectively addressed through careful data collection and analysis, critical reflection, and cautious interpretation by the researcher over time.

System adaptability and regime legitimacy are generated within a complex array of empirical phenomena to be investigated in each zone of (potential) legitimacy building. The legitimacy of a political system or regime must be understood as being composed of partial 'legitimacies' generated in different administrative layers of the system and eventually unfolding in the evaluation zone, where the political authorities receive feedback on implemented policies. I have argued that the 'partial legitimacy' generated in the evaluation zone at the local level weighs more heavily than all other legitimacies generated throughout China's political system. This statement may be confirmed by the plausible assumption that in contemporary China,

41. See Kevin O'Brien and Li Lianjiang, 'Selective policy implementation in rural China', *Comparative Politics* 31(2), (1999), pp. 167–186; Maria Edin, 'Remaking the Communist party-state: the cadre responsibility system at the local level in China', *China. An International Journal* 1(1), (2003), pp. 1–15; Maria Edin, 'State capacity and local agent control in China. CCP cadre management from a township perspective', *The China Quarterly* 173, (2003), pp. 35–52; Susan H. Whiting, 'The cadre evaluation system at the grassroots: the paradox of party rule', in Barry J. Naughton and B. J. Yang Dali, eds, *Holding China Together. Diversity and National Integration in the Post-Deng-Era* (Cambridge: Cambridge University Press, 2004), pp. 101–119.

42. The evaluation of cadres and their performance is a multi-level process that increasingly integrates surveys conducted among party officials and citizens. Although the relative significance of these elements has still been limited in the places I visited during my fieldwork in recent years, they are steadily gaining in prominence and scope.

43. Along the same lines, it is questionable to assume that non-participation, or even resistance, always signals the absence of legitimacy. 'Rightful resistance', as conceptualized by Li Lianjiang and Kevin O'Brien, does indeed confer legitimacy to the political system, though its protagonists distinguish between local officials and the central government, with the former suffering from a deficit in legitimacy. See Kevin O'Brien and Li Lianjiang, *Rightful Resistance in Rural China* (Cambridge: Cambridge University Press, 2006).

systemic delegitimization hinges on protest, which always begins as a local grievance rooted in dissatisfaction over policy implementation.

To make any statement on the Chinese political system's overall adaptability and legitimacy from the perspective of local policy implementation by assessing the degree of (specific and diffuse) support generated among the 'members of society' during the implementation process is certainly a tricky matter. In general terms, it is difficult to aggregate from single cases and, at the very least, as many policy analyses as possible are required to give substance to general claims on the Chinese political system. However, any conclusion drawn from single cases is valid as long as it figures as a hypothesis open to verification or falsification and should thus not be discredited as methodologically untenable. In the theoretical framework proposed above, the link that people make (or do not make) between local policy implementation, on the one hand, and overall system performance and regime legitimacy, on the other, is critical. This also requires more sophisticated inquiries to measure political support and legitimacy.[44] More specifically, comprehensive surveys must be conducted that directly address the people's perceptions of local policy implementation and overall system performance, as well as the importance they assign to political participation, procedural and distributive justice, and specific policy outcomes.[45] However, systematic policy analysis with a focus on implementation and evaluation at the local level remains critical for the study of political legitimacy in contemporary China. Only the investigation of a comprehensive set of 'system-relevant' policies over time and a gradual accumulation of knowledge concerning the interaction of local cadres and the populace, success and failure in policy implementation, and evaluation in terms of both formal performance assessment and public responses, enable us to understand the Chinese political system's problem-solving capacities and its legitimacy. This is certainly a collective effort to be pursued by many China scholars examining different policy fields in different localities. There does in fact appear to

44. There have been recent attempts to measure legitimacy by linking it conceptually to the trustworthiness of government, procedural justice or other categories that are highly relevant in local policy implementation. See, e.g. Margaret Levi, 'Conceptualizing legitimacy, measuring legitimacy beliefs', *American Behavioral Scientist* 53(3), (November 2009), pp. 354–375. In spite of a growing body of literature on public opinion in China, there are only a few studies that directly address the evaluation of policy implementation and link this to an assessment of political support or regime legitimacy in some manner. See, e.g. Jie Chen, Yang Zhong and Jan W. Hillard, 'The level and sources of popular support for China's current political regime', *Communist and Post-Communist Studies* 30(1), (1997), pp. 45–64; Jie Chen, *Popular Political Support in Urban China* (Stanford, CA: Stanford University Press, 2004); Wenfang Tang, *Public Opinion and Political Change in China* (Stanford, CA: Stanford University Press, 2005); Yang Zhong, 'Democratic values among Chinese peasantry: an empirical study', *China: An International Journal* 3(2), (2005), pp. 189–211; Tony J. Saich, 'Citizens' perception on governance in rural and urban China', *Journal of Chinese Political Science* 12(1), (2007), pp. 1–28.

45. Interesting insights have been generated in this context by a thread of research in the field of political psychology. During the past decade, some scholars have become particularly interested in processes of legitimation and reasons behind beliefs in legitimacy. For instance, Tom Tyler has investigated procedural and performance-related factors as variables for the generation of legitimacy in the US and found that the evaluation of procedural fairness (among other factors) in policy making and implementation is more important than an assessment of its outcomes. See Tom R. Tyler, 'A psychological perspective on the legitimacy of authorities and institutions', in John T. Jost and Brenda Major, eds, *The Psychology of Legitimacy: Emerging Perspectives on Ideology, Justice and Intergroup Relations* (Cambridge: Cambridge University Press, 2001), pp. 416–436: John R. Tyler, 'Psychological perspectives on legitimacy and legitimation', *Annual Review of Psychology* 57, (2006), pp. 375–400.

be a new wave of mostly younger China scholars researching local governance along the lines of the agenda I have proposed in the present context.[46]

At this point, a final remark must be made with regard to the 'tautological danger' identified in the Eastonian model, even if it is complemented by policy analysis. This pertains to the argumentative circle that as *long as a political system exists, all policies must be relevant and embedded, and the policy outcomes sufficiently accepted. Hence, the system enjoys critical degrees of specific and diffuse support and, consequently, ensures the perpetuation of its existence.* This circle, I argue, can be avoided in two ways: first, the proposed framework informed by Eastonian systems analysis is simply viewed as a means to structure the field of scientific inquiry and to provide plausible hypotheses open to falsification. Although tracing the policy cycle and translating the findings of such an investigation into the language of Eastonian systems analysis in order to make broader statements on the Chinese political system as a whole is a difficult endeavor, all statements gathered in this process will at least be empirically grounded. The fact that the Chinese political system exists does not say anything about the ways in which it changes, and it is this very *change in persistence* that my approach seeks to highlight. We know that even if the Chinese system persists for the time being, it may suffer from a latent deficit in legitimacy that renders its stability precarious. The proposed framework should, however, help to discover such a condition as it focuses on policy implementation and evaluation at the local level by engaging in systematic empirical research. To put it differently: tautological arguments can be avoided if one takes the empirical opportunities offered by Eastonian systems analysis seriously.

Conclusion

Peter Sandby-Thomas has raised important issues regarding the study of legitimacy in the Chinese political system. I agree with his methodological criticism of my 2008 article on setting up a new research agenda. The turn to legitimation which he proposes sounds consequential; nevertheless, it primarily focuses attention on empirical phenomena that might reveal more about elite discourse and strategy than about public perceptions of the legitimating effects of legitimation. If legitimacy is hard to come by empirically, then the empirical link between legitimation and legitimacy is just as hard to establish. In this article, I have argued that China scholars cannot merely give up on coming to terms with the concept of legitimacy—as 'vague' as it may be. Quite to the contrary, they should stand by their efforts to provide sound theoretical and methodological tools for its investigation. I have suggested a research agenda that does not endeavor to move 'beyond a narrow empirically-measured focus on legitimacy towards a broader conceptually-driven concern with legitimation', as Sandby-Thomas proposes. Instead, I propose a

46. See, e.g. Anna L. Ahlers, *'New Socialist Countryside': Analyzing Contemporary Rural Policy Implementation in China* (London-New York: Routledge, 2014); Chengfang Liu, Linxiu Zhang, Renfu Luo and Scott Rozelle, 'Infrastructure investment in rural China: is quality being compromised during quantity expansion?', *China Journal* 61, (2009), pp. 105–129; Yan Wu and Wen Wang, 'Does participatory budgeting improve the legitimacy of the local government?: a comparative case study of two cities in China', *Australian Journal of Public Administration* 71(2), (2012), pp. 122–135.

systematic approach towards accumulating knowledge on policy implementation in China's local state with regard to procedure, output effectiveness and public responses, even if this does not completely solve the methodological problems of measurement and aggregation that are inherent to an analysis of systems legitimacy. The trick is not to develop a neat solution in theoretical and practical terms, but to apply an analytical framework that helps researchers gather and interpret empirical data in a collective effort with the objective of better understanding the link between local policy implementation and legitimacy building in China's local state.

The Debate on Regime Legitimacy in China: bridging the wide gulf between Western and Chinese scholarship

JINGHAN ZENG

This article identifies continuities, new trends and shifts in emphasis in the Chinese elite debate about political legitimacy by analysing 125 Chinese articles concerning legitimacy published between 2008 and 2012. It reveals a remarkable cleavage between the international perceptions of the Chinese state and the pessimistic views among Chinese intellectuals about the party's ruling. It finds that Chinese scholars often look at Western theories when dealing with the legitimacy conundrum, and rarely look at Chinese philosophy. They focus on ideology much more than Western scholars, and they are more pessimistic about performance legitimacy than the latter. Moreover, this study finds that the legitimacy concerns and policy suggestions of scholars vary significantly depending upon their research locations, institutions and funding sources. This study also finds a distinct rising appeal of social autonomy that runs counter to the dominant official line. Nowadays, value changes, socioeconomic inequality and corruption are considered to be the most perceived threats to legitimacy; ideology, social justice and governance are the leading prescriptions for the party-state. This result is vastly different from the previous study, suggesting a fundamental shift in the legitimacy debate driven by the worsening socioeconomic problems in China.

I. Introduction

Market reforms launched by the Chinese Communist Party (CCP) leadership have fostered remarkable economic growth over the past three decades without triggering a democratic breakthrough. Various survey studies, including the World Values Survey and the Asian Barometer, have found that the Chinese government enjoys strong political support.[1] Conventional wisdom argues that performance legitimacy—economic performance in particular—is a principal (if not the sole) pillar of legitimacy in China.[2] Yet, various problems—socioeconomic inequalities in particular—caused by rapid economic growth have posed an unprecedented challenge to the CCP's monopoly on power. Now more than ever before, the party-state has been concerned that economic performance might not be enough to provide sufficient legitimacy as this article will reveal.

In the meantime, China's economic prosperity has prompted rising schools of thought surrounding the 'China Model' and 'Chinese exceptionalism'. Their proponents argue that China has carved out its own path to modernization without following the West. One of their key theoretical foundations is that China's unique cultural heritage makes it possible for the state to acquire legitimacy without liberal democracy.[3] Many empirical studies have lent strong support to this kind of claim, positioning China as in some way exceptional and built upon different philosophies from those of Western states.[4]

---

1. Jie Chen, *Popular Political Support in Urban China* (Stanford, CA: Stanford University Press, 2004); Bruce Gilley, 'The meaning and measure of state legitimacy: results for 72 countries', *European Journal of Political Research* 45(3), (2006); Bruce Gilley, 'Legitimacy and institutional change', *Comparative Political Studies* 41(3), (2008); Lianjiang Li, 'Political trust in rural China', *Modern China* 30(2), (2004); Tianjian Shi, 'Cultural values and political trust: a comparison of the People's Republic of China and Taiwan', *Comparative Politics* 33(4), (2001); Wenfang Tang, *Public Opinion and Political Change in China* (Stanford, CA: Stanford University Press, 2005); Michael S. Lewis-Beck, Wenfang Tang and Nicholas F. Martini, 'A Chinese popularity function: sources of government support', *Political Research Quarterly*, no. 10.1177/1065912913486196 (2013).

2. Dingxin Zhao, 'The mandate of heaven and performance legitimation in historical and contemporary China', *American Behavioral Scientist* 53(3), (2009); Zhengxu Wang, 'Political trust in China: forms and causes', in Lynn White, ed., *Legitimacy: Ambiguities of Political Success or Failure in East and Southeast Asia* (Hackensack, NJ: World Scientific Pub Co Inc, 2005); André Laliberté and Marc Lanteigne, 'The issue of challenges to the legitimacy of CCP rule', in André Laliberté and Marc Lanteigne, eds, *The Chinese Party-State in the 21st Century: Adaptation and the Reinvention of Legitimacy* (London: Routledge, 2008); David Shambaugh, 'The dynamics of elite politics during the Jiang era', *The China Journal* 45, (2001); Elizabeth Perry, 'Chinese conceptions of "rights": from Mencius to Mao—and now', *Perspectives on Politics* 6, (2008). However, some scholars suggest setting up a new research agenda. Please see Peter Thomas, 'How do you solve a problem like legitimacy?: contributing to a new research agenda', *Journal of Contemporary China* 23(88), (2014); Gunter Schubert, 'Political legitimacy in contemporary China revisited: theoretical refinement and empirical operationalization', *Journal of Contemporary China* 23(88), (2014); Gunter Schubert, 'One-party rule and the question of legitimacy in contemporary China: preliminary thoughts on setting up a new research agenda', *Journal of Contemporary China* 17(54), (2008).

3. For relevant publication about China's political model, see Wei Pan, 'Towards a consultative rule of law regime in China', *Journal of Contemporary China* 12(34), (2003); Wei Pan, ed., *中国模式: 解读人民共和国的六十年* [*The Chinese Model: Interpreting the Sixty Years of the People's Republic of China*] (Beijing: 中央编译出版社 [Central Translation Publishing Press], 2009); Shaoguang Wang, 'Is kingly governance a good thing? An assessment of Confucian constitutionalism', in Daniel Bell and Ruiping Fan, eds, *A Confucian Constitutional Order: How China's Ancient Past Can Shape Its Political Future* (Princeton, NJ: Princeton University Press, 2012); Xiaoguang Kang, '仁政：权威主义国家的合法性理论' ['Benevolent governance: legitimacy theory of authoritarian countries'], *Zhanyue yu guanli* no. 2, (2004); Weiwei Zhang, *中国震撼： 一个文明型国家的兴起* [*China Shock: The Rise of a Civilization State*] (Shanghai: 上海人民出版社 [Shanghai People's Press], 2010); Yang Yao, *中国道路的世界意义* [*The Global Significance of the Chinese Experience*] (Beijing: Peking University Press, 2011). However, please also see Suisheng Zhao, 'The China Model: can it replace the Western model of modernization', *Journal of Contemporary China* 19(65), (2010); Barry Naughton, 'China's distinctive system: can it be a model for others?', *Journal of Contemporary China* 19(65), (2010); Minglu Chen and David Goodman, 'The China Model: one country, six authors', *Journal of Contemporary China* 21(73), (2012).

4. For example, Chinese people's understandings of democracy do not match the definition of liberal democracy. Many find that China's different understanding is influenced by Chinese culture. Please see Tianjian Shi and Jie Lu, 'The shadow of Confucianism', *Journal of Democracy* 21(4), (2010); Doh Shin, *Confucian Legacies and the Making of Democratic Citizens: Civic Engagement and Democratic Commitment in Six East Asian Countries* (Cambridge: Cambridge University Press, 2011).

Beyond the above views, party intellectuals within China may have valuable insights unavailable to those outside and perhaps better understand how China is ruled. As Thomas argues in this special section, elites are crucial in determining regime legitimacy, thus, the views of party intellectual about the party's ruling—the 'intra-elite' legitimacy—is particularly important.[5] No systematic study, however, has been conducted which links party intellectuals' opinions with the English literature—except for Gilley and Holbig's work.[6] Building on the pioneering work of Gilley and Holbig, this study identifies continuities, new trends and shifts in emphasis in the Chinese elite debate about political legitimacy by analysing 125 Chinese articles with 'legitimacy' in the title published between 2008 and 2012. It reveals a remarkable cleavage between the international perceptions of the Chinese state and the pessimistic views among Chinese intellectuals about the party's ruling.

This study departs from the previous research in several important ways. First, this study comprehensively analyses the influence of both Western theories and traditional Chinese philosophies in the Chinese discourse of legitimacy. To date, there has been no systematic attempt to study this issue. This issue is important because it is closely related to the theoretical foundations of the 'China Model' and 'Chinese exceptionalism'. Whilst many observers outside China are increasingly focusing on the search for Chinese philosophies to underpin a new polity,[7] this study finds that Chinese intellectuals are looking to the West instead. In addition, in order to understand better the debate and distinct patterns in the Chinese literature, I have also conducted email interviews with key contributors to this debate.

Second, instead of focusing on the debate alone, this study also examines how the party intellectuals' views are shaped by their backgrounds. As this article reveals, institutions, research locations and funding sources have differentiated Chinese intellectuals' legitimacy concerns and policy suggestions.

Third, as this study covers a more recent period of time, it is able to include critical events such as the 2008 financial crisis. As the world has frequently pointed out the success of the Chinese response to the financial crisis, it would be interesting to hear the perspective of insiders. After the crisis, China's unique developmental model received greater recognition, lending strong support to the existence of the 'China Model'. This study, however, finds that the anxieties about the economy and 'performance dilemma' largely increased in China after the financial crisis, suggesting that Chinese intellectuals seem to have become more pessimistic.

---

5. Thomas, 'How do you solve a problem like legitimacy?'.

6. Bruce Gilley and Heike Holbig, 'The debate on party legitimacy in China: a mixed quantitative/qualitative analysis', *Journal of Contemporary China* 18(59), (2009). In this article, 'the previous study' refers to the study by Gilley and Holbig.

7. For those using Chinese cultural, historical and political traditions to explain political legitimacy in contemporary China, see Vivienne Shue, 'Legitimacy crisis in China?', in P. Gries and S. Rosen, eds, *State and Society in 21st Century China* (New York: Routledge Curzon, 2004); Vivienne Shue, 'Global imaginings, the state's quest for hegemony, and the pursuit of phantom freedom', in Katarina Kinvall and Kristina Jonsson, eds, *Globalization and Democratization in Asia* (London: Routledge, 2002); Yanqi Tong, 'Morality, benevolence, and responsibility: regime legitimacy in China from the past to the present', *Journal of Chinese Political Science* 16(2), (2011); Baogang Guo, 'Political legitimacy and China's transition', *Journal of Chinese Political Science* 8(1&2), (2003); Florian Schneider and Yih-jye Hwang, 'The Sichuan earthquake and the heavenly mandate: legitimizing Chinese rule through disaster discourse', *Journal of Contemporary China* 23(88), (2014).

In addition, China's leadership transition in 2012 has turned a new page. Maintaining the CCP's power in the second largest world economy and the most populous country in the world is the first and foremost task for the *new* leaders. This article provides a guide to understanding what policy options are available and what critical opinions are heard by the new leadership.

Moreover, this study juxtaposes the Chinese literature with the English literature on this subject. It reveals a remarkable cleavage between the international perceptions of the Chinese state and the pessimistic views among Chinese intellectuals about the party's ruling. This study demonstrates how different perspectives of observation on China lead to vastly different perceptions about regime legitimacy in China.

Most importantly, this study reveals a fundamental shift in emphasis around political legitimacy. The top perceived legitimacy threats five years ago—changing interests and the exhaustion of revolutionary-historical legitimacy—have now been replaced by socioeconomic inequality, corruption and incapability of bureaucratic systems, while changing values remains a leading item in both of this study and the previous study. Accordingly, proposed strategies are largely varied. The improvement of bureaucracy,[8] propaganda, rule of law and promotion of equality are the most frequently mentioned strategies in maintaining legitimacy in the debate now compared with the rule of law, economic growth, propaganda and building better party organizations, which were the main strategies five years ago. By using a principle component factor analysis to identify the clusters of strategies, this study finds that social justice and governance have become much more important than before, while ideological change still remains a leading strategy. In addition, this study also finds a distinct rising appeal of social autonomy that runs counter to the dominant official line.

II. Background

II.1. Methodology

In order to understand the legitimacy debate in China, this study developed a coding manual and coded 125 Chinese articles on legitimacy.[9] The coding manual is redesigned from Gilley and Holbig's work, which studies a similar legitimacy debate between 2002 and 2007.[10] The coding of each article starts with the following questions.

- How does the author evaluate political legitimacy in China?
- What are the perceived threats to legitimacy?
- What are the suggested strategies for maintaining legitimacy?
- Whose studies have they cited?

The 125 articles were selected from the China Academic Journals Full-text Database—the largest academic journal full-text database in the world.[11]

8. It generally refers to building a more responsive, transparent and predictable bureaucratic structure that is more efficient and effective.

9. All data are available upon request. The reader can find replication materials on the author's website: https://sites.google.com/site/zengjinghan/data, or by emailing him.

10. Gilley and Holbig, 'The debate on party legitimacy in China'.

11. The database may be accessed at http://www.cnki.net/.

Its humanities and social science database covers 3,300 official social and humanities journals, papers from 9,964 significant conferences, and 515 important newspapers.[12] All articles with 'legitimacy' (合法性) in the title and which include discussions about the legitimacy of the Chinese state and the CCP (published between 2008 and 2012) in this database have been selected.[13]

II.2. Limitations of this study

Owing to the nature of the database and the limitations on what is published in Chinese journals, the selection does not include the opinions of dissidents or confidential discussions about the state. In addition, the database does not include books; however, no cutting-edge Chinese book on state legitimacy was published in the period, and what has been published is typically discussed in articles and thus captured by this analysis (albeit in a secondary manner).

While proposing the dissolution of CCP rule or the move to a competitive multi-party democracy remains taboo, this analysis reveals a remarkably open and plural debate. If the focus is on how to maintain and strengthen CCP rule (rather than replace it), then the debate over legitimacy is an open and public one. This includes ideas that run counter to the dominant official line.

Notably, policies do not always originate from academic debate in China; it can be the other way around, in that academic discussions are sometimes used to test and promote the preferred policies of individual leaders. Either way, this debate about political legitimacy is closely related to the survival strategies of the party-state under the watch of new leaders.

II.3. Composition of the selected articles and the authors

Among the selected articles, 17% are based on government-funded projects.[14] This study finds that those funded projects prefer to advocate improvement in public welfare provision [X^2 (1, $N = 125$) = 6.395, $p < 0.05$].[15] This preference mirrors the way that the regime has shifted its emphasis towards improving people's livelihood.

Interestingly, this study also finds correlations between authors' research locations and their arguments.[16] Intellectuals based in richer regions are less likely to

12. This information is given by the official website of this database, http://ifc.dhbc.net/rewriter/CNKI/http/dmf9bmjh9mds/grid2008/index/ZKSHKX.htm (accessed 15 September 2012).

13. It covers 1 January 2008–1 September 2012. Articles which studied the legitimacy of public policies, ideologies, civil organizations and political parties (other than the CCP) were filtered out.

14. The funding came from various governmental institutions, such as the Ministry of Education, and some large national foundations, such as the National Natural Science Scientific Foundation of China, which is an institution controlled directly by the State Council. The funding source (if there is any) is usually listed on the first page of each Chinese article.

15. For more details, please see the online-appendix on the author's website.

16. I would like to thank Shaun Breslin for suggesting that I study this relationship. The independent variable is coded according to the GDP per capita of the province where the authors' institutions were located in 2009. The reasons why I did not use 'province-year' as the unit and panel data are explained in the online-appendix. $N = 123$ because two articles are filtered: one is anonymous and the other is translated from English articles. In cases where there are two authors, the first author has priority.

worry about socioeconomic inequality [$r = -0.345$, $n = 123$, $p = 0.000$],[17] the sustainability of China's economy [$r = -0.245$, $n = 123$, $p = 0.006$], corruption [$r = -0.200$, $n = 123$, $p = 0.027$] and inadequate political participation [$r = -0.213$, $n = 123$, $p = 0.018$]. One possible reason for this is that richer regions have benefited more from China's economic growth than poorer regions; therefore, they are more capable of solving problems caused by economic growth.

Authors based in poorer regions showed a significant inclination towards suggesting that the government should increase bureaucratic efficiency and transparency [$r = -0.179$, $n = 123$, $p = 0.047$], increase citizen participation [$r = -0.228$, $n = 123$, $p = 0.011$], and encourage the development of civil society [$r = -0.194$, $n = 123$, $p = 0.031$]. Those in richer regions are more likely to propose that the government should improve its ability to guide public opinion [$r = 0.255$, $n = 123$, $p = 0.004$]. These findings indicate very diverse demands and interests among Chinese provinces.

In this debate, the 17 authors are from different party schools, including the Central Party School in Beijing and various provincial and municipal party schools. It is notable that the party school system is the key think tank and the 'incubator of reform ideas and polices' of the CCP.[18] The authors from the party school system and the government were more interested in party democracy [X^2 (1, $N = 125$) $= 7.995$, $p < 0.01$].

Selected articles are written by university professors/researchers (81.7%), party school professors/researchers (13.4%), government officials (2.4%) and military officers (1.6%). Some authors hold positions in both universities and party schools. This needs to be noted, as there is no clear line between officials and scholars in China. For instance, Yu Keping, an author in this debate and one of the most influential party intellectuals, is both the deputy director of the Central Compilation & Translation Bureau and a professor at Peking University.

III. Quantitative results

III.1. Citation rates of scholars

The results of the reference rates are shown in Figure 1.[19] Only 2% of articles in the debate considered Chinese philosophies concerning legitimacy compared with 19% of articles which mentioned the ancient Western philosopher Aristotle. This is interesting because it seems to go against the grain of thinking of China as in some way exceptional and built on different philosophies to Western states. On the one hand, many Chinese officials and scholars have frequently reminded the Western scholars about the uniqueness of China and the move towards the concept of 'harmony' built on China's specific historical traditions. Indeed, the criticism that

17. They are more likely to mention regional inequality.
18. David Shambaugh, 'Training China's political elite: the party school system', *The China Quarterly* 196, (2008).
19. Instead of importing the bibliography into Endnote as the previous study did, this study manually coded the citation and provides specific rates for comparison. This is because sometimes when those Chinese authors simply mention the names of the scholars or their books in the text, this is not reflected in the bibliography. In addition, problems can easily be caused by different Chinese translations of scholars' names.

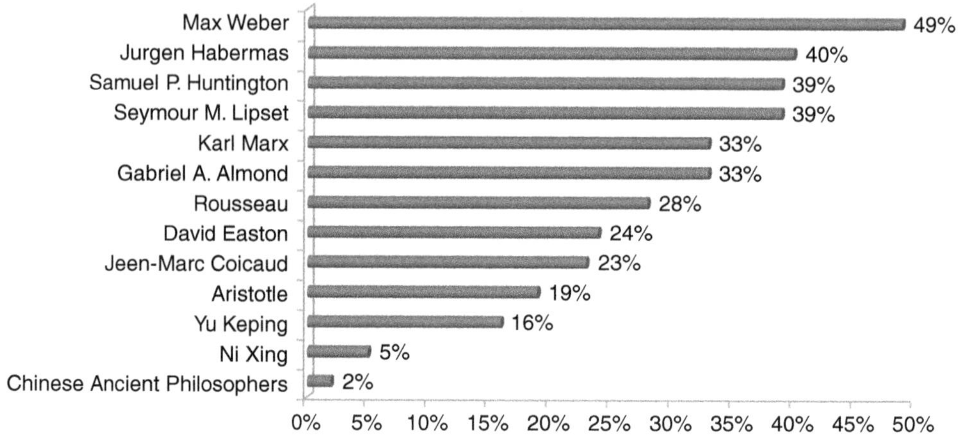

Figure 1. Reference rates of scholars in the Chinese discourse of legitimacy. *Source*: The author's own database.

Western scholars failed to pay enough attention to Chinese culture and misused Western theories in their study of China rose in the very early stages of China Studies.[20] As mentioned, nowadays, many analysts outside China have been increasingly interested in using China's past to explain the present. On the other hand, the Chinese debate is much more influenced by Western theories than traditional Chinese philosophies.

This finding indicates that the advocates of the 'China Model' have not convinced party intellectuals yet. Indeed, Western theories currently dominate the Chinese literature of modern politics. A major reason for this is that traditional Chinese political philosophies have not been sufficiently adapted into modern civilization. Although great efforts are made to modernize Chinese philosophies, they have not yet reproduced a more convincing system to compete with the well-established Western theories. To a certain point, it is true to say that Western theories cannot necessarily easily explain China, and that Western analysts cannot understand China because of its unique historical and cultural traditions,[21] but the alternatives offered (if there are any) tend to be worse. In the words of Ma Deyong, an influential author in the legitimacy debate:

> Currently, none of the Chinese scholars can create a widely accepted academic system. All we can do is to develop new concepts and theories based on the current academic system in order to explain the present.[22]

As indicated in Figure 1, Western scholars dominate not only in ancient but also in modern and contemporary Chinese discourses of legitimacy. The most popular

20. Harry Harding, 'The study of Chinese politics: toward a third generation of scholarship', *World Politics* 36(2), (1984), p. 297.

21. See Yongnian Zheng, '我为什么担忧当前的中国知识界?' ['Why am I worrying about Chinese academia?'], *联合早报网* [*Zaobao*], (2012); Pan, *中国模式* [*The Chinese Model*].

22. Email interview with Ma Deyong, 2 November 2012.

scholars in the debate are all from the West: Max Weber (49%), Jurgen Habermas (40%), Samuel P. Huntington (39%) and Seymour M. Lipset (39%). Interestingly, Karl Marx, the founder of communist ideology, has only been mentioned in 33% of articles—not many in comparison with other Western thinkers.

In the debate, the empirical school of legitimacy is more influential than the critical school and the normative school. This is not only because of the higher reference rate of the empiricists such as Weber and Lipset, but also owing to the fact that the empirical school has been adopted more frequently to approach the issue of legitimacy in a practical way. Weber's framework of legitimacy in particular and the subsequent modified versions are widely endorsed in the debate.

During the coding, I found that almost no author in the debate directly challenged or responded to others although all of them were discussing the same topic and presenting different opinions. A similar pattern was also found in the previous study, in which Chinese elites do not only rarely give a direct response but also avoid citing others.[23] Gilley and Holbig argue that this might be because of 'a latent fear among scholars of being grouped with each other, categories as holding as a partisan view and ending up as representing the "wrong line"'.[24] However, there seems to be less fear now than before. Yu Keping, one of the key authors and also the most cited Chinese scholar in the debate, has been cited by 16% of articles. Yu's 'good governance' (善治) is one of the most popular terms used in this debate.

Indeed, it is a common phenomenon that Chinese literature of political studies has relatively short reviews of other Chinese colleagues' work. This is partly because of the current Chinese academic norms and standards.[25] Chinese intellectuals are reluctant to judge others' articles, especially in terms of giving critical comments, because of '(their) academic culture'.[26]

III.2. Evaluations of political legitimacy

As mentioned, most intellectuals outside China argue that the party-state has enjoyed high popular support or political trust and this view is strongly supported by various cross-national surveys, including the Asian barometer and the World Values Survey. This is a 'consensus' of 'scholars familiar with the field'.[27] Chinese elites, however, seem to be much more pessimistic than this 'consensus'.

As indicated in Figure 2, only two articles argue that regime legitimacy is high or relatively high. Nearly 20% of authors argue that the regime was experiencing a legitimacy crisis (合法性危机) and 21% of authors, including Yu Keping, hold that the party-state is facing some form of challenge or threat to its legitimacy (巨大挑战, 严峻挑战, 威胁, 合法性匮乏, etc.). Possible interpretations of the pessimistic view

23. Gilley and Holbig, 'The debate on party legitimacy in China'.
24. *Ibid.*, p. 342.
25. Email contact with Ma Deyong, 2 November 2012; Huang Jianrong, 3 November 2012, 4 November 2012 and 7 November 2012; and Yu Keping, 4 November 2012.
26. Email interview with Yu Keping, 4 November 2012.
27. Shaoguang Wang, 'Is kingly governance a good thing? An assessment of Confucian constitutionalism' ['王道政治'是个好东西?—评'儒家宪政'], *Open Times* [开放时代] 9, (2010), p. 139; Yun-han Chu, 'Sources of regime legitimacy and the debate over the Chinese Model', *China Review* 13(1), (2013), p. 4; Wang, 'Is kingly governance a good thing?'.

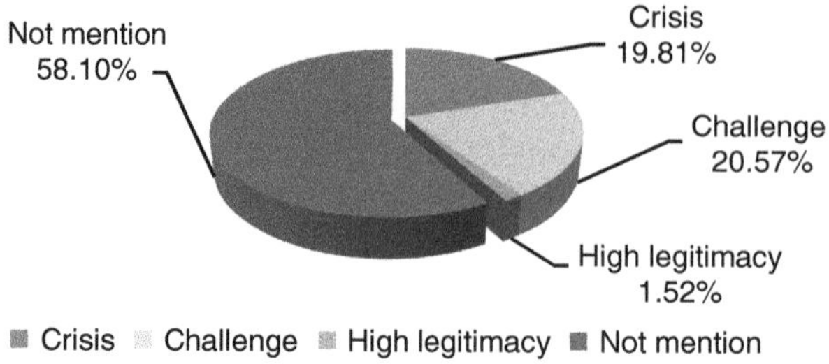

Figure 2. Evaluation of Chinese intellectuals on different levels of regime legitimacy. *Source*: The author's own database.

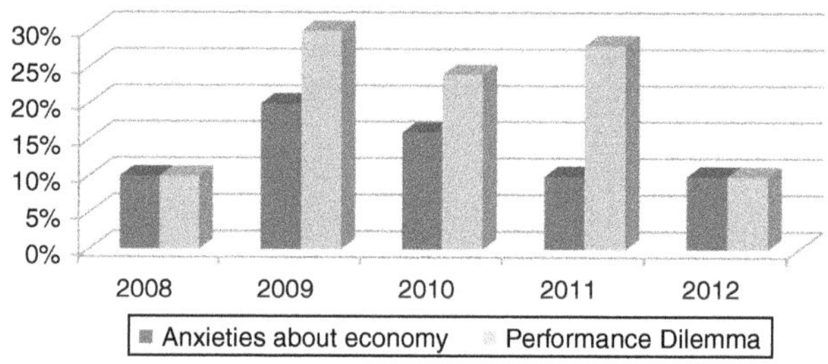

Figure 3. Frequency of performance dilemma and anxieties about the economy between 2008 and 2012. *Source*: The author's own database.

held by Chinese intellectuals are: party intellectuals have insights unavailable to the outside; those whose job it is to look for challenges to legitimacy tend to see problems everywhere; or, most persuasively, both of the above.

III.3. Legitimacy threats

Various domestic (mainly social and political) factors rather than international factors are considered to be the main source of perceived threats in the debate. Only 14% of authors mentioned globalization as a reason why legitimacy has declined and 5% blamed this on the West—the so-called 'foreign or Western hostile forces'. Moreover, 13% of authors expressed their concern that the current pace of economic growth is unsustainable, while 21% were concerned about the on-going or imminent 'performance dilemma' (政绩困局).

As indicated in Figure 3, anxieties about the economy and performance dilemma largely increased after 2008. It suggests that the 2008 financial crisis led to serious concerns about China's economy, although many in the West have looked to China's success in responding to the crisis.[28]

28. For example, see Barry Naughton, 'China's emergence from economic crisis', *China Leadership Monitor* 29, (2009); John Ross, 'China's economic success set an example the world should follow', *The Guardian*, (2012); Heike

Table 1. Threats to political legitimacy in Chinese intellectuals' opinions

Variables	Frequency	Note
Socioeconomic inequality	49%	e.g. the gap between the rich and the poor, social inequality, regional inequality, the gap between the rural and urban areas
Changing values	49%	e.g. weakening of communist ideology, increasing civic awareness and promoting Western political values
Corruption	43%	e.g. corruption (权钱交易, 腐败)
Bureaucracy (threat)	39%	e.g. inefficiency, opacity, incapability of bureaucracy
Inadequate political participation	30%	e.g. inadequate political participation of citizens or NGOs
Interest	21%	e.g. conflicting interests of different social groups, classes, or interest groups (e.g. 社会阶层, 利益团体, 利益集团,利益主体)
Environmental degradation	14%	e.g. environmental pollution, pressures of large population
Inadequate public provision of welfare	13%	e.g. health, education, social security, housing, and pensions
Inadequate rule of law	13%	e.g. poor legislative quality and inadequate judiciary, and implementation of law
Development of technology	5%	e.g. Internet, new mass media, social network

Source: The author's own database.

As indicated in Table 1, almost half of the authors consider socioeconomic inequality (49%) and changing values (49%) to be the major threats to legitimacy, followed by corruption (43%) and bureaucracy (39%). This finding is strikingly concordant with the insights of Chinese leading cadres who considered inequality and corruption to be the most serious social problems, according to a report of the Chinese Social Science Academy.[29] Whyte's survey study is worth mentioning to make some interesting comparisons here. Whyte finds that most Chinese are not bothered by socioeconomic inequality and consider the current system fair.[30] These two seemingly contradictory findings present an interesting phenomenon—that Chinese leaders believe the masses to be worrying about an issue when, in fact, they are not.

Footnote 28 continued
Holbig, 'International dimensions of legitimacy: reflections on Western theories and the Chinese experience', *Journal of Chinese Political Science* 16(2), (2011).

29. Xin Ru, Xueshi Lu and Peiling Li, *中国社会形势分析与预测* [*Analysis and Predication of Chinese Social Situation*] (社会科学文献出版社 [Social Science Literature Press], 2008).

30. Martin King Whyte, *Myth of the Social Volcano* (Stanford: Stanford University Press, 2010). For other relevant literature see Teresa Wright, *Accepting Authoritarianism: State–Society Relations in China's Reform Era* (Stanford, CA: Stanford University Press, 2010).

Regarding the issue of corruption, two contradictory opinions exist in the Chinese mass media. Many argue that the government should immediately promote strong reforms and democratic development to curb corruption.[31] Others hold that corruption will decline in line with socioeconomic development, because the widespread corruption is an issue associated with the modernization of developing countries. Thus, removing corruption from the system is a long process and China should guard against undue haste.[32] Ramirez's optimistic study about corruption in China is worth mentioning here. By comparing China's level of corruption with that of the US at a similar state of development, Ramirez argues that corruption levels in China will gradually decline with further modernization, as was the case with the USA.[33] However, no article provides an in-depth analysis of the latter view in the legitimacy debate, although corruption is frequently mentioned. It indicates that Chinese intellectuals have not examined this issue comparatively and so perhaps miss the 'normalcy' of the Chinese situation.

The finding about technology development is notable. While many contend that the development of the Internet, in particular social networks, has tremendously changed China in many aspects,[34] only 5% of authors mentioned it in the legitimacy debate. Most authors do not perceive the development of technology to be a direct threat to legitimacy. Rather, the Internet is regarded as an intermediary that would enlarge various socioeconomic problems. The authors either argue that strict control over the Internet is not feasible in the long run, or they tend to emphasize solving the root problems over increasing Internet censorship.

III.4. Policy options for maintaining legitimacy

While China watchers tend to explain political legitimacy in terms of economic prosperity, Chinese intellectuals have already realized that economic growth alone will not guarantee the CCP's ruling position. As mentioned, a number of intellectuals expressed anxieties about economic and 'performance dilemma'. Moreover, in the legitimacy debate between 2002 and 2007, 50% of intellectuals suggested promoting better, faster and more sustainable economic growth to maintain legitimacy, but only 21% still insist on doing so now. Many articles continuously warned about the fleeting nature of performance legitimacy and the necessity of establishing more solid legitimacy foundations, especially rational-legal legitimacy. Arguably, in China, it is a near consensus that the state should find sources of legitimacy other than economic performance.

31. Lin Cao, '舍制度和民主之外，反腐无解' ['There is no solution to curb corruption other than institutional building and democracy'], *中国青年报* [*China Youth Newspaper*], (2012).

32. '社评：反腐败是中国社会发展的攻坚战' ['The editorial: anti-corruption is a battle of Chinese social development'], *环球时报* [*Global Times*], (2012).

33. Carlos Ramirez, *Is Corruption in China 'Out of Control'? A Comparison with the US in Historical Perspective*, Department of Economics, George Mason University, 2012.

34. E.g. Richard Baum, 'Political implication of China's information revolution: the media, the minders, and their message', in Cheng Li, ed., *China's Changing Political Landscape: Prospects for Democracy* (Washington, DC: Brookings Institution Press, 2008); Yu Liu and Dingding Chen, 'Why China will democratize?', *The Washington Quarterly* 35(1), (2012).

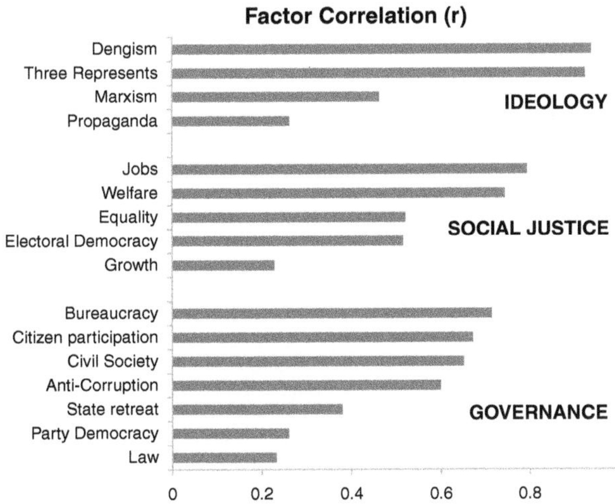

Figure 4. Three dimensions of proposed strategies for maintaining legitimacy (factor correlations *r*). *Note:* No author in the debate advises the separation of the party and the government and the promotion of Maoism; therefore, those two variables are filtered. For more information, please see the online-appendix.

In order to address the threats to legitimacy mentioned above, public intellectuals have suggested a set of diverse solutions. In the debate between 2008 and 2012, the most frequently mentioned strategies are: the improvement of bureaucracy (46%, 25% in the previous study),[35] propaganda (38%), citizen participation (37%) and civil society (27%, 10% previously) compared with rule of law (64%), economic growth (50%), democracy (50%) and propaganda (48%) in the debate between 2003 and 2007.

Among those legitimacy strategies, some might serve as competing alternatives to one another, whilst others—such as citizen participation and civil society—might work to complement each other. To understand better how those strategies knit together and identity specific forms of strategies, I performed a principal component factor analysis on the 29 variables in my coding book. This study labels the top components as ideology, social justice and governance, as indicated in Figure 4. The dispersion of all variables along with ideology (component 1) and governance (component 3) are shown in Figure 5.

As indicated in Figures 4 and 5, bureaucracy, citizen participation and civil society are more likely to be proposed together as ways to address threats to legitimacy. Therefore, they are not only some of the most frequently mentioned strategies, but also more united in their prescriptions for the party-state, which indicates a clear rising appeal of social autonomy. The next section examines proposed strategies through a qualitative analysis.

35. It generally refers to creation of a more responsive, transparent and predictable bureaucratic structure that is efficient and effective.

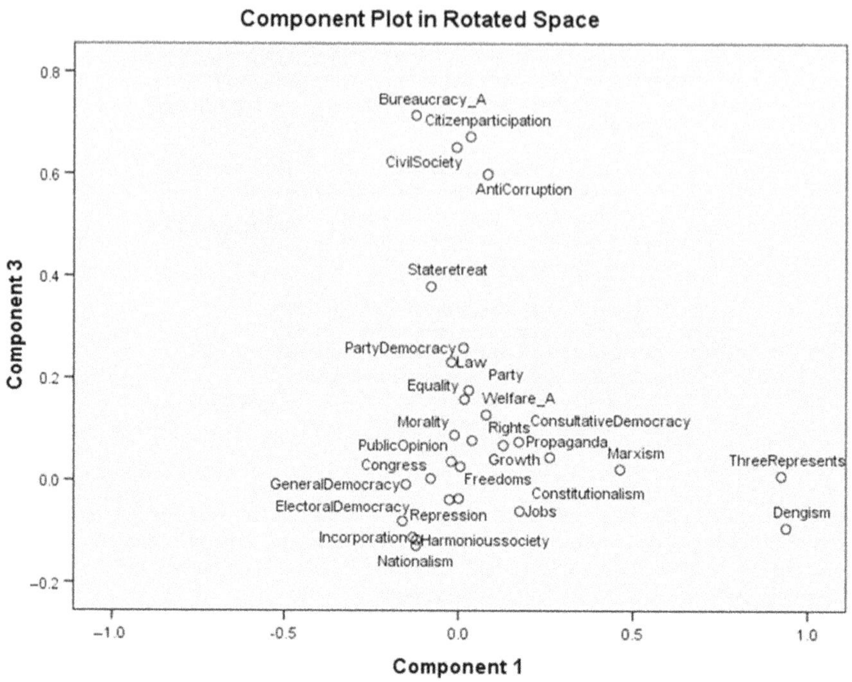

Figure 5. Correlations (r) of variables along ideology and governance.

IV. Qualitative results

IV.1. Ideology

The issue of ideology has been widely neglected in the English literature of contemporary China studies as many considered it obsolete.[36] Chinese leaders and intellectuals, however, have always taken it seriously. In China, ideological changes involve a special meaning of power assertion.[37] It is an attempt to place the new leaders' stamp on the party and history because newly adapted ideologies are clearly identified with specific leaders. When new ideological reform is launched, previous ideologies have been 'discarded' to a certain extent. Mao Zedong's Thought, the bible of China's rising New Leftists (新左派), is completely discarded in the debate, although many observed similar problems—socioeconomic inequality in particular—with the New Leftists. In addition, only three articles mentioned Deng Xiaoping's Theories compared with four articles on Jiang Zemin's Three Represents. Almost all relevant articles symbolically mentioned those previous ideologies by name without giving any detail. This result is completely different from the debate

36. Although many studies have been focused on nationalism, this article does not consider them as political ideology. As Breslin argues, Chinese nationalism 'lack(s) sufficient coherence and guiding principles to be counted as an ideology as such—it is not a "science of ideas"'. Shaun Breslin, 'Democratizing one-party rule in China', in Peter Burnell and Richard Youngs, eds, *New Challenges to Democratization* (London: Routledge, 2009).

37. Jinghan Zeng, 'The Communist Party's right to rule: political legitimacy in contemporary China', working title, University of Warwick, 2014.

five years ago, in which all major ideologies were mentioned: Marxism (34%), Mao's Thoughts (13%), Deng's Theories (24%), Jiang's Three Represents (39%) and Hu's Harmonious Society (18%).

Now, the new fashionable proposition is the Socialist Core Values System. This system is proposed in the new rounds of ideological adaptation in order to strengthen the attractiveness and cohesiveness of socialist ideology. Much of the relevant discourse in the debate is about this adaptation. As proposed in a party report that has been frequently cited in the debate, the construction of a Socialist Core Values System is the foundation of the harmonious culture.[38] This system consists of Marxism (its guiding ideology), socialism with Chinese characteristics, patriotism and the 'Socialist Concept of Honour and Disgrace'.[39] As Chang Sumei put it, 'the diversification and differentiation of values have increased the disorder of social values and have thus reduced party legitimacy'.[40] Thus, some suggest that the state should use the Socialist Core Values System to integrate various social values and form an ideological structure—in which Marxism is the leading ideology coexisting with other diversified thoughts.

IV.1.1. Marxism. Marxism (16%) is proposed as a guiding ideology of the Socialist Core Values System in the debate. Communist ideology in China was established as a distinctive Chinese form of socialism, separate from the Soviet Union and orthodox Marxism. Marxism in the Chinese context refers to Marxism with Chinese characteristics, adapted to China's situation, or the 'Sinification of Marxism'. The CCP has been keen to integrate Marxism with practices in China. This is perhaps because the party might attempt to claim the legitimacy of an independent China as not part of the Soviet Union and to undermine the attacks from culturalists who considered communist ideology to be alien.

Many authors used the party reports and Hu Jintao's report on the 17th Party Congress to highlight the significance of Marxism. For example, Sun Yong and Liu Qingfeng argue that 'the Socialist Core Values System is the very foundation of China's common ideals, which is the premise underlying the party-state. The party-state might be at risk of splitting and collapsing without this foundation'.[41]

Marxism has an irreplaceable role in the past, present and the future of the CCP's ruling according to many in the debate. For instance, Xu Jialing, the visiting scholar of the Central Compilation & Translation Bureau, argues that 'Marxism has been a key legitimacy pillar of the CCP, revolution, and reforms in the past decades, and

38. The Chinese Communist Party, *中共中央关于构建社会主义和谐社会若干重大问题的决定* [*Decisions of the Central Committee of the CPC on Several Important Issues of Construction of Socialist Harmonious Society*] (The Chinese Communist Party, 2006), available at: http://news.xinhuanet.com/politics/2006-10/18/content_5218639.htm (accessed 3 April 2013).

39. *Ibid.*

40. Sumei Chang, '新时期巩固政治合法性基础的路径选择' ['Paths of legitimacy-enhancing in new periods'], *辽宁行政学院学报* [*Jounal of Liaoning Administration College*] 11(2), (2009).

41. Yong Sun and Qingfeng Liu, '坚持科学发展观构建政治合法性多元基础' ['Insist using scientific outlook of development to construct plural foundation of political legitimacy'], *中共合肥市委党校学报* [*Hefei Municipal Party School Journal*] 1, (2009).

only Marxism, rather than any other theory, can provide the legitimacy to combine socialism with Chinese characteristics'.[42]

IV.1.2. Patriotism and nationalism. Nationalism has been discussed in 12% of articles in the debate compared with 15% in the previous study. Similar to the previous study, nationalist positions distributed evenly over the legitimacy debate analysed here. In the debate, nationalism is discussed as a part of the Socialist Core Values System. It is generally considered as a helpful tool to increase Chinese people's national identity. Whilst most relevant articles actually refer to patriotism (爱国主义) rather than nationalism (民族主义), there are two articles published in the *Guangxi Journal of Ethnology* which do refer to nationalism. Zhang Wenjing and Du Jun argue that nationalism is a double-edged sword that can split China because nationalism helps to provide legitimacy and effective political mobilization on the one hand, and promotes separatism and intensifies the contradiction between Han and ethnic minorities on the other hand.[43] They suggested launching patriotic education campaigns and suggested highlighting the fact that China is a united political entity in order to improve ethnic minorities' national identity. It is very important to prevent the ideological infiltration and political propaganda of dissenters from overseas, so they argue that information control is necessary. In another article, they argue that the government should reduce ethnic consciousness and construct a common Chinese culture.[44]

Another article argues that the demonstration of military power can enhance legitimacy by increasing national pride. Wang Haizhou contends that China's National Day Military Parade has enhanced legitimacy by serving as a political ceremony.[45]

IV.2. Governance

Further market reform and rapid economic growth have created many problems in China, which are shaking the legitimacy of the party-state. As mentioned, various social problems—inequality in particular—are the top threats nowadays. Various plans regarding social reforms and the improvement of the bureaucratic system are proposed to help the party-state.

IV.2.1. Citizen participation. As Li Liang warns, if people's desire for political participation cannot be satisfied, they will be easily disappointed with the political system, which will further shake the legitimacy.[46] The problems with citizen

42. Jialing Xu, '中国政治合法性的理论基础及其当代认同' ['Theoretical background and contemporary identity of Chinese political legitimacy'], *科学社会主义* [*Scientific Socialism*] 1, (2009).

43. Wenjing Zhang and Jun Du, '民族主义与多民族国家的政治合法性' ['Nationalism and political legitimacy of multi-ethnic nation'], *广西民族研究* [*Research on Guangxi Ethnics*] 1, (2010).

44. Wenjing Zhang and Jun Du, '多民族中国政治合法性的文化基础构建' ['Cultural construction of multi-ethnic China's political legitimacy'], *广西民族研究* [*Guangxi Ethnic Study*] 2, (2010).

45. Haizhou Wang, '政治仪式中的权力宣展与合法性建构' ['Power assertion of political ceremony and construction of legitimacy'], *学海* [*Academia Bimestris*] 4, (2010).

46. Liang Li, '试论我国政治合法性的系统建构' ['Discussion on systematic construction of political legitimacy in China'], *攀登* [*New Heights*] 29(5), (2010).

participation in China are analysed in the debate in two ways: excessive informal participation and inadequate channels of formal participation. Informal participation refers to illegal and inappropriate ways—such as popular protests and bribes—to influence policy making, and formal participation refers to the institutionalized ways to influence policy making—such as public hearings. Increased informal participation causes either corruption or social instability, both of which are destructive to political legitimacy. Some in the debate consider the inadequate institutionalized channels of citizen participation to be an important factor in the increasing popular protests in China.[47]

The benefits expected from citizen participation are numerous. Liu Dongjie argues that citizen participation in policy making will help to make better policies and strengthen the supervision over policy implementations and evaluations.[48] Xia Jingmei argues that citizen participation will help to maintain stability by 'solving conflicting interests of different social classes, protecting people's rights, increasing bureaucratic efficiency, and enhancing national identity'.[49] Notably, citizen participation is considered by some as a way to unite social forces and to restrict state power. For example, Wang and Li argue that 'dispersed citizens cannot confront the strong administrative power' and thus citizen participation is necessary to help citizens to balance state power.[50]

In order to promote more orderly citizen participation, many urge the state to play a role in nurturing civic spirits. As Yang Xuedong, an associate researcher of the Central Compilation & Translation Bureau pointed out, the government should cultivate the public spirit of participation rather than 'buying citizens' compliances'.[51] Yao Jingjing argues that traditional civic awareness is 'too passive' and the state should cultivate people's willingness to participate through education and official propaganda.[52]

IV.2.2. Civil society, limited government and social autonomy. Civil society (27%) has been much more frequently proposed in the legitimacy debate now compared with five years ago (10%). Modern theories of public administration—limited government and citizen participation in particular—are frequently cited to support relevant arguments. Reasons for supporting civil society and social autonomy in this

47. Wentao Yang, '浅析公民参与的困境及路径选择—以公民参与和政治合法性的关系为视角' ['Analysis on dilemma and choices of citizen participation: from the perspective of the relationship between citizen participation and political legitimacy'], *内蒙古农业大学学报* [*Journal of Inner Mongolia Agricultural University (Social Science Edition)*] 12(5), (2010).

48. Dongjie Liu, '政策公共性与政府执政合法性' ['Policy publicity and political legitimacy'], *中共南宁市委党校学报* [*Journal of CCP Nanning Municipal Party School*] 5, (2009).

49. Jingmei Xia, '公民有序政治参与对党执政合法性的影响' ['Influence of orderly citizen participation on party legitimacy'], *郑州航空管理学院学报* [*Journal of Zhengzhou Institute of Aeronautical Industry Management (Social Science Edition)*] 27(1), (2008).

50. Guiyun Wang and Tao Li, '巩固和加强政府合法性基础的路径选择' ['Ways of consolidating and strengthening political legitimacy'], *兰州大学学报* [*Journal of Lanzhou University (Social Sciences)*] 39(1), (2011).

51. Xuedong Yang, '公共权利，合法性与公共服务型政府建设' ['Public power, legitimacy and construction of public service government'], *华中师范大学学报* [*Journal of Huazhong Normal University (Humanities and Social Sciences)*] 46(2), (2007).

52. Jingjing Yao, '行政参与的合法性与参与式治理的构建策略' ['Legitimacy of administrative participation and strategies of participation governance'], *今日南国(理论创新版)* [*The South of China Today*] 4, (2009).

debate are manifold: the changing values, the rise of the third sector, the inability of the traditional bureaucracy and corruption.

Consequently, many in the debate suggest a new governance model that is co-managed by the society, the state and the market. For instance, Huang Jianrong argues that 'the current management model of the state has becomes a barrier to political and economic developments', and the state should 'face the fact that both social and public affairs cannot be well managed by the government alone'.[53] In Huang's opinion, civil society and NGOs are the main forces to harness in order to supervise and restrict state power, which eventually can prevent and reduce corruption. Civil society is also suggested in order to consolidate the CCP's ruling in ethnic minority areas. Deng Mei argues that civil organizations will increase interactive communications between the political system and the citizens, strengthen the uptake rate of social resources, and maintain social order.[54]

The rising recognition of civil society is partly because of civil organizations' constructive roles in the 2008 Sichuan earthquake. Various NGOs have helped the government through the entire process of disaster relief and reconstruction. They have been considered by many as a helping hand rather than a threat. For instance, Chun Yumiaoling and Liang Xiao argue that the government should promote the development of NGOs as complementary to the state in order to maintain legitimacy and to overcome future crisis.[55]

IV.2.2.1. Pitfall of civil society (公民社会陷阱) vs. cooperated governance. Clearly, the government might be reluctant to share power with the social forces. According to Xue Tao, 'some party cadres regarded civil society as alien to resisting or confronting the state power; some even argued that the development of civil society would reduce the party's capability of leading and managing society'.[56]

The 'pitfall of civil society' is a notable and controversial idea which serves to resist the development of civil society; it is proposed by the Secretary-General of the Central Commission for Politics and Law (中央政法委) and the deputy director of the Central Commission for Comprehensive Management of Social Security (中央社会治安综合治理委员会), Zhou Benshun. Considering its significance, it is necessary to introduce briefly the cleavage over civil society, although it is not a part of the legitimacy debate. Zhou argued that the current mode of social management is an 'advantage'; thus, the regime should not promote civil society—'a pitfall designed by some Western countries'—to govern the society.[57] Zhou argues

53. Jianrong Huang, '论现代政府合法性递减' ['Discussion on the decreasing legitimacy of modern governmen32s'], *浙江大学学报* [*Journal of Zhejiang University*] 1, (2010).

54. Mei Deng, '政治合法性与公民积极政治心理—西部民族地区公民积极政治心理的政治环境优化研究' ['Political legitimacy and citizen's positive political psychology'], *西北工业大学学报* [*Journal of North-western Polytechnical University (Social Sciences)*] 29(2), (2009).

55. Yumiaoling Chun and Xiao Liang, '公共危机的应急管理与政治合法性的关系—以汶川大地震为个案' ['The relationship between public crisis management and political legitimacy—a case study on Wenchuan earthquake'], *云南行政学院学报* [*Journal of Yunnan Administration College*] 6, (2009).

56. Tao Xue, '论公民社会的兴起对中共执政合法性基础的影响' ['Discussion on the influence of rising civil society on the CCP's legitimacy'], *理论研究* [*Theoretical Research*] 3, (2008).

57. Benshun Zhou, '防止落入所谓公民社会陷阱' ['Preventing falling into the so-called pitfall of civil society'], *求是* [*Seeking Truth*], (17 May 2011).

that the state and party committees should 'put social management and public services in place rather than let society be in charge'.

Partly because of Zhou's official capacity, this article, published in the party's primary mouthpiece *Seeking Truth* (求是), reflected the official position of civil society to a certain extent and thus received wide attentions. However, no author in the legitimacy debate openly endorses this position. All relevant articles mentioning civil society endorse the development of civil society.

IV.2.2.2. Limited government (有限政府). 'Limited government' is another popular term in the debate. Some 20% of authors suggested that the government should retreat from social areas and return power to society. For example, Yu argues that the state withdrawal/retreat can help to avoid bureaucratic inefficiency and thus can help to increase the effectiveness of governance.[58] According to Yu, state withdrawal/retreat is an important step towards good governance. Jian Zhang argues that the rising civil society and the ideas of limited government are 'historical tendencies' that are unavoidable in a market economy; for this reason, the state should follow those tendencies.[59]

Many argue that traditional political totalism and the 'big government, small society' mode should be abandoned in order to face up to the legitimacy crisis.[60] Some argue that corruption will be reduced if the state restricts its field of activities.[61] The state is offered as an option that can allow the market to provide more public services.[62]

IV.2.2.3. 'Strong state and weak society' (大政府，小社会) vs. 'weak state and strong society' (小政府，大社会) = 'strong state and strong society' (大政府，大社会)?. In the debate, some criticized the state's strict control over social affairs and the 'strong state and weak society' model. For example, Xu Chengyu argues that the state's monopoly on power and information has made its relationship with citizens more intense.[63] In addition, it also leads to inefficient resource allocation and unfair competition.

Even though Chinese intellectuals recognized the problems of the 'strong state and weak society', none openly advised a 'weak state and strong society' model in the debate. Zhou Benshun's 'pitfall of civil society' article partly explains why. Zhou was directly critical of those 'who do not understand the social management model in foreign countries' and argues that 'not all the developed countries adopt the "weak government and strong society" model' and many of them have 'strong states; many social organizations have government backgrounds and are under the control of their governments'.[64] In Zhou's opinions, China must tighten its control over social

58. Keping Yu, '善治：政治合法性主要来源' ['Good governance: the main source of political legitimacy'], *社会科学报* [*Newspaper of Social Sciences*], (27 July 2010).
59. Jian Zhang, '当代中国政府合法性问题探讨' ['Discussion on political legitimacy in contemporary China'], *唯实* [*Truths and Facts*] 7, (2008).
60. E.g. Tao Li, '中国公民社会的兴起于政府合法性构建' ['Rising civil society and constructions of legitimacy in China'], *陇东学院学报* [*Journal of Longdong University*] 22(5), (2011).
61. Chongming Zheng and Xupeng Tu, '论我国公共权力合法性及其变迁' ['Discussion on legitimacy and changes in China's public power'], *岭南学刊* [*Lingnan Journal*] 5, (2008).
62. Jingchen Shen and Dawei Zhang, '当代中国政府合法性危机分析' [Analysis of the legitimacy crisis in contemporary China'], *商品与质量* [*Commodity and Quality*] 3, (2010).
63. Zhengyu Xu, '关于增强政府执政合法性的若干思考' ['Several thoughts on strengthening political legitimacy'], *中共太原市委党校学报* [*Journal of Taiyuan Municipal Party School of CPC*] 3, (2011).
64. Zhou, '防止落入所谓公民社会陷阱' ['Preventing falling into the so-called pitfall of civil society]'.

organizations and prevent the multiplication of those organizations with 'ulterior motives'.

Interestingly, 'strong society and strong state' is proposed as an alternative in order to balance 'strong state and weak society' and 'weak state and strong society'. Ma Xiaoni and Cheng Weijie, for example, argue that only 'big society and big government' can help the state to win more support.[65] It seems that this alternative could solve the problems of 'weak society' by promoting a 'strong society' and avoid conflicting with the state by maintaining a 'strong state'.

IV.2.3. Bureaucracy (solution). Under the guidance of the Scientific Outlook of Development, the idea of People-Oriented (以人为本) has been promoted as a basic value of the entire state. It attempts to change the ruling philosophies and functions of the state from growth-oriented to public service-oriented. In this special section, Schneider and Hwang examine this official discourse of 'people-oriented'—which they translate as 'putting people first'—in the management of disaster.[66] In the legitimacy debate, this idea is frequently used to highlight the importance of rebuilding bureaucracy. Many argue that the state should change its main priority from economic growth to social management in order to build a public service-oriented government and to strengthen the provision of public service.[67]

Chinese intellectuals propose both external and internal ways to restrict state power and officials. Externally, they suggest public supervision and transparency. For instance, Chen Bohui argues that public overseeing is the most effective way to restrict state power. According to Chen, 'Chinese mass media does not dare and is not willing to investigate corruption because of the government interventions'; therefore, China should enact laws to protect mass media.[68] The establishment of internal institutions and regulations are also advised for the purposes of preventing corruption and increasing performance.[69]

Promoting transparency of information is considered to be a way to maintain stability and legitimacy. For example, Li Chuxue and Luo Zhang argue that the development of the Internet and mass media provide channels for rumours and inaccurate information.[70] Therefore, local governments should objectively publicize

65. Xiaoni Ma and Weijie Cheng, '转型期的合法性变迁： 利益，权力，权利' ['Changing legitimacy at the transformation stage: interests, power and rights'], *河北青年管理干部学院学报* [*Journal of College of Hebei Young Managing Cadres*] 4, (2011).

66. Schneider and Hwang, 'The Sichuan earthquake and the heavenly mandate'.

67. For example, Chunlei Zhu, '乡镇改革： 乡镇制度的重建- 基于基层政权合法性于有效性的视角' ['Reforms of villages and towns: reconstruction of village and towns institutions—from the perspective of legitimacy and performance of local regimes'], *湖北社会科学* [*Hubei Social Sciences*] 12, (2008); Caihui Shong and Fangzhi Wang, '合法性视野下乡镇政府改革探析' ['Analysis of village and town governments' reform from a legitimacy perspective'], *中共乐山市委党校学报* [*Journal of the Party School of Leshan Municipal Committee of CPC*] 11(4), (2009).

68. Chen Bohui, '对社会转型期我国政治认同重构的新思考' ['New thoughts on the reconstruction of national identity at the transformation stage—based on Habermas' legitimacy theory'], *上饶师范学院学报* [*Journal of Shangrao Normal College*] 28(1), (2008).

69. For example, Wang and Li, '巩固和加强政府合法性基础的路径选择' ['Ways of consolidating and strengthening political legitimacy'].

70. Chuxue Li and Zhang Luo, '预防群体性事件与完善基层政治合法性基础探究' ['Exploration on prevention of popular protests and increase legitimacy of local governments'], *领导视角* [*Science of Management*], (July 2012).

rather than attempt to hide the relevant information. In Yu's 'good governance', transparency is a basic component of modern states and is popular with supporters of 'good governance'.[71]

The rapidly changing circumstances have led to concern about the state's decision-making capabilities. By listing past problematic policies, Huang Jianrong argues that the government should strengthen its decision-making ability by changing its ruling philosophies from economic efficiency-oriented to people-oriented.[72] Ren Hongjie, a professor at the People's University of Public Security, warns that the information explosion led by the Internet's development has made it more difficult for the state to make scientific decisions: 'Once the inappropriate policies and their consequences were exposed on the Internet, legitimacy would be significantly reduced'.[73] Therefore, Ren suggests that the government should 'establish special mechanisms to collect and filter Internet information for decision-making, build channels to communicate with the public about important policies, and increase the leaders' decision-making abilities by providing sufficient training'.

Moral education is also suggested as complementary to bureaucratic rebuilding. For example, Xia Lei argues that 'the entire moral image of the party-state is reflected in each civil servant or party cadre'; as such, strengthening moral education for civil servants is essential.[74] In addition, Shen Jingchen and Zhang Dawei argue that 'the political education of civil servants should move from general, ideological education to a more specific education of administrative accountability'.[75]

IV.3. Social justice

The promotion of social justice is the most direct way to respond to rising legitimacy concerns with regard to social problems. Inadequate social justice is considered both a direct and an indirect threat to party legitimacy: it leads to decreased support from disadvantaged groups and the poor, and also shakes social stability. As Yang Songlu warns, if the state fails to improve people's livelihood, 'it will not only slow down economic growth and damage social stability, but also threaten the regime's legitimacy'.[76] Peng Hua, writing in the in-house journal of the Beijing Youth Politics College, finds that social inequality and inadequate public provision of welfare have led to low political identities of the rural youth—a dangerous sign of social instability.[77] Peng further argues that market reform in China has led to many

71. Yu, '善治：政治合法性主要来源' ['Good governance: the main source of political legitimacy'].

72. Huang, '论现代政府合法性递减' ['Discussion on the decreasing legitimacy of modern governments'].

73. Hongjie Ren, '试论网络文化放大效应对政府合法性的新挑战' ['New challenges of Internet culture to political legitimacy'], *社科纵横* [*Social Sciences Review*] 11, (2011).

74. Lei Xia, '塑造柔性权威：提高政府合法性的根本出路' ['Constructions of soft authoritativeness: the fundamental way to increase political legitimacy'], *天府新论* [*Tianfu New Ideas*] no. 2, (2008).

75. Shen and Zhang, '当代中国政府合法性危机分析' ['Analysis of the legitimacy crisis in contemporary China'].

76. Songlu Yang, '试论社会转型期面临的合法性挑战及政策选择' ['Discussion on the legitimacy challenge and policy options at the transformation stage'], *内蒙古农业大学学报* [*Journal of Inner Mongolia Agricultural University (Social Sciences)*] 12(1), (2010).

77. Hua Peng, '合法性视阈下农村青年政治认同研究' ['Study on political identity of rural youth from a legitimacy perspective'], *北京青年政治学院学报* [*Journal of Beijing Youth Politics College*] 21(2), (2012).

socioeconomic problems and the government should take responsibility to improve people's livelihood and promote equality.

IV.3.1. People's livelihood (民生). With widening social inequality, focusing on people's livelihood is very critical to winning support from the poor. Jing Haixin argues that the issue of people's livelihood has become the root cause of social conflict in China.[78] Notably, the term 'people's livelihood' is not new to China as it used to be a part of Sun Yat-sen's 'Three Principles of the People'. The exact definition of 'people's livelihood' is never settled because Sun never clearly or fully explains it, but the equal ownership of land is fairly clear as it is based on Henry George's Georgism.[79] In the current context, people's livelihood represents a much broader spectrum. Both the ideas of 'people-oriented' and people's livelihood imply a similar message: that economic means alone cannot sustain the CCP's ruling, but being 'people-oriented' focuses more on ideological values and the latter is more like a direct policy responding to the inadequate provision of public welfare.

Nowadays, an improvement in people's livelihood is regarded by many as the new source of legitimacy in China.[80] Based on two influential government-funded survey projects in 2012, some even argue that the provision of public goods has replaced economic performance to become the most important legitimacy source. Ma Deyong and Wang Zhengxu, for example, argue that the public provision of welfare and the fairness of institutional arrangements are the keys for local governments to overcome a legitimacy crisis.[81] In another survey, Peking University's Meng Tianguan and Yang Ming found that 'economic growth can no longer help to maintain political trust, yet the increasing provision of public services—such as reducing the unemployment rate and Gini coefficient—and public welfare expenditure are still effective'.[82]

IV.3.2. Equality. As mentioned above, socioeconomic inequality has become the top legitimacy threat. Recognizing the widening of social inequality, the Scientific Outlook of Development intended to move the state's priority from efficiency-oriented to a more balanced position of equity and efficiency.

78. Haixin Jing, '政治合法性与改善民生' ['Political legitimacy and improvement of people's livelihood'], *行政论坛* [*Forum of Administration*] 18(4), (2011).

79. Yat-Sen Sun, *The Three Principles of the People* (Beijing: Commercial Press, 1930).

80. For example, Yongjuan Lu and Ronghua Shen, '反思我国地方政府的合法性资源' ['Rethinking legitimacy sources of local governments in China'], *天水行政学院学报* [*Journal of Tianshui Administration College*] 5, (2011).

81. Deyong Ma and Zhengxu Wang, '民主，公正还是绩效？ 中国地方政府合法性来源及其分析' ['Democracy, justice or performance? The legitimacy sources of local governments in China'], *经济社会体制比较* [*Comparative Economic & Social Systems*] 161(3), (2012).

82. Interestingly, their articles specifically point out that effective provision of welfare, rather than elections and citizen participation, is the main source of legitimacy in contemporary China. They also mention that this finding has confirmed the previous studies published in another legitimacy article in 2007. As mentioned, most articles did not directly challenge or respond to other competing views; however, this is the only exception. This is also the only article that mentioned citizen participation and elections but did not support them. See Tianguang Meng and Ming Yang, '转型期中国县级政府的客观治理绩效于政治信任—从经济合法性到公共产品合法性' ['Performance and political trust of China's town-level governments at the transformation stage—from economic growth legitimacy to public goods legitimacy'], *经济与社会体制比较* [*Comparative Economic & Social Systems*] 162(4), (2012).

In the debate, some argue that the government should play a role in compensating for market deficiencies and promoting equality. For example, Qu Wanhong argues that the government should compensate for market deficiencies, provide fairer competition in the market and promote social justice—in particular regional equality.[83] Specific economic policies to reduce inequality are also proposed. For example, Fu Jingtao and Li Ming suggest adjusting the structures of income tax and financial expenditure.[84]

IV.3.3. Grassroots democracy/basic level democracy (基层民主). As noted above, intellectuals have been looking for more solid legitimacy sources other than economic performance; democracy is clearly a key way of establishing Weber's rational-legal legitimacy. In Hu Jintao's speech at the 17th Party Congress, socialist democracy—grassroots democracy in particular—was proposed as a way to promote social justice. In the debate, grassroots democracy is considered by 13% of the articles as an effective way of promoting social justice and satisfying people's rising demands to participate in the political process.

Grassroots democracy is also considered an effective way of increasing the political legitimacy of local governments. For example, Ma and Wang's study finds that the effective implementation of direct elections in villages and towns can enhance the legitimacy of the local states.[85] Therefore, they suggest that the implementation of electoral democracy at local levels is worth trying.

Interestingly, the debate seems to be systematically refraining from any conceptualization of the term 'grassroots democracy'. Although it is mentioned frequently in the debate, no author has an interest in defining what 'basic' (基层) is. Also, no author mentions what should follow after the success of basic democracy. Li Meiling argues that 'democratic development has to be gradual because of the inadequate democratic traditions and values in Chinese history' and emphasizes that both high-level democracy and grassroots democracy are important.[86] However, Li does not explain this so-called 'high-level' in detail.

Elections are, of course, an essential component of grassroots democracy. In the debate, only an article written by a senior colonel of the Chinese military openly opposes electoral democracy. It argues that the benefits of electoral democracy—such as increased political identity and stability—cannot compensate for the cost—such as decreased national identity, increased ethnic separatism and low efficiency.[87] According to this article, 'the West attempts to use electoral democracy

83. Wanhong Qu, '转型期政治合法性流失对政治稳定的影响' ['The impacts of decreasing political legitimacy on political stability at the transformation stage'], *云南行政学院学报* [*Journal of Yunnan Administration College*] 1, (2011).

84. Jingtao Fu and Ming Li, '政府合法性的社会群体结构及其合作博弈' ['Social groups of political legitimacy and its cooperation game'], *湖北行政学院学报* [*Journal of Hubei Administration Institute*] 43, (2009).

85. Ma and Wang, '民主，公正还是绩效？' ['Democracy, justice or performance?'].

86. Meiling Li, '民主是党的执政合法性的动力和源泉' ['Democracies are the driving forces and sources of the party's legitimacy'], *中共山西省委党校学报* [*Journal of Shanxi Provincial Committee Party School of CPC*] 32(2), (2009).

87. Yanzhong Cao, '试析民主的形式与政治合法性的认同' ['Democratic forms and identities of political legitimacy'], *新视野* [*Expanding Horizons*] 5, (2010).

to bring disorder and chaos to China under the guise of protecting human rights'. The article considers party democracy as an alternative to electoral democracy.

Elections are also suggested in order to strengthen the party's ruling capabilities and subsequently its legitimacy. The Central Party School's Zhao Yao argues that the party's personnel system should make efforts to increase elections and gradually reduce appointments from the top.[88] Zhao considers the electoral system to be a revolution of the appointment system and advises the implementation of gradual reforms, although he clearly recognizes that the electoral system might have risks associated.

V. Concluding remarks

This article studies the legitimacy debate in China between 2008 and 2012. Several findings can be highlighted. First, while many overseas China observers are focusing on the search for Chinese philosophies to underpin a new polity, the Chinese intellectuals are looking to the West instead. It suggests that those who thought concertedly of China as in some way exceptional and built on different philosophies from Western states have not yet fully convinced their peers within China.

Second, most China watchers emphasized performance legitimacy and paid almost no attention to ideology; however, the analysts within China still consider ideology to be crucial and express serious concern about performance legitimacy. Continuous efforts towards ideological adaptation indicate party leaders' increasing concerns about the CCP's declining ideological legitimacy at the transformation stage. The party has realized the gap between social reality and ideology, and thus many modern political values have been absorbed so as to make a successful adaptation. Nowadays, democracy and rule of law have been considered as the only solid ground for Weber's rational-legal legitimacy. As Li Meiling put it, 'party legitimacy can only be gained from democracy'.[89] Whether or not China should be more democratic is no longer the question; the focus is on which forms of democracy China should embrace.

Third, there is a distinct rising appeal of social autonomy that runs counter to the dominant official line in this debate. The increased recognition of social autonomy has indicated the growing power of social forces; this tendency might shape China's political development. Although there is still some resistance, the findings of this study indicate that Chinese intellectuals have increasingly realized the fact that social autonomy is an unavoidable tendency and advised the party-state to promote rather than to repress it. However, it should not be interpreted as a sign of moving toward a more liberal and electoral democratic system. Rather, those suggestions are designed to strengthen the one-party system. Whether the development of civil society will achieve their expected outcomes or whether it will threaten the party's control as some have warned still needs further investigation.

Fourth, this study finds a correlation between authors' backgrounds (institutions, research locations and funding sources) and their dominant arguments about

---

88. Yao Zhao, '选人用人制度改革探析—基于政治合法性的视角' ['Analysis and exploration on personnel system—from political legitimacy perspective'], *湖北行政学院学报* [*Journal of Hubei Administration Institute*] 4, (2011).

89. Li, '民主是党的执政合法性的动力和源泉' ['Democracies are the driving forces and sources of the party's legitimacy'].

legitimacy. Chinese intellectuals based in more affluent areas are less concerned with inequality, the sustainability of China's economy, corruption and inadequate political participation. Those based in poorer regions prefer to suggest the improvement of bureaucracy, increase citizen participation and encourage the development of civil society; those in affluent regions are more interested in suggesting that the regime should improve its capability to guide public opinion. In addition, government-funded projects are more likely to endorse the improvement of public welfare and intellectuals based in the party school prefer party democracy. Those differentiated legitimacy concerns and strategies deserve further study.

Moreover, while the world has pointed out the successes of the Chinese response to the financial crisis, Chinese intellectuals seem to have become more pessimistic. This again indicates that Chinese intellectuals are concerned that economic performance alone cannot sustain the CCP's ruling.

Most importantly, this study finds a fundamental shift in the legitimacy debate in China. It is driven by various worsening problems caused by economic growth—socioeconomic inequality in particular. As this study reveals, it is clearly recognized that simply relying on economics is not sufficient—even if the economy continues to do well (and of course, there is a clear understanding that bad economic performance will harm legitimacy).

Indeed, economic growth is not a direct source of legitimacy; the regime gains legitimacy only if economic performance is transformed into actual material benefit which is delivered to its citizens.[90] In the modern 'social contract', provision of public welfare is the key to the communist states being able to trade economic benefits with the civil rights of citizens.[91] Nowadays, the party-state has been increasingly urged to put more effort into providing public welfare. Some recent surveys in this debate even find that the provision of welfare has already replaced economic growth to become the principal pillar of legitimacy of local governments.[92] Schubert's new research agenda that is debated in this special section shed lights on how to better catch this changing dynamics of legitimacy of local governments.[93]

All in all, this study reveals a remarkable cleavage between the international perceptions of the Chinese state and the pessimistic views among Chinese intellectuals about political legitimacy. The cleavage between the Western and the Chinese literature over this issue is perhaps owing to different perspectives: party intellectuals have more insights which are unavailable to the outside, and analysts outside China are looking comparatively and so perhaps better understand the 'normalcy' of the Chinese situation. This might reflect a general pattern of area studies. Outsiders and insiders are observing the research object from different angles, and they therefore might reach different observational results.

90. Bruce Gilley and Heike Holbig, 'Reclaiming legitimacy in China', *Politics& Policy* 38(3), (2010).

91. Vladimir Victor Kusin, *From Dubcek to Charter 77: A Study of 'Normalisation' in Czechoslovakia, 1968–1978* (Edinburgh: Q Press, 1978).

92. Ma and Wang, '民主，公正还是绩效？' ['Democracy, justice or performance?']; Meng and Yang, '转型期中国县级政府的客观治理绩效于政治信任' ['Performance and political trust of China's town-level governments at the transformation stage'].

93. Schubert, 'Political legitimacy in contemporary China revisited'; Schubert, 'One-party rule and the question of legitimacy in contemporary China'.

Political Process and Widespread Protests in China: the 2010 labor protest

RAY OU YANG

Existing studies of collective actions in China pay most attention to frequent but localized protests, but such protests are less likely to deeply drive China's political and social prospect. By contrast, widespread protests are more likely to affect the Chinese Communist Party's authority and policies once they emerge. The goal of this article is thus to probe the conditions under which a widespread protest can happen in China today. This article proposes four necessary conditions grounded in the political process model and tests them by explaining the successful outbreak of the 2010 labor protest. Identifying these conditions helps us understand and predict the political and social development of China.

I. Introduction

This article seeks to identify the conditions under which a widespread protest is likely to emerge in China today. Activists may attempt to initiate a widespread protest for any public issue, whether directly or indirectly relevant to governments, but not all trials will succeed. Widespread protests are indeed rare phenomena. However, as highlighted in this article, these protests will be more likely to influence the Chinese Communist Party's (CCP) authority and policies once they emerge, even if their issues are indirectly relevant to the government. Compared to probing those frequent but localized protests to which existing studies pay most attention, probing widespread protests thus helps us more comprehensively understand and predict China's political and social development.

Scholars still use widespread protest as a term without a clear common definition. What further confuses people is that scholars sometimes also apply other terms that sound similar, such as popular protest and large-scale protest, and these terms are also not well defined. Nonetheless, we are able to find a subtle demarcation in fact. The latter two terms seem to focus more on the number of protesters, while 'widespread' is seemingly applied to describe a protest that spreads over many areas.[1] To avoid any confusion, this article forms a minimum definition of widespread protest applicable to China, highlighting spatial diffusion. A protest is 'widespread' if it satisfies the following criteria: (1) it consists of multiple collective action events aiming at the same goals; and (2) these events must simultaneously or sequentially happen in at least two provincial-level administrative divisions.[2]

This definition indicates that the collective action events in a protest must not be regarded as a whole. Instead, in a widespread protest, the first event directly conducted by initiators is like a bellwether, while all other events are like followers. However, the definition does not assume a connection that these events must have. In theory, we can sum up possible connections into two types, unitary and federal. For the first type, this means that initiators, as well as their local agents, directly conduct not only the first event but also every sequent event. For the second type, it says that the collective action events in a widespread protest are affiliated but independent. Initiators only plan and organize the first event at most, and then other activists separately follow the spark to carry out collective actions with the same goal.

This article cares only about a widespread protest's emergence. Grounded in McAdam's political process model, I propose several general conditions.[3] These conditions are all necessary for a widespread protest to emerge in China, whether unitary or federal. The conditions are tested and supported by a rare case, a widespread labor protest, which broke out in 2010.

II. A review of the current focus: individual motivation

In existing research, exploring what can motivate Chinese people to protest still accounts for a major part. Scholars mostly accept the factors reviewed below as key individual motivation. The factors are directly or indirectly related to the CCP, but none of them is totally unrelated to the party. This is because the CCP and the state are still highly intertwined in China today.[4] The CCP's branches exist everywhere in people's daily life, driving policies in public institutions and endorsing those in private institutions. In this context, all protests need the CCP to do something for them in the end once they successfully emerge. This situation is not only the case in China. In fact, protesters in democracies also tend to see officials as 'responsibility takers of last resort'.

1. See for example, Kevin J. O'Brien, ed., *Popular Protest in China* (Cambridge, MA: Harvard University Press, 2008); Xiuying Cheng, 'Dispersive containment: a comparative case study of labor politics in central China', *Journal of Contemporary China* 22(79), (2013), pp. 131–147.

2. The reason why this article defines that a widespread protest must have multiple collective action events in at least two provincial areas is that, by the definition, a widespread protest thus can be a cross-provincial issue involving the central government, which is more likely to affect the authority and policies of the CCP.

3. Doug McAdam, *Political Process and the Development of Black Insurgency, 1930–1970* (Chicago, IL: University of Chicago Press, [1982] 1999).

4. Cheng Li, 'China's communist party-state: the structure and dynamics of power', in William A. Joseph, ed., *Politics in China: An Introduction* (New York: Oxford University Press, 2010), pp. 166–177.

Those affecting Chinese people's attitudes toward the CCP are the factors more directly related to the party. Traditional values, the state-controlled media and striking economic records are often expected to drive the attitudes.[5] The traditional values refer to the sense of guardianship stemming from Confucianism. People define their relationship with authority as hierarchical in China, obligating them to respect and follow authority.[6] The CCP thus tends to be regarded as a guardian. This sense allows the CCP to make decisions according to the party's judgments on the collective interests of China, and it does not allow people to withdraw their support for the CCP once their personal interests are harmed.[7] The sense of democracy is contrasted to the sense of guardianship.[8] The weaker the later, the stronger the former will be.[9] Therefore, those people who are not driven by traditional values tend to prefer democracy, and they are often expected to be more likely to challenge the CCP's authority.[10]

With respect to media, the CCP controls the full scope of media programming. The CCP mobilizes Chinese people's political support through political control and censorship.[11] However, many observers have argued that the Internet is much less controlled by the CCP than traditional media (TV, newspaper and broadcast) in China.[12] Through the Internet, people are more likely to hear different voices and know the truth that differs from the CCP's propaganda. For example, Lei applies the 2007 World Value Survey to reveal that those who use the Internet as their main news source are expected to be more dissentient and more inclined to protest against the CCP's positions in China, compared with those who use traditional media as their main news source.[13]

China's economic development is another important factor commonly expected to affect Chinese people's political attitudes. For instance, drawing on the 2001 World Values Survey and the 2002 East Asian Barometer, Wang indicates that over 90% of the Chinese respondents had a high level of confidence in the national government and the CCP.[14] He highlights that the CCP government succeeds in improving

5. See for example, Pippa Norris, *Democratic Deficit: Critical Citizens Revisited* (New York: Cambridge University Press, 2011), pp. 114–115.

6. Lucian W. Pye, *The Mandarin and the Cadre: China's Political Cultures* (Ann Arbor, MI: Center for Chinese Studies, The University of Michigan, 1988).

7. Tianjian Shi and Jie Lu, 'The shadow of Confucianism', *Journal of Democracy* 21(4), (2010), p. 126.

8. Robert A. Dahl, *Democracy and Its Critics* (New Haven, CT: Yale University Press, 1989), p. 52.

9. Another political value discussed by Dahl is the sense of anarchism. To make this article compatible with existing studies and data, however, I only consider the contrast between guardianship and democracy. See *Ibid.*, pp. 37–51.

10. See for example, Jian-Hua Zhu, 'From discontent to protest: individual-level causes of the 1989 pro-democracy movement in China', *International Journal of Public Opinion Research* 5(3), (1993), pp. 234–249.

11. Wenfang Tang, *Public Opinion and Political Change in China* (Stanford, CA: Stanford University Press, 2005), p. 99.

12. See Tom Downey, 'China's cyberposse', *The New York Times Sunday Magazine*, (7 March 2010); Qiang Xiao, 'The rise of online public opinion and its political impact', in Susan L. Shirk, ed., *Changing Media, Changing China* (London: Oxford University Press, 2011).

13. Ya-Wen Lei, 'Political consequences of new media: the beliefs and practices of Chinese netizens', *Political Communication* 28(3), (2011), pp. 291–322. Also, see for example, Guobin Yang, 'The Internet and civil society in China: a preliminary assessment', *Journal of Contemporary China* 12(36), (2003), pp. 453–475.

14. Zhengxu Wang, 'Explaining regime strength in China', *China: An International Journal* 4(2), (2006), pp. 220–222.

Chinese people's financial well-being and living standards, which leads to a high level of confidence in the regime.[15]

Nonetheless, not all people are winners in the economic reform since 1978; injustice has risen to be a detrimental side effect. Summarizing existing studies, injustice is mainly composed of social inequality, unfair working conditions and land expropriation. In regard to inequality, in order to pursue a rapid economic growth the CCP disregarded redistribution over the past decades; instead, it concentrated on developing the most profitable sectors' productivity by a continuous increase in large-scale investment and capital–labor ratio.[16] A 'deep reform' aiming for greater economic openness and the cuts in public service expenditures from 1994 to 2002 aggravated inequality.[17] Since the growth cannot be converted into personal income to enrich their lives, disadvantaged people are more likely to protest against the CCP for economic equality.[18]

Moreover, for lower classes, the working class in particular, job security has been eroded by marketization.[19] Employees in state-owned enterprises, as well as those in private enterprises, are all involved in job competition now. Nevertheless, local GDP is a criterion for the performance evaluation of local officials, so the officials usually have a close tie with employers who decide investment. Once people dispute against their employers over working conditions, local officials will take the employers' side.[20] Unfortunately, employees cannot easily give up their jobs even if they suffer injustices, because it is difficult to maintain daily life without any income, given the CCP's withdrawal from public services (e.g. medical care). This dilemma is expected to lead Chinese people to protest against the CCP as well as their employers.[21]

As another major source of injustice, land expropriation fuels social tension in China. This means that the needs of economic development are still likely to be satisfied at the expense of individual rights. In urban China, the expropriation is usually reflected by home demolition and eviction for development projects, which has been believed to push urban people to protest with a growing sense of property rights.[22] In rural China, the expropriation is often equal to farmland deprivation.

15. Zhengxu Wang, 'Before the emergence of critical citizens: economic development and political trust in China', *International Review of Sociology* 15(1), (2005), pp. 155–171; Wang, 'Explaining regime strength in China', pp. 225–226.

16. See for example, Louis Kuijs and Tao Wang, 'China's pattern of growth: moving to sustainability and reducing inequality', *China & World Economy* 14(1), (2006), pp. 1–14.

17. Shaoguang Wang, 'Openness and inequality: the case of China', in Lowell Dittmer and Guoli Liu, eds, *China's Deep Reform: Domestic Politics in Transition* (Lanham, MD: Rowman & Littlefield, 2006), pp. 252–258.

18. Steve Hess, 'Land rights, and frames of injustice on China's protest landscape', *Asian Survey* 50(5), (2010), p. 911.

19. Feng Chen, 'Subsistence crises, managerial corruption and labor protests in China', *The China Journal* 44, (2000), pp. 45–46.

20. Yang Su and Xin He, 'Street as courtroom: state accommodation of labor protest in South China', *Law & Society Review* 44(1), (2010), p. 162.

21. See William Hurst and Kevin O'Brien, 'China's contentious pensioners', *China Quarterly* 170, (2002), pp. 345–360; Feng Chen, 'Industrial restructuring and workers' resistance in China', *Modern China* 29(2), (2003), pp. 237–262; Simon Gilbert, 'China's strike wave', *International Socialism*, (29 June 2005), available at: http://www.isj.org. uk/index.php4?id=125 (accessed April 2012).

22. See for example, Hess, 'Land rights, and frames of injustice on China's protest landscape'.

Losing farmland is expected to elevate peasants' protest tendencies, since it deprives them of their means of livelihood and their chances of engaging in the land market.[23]

Besides the above factors, there are still some other factors commonly expected to affect Chinese people's protest tendencies, such as corruption and pollution. Regarding corruption, to ensure that the economic reform can be smoothly carried out, the CCP allowed officials to retain some of their old powers and to get new powers over the economy in the marketization process.[24] This strategy removed political resistance to the reform but also led to pervasive corruption problems. Some scholars show that although Chinese people tend to acquiesce to corruption, they will fight against it if they believe that it hurts them.[25] Finally, following a growing sense of environmental protection in China, the impact of pollution is also increasing. If the damages from a pollution event are known, it may motivate victims to protest against troublemakers and relevant officials.[26]

III. Theoretical expectations: from individual motivation to the entire political process

Even if the factors reviewed above combine, this does not mean that a widespread protest will definitely break out in China once there is a group of people preferring democracy, using the Internet as the main news source, feeling relatively deprived, or suffering from poor working conditions, land expropriation, corruption and pollution. Individual motivation should be incorporated into a broader political process. In the field of contentious politics, McAdam's synthetic model looking at such a process has been widely applied. From his position, the political process transforming individual motivation into actual collective actions consists of three integral elements: expanding political opportunities; indigenous organizational strength; and cognitive liberation.[27] To simplify the following discussion, I employ the corresponding terms from Tarrow to discuss the later two elements: mobilizing structures and framing.[28]

Political opportunities are more important for the emergence of collective actions in non-democracies.[29] When existing studies of protests in China investigate this variable, most of them pay attention to the decline in the state's repression. Since China's former president Hu Jingtao began to promote the ideas of a 'harmonious society' to bolster the CCP's legitimacy in 2003, the CCP has altered its tendency to

23. See for example, Ray Yep, 'Containing land grabs: a misguided response to rural conflicts over land', *Journal of Contemporary China* 22(80), (2013), pp. 273–291.

24. Yan Sun, 'Reform, state, and corruption: is corruption less destructive in China than in Russia?', *Comparative Politics* 32(1), (1999), pp. 2–5.

25. See for example, Chen, 'Subsistence crises, managerial corruption and labor protests in China'.

26. See for example, Benjamin Van Rooij, 'The people vs. pollution: understanding citizen action against pollution in China', *Journal of Contemporary China* 19(63), (2010), pp. 55–77.

27. McAdam, *Political Process and the Development of Black Insurgency*, pp. 40–51.

28. Sidney G. Tarrow, *Power in Movement: Social Movements and Contentious Politics* (New York: Cambridge University Press, [1994] 2011), pp. 30–32.

29. Jeff Goodwin, 'Conclusion: are protestors opportunities? Fifty tests', in Jeff Goodwin and James M. Jasper, eds, *Contention in Context: Political Opportunities and the Emergence of Protest* (Stanford, CA: Stanford University Press, 2012), pp. 284–286. Goodwin concludes that, regarding the emergence of political contention, political opportunities matter in about 40.9% of the democratic cases and 83.3% of the non-democratic cases that are studied in the book.

repress protests.[30] Some analyses even highlight the point that the CCP is specifically satisfying people who demonstrate their particular demands through political actions given political risks.[31] The window of opportunity is opened for protests in China today, though the CCP will still repress those protests threatening its political survival.[32]

When this 'window' is likely to be closed is a question further related to the link between state repression and movement mobilization.[33] The classic perspective is that state repression has a negative effect on the magnitude of collective action.[34] By contrast, many recent analyses point out that the link is actually curvilinear.[35] State repression sometimes may incubate the formation of revolutionary movements, since it has the potential to push those who are oppressed to take more radical actions.[36] Interestingly, the CCP is indeed concerned about this curvilinear link.[37] We can thus expect that the CCP's responses to a protest's forerunners influence whether the following collective action events will happen in different areas. As long as the CCP believes that a protest will not readily and directly threaten its political survival, it will tend to not repress the protest's forerunners to avoid arousing more resentment.

Another variable is mobilizing structures. These are the resources of a group of aggrieved people that enable them to utilize political opportunities.[38] Social networks and organizations are two major resources.[39] Organizations further provide four different resources: members recruited along established lines of interaction; an internal communication network; an established structure of solidary incentives; and leaders.[40] However, the importance of social networks is much greater in China, where every social group should be officially sanctioned in order to exist. Social organizations are controlled and included in the CCP's party-state system, so they are hardly likely to be hosts of collective action. What Chinese people can rely on are social networks that help them translate their interpersonal trust and shared perceptions into collective action. On the other hand, scholars have shown the Internet's contributions to the establishment of social networks.[41] Therefore, in addition to the traditional sources of social networks (i.e. face-to-face interactions,

30. Su and He, 'Street as courtroom', p. 162.

31. See for example, Benjamin Liebman, 'A populist threat to China's courts?', in Margaret Y. K. Woo and Mary E. Gallagher, eds, *Chinese Justice: Civil Dispute Resolution in Contemporary China* (New York: Cambridge University Press, 2011).

32. Chen, 'Subsistence crises, managerial corruption and labor protests in China', p. 61.

33. Some scholars have highlighted the existence of other political opportunities in China. See for example, Xi Chen, 'Collective petitioning and institutional conversion', in O'Brien, ed., *Popular Protest in China*. However, it is reasonable to argue that the decline in the CCP's repression should be the most critical opportunity.

34. See for example, David Snyder and Charles Tilly, 'Hardship and collective violence in France, 1830 to 1960', *American Sociological Review* 37(5), (1972), pp. 520–532.

35. See for example, Jeff Goodwin and James M. Jasper, 'Caught in a winding, snarling vine: the structural bias of political process theory', *Sociological Forum* 14(1), (1999), p. 38.

36. Jeff Goodwin, *No Other Way Out: States and Revolutionary Movements, 1945–1991* (New York: Cambridge University Press, 2001), pp. 27–30.

37. Chen, 'Subsistence crises, managerial corruption and labor protests in China', p. 61.

38. McAdam, *Political Process and the Development of Black Insurgency*, p. 43.

39. Tarrow, *Power in Movement*, pp. 119–139.

40. McAdam, *Political Process and the Development of Black Insurgency*, p. 43.

41. See for example, Victoria Carty, 'Bridging contentious and electoral politics: Moveon and the digital revolution', in Patrick G. Coy, ed., *Research in Social Movements, Conflicts and Change, vol. 30* (Bingley, UK: Emerald Group Publishing, 2010).

native-place solidarity, kinship and transactions), the Internet is likely to afford Chinese people a new source, since the Internet is much less controlled by the CCP.[42]

Finally, as McAdam highlights, people and the subjective meanings they attach to their situations mediate between political opportunities and collective action.[43] People only jointly act for what they jointly define as meaningful. This highlights the importance of framing. In general, framing means the strategic alignment of activities, goals, and the ideology of a movement with potential participants' interests, values and beliefs.[44] However, Diani has shown the importance of the congruence between mobilization frames and political opportunities.[45] As discussed above, political opportunities are more critical for the rise of collective action in non-democracies. Thus, we can expect that Chinese protesters must also frame the strategies they are supposed to use in a way consistent with the political opportunity structure.

Taking into account individual motivation, political opportunities, mobilizing structures and framing, I propose four general expectations about the conditions under which a widespread protest is likely to emerge in China.[46] Because the conditions do not depend on the types of intra-protest connections, they must be necessary for the outbreak of any widespread protest in China, whether unitary or federal.

a. There should be some individual motivation factors pushing Chinese people across different areas to popularly join a protest (logically, there should be at least one such factor).
b. A protest based on the above factors should not fundamentally threaten the CCP's political survival, so that the CCP is more likely to moderately respond to the protest's forerunners in order to avoid arousing more resentment.
c. There must be some social networks that help protesters translate their interpersonal trust and shared perceptions into collective actions.

---

42. Political process theorists are criticized for their ignorance of collective identity. See Aldon D. Morris, 'Political consciousness and collective action', in Aldon D. Morris and Carol McClurg Mueller, eds, *Frontiers in Social Movement Theory* (New Haven, CT: Yale University Press, 1992). A more moderate view is that political process theorists see the formation of collective identity as embedded in the process of framing. See for example, McAdam, *Political Process and the Development of Black Insurgency*. A derivative assumption is that a useful injustice framing establishes a collective identity. See Hess, 'Land rights, and frames of injustice on China's protest landscape'. This article accepts this assumption without discussing collective identity. Moreover, it is difficult for a collective identity to last for a long time in China due to the state's intervention. See George T. Crane, 'Collective identity, symbolic mobilization, and student protest in Nanjing, China, 1988–1989', *Comparative Politics* 26(4), (1994), pp. 395–413. Hence, every protest in China may need to form a new collective identity through framing. In addition, elite allies are sometimes seen as mobilization resources, but so far they are still unavailable in China.

43. McAdam, *Political Process and the Development of Black Insurgency*, p. 48.

44. David A. Snow, E. Burke Rochford, Jr, Steven K. Worden and Robert D. Benford, 'Frame alignment processes, micromobilization, and movement participation', *American Sociological Review* 51(4), (1986), pp. 464–481.

45. Mario Diani, 'Linking mobilization frames and political opportunities: insights from regional populism in Italy', *American Sociological Review* 61(6), (1996), pp. 1053–1069.

46. The political process model is good at probing the 'structural' conditions for protests, and such structures are the interest of this article. Nevertheless, for those who care about the behavioral and psychological processes within (or between) groups as the conditions for protests, they should refer to the theories of group dynamics that are better at analyzing relevant issues: the formation of group norms and culture, exchange behavior and cost–benefit calculation, members' cohesion and assembly, and symbolic convergence. See for example, Ernest G. Borman, *Discussion and Group Methods: Theory and Practices* (New York: Harper and Row Publishers, 1975).

d. A protest's initiators not only must frame the protest congruent with the factors motivating Chinese people, but also must frame the strategies that they are supposed to employ in a way consistent with the political opportunity structure in China.[47]

IV. The 2010 labor protest as a case study: research design and data sources

On 17 May 2010, a widespread labor protest broke out at Honda's Foshan factory in the south of China. After the first collective action event occurred at that factory, the protest quickly spread to Honda's other factories as well as other companies' factories in Guangdong and other provinces. Because of space limitations, Table 1 only lists some popular collective action events in the protest. The protest spread to at least ten provincial areas. The collective action events happened not only in foreign-owned corporations, but also in China's government-owned corporations and private enterprises. The protest climaxed in June 2010, and then it gradually subsided.

The labor protest is the only widespread protest that has successfully emerged in China in recent years. I use this case to test the general expectations. Since survey data are better at reflecting the general attitudes of people across different areas, Expectation A is tested using the 2008 China Survey. The survey is the work of the College of Liberal Arts at Texas A&M University, with the collaboration of the Research Center for Contemporary China at Peking University. The survey's data are from a multi-stage stratified random sample containing 3,989 respondents from China's seven geographic regions.[48] A critical advantage of the survey is that it asked people's tendencies to protest in the future. The survey is thus good for testing Expectation A, since it was conducted before the labor protest.

Unfortunately, surveys often cannot show enough information on political opportunities, mobilizing structures and framing. This is also the case for the 2008 China Survey. Expectations B, C and D are thus tested through an intensive analysis of the labor protest, taking into account the survey finding about individual motivation. This analysis employs secondary data including: studies generally examining China's political structure and the CCP's intraparty politics (they are relevant to China's political opportunity structure), the field studies of how the party

47. Some scholars have demonstrated the effects of social movement spillover. One possible spillover effect is that a movement can affect subsequent movements by altering the political and cultural conditions it confronts. See David S. Meyer and Nancy Whittier, 'Social movement spillover', *Social Problems* 41(2), (1994), pp. 277–297. This article does not totally reject the possibility of this spillover effect, while this article does argue that we need to hold a reserved opinion on the extent to which this effect can really work in China. At least for localized protests, scholars did not observe a clear change in China's political and cultural conditions with the increasing number of localized protests.

48. In the sampling process, 75 counties and county-level districts were first selected from seven geographic regions. The number of counties from a region is proportionate to its population. Two townships or township-level districts were then drawn from each county-level unit. After that, two half-square minutes of longitude and altitude were drawn from each township-level unit. Furthermore, 25 dwellings were selected from each minute using the dwelling lists of spatial square seconds that were also drawn from the same minute based on the population density. Finally, applying the Kish Grid method, the respondents were selected from each dwelling. In the end, 438 respondents were selected from the Northeast, 730 from the North, 555 from the East, 338 from the South, 848 from the Central, 435 from the Northwest, 541 from the Southwest and 104 from the municipalities.

Table 1. China's labor protests in 2010 (partial list)

Date	Factory company	Owner origin	Location	Number of participants (approximate)
17 May 2010	Honda	Japan	Foshan, Guangdong province	1,700
30 May 2010	Lanchow Vinylon	Government-owned	Lanchow, Gansu province	2,000
3 June 2010	Brother Industries	Japan	Xian, Shaanxi province	900
5 June 2010	KOK Machinery	Taiwan	Kunshan, Jiangsu province	2,000
6 June 2010	AZ-Instrument	Taiwan	Shenzhen, Guangdong province	2,000
7 June 2010	Yacheng Electronics	South Korea	Huizhou, Guangdong province	2,000
8 June 2010	Henan Pingmian Textiles Group	Government-owned	Pingdingshan, Henan province	5,500
9 June 2010	TPO Displays	Taiwan	Shanghai City	2,000
10 June 2010	Flextronics	United States	Zhuhai, Guangdong province	1,000
15 June 2010	EPSON	Japan	Shenzhen, Guangdong province	N/A
17 June 2010	Toyota	Japan	Tianjin, Hebei province	N/A
21 June 2010	Denso	Japan	Guangzhou, Guangdong province	N/A
1 July 2010	Mitsumi Online	Japan	Tianjin, Hebei province	N/A
5 July 2010	Fangzhi Textile	Government-owned	Xianyang, Shaanxi province	10,000
28 July 2010	Dalian Shaft	Government-owned	Dalian, Liaoning province	N/A
13 August 2010	Kunming Machine Tool	Private	Kunming, Yunnan province	N/A
16 August 2010	LOTTE	South Korea	Beijing City	300

Source: Chan, 'Honda lock strike in China continues as industrial unrest spreads'; CLW (China Labor Watch), *The 2010 Annual Report on the Working Conditions of Migrant Workers in China* (New York: CLW, 2011) [in simplified Chinese].

responded to the protest, and news reports about how the protest's framing and participants' social networks worked.

V. The test on Expectation A

If Expectation A is really a necessary condition, there should exist fuel for protests before May 2010. We must see that there were indeed some factors propelling Chinese people to protest before the labor protest was initiated, although whether the protest was framed as consistent with the factors is another question analyzed in the next section. I use those factors noted in Section II as candidates.

The 2008 China Survey has an item (e5g) asking whether respondents would protest in the future and whether they had ever taken part in a protest. Their answers to the former question might be affected by their answers to the latter one. I thus must control for their protest histories when I test what factors increase their future protest tendencies. Nonetheless, the protest histories cannot be directly put into a model. It may cause a recursiveness problem, because the histories are also likely to be affected by other variables expected to affect the future protest tendencies. Thus, this article utilizes a two-stage model to handle this issue. I look at respondents' protest histories in Model 1 and then use the predicted values of the histories as an instrumental variable in Model 2 that focuses on respondents' future protest tendencies.

The dependent variable of Model 1 is whether respondents had ever engaged in a protest (1 = yes and 0 = no), and that of Model 2 is whether respondents said that they would protest in the future (1 = yes and 0 = no). Only 92 respondents had ever joined a protest, while 382 respondents said that they would protest in the future. The models use the same independent variables, except for *Predicted protest history* in Model 2.

The sense of democracy measures whether respondents believed that: (1) demonstrations can easily disturb social stability (item e14a); (2) they should have a strong government to handle complex economic problems (item e14d); (3) their society can be chaotic if they do not share the same thinking (item e14e); and (4) a multiple-party system can cause political chaos (item e14g). I combine the responses to all statements into a 17-point scale to reflect the influence of political values (0 = extremely pro-guardianship and 16 = extremely pro-democracy).

Main news source reflects respondents' major sources of news. The possible sources are: TV (items d6a–d6c), radio (items d8a–d8c), newspapers (items d13a–d13c), magazines (item d20) or the Internet (items d26s1–d26s6). The first four are traditional media. I combine the responses into an ordinal variable to show the influence of media (0 = did not read news, 1 = only traditional media, 2 = both traditional media and the Internet, and 3 = only the Internet).

Macro economic problem evaluation represents the extent to which respondents thought that economic development was a serious problem in China (item g6b), which is measured by an 11-point scale (0 = not a problem at all and 10 = an extremely serious problem). I use this variable to reflect the effect of the inconsistency between China's economic growth and Chinese people's macro-economic evaluation.

The sense of inequality is based on two indicators. One is how respondents ranked their social status (item h3), measured by an 11-point scale (0 = very low and 10 = very high). The other one is at what level respondents felt that their income was situated (item h5) as compared with the average in their residence areas, measured by an 11-point scale as well (0 = low-level income and 10 = high-level income). I reverse the original scales of these indicators and then combine them into a 21-point scale (0 = not unequal at all and 20 = extremely unequal).

Personal hardship evaluation contains three indicators: the extent to which respondents feel pleased with their life as a whole (item h2b); financial situations (item h2a); and current jobs (item h2c). They are measured by an 11-point scale (0 = satisfied very much and 10 = not satisfied at all) separately. This variable is employed to capture the influence of the gap between China's economic growth and individual Chinese people's lives.

Land expropriation shows whether respondents had ever suffered from land confiscation or resettlement (items g8 and g8a–g8c). *Corruption experience* denotes whether respondents had ever personally experienced cadre corruption (item e11). *Pollution damage* indicates whether respondents had ever suffered from any pollution incident (items g9 and g9a–g9c). These three variables are all binary (1 = yes and 0 = no). Based on Section II, the above eight key explanatory variables are expected to have a positive relationship with respondents' protest histories and their tendencies to protest in the future.

Besides, I also consider whether respondents belonged to social groups (items e6d–e6j) and whether they communicated with other people through the Internet for public issues (items d27s1–d27s3 and e3as4). In theory, social networks and organizations can serve as either social capital or mobilizing structures. However, when they serve as mobilizing structures, their effects must be examined in the context of a collective action (which I will do in the next section), but the models in Table 1 are not estimated in such a context. On the other hand, when social networks and organizations serve as social capital, they are expected to make people more likely to engage in collective actions in general. This is what I test in the models.[49]

Social group membership is measured by whether respondents were members of trade unions, business associations, professional associations, religious organizations, cultural groups, community residence groups or any other social groups. I code it as a binary variable (1 = yes and 0 = no). Due to China's party-state system, this variable is hardly likely to significantly affect respondents' protest tendencies. *Communication through the Internet* shows whether respondents communicated with other people on public issues via blogs, chat rooms, bulletin board services (BBS) or emails. This is also coded as a binary variable (1 = yes and 0 = no). Given the context of China, I expect that this variable has a positive effect on respondents' tendencies to protest.

49. See for example, Robert Putnam, Robert Leonardi and Raffaella Y. Nanetti, *Making Democracy Work: Civic Traditions in Modern Italy* (Princeton, NJ: Princeton University Press, 1993); Amber L. Seligson, 'Civic association and democratic participation in Central America: a test of the Putnam thesis', *Comparative Political Studies* 32(3), (1999), pp. 342–362.

I consider four critical control variables. *Political efficacy* measures whether respondents agreed with three statements: (1) 'people like me don't have any say about what the government does' (item e8a); (2) 'I don't think the government cares much what people like me think' (item e8b); and (3) 'sometimes politics and government seem so complicated that a person like me can't really understand what's going on' (item e8g). I combine the responses into a 13-point scale (0 = extremely low efficacy and 12 = extremely high efficacy). *The CCP membership* reveals whether respondents were members of the CCP, which is a binary variable (1 = yes and 0 = no). *Safety experience* indicates whether respondents had ever suffered from robbery or theft, which is coded as binary as well (1 = yes and 0 = no). *Health care* shows the extent to which respondents saw health care as a serious problem in China (item g6a) with an 11-point scale (0 = not a problem at all and 10 = an extremely serious problem).

Last, I control for demographical variables. They are age, gender (1 = male and 0 = female), race (1 = non-Han and 0 = Han), education (0 = no education, 1 = elementary, 2 = junior high, 3 = senior high, 4 = college and 5 = postgrad), marital status (1 = non-married and 0 = married) and residency (1 = urban resident and 0 = rural resident). The descriptive statistics and the correlation matrix of all variables in the models are respectively reported in Tables A1 and A2 in the Appendix.

The models are run by the logistic regression method with weighted data. As displayed in Table 2, none of the key explanatory variables significantly drives respondents' protest histories in Model 1 (even the control variables almost all fail to produce a significant effect). A technical explanation is that only a few respondents had ever joined a protest before the survey's interview, so the poor variance in the dependent variable does not allow for many significant relationships in the model.

Table 2. Individual motivation and protest in China

	Model 1		Model 2	
	Protest in the past		Protest in the future	
	b/se	*p*	*b/se*	*p*
Key explanatory variables				
The sense of democracy	−0.0438 (0.044)	0.325	−0.0121 (0.029)	0.681
Main news source	0.1093 (0.260)	0.674	0.0362 (0.173)	0.834
Macro economic problem evaluation	0.0138 (0.065)	0.830	0.0018 (0.030)	0.952
The sense of inequality	−0.0289 (0.044)	0.513	−0.0257 (0.034)	0.452
Personal hardship evaluation				
Life (as a whole)	−0.0924 (0.083)	0.265	−0.0549 (0.047)	0.240

(continued)

Table 2. (***Continued***)

	Model 1		Model 2	
	Protest in the past		Protest in the future	
	b/se	*p*	*b/se*	*p*
Financial situation	0.1451 (0.124)	0.241	0.0081 (0.046)	0.859
Job	0.0680 (0.060)	0.260	*0.0658* (0.035)	0.059
Land expropriation	−0.4103 (0.523)	0.433	0.2443 (0.233)	0.294
Corruption experience	0.2064 (0.340)	0.544	*0.3743* (0.191)	0.051
Pollution damage	0.5087 (0.346)	0.142	0.3050 (0.259)	0.238
Social capital variables				
Social group membership	0.1819 (0.395)	0.645	−0.2426 (0.241)	0.314
Communication through the Internet	0.7687 (0.609)	0.207	0.4223 (0.324)	0.193
Control variables				
Political efficacy	*−0.1045* (0.048)	0.028	*−0.0819* (0.032)	0.010
The CCP membership	−0.0602 (0.440)	0.891	0.1154 (0.197)	0.558
Safety experience	−0.5265 (0.416)	0.205	0.0244 (0.200)	0.903
Health care	−0.0177 (0.089)	0.843	0.0230 (0.038)	0.544
Age	0.0030 (0.009)	0.738	*−0.0186* (0.006)	0.003
Male (compared to female)	0.3750 (0.416)	0.367	0.2480 (0.152)	0.102
Non-Han (compared to Han)	0.0270 (0.433)	0.950	−0.1658 (0.242)	0.493
Education	0.4117 (0.327)	0.207	−0.0932 (0.158)	0.556
Non-married (compared to married)	−0.2796 (0.463)	0.546	0.0224 (0.205)	0.913
Urban resident (compared to rural resident)	0.2383 (0.312)	0.445	0.0930 (0.205)	0.651
Predicted protest history			−6.2633 (5.844)	0.284
Constant	*−3.9034* (0.938)	0.000	−0.6446 (0.653)	0.324
N	3132		3091	
Pseudo R^2	0.0523		0.0340	
Prob > chi^2	0.0000		0.0000	

Notes: 1. The models are estimated by the logistic regression method with weighted data. 2. The significance level is 0.1 (two-tailed test). 3. Robust standard errors are shown in the parentheses.
Source: The 2008 China Survey.

The survey also may not have appropriate items to measure the effects of some of the variables. For example, the survey asked respondents whether they had suffered from land expropriation and corruption in the last year before the interview. This might conflict with the measurement of the dependent variable, because item e5g allowed respondents to answer if they had ever joined a protest in the further past.

However, a theoretical explanation mainly attributes this finding to the CCP's tendency to satisfy protesters' particular demands during the past decade. For those respondents having protest experience, the survey may not reflect their values for the sense of democracy, macro-economic problem evaluation, the sense of inequality and personal hardship evaluation at the time when they joined a protest, since the values perhaps had altered due to the protest's outcome when the respondents were interviewed.

Model 2 plays the core role in testing Expectation A, which indicates that two of the key explanatory variables significantly fuel respondents' future protest tendencies: the level to which respondents were satisfied with their current jobs and whether they experienced cadre corruption. As for social capital, social group membership does not have a significantly positive impact, which matches my expectation, whereas Internet communication also has no such effect, which violates what I expect. As for the most critical control variables, CCP membership, safety experience and health care fail to exert a significant effect, but political efficacy has a significantly negative effect, contradicting the mainstream position that people with higher efficacy are more likely to participate. This finding implies that, in China, high political efficacy reflects that people believe they do not need to push the government to serve them, since they already obtain what they want from the government.

Nevertheless, overall, there are still only a few variables with significant effects in Model 2. My position is to understand most variables' lack of significant effect via a technical explanation. It must be stressed that this article never theoretically rejects the impact of those key explanatory variables other than working conditions and corruption. Those variables indeed have been found to motive Chinese people in many case studies. The problem is that the impact of those variables is very likely to be diluted in a national sample. This is because the proportion of motivated people is relatively small in China's population, making the variance in the dependent variable low. This low variance also makes it hard for the independent variables in Model 2 to generate significant effects. Of course, the low variance may result from the fact that respondents did not honestly report their protest tendencies due to sensitivity. From another view, however, given the difficulty of finding significant relationships, we actually can be confident of the impact of working conditions and corruption.

VI. The test on the other expectations

We cannot explain the outbreak of the 2010 labor protest without understanding why the CCP's tendency to repress declines. As a state with strong infrastructural power and bureaucratic institutions, the Chinese government undoubtedly has a great capability to repress a protest. Thus, the political opportunity structure in China must be illustrated first.

How splits within the ruling elites influence the state's use of force have been analyzed in some cases of other countries.[50] For the CCP, factionalism is its long-standing feature. The CCP leadership is structured into two informal coalitions today: populist and elitist.[51] Most members of the populist coalition are from the Communist Youth League of China and the populace, while most members of the elitist coalition are from the CCP founders' families, the former president Jiang's followers, and high-ranking officials' families. To balance the background advantages of the elitist coalition, the populist coalition resorts to ordinary Chinese people's support. While the elitist coalition defends 'the-growth-at-any-cost strategy of development', the populist coalition wants to solve some serious problems caused by the economic reform.[52]

Since former president Hu Jingtao and former premier Wen Jiabao (both assumed office in 2003) are from the populist coalition, it is not surprising to see the CCP's downward tendency to repress protests over the past decade. Hu began to promote the idea of a 'harmonious society' for the CCP's legitimacy in 2003. This policy changed the party's attitude toward protests. A more neutral official term used to describe protests, 'mass incidents', replaced the traditional derogatory official terms, 'mobbing crowds' or 'illegal associations'.[53] Another instance is that, in 2008, the minister of public security asked the police to avoid using force to handle mass incidents.[54] Also, the party's Disciplinary Investigation Committee warned local officials against indiscriminately using force by threatening to dismiss them from office and the party.[55]

However, the elite and the populist coalitions still share the same goals. The most critical one is to ensure the CCP's rule in China.[56] Therefore, no matter which coalition controls the top positions in the party, any protest pursuing a political change will be repressed. The good news is that unless a protest fundamentally threatens the CCP's political survival, the party will tend not to use force. Repressing people who demand a minimum livelihood without making political claims would place the CCP in a 'morally and politically indefensible position', which is likely to arouse even greater resentment.[57]

As a result, the initiators of the 2010 labor protest had to make the protest meaningful for Chinese people, but they also had to avoid making the protest too provocative to the CCP when they appealed to them to alter the labor–capital relationship endorsed by the party. The initiators met these conditions. The key initiator, Guocheng Tan, worked at Honda's Foshan factory until the protest occurred. Before he left his hometown in

50. See for example, J. C. Sharman, 'Culture, strategy, and state-centered explanations of revolution, 1789 and 1989', *Social Science History* 27(1), (2003), pp. 1–24.

51. Li, 'China's communist party-state', pp. 183–184.

52. *Ibid.*, p. 184.

53. Su and He, 'Street as courtroom', p. 162.

54. Guoan Yin, 'Listen to the "three careful usages" from the minister of public security', *Xinhuanet*, (5 November 2008), available at: http://news.xinhuanet.com/comments/2008-11/05/content_10305020.htm (accessed April 2012) [in simplified Chinese].

55. Yajie Li and Qinghong Yu, 'An abuse of police force to handle mass incidents can be subject to double dismissals, applicable to party and government chief leaders', *Xinhuanet*, (25 July 2008), available at: http://news.xinhuanet.co m/legal/2008-07/25/content_8765331.htm (accessed April 2012) [in simplified Chinese].

56. Li, 'China's communist party-state', p. 188.

57. Chen, 'Subsistence crises, managerial corruption and labor protests in China', p. 61.

Hunan province, he believed that working for a global company would provide him with a middle-class life.[58] However, the truth was that he worked for at least nine hours per day with a low salary. When Honda raised his monthly salary from US$175 to US $182 in January 2010, which was still not enough for him to get married, he decided to overturn this unfair labor–capital relationship.[59]

Tan was one of China's migrant workers who have been moving from interior areas to coastal cities for jobs. In 2010, the total number of migrant workers in China was about 230 million.[60] Tan's story was a common experience for most migrant workers.[61] Hence, when Tan and other initiators used this experience to call for a protest against working conditions, the response was strong. Section V has revealed that Chinese people's concerns about job situations did motivate them to protest before the labor protest was initiated. The appeal by Tan and the other initiators basically matched these concerns, so the response came not only from migrant workers but also from those who worked locally. The protest's participants were actually from interior provinces as well as coastal areas.

The framing by Tan and the other initiators was simple but discreet. They stressed the injustice faced by workers in China (i.e. no fair compensation for their hard work), attributed the responsibility for it to the employers, and then demanded higher wages, better conditions and more secure jobs.[62] They neither connected the injustice with the CCP nor made political demands refusing the CCP's rule, although their ultimate target was the CCP's authority over the labor–capital relationship.[63] The low political ambition of the framing by Tan and the other initiators allowed the protest to benefit from Hu's policy of the 'harmonious society'. Su and He's field study depicts the pattern of the CCP's response to the protest, which they named 'street as courtroom', that is, local courts and related government agencies engaged protesters on the street and tended to provide a favorable resolution; in the process, the court staff behaved like 'firefighters' rather than judges.[64]

The CCP modestly responded to the collective action event at Honda's Foshan factory.[65] This non-violent response signaled that subsequent collective actions

58. David Barboza, 'In China, unlikely labor leader just wanted a middle-class life', *The New York Times*, (13 June 2010), available at: http://www.nytimes.com/2010/06/14/business/global/14honda.html?_r=2&scp = 13&sq = june%2014%202010&st = cse (accessed April 2012).

59. *Ibid.*

60. Zheng Liu, 'National bureau of statistics: the number of migrant workers will reach 2.3 million with a 1417 yuan average monthly wage', *The People's Daily*, (24 March 2010), available at: http://finance.people.com.cn/GB/11208775.html (accessed April 2012) [in simplified Chinese].

61. Daniel Fu Keung Wong, Chang Ying Li and He Xue Song, 'Rural migrant workers in urban China: living a marginalised life', *International Journal of Social Welfare* 16(1), (2006), pp. 32–40.

62. John Chan, 'Honda lock strike in China continues as industrial unrest spreads', *World Socialist Web Site*, (12 June 2010), available at: http://www.wsws.org/articles/2010/jun2010/hond-j12.shtml (accessed April 2012).

63. See for example, Barboza, 'In China, unlikely labor leader just wanted a middle-class life'. In an interview with the *Wall Street Journal*, nonetheless, Tan indirectly confessed that his ultimate goal behind the injustice framing was to make the CCP government revoke its endorsement of the unfair labor–capital relationship. See Norihiko Shirouzu, 'Honda offers strikers in China 24% pay boost', *The Wall Street Journal*, (1 June 2010), available at: http://online.wsj.com/article/SB10001424052748703406604575278501916351546.html?mod=rss_whats_news_us#articleTabs%3Darticle (accessed April 2012).

64. Su and He, 'Street as courtroom', pp. 169–170.

65. Katherine Ryder, 'Why is the Chinese government allowing workers to strike?', *CNNMoney*, (10 June 2010), available at: http://money.cnn.com/2010/06/10/news/international/china_labor_strikes.fortune/index.htm (accessed April 2012).

would be allowed to break out. In particular, when the collective action event at Honda's Foshan factory was settled with a 24–32% monthly wage increase, which was mediated by the local government, it became a symbol for the subsequent collective actions.[66] Protesters at other factories also wanted the same increase.[67]

However, even though Tan and the other initiators made the protest meaningful for Chinese people and carefully avoided provoking the CCP, this is still not enough to explain why the protest successfully emerged and became widely spread. We must examine the protest's mobilizing structure. As mentioned above, in China a collective action can only rely on social networks instead of organizations as mobilizing structures, and the Internet is likely to afford Chinese people a new source of social networks. This was indeed the case in the 2010 labor protest, given that all labor unions in China were controlled by the state. The protest's mobilizing structure can be divided into three levels as shown by Figure 1.

In general, there was a group of workers serving as 'leaders' to mobilize and coordinate other workers at each factory. Level 1 in the mobilizing structure refers to how the members of these core groups could collectively act, based on face-to-face interactions and native-place solidarity. A critical case is the collective action event at Honda's Foshan factory. The core group consisted of Tan and other protest initiators in that case. In the beginning, Tan tried to share his protest idea with five or six senior workers on his assembly line; although the workers said that they lacked bravery, they agreed to support Tan when he promised to lead them.[68] More importantly, another key initiator, named Lang Xiao, was also from Hunan province. In fact, native-place solidarity was an important pillar of the protest's mobilizing structure. On 17 May 2010, when Tan hit his production line's emergency stop button, Xiao also did so on another line.[69]

When Tan and Xiao stopped their production lines, they knew those workers outside the core group would follow the group in protest. Level 2 in the mobilizing structure addresses how a core group could mobilize other workers at a factory, given that other workers might not have face-to-face interactions with the group's members and might come from distinct provinces. The answer is the Internet. The Internet allowed a core group to mobilize other workers under their employer's surveillance. For example, Tan and the other protest initiators used Internet chat rooms and other means to communicate with more than 600 workers at Honda's Foshan factory.[70]

Finally, the Internet provided the protest with a channel with which to spread. This is Level 3 in the mobilizing structure. Core groups at different factories utilized the Internet to share experience, framing and strategies. Core groups then mobilized other workers at their factories. Sometimes, core groups even coordinated in order to

66. David Barboza and Hiroko Tabuchi, 'Power grows for striking Chinese workers', *The New York Times*, (8 June 2010), available at: http://www.nytimes.com/2010/06/09/business/global/09labor.html?pagewanted=all (accessed April 2012).

67. See for example, Chan, 'Honda lock strike in China continues as industrial unrest spreads'.

68. Barboza, 'In China, unlikely labor leader just wanted a middle-class life'.

69. *Ibid.*

70. David Barboza and Keith Bradsher, 'In China, labor movement enabled by technology', *The New York Times*, (16 June 2010), available at: http://www.nytimes.com/2010/06/17/business/global/17strike.html?src=busln (accessed April 2012).

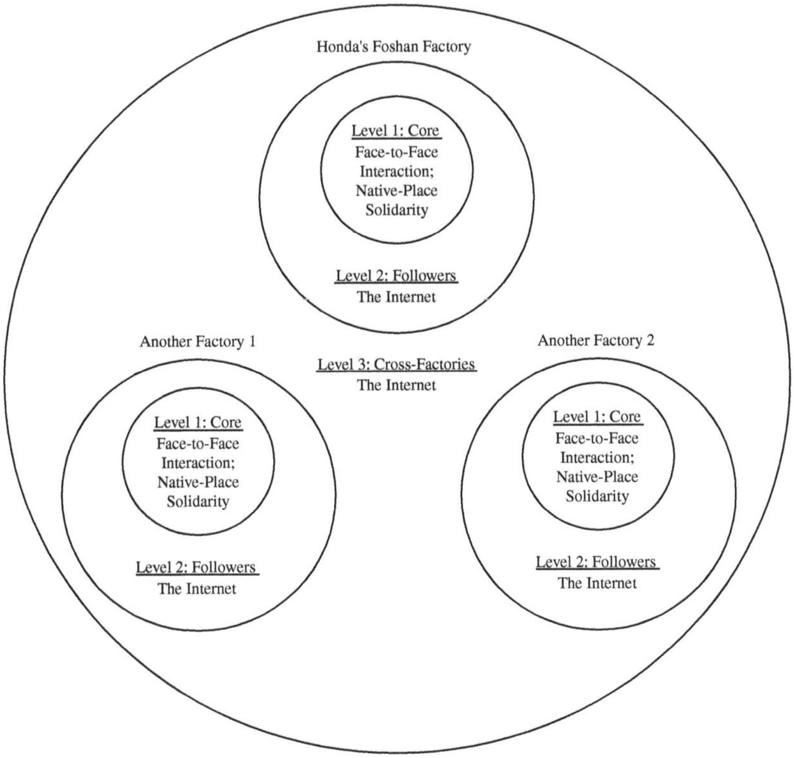

Figure 1. The mobilizing structure of the 2010 labor protest.

act. The core group at Honda's Foshan factory played the most critical role in this process. What the group shared and discussed via Internet chat rooms provided not only a guide for workers at other Honda factories to use when thinking about their actions, but also some ideas for disgruntled workers in other areas.[71] For instance, just a few hours after collective action broke out at another Honda factory in Zhongshan participants started posting records of their actions online, following Tan and the other protest initiators' strategy of using the Internet.[72]

Within minutes of Tan and Xiao stopping the production lines on 17 May 2010, workers at Honda's Foshan factory had begun to march. This was followed by a number of collective action events at other factories across at least ten provincial areas. This protest forced employers to pay more to workers and improve working conditions. It also stimulated the CCP to review the labor–capital relationship. As a result, more than half of China's provincial governments (17 out of 31) increased the minimum wage before the end of 2010, a double-digit raise on average.[73] The CCP,

71. *Ibid.*
72. *Ibid.*
73. EIU (The Economist Intelligence Unit), 'China business: rising industrial unrest', *The Economist Intelligence Unit*, (16 June 2010), available at: http://www.eiu.com/index.asp?layout=VWArticleVW3&article_id=157207800&country_id=1800000180&channel_id = 180004018&category_id = 500004050&refm=vwCat&page_title=Article &rf = 0 (accessed April 2012).

nevertheless, sought to satisfy protest participants at different factories separately. To date, it is still unclear whether the CCP's division strategy caused the protest to eventually subside. Since this article cares only about the emergence of a widespread protest, I do not discuss this question about protest duration.

In sum, Sections V and VI support this article's general expectations about the conditions under which a widespread protest is likely to take place in China. A widespread protest in China must be an outcome of a political process composed of several elements that convert individual motivation into actual collective actions. The labor protest with a federal internal connection met all of the expected conditions and successfully emerged.

VII. Conclusions and future research

Grounded in McAdam's political process model, I expect four conditions for widespread protests in China: (1) there must be some factors propelling Chinese people across different areas to popularly join a protest; (2) a protest should not fundamentally threaten the CCP's survival, so that the CCP may moderately respond to the protest's forerunners, affecting whether the subsequent collective actions will occur in different areas; (3) there should be some social networks helping protesters translate their interpersonal trust and shared perceptions into collective actions, and the Internet and traditional sources of social networks are all essential; and (4) a protest's initiators must frame the protest congruent with not only the factors motivating Chinese people but also China's political opportunity structure.

I argue that these conditions are all necessary for a widespread protest in China, whether unitary or federal. The case study of the outbreak of the 2010 labor protest, in which a survey analysis (Section V) tests the first condition indicated above and an intensive analysis (Section VI) tests the other three conditions, supports this argument. Of course, widespread protest is still rare in China, so at this point I do not have many available cases to further test the argument. This is a research limitation.

This article helps us understand and predict China's political and social development. We can use the above conditions to estimate China's prospects for democratization; this is an implication of this article. A long-standing question is whether Chinese people across different areas can jointly challenge the CCP's rule, or, at least, whether they can accept the CCP's legitimacy but struggle for more political rights. Unfortunately, this article implies that we have no reason to expect the outbreak of such widespread protests in the near future.

So far, it is still hard for a pro-democratic protest to achieve comprehensive support from the Chinese people across different areas, since democratic values cannot motivate the Chinese people to engage in a protest. It is thus most unlikely for us to see a direct clash between Chinese people and the CCP in the near future, in which a large number of Chinese people across different areas take to the streets to struggle for greater political rights, and the CCP represses them to maintain its political survival. A widespread protest is still likely to take place in China again, but it would be a protest without political demands directly threatening the CCP's rule, like the 2010 labor protest.

Finally, I have noted some research limitations above, but there are further limitations that must be addressed. At this point, we do not have enough data to capture any further details of the causal mechanisms behind the above conditions for widespread protests in China. This shortage needs to be supplemented by future research. If we care about the prospects for democratization in China, for example, then future research should answer at least two questions: why can't democratic values motivate Chinese people to protest; and does the CCP's potential repression make even those pro-democratic Chinese people unwilling to act to gain greater political rights? To answer these questions, future research must use qualitative approaches to gather more in-depth data.

Appendix

Table A1. The descriptive statistics of the variables

Variable	Observations	Mean	Standard deviation	Min	Max
Protest in the future	3,398	0.112	0.316	0	1
Protest in the past	3,446	0.027	0.161	0	1
The sense of democracy	3,989	5.197	2.818	0	16
Main news source	3,989	0.855	0.585	0	3
Macro economic problem evaluation	3,989	4.901	2.387	0	10
The sense of inequality	3,989	10.903	3.465	0	20
Personal hardship evaluation (life)	3,989	4.088	2.538	0	10
Personal hardship evaluation (financial situation)	3,989	4.980	2.633	0	10
Personal hardship evaluation (job)	3,989	4.762	2.341	0	10
Land expropriation	3,989	0.072	0.258	0	1
Corruption experience	3,619	0.135	0.342	0	1
Pollution damage	3,989	0.158	0.365	0	1
Social group membership	3,989	0.079	0.269	0	1
Communication through the Internet	3,989	0.053	0.223	0	1
Political efficacy	3,989	5.470	2.882	0	12
The CCP membership	3,989	0.148	0.355	0	1
Safety experience	3,989	0.142	0.349	0	1
Health care	3,989	5.591	2.853	0	10
Age	3,989	45.986	15.633	18	92
Gender	3,989	0.482	0.500	0	1
Race	3,900	0.126	0.332	0	1
Education	3,989	0.800	0.453	0	4
Marital status	3,989	0.183	0.386	0	1
Residency	3,969	0.246	0.431	0	1

Table A2. The correlation matrix of the variables

	Protest (future)	Protest (past)	Democracy	Media	Economy evaluation	Inequality	Life	Financial situation	Job	Land expropriation	Corruption	Pollution	Group membership	Internet communication	Efficacy	CCP membership	Safety experience	Health care	Age	Gender	Race	Education	Marital status	Residency
Protest (future)	1																							
Protest (past)	−0.0403	1																						
Democracy	0.0356	−0.0011	1																					
Media	0.078	0.0364	0.0525	1																				
Economy evaluation	0.0137	0.0052	0.0441	0.0686	1																			
Inequality	−0.0261	0.0138	0.0016	−0.181	0.0481	1																		
Life	−0.0039	0.0406	0.1052	−0.0805	0.1404	0.4692	1																	
Financial situation	−0.0133	0.0398	0.0525	−0.0908	0.1247	0.5385	0.6596	1																
Job	0.011	0.0444	0.0571	−0.078	0.1293	0.4443	0.5327	0.5284	1															
Land expropriation	0.0268	0.0025	−0.0528	0.0191	0.0173	0.0676	0.0527	0.0559	0.0495	1														
Corruption	0.0353	0.0058	0.0033	0.0567	0.0649	0.0599	0.0334	0.0362	0.0435	0.0732	1													
Pollution	0.03	0.0197	0.0012	0.1058	0.0444	−0.0141	−0.0308	0.0157	−0.0033	0.1304	0.0728	1												
Group membership	0.0076	0.0086	−0.0495	0.1145	0.0084	−0.0605	−0.0489	−0.0351	−0.0885	0.0272	0.0094	0.102	1											
Internet communication	0.0853	0.0519	0.0882	0.4618	0.0656	−0.0921	−0.0046	−0.0225	−0.016	−0.0114	0.0205	0.0607	0.0788	1										
Efficacy	−0.0944	−0.0506	−0.016	−0.172	−0.0245	0.1329	0.0464	0.0493	0.0363	0.0451	0.0244	−0.0305	−0.0818	−0.0931	1									
CCP membership	0.0354	0.0073	−0.0534	0.2336	0.034	−0.1522	−0.056	−0.0979	−0.0864	−0.0108	0.0453	0.039	0.2405	0.1632	−0.1162	1								
Safety experience	0.0291	−0.0051	−0.0074	0.0986	0.064	0.0115	−0.0014	0.0079	−0.0032	0.0756	0.116	0.1553	0.0484	0.0633	−0.0003	0.0642	1							
Health care	0.0226	−0.03	0.0292	0.0947	0.4433	0.0771	0.12	0.1304	0.0916	0.0523	0.1116	0.0881	0.0597	0.0528	0.0157	0.0572	0.0755	1						
Age	−0.0977	−0.0154	−0.1257	−0.2428	−0.1306	0.003	−0.0833	−0.0716	−0.0453	−0.0003	0.0028	−0.04	−0.0141	−0.2304	0.116	−0.0404	−0.0869	−0.0295	1					
Gender	0.0067	0.0194	0.0008	0.152	−0.0137	−0.0499	0.0078	−0.0251	−0.0155	−0.0129	0.0307	0.0184	0.0223	0.0254	−0.0527	0.1331	−0.0034	0.0322	0.0738	1				
Race	0.0058	−0.0119	0.0918	−0.0194	0.106	0.0572	0.0957	0.0713	0.0548	−0.0371	−0.0403	−0.0553	0.0105	−0.0254	−0.0347	−0.0327	−0.0013	0.0697	−0.0927	−0.0025	1			
Education	0.0309	0.0273	−0.0337	0.2339	0.0321	−0.1004	−0.0697	−0.0544	−0.0575	0.013	0.0411	0.0941	0.092	0.0907	−0.0888	0.142	0.0506	0.07	−0.2517	0.1011	−0.1185	1		
Marital status	0.0545	0.0019	0.0616	0.1	0.0197	0.0187	0.059	−0.0017	0.0486	−0.0135	−0.0482	−0.0284	−0.0306	0.1909	−0.0386	0.1133	−0.0028	−0.0068	−0.1172	0.0235	0.0434	−0.0751	1	
Residency	0.0257	0.0252	−0.0074	0.2881	0.0956	−0.0847	−0.0398	−0.0164	−0.0445	0.0039	0.0529	0.112	0.2307	0.2136	−0.044	0.2195	0.0873	0.1524	0.0213	0.0059	−0.0816	0.1781	0.053	1

Disorganized Popular Contention and Local Institutional Building in China: a case study in Guangdong

Feng Chen and Yi Kang

Hong Kong Baptist University, Hong Kong

ABSTRACT

Concurring with the approach stressing the role of contentious politics in (re)shaping state institutions, this study explores how *disorganized* popular contentions configure local institutional building in China. As Chinese citizens are not legally allowed to take organized collective action to express their grievances and demands, popular contentions, despite their common origins, similar claims and identical targets, break out here and there in large numbers without clear organizational shape. This compels the government to build institutions able to map scattered conflicts, detect potential problems and defuse them on a case-by-case basis in a timely fashion. Such a *dissipative* approach is distinguished, by its purpose, format and mechanism, from two common types of state responses to popular contentions—incorporation and repression—which are typically linked to democracies and authoritarian developing states where popular contentions are often organized in various ways.

The past two decades have witnessed a dramatic increase in social conflict in China. Demanding *hefa quanyi* [legitimate rights and interests] has motivated numerous popular actions—petitions, protests, strikes, demonstrations, riots, etc.—by people from different walks of life seeking redress of various grievances. They are driven in part by the sweeping market reforms that have increasingly polarized Chinese society, but also by perceived flaws in governance. Deep resentment has accumulated over the years in the face of injustices and abuse of power perpetrated by government officials at various levels. To keep social conflict at bay and shore up stability, the government has identified *weiwen* [maintaining stability] as a top priority.

The government's efforts toward *weiwen* have relied heavily on the coercive apparatus. However, the sheer use of force is not the routine practice when dealing with the contentious incidents that occur in China on a daily basis. Over the past few years, the Chinese Communist Party (CCP) has been vocal in calling for the strengthening of 'social management' for building a 'harmonious society'. At the front line, local authorities have responded to this call by institutional reorganization and innovation for conflict resolution and prevention, which has constituted a 'soft' part of the *weiwen* system. Despite individual variations, the new institutional arrangements across the country share the common features of realigning conflict management agencies, pooling diverse resources and combining different modes of mediation in dispute resolution.

Why have local authorities responded to rising popular unrest with those distinct institutional practices? This article seeks to answer this question by examining the mutually reconfiguring effect of state institutions and contentious politics, with a focus on the effect of the latter in shaping the former. Most previous research has treated popular contention as an outcome to be explained while taking state institutions as the key independent variable. Many scholars have written on how political institutions define opportunities for, as well as constraints on, social actors; inform the way they make claims; and shape final outcomes. Less attention is paid to the causal effect working the other way round, i.e. the features of social contention shaping the state apparatus. The most prominent effort in this regard has been made by Charles Tilly, whose 'war-makes-state' thesis has become the touchstone of this approach.[1] Studies within this analytical tradition view popular contention as major stimuli to institutional building. They demonstrate that state actions in response to such challenges 'often lead to the establishment of new institutional forms, powers, and precedents'.[2] Popular contention, as Slater argues, is not only a product of political institutions, but also a producer of them. Internal conflicts, in his words, can also 'make the state'.[3] Students of social movements see their impact on state institutions in terms of 'consequences', which often take on states' concessions to, or acceptance of, challengers' claims. At the structural level, they include 'the extension of democratic rights and practices and the formation of new political parties'.[4] At a more intermediate level, consequences are embodied in 'political public goods' or 'consistent benefits' provided for a movement's constituency and enforced collective identity, and aid challengers in making demands.[5]

With the surge in social conflict in China, research on contentious politics has become a booming enterprise, with an impressive academic output relating to the state's role in motivating and shaping social protests.[6] Some studies have examined the impact of contentious politics at the micro level, reflected in improved policy implementation and concessions by the authorities, as well as increased public awareness of particular issues and a boosting of activism.[7] Others have explored the state's tactical responses to popular contentions and their micro-foundations.[8] However, like the research on contentious politics elsewhere, insufficient efforts have been made so far to investigate the configuring effect of popular contention on China's institutional building.

This study will demonstrate that while the state shapes popular contention as it defines its political and institutional parameters, this in turn (re)configures the institutions that serve to enhance states' capacity to manage social conflict. Here, the nature and form of contention is important. The authors contend that the most striking feature of Chinese popular contention is that it is disorganized and dispersive. Various conflicts, despite their common origins, similar claims and identical targets, break out here and there in large numbers without clear and sustainable organizational shape. Such a pattern of contention is, of course, preordained by the political system itself. The state's *de facto* ban on the exercise of the rights of assembly and association[9] as well as the absence of a genuine system of representation creates formidable barriers to organized claim making in Chinese society. With the surge and intensification of such conflict in recent years, however, the state is compelled to adjust its own institutional arrangements for better social control. The primary goal is to nip popular contention in the bud at the grassroots and prevent actions from spreading, coalescing or flowing toward the top. The

[1]Charles Tilly, 'Reflections on the history of European state-making', in Charles Tilly, ed., *The Formation of National States in Western Europe* (Princeton, NJ: Princeton University Press, 1975).

[2]Stephen Skowronek, *Building a New American State: The Expansion of National Administrative Capacities 1877–1920* (Cambridge: Cambridge University Press, 1982), p. 10.

[3]Dan Slater, *Ordering Power: Contentious Politics and Authoritarian Leviathans in Southeast Asia* (Cambridge: Cambridge University Press, 2010).

[4]Edwin Amenta, Neal Caren, Elizabeth Chiarello and Yang Su, 'The political consequences of social movements', *The Annual Review of Sociology* 36(14), (2010), pp. 1–21.

[5]*Ibid.*

[6]See, for example, Kevin O'Brien, ed., *Popular Protest in China* (Cambridge, MA: Harvard University Press, 2008).

[7]Kevin O'Brien and Lianjiang Li, 'Popular contention and its impact in rural China', *Comparative Political Studies* 38, (2005), pp. 235–259.

[8]Ching Kwan Lee and Yonghong Zhang, 'The power of instability: unraveling the microfoundations of bargaining authoritarianism in China', *American Journal of Sociology* 6, (2013), pp. 1475–1508.

[9]Constitutionally, Chinese citizens have the freedom of assembly and association.

need to contain disorganized popular contention in China thus generates a *weiwen* regime that differs, in terms of purpose, format and mechanism, from the two common types of state responses to popular contention: incorporation and repression—they are typically linked to democracies and authoritarian developing states, respectively, where popular contention is often organized in various ways. China's emerging institutions, neither incorporative nor across-the-board repressive, aim to defuse, dissipate and contain popular contention from below on a case-by-case basis.

In the following sections, the authors firstly contrast the Chinese practices with two other types of state responses to popular contention, and then examine the distinctive impact of disorganized contention on institutional building. A case study of City AB, an administrative district in Guangdong Province, is conducted in order to elaborate the processes and features of the adjustment in conflict management institutions in local China. AB is chosen on the basis of both analytical purposes and practical concern. While local institutional building in response to disorganized contention is a widespread undertaking across the country, Guangdong has pioneered the promotion of institutional realignment to implement the dissipation of social conflict. As one of the most prosperous yet conflict-ridden cities in Guangdong, AB was selected by the provincial government as an experiment site for institutional innovation in conflict management. Its experience and practices thus provide a window for us to probe the interaction between popular contention and institutional (re)building. Data were collected through site-intensive research, i.e. interviews and participant observation. Extensive background information was also derived from government documents, officials' speeches and media reports.

Popular contention and institutional building

As a transgressive form of interest articulation by rank-and-file citizens, popular contention occurs in various social contexts, particularly where there is a lack of institutional channels for representation and participation. History shows that organized contention, which challenges state power and disrupts institutional patterns of social relations, engenders two types of state response: incorporation and repression. The former refers to the state's attempt to channel popular contention into the political system through the institutionalization of political representation and participation, while the latter involves negative sanction of people's civil and political liberties and the exercise of state terror. In Western capitalist states, the existence of civil rights and minimalist democratic institutions provides the preliminary social conditions for organized popular contention.[10] Having wrestled with protracted popular struggles, often using repressive means, states began incorporating them through structural and institutionalized accommodations, a process that transformed organized social contention from *de facto* into *de jure* power.[11] The major institutions that underpin modern democracies all resulted from protracted popular struggles. As Tilly points out, for example, 'citizenship rights came into being because relatively organized members of the general population bargained with the state authorities for several centuries'.[12] Specifically, three basic institutional mechanisms have been constructed to channel popular contention into the existing political framework. Firstly, electorally representative arrangements allow political parties to aggregate and represent diverse societal interests, thus organizing them into a large coalition for the purposes of winning elections.[13] Secondly, interest group politics, using either pluralist or social corporatist models, institutionalizes the representation of group interests in the process of policy making.[14] Thirdly, states allow civil society and social movements to be a direct form of representation

---

[10]T. H. Marshall, *Citizenship and Social Class* (London: Pluto Classic, 1992), p. 199.

[11]Daron Acemoglu and James Robinson, *Economic Origins of Dictatorship and Democracy* (Cambridge: Cambridge University Press, 2006).

[12]Charles Tilly., 'Where do rights come from', in Theda Skocpol, ed., *Democracy, Revolution, and History* (Ithaca, NY: Cornell University Press, 1998), p. 57.

[13]See, for example Frances Fox Piven, *Challenging Authority: How Ordinary People Change America* (Lanham, MD: Rowman & Littlefield Publishers, 2006).

[14]See, for example, Phillips Schmitter, *Modes of Interest Intermediation and Models of Societal Change in Western Europe* (London and Beverly Hills, CA: Sage Press, 1973); Suzanne Berger, ed., *Organizing Interests in Western Europe: Pluralism, Corporatism, and the Transformation of Politics* (Cambridge: Cambridge University Press, 1983).

and an alternative way for representing and articulating the demands of the under-represented.[15] All these mechanisms have translated the myriad of bewildering social conflicts into legible formats and manageable dimensions, channeling them into institutionalized conflict resolution.

In many authoritarian developing nations, on the other hand, forms of organized resistance such as communal and guerrilla actions or social and labor movements have become widespread, because states have lacked the capacity to penetrate and exercise total control over society. Popular resistance in such countries is often met with heightened use of repressive state apparatus. Protesters and activists have been imprisoned, tortured or killed.[16] Some scholars argue that class conflicts in the Latin American authoritarian countries have had a causal effect on repressive regime institutions, and view the existence of anti-labor regimes as a function of their hostility toward working-class movements.[17] Bureaucratic authoritarianism is another institutional response to the increasing power of organized labor movements.[18] Some Latin American authoritarian states have attempted to co-opt or incorporate organized movements. For instance, they have established a system of officially sanctioned, non-competitive and compulsory trade unions, subsidizing them and imposing constraints on their demand making, leadership and internal governance, so that the labor movement could be depoliticized, controlled and penetrated by the state.[19]

However, the huge popular conflicts that have emerged since the market reforms in China have been largely disorganized. They differ from the social movements or rebellions seen in other contexts, in that they seek neither class-based solidarity nor cross-cutting collaborations, even if they have shared interests, pursue similar goals, or have common targets for their grievances. Nor do they typically employ violent means, although a few localized riots have occurred. Contentious incidents in China are characterized by 'large numbers of individual behaviors with similar claims, patterns, and targets'.[20] They often take the form of individual petitioners, plaintiffs and complainers, or involve groups engaged in contentious gatherings, many of which are spontaneous and leaderless. Conflicts of similar content and nature have arisen in different settings, with their claims framed in diverse languages and expressed in various forms, and their ways of seeking resolution vary somewhat haphazardly across cases. However, disorganized contention does not mean that all such conflicts are unorganized. In fact, scattered group activism and organized protests can be found from place to place, but they are often poorly organized and less sustainable. They do not represent organized movements or organized interest articulation. Reflecting what Tilly calls 'embedded identity' configured in 'sites of wrongdoing'[21] protesters have made claims stemming from specific grievances linked to a particular factory, village or residential community, and demanded immediate redress. As Perry points out, they have rarely made broad claims on political and citizenship rights.[22]

While such disorganized contention may not necessarily constitute an imminent and credible threat to the existing political order, the government is afraid of such conflict spreading, escalating, linking up and flowing towards the top. It is obvious that institutionalized incorporation is not likely to be a solution where societal interests are highly scattered and atomized, and there are no representative bodies serving as aggregator and bridge. Violent repression, on the other hand, is apparently not a preferred option for the government either, even though some local authorities have occasionally

[15]Craig Jenkins, 'Social movements, political representation, and the state: an agenda and comparative framework', in Craig Jenkins and Bert Klandermans, eds, *The Politics of Social Protest: Comparative Perspectives on States and Social Movements* (Minneapolis, MN: University of Minnesota Press, 1995), pp. 14–38.

[16]Christian Davenport, ed., *Paths to State Repression* (Lanham, MD: Rowman & Littlefield Publishers, 1996).

[17]Paul Drake, *Labor Movements and Dictatorship* (Baltimore, MD: Johns Hopkins University Press, 1996).

[18]Guillermo O'Donnell, *Modernization and Bureaucratic-Authoritarianism: Studies in South American Politics* (Berkeley, CA: Institute of International Studies, University of California, 1973).

[19]Ruth Collier and David Collier, *Shaping the Political Arena: Critical Junctures, the Labor Movement, and Regime Dynamics in Latin America* (Princeton, NJ: Princeton University Press, 1991).

[20]Xueguang Zhou, 'Unorganized interests and collective action in Communist China', *American Sociological Review* 58, (1993), pp. 54–73.

[21]Charles Tilly, *Contention and Democracy in Europe, 1650–2000* (Cambridge: Cambridge University Press, 2004), p. 59.

[22]Elizabeth Perry, 'A new rights consciousness?', *Journal of Democracy* 20(1), (2009), pp. 17–20.

Table 1. Differences between organized and disorganized popular contentions.

Type	Organized contention	Disorganized contention
Form	Political and social movements, labor movement, guerrilla war, revolution	Petitions, protests, strikes, demonstrations, riots
Aim	Shared interests or grievances pointing to common targets, pursuing broad goals of rights and social changes	Making claims stemming from a specific grievance linked to a particular setting (factory, village, etc.) and demanding immediate redress. Broad political and rights demands are rarely made
Pattern	Seeking class-based solidarity or cross-cutting collaborations	Large numbers of conflicts with similar contents emerging scattered and expressed in diverse ways
Effect	Challenging state power and disrupting existing institutional patterns	Hardly constituting imminent and credible threat to the existing political order, but disturbing local governance
State response	• Incorporation: • Elections • Organized interests representation (interest groups, social movements, etc.) • Repression	• Dissipation: to reduce or exhaust the energy of contention by dispersion • Concerted institutional arrangements • Case-by-case problem solving through multiple and mandatory mediation • Community surveillance

forcibly dispelled riots. Such a response would be costly given that disorganized popular actions are so widespread and pervasive. The government also has to be aware of the political price of using force against its own citizens. Thus, instead of incorporation or outright coercion, the Chinese government has chosen an approach of *dissipation*: preventing, defusing and settling conflicts on a case-by-case basis, and dispelling their elements before they can fester and grow (see Table 1).[23] This requires corresponding institutions to be built.

Institutional trajectory of conflict management

The emerging institutions of conflict management in China reflect the changing interplay of the state and disorganized popular contention. Before the economic reforms commenced in 1978, the independently organized articulation of societal demands was rare. The Chinese state denied the legitimacy of any interest-based groups, and did not acknowledge the people's right to express demands in a collective way. This, however, did not mean that political leaders ruled without regard for societal interests. Coupled with negative sanctions such as repression and extensive organizational control were some unique institutional arrangements designed to accommodate such interests. For example, societal interests were represented through the setting up of functional government agencies to reflect the interests of certain sectors in society. The All-China Federation of Trade Unions (ACFTU) and the Women's Federation are *de facto* government bodies with workers and women as their constituencies. The Work Unit (*danwei*) system, furthermore, took care of most urban citizens' basic economic interests and social welfare.[24] Mass campaigns and the mass line were carried out to allow people to express their views in a way strictly delimited by the Party-state.[25]

Nevertheless, incorporating citizens into these webs of organizational control and socialist paternalism did not eradicate the collective expression of grievance. Rather, it produced a unique form of contention. As Kelliher notes, state socialism places a great number of people in very similar and prescribed circumstances in which they confront 'a nearly identical face of state power', hence creating the possibility of mass action by disorganized and atomized individuals.[26] Zhou also points out that the authoritarian institutional structure that prevents organized interests from forming facilitates collective

[23]The table is prepared by the authors.

[24]Andrew Walder, *Communist Neo-traditionalism: Work and Authority in Chinese Society* (Berkeley, CA: University of California Press, 1986).

[25]Kenneth Lieberthal, *Governing China: From Revolution to Reform* (New York: W. W. Norton & Company, 2003).

[26]Daniel Kelliher, *Peasant Power in China: The Era of Rural Reform, 1979–1989* (New Haven, CT: Yale University Press, 1992), pp. 20–21.

action based on unorganized interests.[27] However, mass protests occurred only at certain unusual moments when there was a sudden opening up of opportunities that allowed disorganized people to air their grievance collectively. The Hundred Flower Campaign in 1957, the Cultural Revolution in 1966 and the Tiananmen Movement in 1989, were all such instances. Pre-reform China otherwise saw little of the popular contention.

The market economy has transformed China's social and economic landscape, engendering means of articulating interests that are in many ways distinct from those of the pre-reform period. Above all, the explosion of grievances and claims is attributable to changes in economic relations. For example, market-based labor relations produce conflicts between labor and capital, leading to widespread labor protests. The state *per se* also constitutes a source of contention. Its retreat from socialist paternalism has affected the lives of millions of state workers, forcing many of them to take to the streets. The state's developmental strategy, prioritizing economic growth, has encouraged rampant labor exploitation, house demolitions, land grabs, environmental damage, etc., all of which has fueled people's resentment and motivated them to protest. Indeed, drastic socioeconomic change and the relaxation of political control over society all provide opportunities for popular contention.[28] At the same time, however, the Leninist regime is far from ready to permit organized actions, which are still perceived as a threat to political order. Consequently, it has failed to provide any meaningful institutional channels for citizens' representation and participation, despite the drastic rise of popular demands. As citizens are not allowed to organize and coordinate themselves, the expression of their grievances and demands, even when they are homogeneous and interlinked, becomes amorphous, disorderly and chaotic. Dispersive and disorganized popular contention in China is therefore a distinctive phenomenon resulting from a socioeconomic transformation without corresponding change of political institutions.

Before its latest drive to rebuild the conflict management institutions, the Chinese state already had in place a set of institutions for maintaining social stability. These were composed of people's mediation, judiciary procedures, the *xinfang* system and various means of administrative interference. Each, in theory, has a defined jurisdiction as well as distinct powers and resources for coping with social conflict. However, this conflict management system has come to appear insufficient for dealing with the mounting pressure of disorganized contention over recent decades. For example, as one of the primary institutions for handling petitions, the *xinfang* system lacks the real enforcement power to resolve disputes. But since people have had few alternative channels for redressing their grievances, they have kept flooding the *xinfang* offices in Beijing and across the country. Indeed, the *xinfang* system has come to symbolize bureaucratic incapacity and the inefficiency of the Chinese state in handling popular contention.

The government has also tried to channel various disputes into legal procedures, as part of its endeavor to establish the rule of law in China. However, the soaring number of legal disputes has overloaded many local courts. Overwhelming volumes of cases, cumbersome trial processes and the poor execution of court decisions have often led to petitions. Local officials have become frustrated and eager to arrive at quick solutions to disputes. For them, judicial processes have reduced their flexibility and discretionary power in problem solving. Moreover, the last decade has seen the rapid growth of interest-based disputes that can hardly be resolved through the judicial process.[29] For the government, the judicial system is no longer adequate for dealing with rising levels of disputes.

Obviously, disorganized contention confronts the Chinese state with challenges that are quite different from those posed by organized conflict. Since numerous messy, isolated and dispersive disputes cannot be automatically converged and classified through group representation and organized social action, the state cannot incorporate or routinely repress them. It therefore has to create institutions that enable bureaucrats to identify, map and categorize contentious incidents with concerted efforts and control them in a scattered, case-by-case manner. Such an approach engenders an institutional

---

[27]Zhou, 'Unorganized interests and collective action in Communist China'.
[28]Yongshun Cai, 'Managed participation in China', *Political Science Quarterly* 119(3), (2004), pp. 425–451.
[29]Feng Chen and Mengxiao Tang, 'Labor conflicts in China: types and their implications', *Asian Survey* 5(3), (2013), pp. 559–583.

alignment that provides a platform for facilitating cross-departmental collaboration. The new institutional arrangement has developed three key mechanisms, aimed to reduce or exhaust the energy of contention and defuse it at the grassroots level.

Firstly, there is concerted conflict management. Given that popular contention involves issues that cover multiple policy areas or which cannot be solved by a single agency, concerted settlement, based on intra-institutional collaborations, allows them to work together to seek solutions and expedite problem solving. To a large extent, this can overcome previous institutional fragmentation in the handling of social conflict.

Secondly is mapping and surveillance, accomplished through weaving an extensive web of street-level conflict control agencies. They constitute the 'trenches' where the street bureaucrats fight for executing state directives in the face of social resistance.[30] As grievances are prevalent, popping up randomly anytime and everywhere, these agencies can quickly reach out to the grassroots as well as being accessible to disputants. They function like firefighters, ready to stamp out any conflicts in townships, communities, villages and factories. They are also the antennae of government, responsible for gathering information and providing first-hand data for higher authorities to map dispersive conflicts and assess the state of local public order.

Thirdly is the use of mandatory and multiple mediation methods. As disorganized contention takes the form of numerous isolated incidents, the government has had to adopt a case-by-case approach to settlement. Mediation best fits this approach, because it is less constrained by formal rules, offering considerable flexibility and discretion which enables officials to maneuver, manipulate and play around with 'divide and rule' in dispute resolution. To maximize the effect of mediation, the government promotes what is called 'grand mediation' that links different modes (people's, administrative and judicial) to enhance multiple and coerced mediation.

Emerging institutions: structures, mechanisms and actors

The creation of local institutions for conflict management originates in the practice of comprehensive governance that can be traced back to early 1981 in some major cities such as Beijing, Tianjin, Shanghai, Guangzhou and Wuhan. The initial purpose was to prevent crime and maintain public security. The Standing Committee of the National People's Congress passed the Decision on Strengthening the Comprehensive Governance of Public Security in 1991, which led to the widespread establishment of Comprehensive Governance Offices at different administrative levels. These offices were responsible for coordinating relevant governmental departments, such as *xinfang*, Public Security and so on, and involving villages/streets, workplaces and ordinary citizens in combating crime and maintaining public security. However, comprehensive governance initially remained loosely structured and less standardized. A rapid surge of disorganized contention in the years that followed proved that casual and irregular institutional collaboration was ineffective. The government was therefore compelled to intensify efforts to strengthen its administrative arm. Building on earlier practices, the government deepened comprehensive governance by promoting local institutional realignment and the integration of different dispute mechanisms, as well as enhancing control over the grassroots.

City AB in Guangdong Province is composed of four sub-districts and six townships, with a population of 2.4 million in total. Over the last three decades, AB has experienced rapid economic development and urbanization. Such impressive economic growth, however, has been accompanied by tense social conflict arising from land disputes, 'not-in-my-backyard' issues, layoffs and the grievances of demobilized soldiers. In 2010, of over 2,000 people petitioning the Provincial Government more than half came from AB. CC, the township adjacent to Guangzhou and with the highest incidence of conflict in the AB district, is a favorable site for foreign investors, and the commercial value of its land has also attracted numerous development projects, all of which brought various disputes. In 2010 alone, there were 34

[30]Joel Migdal, Atul Kohli and Vivienne Shue, *State Power and Social Forces: Domination and Transformation in the Third World* (Cambridge: Cambridge University Press, 1994), p. 16.

petitions to the provincial government, involving 3,726 people. This ranked CC first in the Province in terms of the number of *shangfang*. There were also numerous *shangfang* to the city, district and township governments. In one incident, more than 600 petitioners from the township surrounded the Provincial Party Committee demanding a settlement of land disputes. A couple of riots erupted in the same year. The provincial government thus identified the CC Township as a 'key unit' to be managed. Thus, the district governments of both AB and CC Township were under pressure from the provincial authorities to stop *shangfang* from disturbing higher authorities.

Concerted conflict management

In societies where citizens organize themselves and voice their problems through institutionalized channels, the myriad popular contentions are hence translated into legible formats for states. Abhorring any form of autonomous societal interest organization and representation, however, the Chinese state has stifled the 'interest aggregation' initiatives of the society. As a result, state administration comes face-to-face with the wilderness of popular contentions.

To make things worse, existing institutions have suffered from the fragmentation of power and resources and poor intra-institutional coordination.[31] Bureaucratic agencies, courts, *xinfang* offices, trade unions and mediation agencies dealt separately with cases that were probably quite similar in nature, with lots of resources wasted on redundant efforts. Various self-interested state agencies have found it important to compete for resources and jurisdiction on the one hand, and convenient to shy away from responsibilities on the other. Such institutional fragmentation weakened the government's ability to control conflict. It also created opportunities for contending parties to exploit such fragmentation by petitioning different agencies with a similar grievance, which further aggravated the waste of institutional resources and effort.

Thus, Guangdong Province took the national lead in the move toward integrating various government agencies into a single center, named the Center of Comprehensive Governance, Letters & Visits, and Stability Maintenance (CCG for short). This was established in 2009 at both county and township levels in response to widespread social conflict. Huang Huahua, the then governor of the Province, described the intention of such an institutional effort as follows: 'Setting CCGs can solve various difficult problems caused by the insufficiency of the previous system in dealing with the increasing number of conflicts and enhance grassroots Party committees' and governments' ability to control the situation of public security'. He declared that the widespread presence of CCGs would mean that 'small things can be solved within the village, big things within the township, and contradictions are not handed over to higher authorities'.[32] Very soon, the Central Committee of Comprehensive Governance endorsed Guangdong's experiment, which resulted in the widespread adoption of CCGs or similar institutions across the country.

As the authors found in AB, CCGs are organizationally subordinate to the Party Committee of the county/district and township/sub-district and directed by the Vice-Party Secretary in charge of political and legal affairs. CCGs have separate budgets and office space of their own. Their stated aims include the comprehensive governance of social and public security, coordinating the settlement of emergency incidents, handling petition letters and receiving petitioners, carrying out people's mediation and legal assistance, and so on.[33] Their core member units include the Comprehensive Governance Office, Stability Maintenance Office, *Xinfang* Office, Public Security Branch, Judicial Bureau (or Judicial

---

[31]For the fragmented decision-making process, see Kenneth Lieberthal and Michel Oksenberg, *Policy Making in China: Leaders, Structures, and Processes* (Princeton, NJ: Princeton University Press, 1988).

[32]Huang Huahua, 'Xunsu quanmian pukai zhenjie zongzhi xinfang weiwen zhongxin jianshe' ['Establishing the county/township Center of Comprehensive Governance, Letters & Visits, and Stability Maintenance in a swift and comprehensive manner'], *Southcn.com*, (30 May 2010), available at: http://www.southcn.com/jsfw/zt/wsxfjf/zdgz/content/2010-05/30/content_12378439.htm (accessed 10 November 2014).

[33]Interview, 14 April 2014.

Administrative Office in a township), Procuratorate and the Court. These units collaborate with the functional departments dealing with civil affairs, labor affairs, urban construction, urban management, housing management, traffic, food safety, as well as trade unions, youth leagues and women's federations. The Comprehensive Governance Office, which is also headed by the Party Secretary of political and legal affairs, takes the lead in coordinating all other member units. With the establishment of CCGs, local conflict management has now revolved around an administrative team rather than individual governmental organs. The new institutions work as an efficient communication platform and collaborative mechanism, enabling different government agencies to solve problems together.[34]

In seeking conflict resolution, the key member units have a clear division of labor. The Comprehensive Management and Stability Maintenance Offices are in charge of daily routines. They classify incoming cases, assign them to relevant units or factional sectors, coordinate the process of settlement, and follow the cases until they are closed. The *Xinfang* Office, which used to operate separately from other government agencies, is now at the entry point of the CCG's settlement process. Visitors who come to the CCG to file complaints are dealt with by this office. *Xinfang* staff will try to effect a settlement on the spot or refer petitioners to relevant units for further consultation. This office also identifies protracted and difficult cases and forwards them to the Director of the CCG. The Judicial Office is responsible for providing guidelines for people's mediation and legal services for people who need them. It also provides legal advice to grassroots authorities and assists them in dealing with various disputes. Some functional departments are perhaps more important than others in dealing with contentious incidents. For example, in the Guangdong area, where industries boom, labor conflict is tense, so the Labor and Social Security Agency is crucial in managing labor disputes. It is charged with the task of making sure that labor laws are followed in settlements and also mediates individual and collective labor disputes. It is also responsible for monitoring enterprises' compliance with labor standards in their operations. The trade unions are required to defuse workers' collective actions as well as mediate in disputes between labor and management. A strong arm of the CCG is the Joint Enforcement Team, composed of members from different agencies. This is further broken into task groups based on issues such as house demolition, labor disputes, migrant populations and food safety, which are often the causes of conflict. The Team's chief responsibility is to carry out inspections in its jurisdiction and make sure that settlements, as well as laws and regulations, are implemented. In this way, the CCG has lumped together the relatively homogeneous and interlinked tasks and synthesized the functions of gathering, processing, tracking and transmitting information as well as directing and coordinating operations in social conflict prevention and settlement.

A close look at the CCG in CC Township in AB illustrates its processes and mechanisms. The township's CCG is composed of four sections: Comprehensive Affairs, *Xinfang* and Stability Maintenance, Judicial Affairs, and Floating Population Management. Each includes staff members from different functional departments of the government. Previously, when a conflict occurred, different government agencies had to act separately to deal with it. If they were unable to resolve the issue, their heads of service were required to seek guidance from the Party Secretary or Deputy Secretary in charge of political and legal affairs. This often slowed the process of dispute resolution. However, since the CCG is an extended arm of the Party committee and headed by the Party Secretary in charge of political and legal affairs, it can take quick and coordinated moves to respond to conflict.

Such a concerted approach to conflict management is epitomized by the CCG's six-step procedure of dispute resolution: (1) *xinfang* officials receive letters and calls from the public, and meet petitioners. They try to resolve disputes on the spot, if possible; (2) if this is not possible, the disputes are channeled into either people's or administrative mediation; (3) relevant functional departments are assigned the administrative mediation, while the Judicial Office is responsible for people's mediation. In both cases the CCG will follow up the process; (4) if a functional department fails to mediate the dispute successfully, the Director of the CCG will hold a joint meeting with members of the various functional departments involved and seek a solution; (5) if this procedure does not lead to settlement, the dispute will be brought

---

[34] *Ibid.*

to the Committee of Comprehensive Governance, which is chaired by the Party Secretary of the township. The Party Secretary will seek a resolution by mobilizing all necessary institutional resources; (6) failure of this step will lead to arbitration and adjudication.[35] The government hopes that this procedure can provide claimants with a one-stop shop for dispute resolution and keep disputes within officially sanctioned channels. Ultimately, it aims to reduce *shangfang* and nip grassroots conflicts in the bud. As one official interviewed emphasized:

> We need this platform, because without it, villagers would go directly to the township government or higher governments and demand to meet the leaders. How can the Party secretary and chief of the township have the energy and time to meet them? Now if they have any complaints, they can come to us here. We have places for them to sit down, talk and settle their problems.[36]

Community surveillance

While institutional realignment facilitates information sharing and administrative coordination, which enables state agencies to take prompt and concerted actions in response to any developing popular contention, it alone does not relieve the government from the stress. The vast dispersion and randomness of disorganized contention poses a serious challenge for local governance. To exercise effective control, the authorities need to improve not only their capacity to act but also their acuteness of perception. Thus the top leaders have urged local governments to devote more attention and resources to gathering and analyzing information on existing and potential social contention and set up early warning mechanisms. At the Central Public Security and Legal Working Conference in 2007, the former President Hu Jintao stressed the necessity of establishing an effective system for social stability risk assessment and early alarms. 'This system should be established as soon as possible', he said, 'as it will permit us to detect problems early, make timely interventions, and resolve conflicts in the bud and at the lowest level'.[37] This drove local governments to make various efforts to map scattered conflict, gather and sort out information, and monitor potential destabilizing elements. Information gathering and community surveillance thus became an integral part of concerted conflict management.

In the CC Township, one of the jobs of the CCG is to gather, transmit information about conflict and assess its potential influence. Village Committees or Street Offices are required to report regularly to the CCG on problems that are perceived to threaten social stability. Upon receiving these reports, the CCG holds joint meetings of member units to discuss the problems identified, devise coping strategies and divide tasks among different agencies. These functions used to be performed separately within different bureaucratic units. The new institutional arrangement allows the CCG to follow up various types of conflicts, detecting and targeting problems at the embryonic stage.

To standardize information processing and problem solving, the township government has set out the procedure of 'examining (*paicha*) the information on the elements of instability and handling major instability incidents'. The Information Section of the CCG is responsible for collecting and assessing information on the state of public order, while the CCG makes an overall assessment of the information on a weekly basis and issues a wrap-up report every ten days. The CCG also ranks villages and communities in terms of the effectiveness of their *weiwen* work. For those villages and communities identified as unstable, the CCG will set up a special network for gathering information and watching those targeted persons closely. The CCG claimed that in 2013, it collected 1,220 pieces of information about instability. Moreover, the CCG enhanced its surveillance capability by aggressively recruiting informants as well as security staff. In 2013, in a township with a population of 150,000, there were 68 CCG staffers in charge of monitoring public order in the community, 415 members of the security patrol, 72 monitors

---

[35]The Work Manual of CCG of CC Township, 2013.

[36]Interview, 14 April 2014.

[37]Hu Jintao, 'Zhazhashishi kaichuang woguo zhengfa gongzuo xin jumian' ['Creating a new future for our country's political and legal work'], *www.news.cn*, (25 December 2007), available at: http://news.xinhuanet.com/newscenter/2007-12/25/content_7312439.htm (accessed 10 November 2014).

of video surveillance and 120 'village defenders'. They were all under the supervision of the Head of the township's Public Security, who reported to the CCG.

Community surveillance is also carried out through the experiment of 'grid management'. Dividing residential communities into smaller grids, the authorities attempt to multiply the 'nerve centers' at the grassroots level in order not only to help sharpen government sensitivity to societal grievances which randomly pop up everywhere, but also to enable them to respond promptly to a variety of contingencies before they develop into more worrying threats to social stability. Specifically, each geographic grid cell is assigned functionally differentiated staff. For example, in some townships in AB, the authorities equipped each of their grid cells with five types of staff, including supervisors, managers, police officers, assistants and property managers. These personnel served as the government's designated liaisons at the grassroots level, assisting local officials to carry out various administrative control and service programs on the one hand, and monitoring neighborhoods for the purposes of public security on the other. In addition, they played a crucial role in preempting disruptive popular contention. For instance, they collected input from residents, and divided labor among themselves to act on relatively trivial complaints and suggestions over issues such as noise, dirt in the environment and crimes in the neighborhood. If more demanding requests emerged, they would convey the message upward. They also gathered information about people in need such as migrants, lonely elderly, families in financial difficulty and so on, and helped the Residents' Committee assess what kind of aid would be sufficient to prevent grievances from arising among these groups. Furthermore, they kept an eye on disputes and discontent, watching out for petitions and any other activities that they considered unusual and that might upset social stability. Besides those five types of staff, the Residents' Committees also had dozens of assistants on the ground within each grid cell, including residents' small group leaders, courtyard liaisons, block and floor representatives, security patrols and so on. These ordinary residents could not only gather household information to which administrators at higher levels would have no access, but also served as a bridge between state cadres and residents, helping the former to create more intimate ties with the latter. Furthermore, all the people's mediation organizations in AB identified a number of mediators as informants (*xinxiyuan*) responsible for collecting information on social conflict in their neighborhoods.[38]

A more drastic measure introduced by the AB government was the establishment of enclosed communities with extensive use of surveillance cameras. According to a document issued in 2012, the government called for 'adopting a thorough physical enclosure of communities if geographical conditions permit, and adding more surveillance cameras otherwise'. The CC Township reports that all 14 of its villages were turned into such gated communities. Accompanying this measure was an enhanced monitoring of the floating population, which is thought to be a potentially unstable element. CCG staff regularly inspects the areas where migrants reside.

To ensure that disputes were solved within communities, the AB government purchased legal services from law firms and guaranteed that each community/village would be assigned one lawyer. He or she would be on site within 24 hours of a conflict emerging, as well as providing legal advice to people requiring it. Lawyers who took on dispute cases independently were required to report to the city's authorities about the nature and status of their cases. As one of the city's top officials described it,

> we have the internal mechanisms to follow up the cases being handled by commissioned lawyers. If they find any sign of escalation of conflict or anything that involves sensitive issues, they must report to us the first time. If they (lawyers) are handling collective cases, they must inform us. If they inform us of anything serious, we will report it to the Party secretary in charge of political and legal affairs. The advantage of the current system is that the information about mass incidents that occurred in communities or villages can quickly be transmitted to the leading officials and we can respond quickly.[39]

In this top-down grid management that aims to reinvigorate and re-equip the Party-state's grassroots governing infrastructure, local governments have made their utmost efforts in weaving denser

[38] 'Shunde jiji goujian "da tiaojie" geju' ['Shunde actively building institutional apparatus for "grand mediation"'], *Zhujiang Shangbao*, (23 May 2011), available at: http://www.sdpma.com/news.aspx?id=370 (accessed 10 November 2014).
[39] Interview, 23 July 2013.

Table 2. Facts about the mediation network in AB.

	N
Mediation Committees (in the district and townships/subdistricts)	299
Village Mediation Committees	108
Neighborhood Mediation Committees	92
Small Mediation Groups in Villages	1,090
Small Mediation Groups in Neighborhoods	654
Enterprise Mediation Committees	45
Sectorial Mediation Committees	7
Professional Mediation Committees	36
Commercial Mediation Committee	1
Mediators	18,715

governance networks that permit more precise, penetrating and systematic state control over the Chinese society. Dividing neighborhoods into even smaller grid cells, the authorities have multiplied the 'nerve centers' that sharpen local authorities' sensitivity to the social conflicts and enable them to respond promptly before the escalation of tensions.

Collaborative and mandatory mediation

Disorganized contentions often take the form of numerous isolated incidents, disputes or complaints. The government has to adopt a case-by-case approach to settlement. Mediation fits this approach best, because it is not only low-cost and widely applicable, but also less constrained by formal rules and offers considerable flexibility and discretion, enabling local officials to play divide-and-rule tactics in dispute resolution.

Mediation has been used as a method of conflict resolution in urban neighborhoods, rural communities and workplaces since the founding of the People's Republic of China. However, the process of market reform since the 1980s stimulated the rule of law movement, which sidelined mediation for some time. The surge in social conflict over the past decade or so has once again restored mediation as a key mechanism of conflict resolution. What is striking is that the form of mediation that has re-emerged has been considerably enhanced as an instrument of the state to handle disorganized contention. For the government, mediation is especially suitable for controlling and defusing disorganized contention, due to its flexible manipulative nature. Mediation used to be carried out separately by different agencies. To maximize its impact, some local governments sought to combine different modes of mediation called 'grand mediation'.

This approach quickly gained momentum in other parts of the country. The reason for this is that each mode of mediation has its limitations. For example, while judicial mediation is more authoritative, it is relatively costly and time consuming. The rapidly growing numbers of cases also create a heavy burden on the courts. People's mediation is highly flexible but its decisions appear to lack authority. Administrative mediation is often perceived as biased, arbitrary and uncertain, as citizens' trust in local government agencies is currently remarkably low.

To enforce collaborative mediation, the AB government rebuilt a huge network of people's mediation as the frontline of dispute settlement and extended it down to the grassroots with a four-level structure (that is, at the district, township/sub-district, village/residential community and subgroup of village/residential community levels). In the meantime, it also set up some specialized and trade-based mediation committees for labor, medical and housing disputes. Such a network constitutes a micro-foundation of the mechanism of conflict resolution. People's mediation has been promoted because mediators embedded in grassroots society are accessible, sensitive to local disputes, and can be quickly mobilized for conflict resolution. Table 2 provides some facts about the mediation network in AB.[40]

[40] 'Shunde jiji goujian "da tiaojie" geju', *Zhujiang Shangbao*.

While people's mediation is considered crucially important for conflict management at the grassroots, the CCG provides an institutional platform linking it to both judicial and administrative mediation as well. The CCG is responsible for coordinating and supervising mediation by different agencies, integrated into a single center. However, it is the court that plays a pivotal role in steering the process of mediation, particularly in enhancing people's mediation. People's mediation has been aggressively promoted by the government, as it is flexible, less constrained by formal rules and accessible. Nevertheless, it suffers from lower prestige and authoritativeness, which often leads to non-compliance with its decisions. Under the new institutional framework, the court is allowed, with the consent of the disputing parties, to approve mediation agreements so that they become legally valid and binding. The court also screens numerous litigation actions and channels many of them, again with the consent of parties, to mediation agencies. The court endorses successfully mediated cases to place them on the same footing as those that have been legally settled.

Under grand mediation, the courts are linked to administrative agencies through the joint conference and other *ad hoc* arrangements. Participants in the joint conference include officials from the judicial and public security bureau as well as representatives from trade unions, youth leagues and women's federations. The joint conference aims to share information on local conflicts, examine difficult and complex cases, assess potential problems and discuss collaboration. The courts also channel lawsuits to relevant administrative agencies (such as the public security and labor bureau) for mediation. The courts even invite government agencies to carry out joint mediation in some complex and sensitive disputes. Administrative mediation agreements can also be judicially endorsed in the form of civil dispute resolution.

The courts themselves are also actively involved in mediation under grand mediation. Judicial mediation takes place not only before but also during court trials. In AB, mediation offices have been widely set up within the courts. Representatives from other agencies, such as arbitration committees, trade unions and women's federations, have been invited to join the process.[41] Mediation allows the courts to use various non-judicial approaches, such as divide and rule, persuasion and intimidation, to seek plaintiffs' withdrawal from lawsuits, or to strike a compromise and ensure a legally binding agreement between parties. For court officials, mediation can reduce the tension between parties, as it is undertaken in a closed-door setting and open confrontation can be avoided. Unlike an open trial, closed-door mediation is less likely to attract media attention and hence heighten the antagonism between the parties. Another reason mediation is encouraged is because controversial verdicts are believed to risk arousing more controversy and *shangfang*.

The consequences of the new institutional practice

Disorganized contention has taken the form of numerous scattered and dispersive conflicts or *shangfang*, which disturb the local social order. Thus, from the government's perspective, defusing them and reducing their number is the primary indicator of the effectiveness of the new institutions of conflict management. Local governments have claimed that the implementation of these so-called innovative measures has enabled them to bring conflict under control and contain *shangfang*. For example, the AB government reports that in the past three years 22,530 out of 23,347, or 97%, of disputes raised in the city were successfully mediated by various agencies. Also, 63.5% of civil cases brought to the courts in 2010 were settled or withdrawn after mediation. In the same year, 6,846 disputes were resolved through collaborative mediation prior to court trials commencing. 2010 also saw a 31% drop in *shangfang* compared to the previous year.[42]

One of the thorniest challenges to the AB government was the recurring collective petitions and protests by demobilized soldiers who fought in the Sino–Vietnamese War in 1979. This is a nationwide

[41] Interview, 14 April 2014.

[42] Foshangshi Yifa Zhishi Ban [Office of City Governance by Law of Foshan City], 'Foshanshi "da tiaojie jizhi" jianshe qingkuang de diaoyan ji jianyi' ['Investigations and suggestions on Foshan's "grand mediation" development'], *Fazhi guangdong wang*, (21 November 2011), available at: http://www.fzgd.org/gzdy/201111/t20111121_213754.htm (accessed 10 November 2014).

Table 3. Number of shangfang raised with the provincial government.

Year	Times	Number of people involved
2010	34	3,720
2011	45	1,782
2012	1	15
2013	0	0

issue but Guangdong witnessed a few big rallies and demonstrations in a number of its cities as well as numerous *shangfang* to city and provincial governments. On 9 May 2012, hundreds of former soldiers marched in the streets in AB and blocked the traffic, demanding jobs and economic improvement. Many of them had also been among the more frequent petitioners in the city. The CCG was fully mobilized to pacify this highly contentious group. Besides adopting various measures to keep them out of the streets and punishing those whose behavior was illegal, the CCG sought to provide them with employment opportunities. It managed to recruit a number of former soldiers to the *weiwen* apparatus through community security teams and various security positions as well as the CCG itself. It was hoped that such offers of employment could defuse the soldiers' contention. As one CCG official put it,

> they wanted employment and we arranged it for them. We introduced them to community security teams or security positions in various departments. We pay them a salary even if they do not work normally or very hard, as long as they do not make trouble anymore.[43]

The authorities in AB claimed that the contention caused by demobilized soldiers had been largely settled over the past two years. The CC Township also reported that the new institutions of conflict management had been successful. According to its statistics, there had been a drastic drop in the number of *shangfang* raised with the provincial government in the past three years (see Table 3).[44]

In the meantime, the Township government also reported that using the mechanism of concerted conflict settlement, it resolved 178 out of 189 *xinfang* received by its CCG in 2013. The CCG also defused and resolved 32 mass incidents involving a total of over 900 people, while all 103 cases channeled to people's mediation were successfully settled in the same year. Some villages in AB reported that 90% of disputes had been internally solved without involving *shangfang*.[45] This change matches the national data, which recorded a 75.5% reduction of *shangfang* in 2012.[46]

The accuracy of these data may be open to question as there is always an element of exaggeration and cherry-picking in China's official statistics. However, in our interviews with grassroots officials in the CC Township our respondents unanimously concurred that *shangfang* had been reduced. The Party Secretary in AB claimed that 'with the CCG, we have finally got rid of the previous "on-the-run-all-the-day situation"' in dealing with disputes and *shangfang*.[47] The intensification and acceleration of governmental *weiwen* efforts seemed to have contributed to this trend. The new institutional arrangements had significantly reinvigorated and extended local governments' organizational web of control over grassroots society. What still needs to be pointed out, however, is that the new conflict management institution does not function without coercion. The police are often used to disperse contentious gatherings. Protest organizers are likely to face harsh punishment. In handling the former soldiers' protests, for example, the AB authorities used the carrot and stick method. While they placated protesters by

[43]Interview, 14 April 2014.

[44]Pan Jiying, 'Shunde chencun zhen: jianli jizhi an fazhi kuangjia jiejue jiceng maodun' ['Shunde Chencun Township: establishing legal mechanisms to resolve grassroots conflicts'], *South.com*, (11 September 2014), available at: http://www.fzgd.org/xczb/fzpt/mtssd/201409/t20140911_508974.htm (accessed 10 November 2014).

[45]Foshangshi Yifa Zhishi Ban, 'Foshanshi "da tiaojie jizhi" jianshe qingkuang de diaoyan ji jianyi'.

[46]Wang Shengjun, 'Xinfang renshu wunian xiajiang 75.5%' ['A 75.5% reduction in the size of the letters & visits population'], *Xinhua*, (10 March 2013), available at: http://3g.163.com/news/13/0310/09/8PJIE33Q0001124J.html (accessed 12 November 2014).

[47]Chen Yu, 'Liang Weidong: Shunde weiwen buzai piyubenming' ['Liang Weidong: social stability maintenance in Shunde is no longer overly exhausting'], *Southern Metropolis Daily*, (16 January 2013), available at: http://roll.sohu.com/20130116/n363575510.shtml (accessed 12 November 2014).

providing them with employment opportunities, they also arrested two organizers and sentenced them on charges of disturbing public order. As the District Mayor of AB made clear,

> nobody should *shangfang* or *naoshi* without reason. Don't assume that the government would yield under unreasonable pressures ... We will use all means to maintain stability. If anyone challenges us, we will show no mercy on him according to the law.[48]

Needless to say, the local institutional (re)building designed to contain disorganized contention has also had broad political and institutional consequences. One of its most notable corollaries is a re-enhanced presence of Party power in the grassroots. This is reflected in the ascending position of the Party's political and legal commission, dominating the work on stability maintenance. As described above, all CCGs are concurrently headed by Vice-Party Secretaries in charge of political and legal affairs, while the Comprehensive Governance Office directed by the same officials assumes the leading role in CCGs. Institutional realignment, concerted action of agencies and the incorporation of non-governmental actors in conflict resolution are all decisively reliant on the Party's organizational power and authority to direct, mobilize and coordinate.[49] The CCG framework, in turn, allows the Party via its political and legal authority to amass administrative, legal and human, as well as financial, resources. The Party's political and legal commissions are the final decision makers on the settlement of major mass incidents. The Party-directed institution of conflict management does not amount to the institutionalization of dispute resolution. In fact, CCGs rely heavily on *ad hoc* measures to operate, despite their stated working rules and procedures. This is largely forced upon them by the nature of disorganized contention, whose dispersal and unexpectedness require quick, flexible and niche-targeting responses. The Party's increasing discretionary power further encourages *ad hoc*-ism, which undermines the institutionalization of conflict resolution.

Furthermore, the Party-dominated institutional realignment and concerted actions undermines the distinctive role of the judicial offices in mediation. The judicial offices in sub-districts or townships used to be subject to the district judicial bureau and more or less independent of sub-district or township governments. They were perceived by the people as relatively impartial in conflict settlement, as they were not organizationally entangled with other arms of local government. Nevertheless, the incorporation of the judicial offices into the CCGs in sub-districts or townships has compromised their impartiality and hence weakened people's trust. As one official described it,

> ... before, the judicial offices in the sub-district and townships played an impartial role in dispute settlements and could win people's trust. If villagers had an argument with villagers' committees or the township government, the staff from judicial offices could mediate as a third party on behalf of the district judicial bureau. However, since the judicial offices part of the CCGs of townships, the people have come to lose trust in them, for they now perceive them as a part of township governments. We told the villagers that the judicial offices did not represent the township government, but they simply did not believe it. As some villagers said, 'they [staff from judicial offices] were working with township officials in the same office (that is, the office hall of CCGs), so how can you say that they do not represent the government?'.[50]

Similarly, the new institutions of conflict management also distort the role of the courts and hence weaken the rule of law. As some studies have already pointed out, the Party-state's *weiwen* drive has pushed local courts to engage in extrajudicial activities and mediation, and collaborate with government agencies.[51] In other words, in order to serve the government's priority of maintaining stability, courts tend to seek pragmatic solutions rather than applying the law to disputes. This is also the case in AB:

---

[48] 'Qunian 31 Shunde ganbu tanwu weiji shou chufen' ['31 cadres in Shunde penalized for corruption and disciplinary violations last year'], *Southern Metropolis Daily*, (31 March 2011), available at: http://www.citygf.com/FSNews/FS_002008/201103/t20110331_1424867.html (accessed 12 November 2014).

[49] Xie Yue, 'The political logic of weiwen in contemporary China', *Issues and Studies* 48(3), (2013), pp. 1–41.

[50] Interview, 23 July 2013.

[51] See, for example, Xin He and Yang Su, 'Street as courtroom: state accommodation of labor protest in South China', *Law and Society Review* 44(1), (2010), pp. 157–184; Feng Chen and Xin Xu, '"Active judiciary": judicial dismantling of workers' collective action in China', *The China Journal* 67, (2012), pp. 87–108.

> Since joining the office (that is, CCGs) and working together with other government agencies, the courts and lawyers have had to pay more attention to stability maintenance. Before, the courts and lawyers followed laws and legal procedures to settle collective disputes. Now it is different. They must report their cases to us and solve disputes in the light of stability maintenance. We will work together with them to settle the problems.[52]

In short, the incorporation of the local courts in the new institutions of conflict management has led to them becoming increasingly subsumed into the Party's prioritization of stability. As a result, political and administrative tactics often, and indeed routinely, prevail over the rule of law.

Conclusion

Because of structural and institutional constraints, Chinese citizens cannot legally organize themselves to articulate their interests. The explosion in the number of claims and demands made during the market-driven reform process has consequently taken the form of widespread and disorganized incidents of contention, which are dispersive and scattered. They cannot be incorporated as they are not organized; nor can they be totally eradicated by force, given their quantity and frequency as well as the political cost of such suppression. Disorganized contention thus produces a state response that differs from those found in countries where popular struggles can be organized to varying degrees. This research shows that disorganized contention has left a significant imprint on the evolutionary trajectory of the country's institutions of conflict management, which has several prominent characteristics. Firstly, as disorganized contention usually takes the form of isolated conflict and disputes, the institution has developed strong mechanisms for case-by-case dispute resolution. The CCG framework provides institutional platforms that enable dispute cases to be handled by different modes of settlement or government agencies in coordinated and collaborative ways, in order to secure quick and effective solutions to conflicts and prevent them from escalating and spreading. Secondly, the new arrangements use mediation as the principal means of conflict resolution, because it is most suitable for the case-by-case problem solving approach. Mediation is widely applied to almost all types of dispute cases. Without the need to follow any specific rules, it allows the authorities to flexibly apply a range of means, from persuasion, intimidation, and divide and rule, to defuse conflict. Thirdly, to cope with the pervasiveness, unexpectedness and randomness of disorganized contention, conflict management institutions have evolved into a network of social monitoring agents involving information gathering, risk assessment and the micro-governance of communities. This reinforces the government's capacity to reach out into grassroots society and prevent and preempt social conflicts.

Institutional (re)building for conflict management is a robust return of state power to grassroots China, which had weakened during the market reforms. It relies on the old institutional structure and resources but reconfigures and refurbishes them into a new form of power to penetrate society. Through weaving denser governance networks, this permits more precise, targeted and systematic state control over society, and strengthens local authorities' ability to contain grassroots social conflict. The almost ubiquitous presence of government units and state-designated liaisons on the ground demonstrate the government's intention to maintain a stern grip on society and to squeeze the more autonomous civil associations out.

Whether the new institutional arrangements can cope effectively with the challenge of mounting levels of popular contention remains to be seen.[53] However, as long as citizens are denied the right to organize and the opportunity for representation and participation, they will continuously create new forms of expression of their discontent and demands. The resulting duplication and chaos may block and even overturn any categories officials devise and impose upon social problems. Moreover, since people's voices can pop up at any time and everywhere, even the most refined organizational networks can fail to prepare administrators properly to hear their voices clearly and silence them all at once. *Ad*

---

[52] Interview, 23 July 2013.

[53] One recent study shows that mediation in the Guangdong area did reduce workers' collective actions. See Wenjia Zhuang, 'Can "mediation first" reduce collective labor disputes?', *Shehuixue yanjiu* [*Sociological Studies*] 5, (2013), pp. 145–171.

hoc-ism and improvisational tactics have to be frequently used to handle unexpected and complicated situations. It can be argued that without providing more representative and participatory channels, the institutions built to contain disorganized contention will continue to keep popular resistance atomized and disorganized and (re)produce and entrench the current pattern of popular contention. If so, China will continue to face the challenge of disorganized contention in the years to come.

Acknowledgements

Feng Chen would like to thank the Research Grants Council of Hong Kong, Chiang Ching-kuo Foundation and Faculty Research Grants of Hong Kong Baptist University for funding the writing of this article. Yi Kang wishes to thank the Faculty Research Grants of Hong Kong Baptist University for the financial support of this research.

Pollution, Institutions and Street Protests in Urban China

Yang Zhong[a,b] and Wonjae Hwang[b]

[a]Shanghai Jiao Tong University, China; [b]University of Tennessee, USA

ABSTRACT

Street protests have become commonplace in China. Utilizing extensive survey data, this study attempts to shed light on the nature of environmental street protests in China. The key question to be answered in the article is: why, facing the same issue, do some people choose the option of participating in street protests while others do not? Multivariate analytical findings indicate that Chinese urban residents' willingness to participate in street protests over a hypothetical pollution issue in China is significantly related to their attitudes toward institutions in China. What motivates people to participate in street protests has a lot to do with their trust and support of the political system in China and their perceived government transparency. In other words, these protests are not just what Lewis Coser calls 'realistic conflicts' which primarily involve specific issues and solutions. One implication from this study is that street protests in China may not be as benign and non-regime threatening as some scholars might think.

Introduction

Looking from outside, the Chinese government has been stable and is described as 'resilient'[1] despite the third wave of democratization and, recently, the Arab Spring. However, the picture is not so rosy inside China. In fact, street protests [or *quntixing shijian*], one form of contentious politics,[2] have become commonplace in China. The most cited official figure of social protests in China was 87,000 that occurred in 2005.[3] According to a *Wall Street Journal* report, the figure reached 180,000 in 2010.[4] Due to the frequent occurrences of street protests the Chinese government has made maintaining stability [*weiwen*] a top priority for all levels of government in China. It is reported that China currently spends more on domestic security than on its military.[5] What is the nature of these street protests? Do these activities pose a potential threat to destabilize the political regime in China? Answering these questions is critical for understanding contentious politics in China and assessing the prospect of change in the country.

---

[1]Andrew Nathan, 'Authoritarian resilience', *Journal of Democracy* 14, (2003), pp. 6–17.

[2]On contentious politics, see Doug McAdam, Sidney Tarrow and Charles Tilly, *Dynamics of Contention* (New York: Cambridge University Press, 2001).

[3]Zhao Peng *et al.*, 'The warning signal of "typical social protests"', *Outlook Weekly*, (8 September 2008), p. 36. For whatever reason, the Chinese government stopped publishing statistics with regard to street protests after 2006.

[4]Tom Orlik, 'Unrest grows as economy booms', *Wall Street Journal*, (26 September 2011), available at: http://online.wsj.com/news/articles/SB10001424053111903703604576587070600504108?mg=reno64wsj&url=http%3A%2F%2Fonline.wsj.com%2Farticle%2FSB10001424053111903703604576587070600504108.html (accessed 26 September 2011).

[5]Ben Blanchard and John Ruwitch, 'China hikes defense budget, to spend more on internal security', *Reuters*, (5 March 2013), available at: http://www.reuters.com/article/2013/03/05/us-china-parliament-defence-idUSBRE92403620130305 (accessed 11 January 2014).

There are different assessments among China scholars on the nature of street protests in China. Some believe that social protests pose serious threat to social stability in China and may lead to significant political changes.[6] Others argue that social protests in China are primarily issue-driven and, therefore, they do not undermine the fundamental structure of the existing political system.[7] Elizabeth Perry, an influential scholar on contentious politics in China, even argues that social protests have become a normal form of political participation for ordinary Chinese in Chinese politics and these activities actually contribute to social stability in China because protesters use these occasions to vent their anger and have their demands met.[8]

One way to shed light on the nature of street protests in China is to study what motivates people to participate in likely street protests. A key question in this debate involves whether these street protests are purely issue-driven or are also motivated by other factors, especially institutional factors? Why, facing the same issue, do some people decide to participate in street protests while others do not? If institution-related factors significantly affect street protest participation, these social activities can be perceived as a challenge to the stability of the authoritarian regime. A missing piece in assessing the danger of street protests in China is the type of street protest. Common causes for most street protests in China in the last two decades fall into the following categories: inadequate compensation for land-related disputes in both rural and urban areas of China; abuse of power by local Chinese officials; China's one-child policy; labor disputes; environmental pollution; and religious and secessionist movements.[9] Some of the street protests, such as land- and labor-related conflicts, involve small groups of people and are clearly narrow and specific-issue-driven. However, some other contentious conflicts are more general in nature. Most environment-related street protests are such conflicts because the environmental issues involved in the conflicts may carry potentially long-term detrimental health effects and affect a relatively large number of people. As such, people may have less incentive to participate in street protests over these issues (free ride problem). Therefore, this article picks environmental protests as the focus of study. The authors believe that environment-related street protests are better cases to test the effect of institutional factors in motivating people to participate in street protest activities in China.

Environment-related protests, which have experienced an annual increase of close to 30% since the mid-1990s in China,[10] have attracted scholars' attention in recent years.[11] This type of conflict is worthy of our attention for the following additional reasons. First, unlike land or labor dispute issues which only concern a small specific group of people, environmental pollution and degradation are of wide concern to the general population and can arouse widespread societal reaction due to the fact

---

[6]Li Zhu, 'Analysis of China's social risk: the social conflict nature of mass protests', *Xuehai* 1, (2009), pp. 69–78; Kevin O'Brien and Lianjiang Li, *Rightful Resistance in Rural China* (Cambridge: Cambridge University Press, 2006); Merle Goldman, *From Comrade to Citizen: The Struggle for Political Rights in China* (Cambridge, MA: Harvard University Press, 2005).

[7]Yu Jianrong, 'Categories and main features of China's current mass protests', *Zhongguo zhengfa daxue xuebao* 6, (2009), pp. 114–160; Elizabeth Perry, 'Chinese conceptions of "rights": from Mencius to Mao—and now', *Perspectives on Politics* 6, (2008), pp. 37–50.

[8]Elizabeth Perry, *Challenge the Mandate of Heaven: Social Protest and State Power in China* (Armonk, NY: M. E. Sharpe, 2002).

[9]Peter Ho, 'Who owns China's land', *The China Quarterly* 166, (2001), pp. 394–442; Xiaolin Guo, 'Land expropriation and rural conflict in China', *The China Quarterly* 166, (2001), pp. 422–439; Tyrene White, 'Domination, resistance and accommodation in China's one-child campaign', in Elizabeth Perry and Mark Selden, eds, *Chinese Society: Change, Conflict and Resistance* (London: Routledge, 2000), pp. 171–196; Jun Jing, 'Environmental protests in rural China', in Perry and Selden, eds, *Chinese Society*, pp. 297–214; David Zweig, 'To the courts or to the barricades: can new political institutions manage rural conflict?', in Perry and Selden, eds, *Chinese Society*, pp. 123–147; Ching Kwan Lee, 'Pathways of labor insurgency', in Perry and Selden, eds, *Chinese Society*, pp. 57–79; William Hurst, 'Understanding contentious collective action by Chinese laid-off workers: the importance of regional political economy', *Studies in Comparative International Development* 39, (2004), pp. 94–120; Feng Chen, 'Subsistence crises, managerial corruption and labor protests in China', *The China Journal* 44, (2000), pp. 41–63; Jae Ho Chung, Hongyi Lai and Ming Xia, 'Mounting challenges to governance in China; surveying collective protestors, religious sects and criminal organizations', *The China Journal* 56, (2006), pp. 1–32.

[10]'China experiences 23% annual increase in environment-related protests and the Chinese court refuses to litigate these cases due to their sensitivity', *News*, (28 October 2012), available at: http://news.163.com/12/1028/02/8ESBJE2B00014AED.html (accessed 28 October 2012).

[11]Fengshi Wu, 'Environmental politics in China: an issue area in review', in Sujian Guo, ed., *Political Science and Chinese Political Studies: The State of the Field* (London: Springer, 2013), pp. 103–124.

that environmental problems are getting worse every day in China and they affect people's health and livelihood directly. According to an official report by China's Ministry of Environmental Protection, 57.3% of groundwater in 198 Chinese cities was described as 'bad' or 'extremely bad', 30% of the country's major rivers were polluted or seriously polluted, and over 85% of Chinese key cities did not meet air quality standards in 2012.[12] The survey in this article found that 72.4% of our surveyed urban residents said that the city they lived in was polluted or seriously polluted and 68% of them believed that pollution in their city affected their health. Environmental problems have drawn by far the largest crowds of protesters in China since Tiananmen. Planned construction of polluting chemical and power plants in Xiamen in 2007, Dalian in 2011 and Kuming in 2013 drew tens of thousands of urban protesters to the streets. Second, unlike rural land conflicts and urban labor disputes, environmental movements and campaigns particularly attract urban middle-class participants who have been understudied.[13] The urban environmental movement is probably the most vigorous civil society force in China.[14] One scholar claims that the urban environmental movement is the style of the new citizen activism in China.[15] Third, environmental protests seem to be more successful in achieving their goals due to the large number of participants (resulted partly from the use of new technologies in mobilization) and the wide appeal to the general population. A number of high-profile environmental protests have led to either the shutdown of existing polluting factories or the cancellation of proposed environmentally hazardous facilities.[16]

Despite the importance of the question, there have been few empirical studies focusing on street protests in China. This study, based on a large-scale random survey conducted in 34 Chinese cities, attempts to shed some light on the factors that contribute to Chinese people's willingness to participate in street protests and, therefore, the nature of street protests in China. Specifically, this article tests two models concerning Chinese urban residents' propensity to participate in environment-related street protests: the issue-oriented model vs. the institutional model. These two models are not necessarily mutually exclusive, since all protests are issue-driven to some extent. Nevertheless, if it is issue or grievance-relevant factors that solely drive people's willingness to participate in this form of public demonstration, it can be said that street protests may not pose a serious threat to the stability of the political regime. On the other hand, if it is also their distrust or dissatisfaction with the government that mobilizes people in a country where many open forms of political activities are discouraged or forbidden, the growing street protests can be a serious threat to the Chinese authorities and a destabilizing factor of the authoritarian regime. The findings of this article lend support to the institutional model.

This article makes several contributions to the current literature on contentious politics in China. First, unlike some other studies which explain the dramatic rise of social protests or the success or failure of popular protests,[17] this article focuses exclusively on the motivational factors, both issue-related and institutional, explaining people's willingness to participate in street demonstrations in urban China. Second, this article chooses environmental pollution as the protesting issue for the study. Environmental pollution has no doubt become a significantly serious challenge in China's economic development. Since pollution affects people's livelihood directly, it has also become a new focus for street protests in China, and, therefore, a serious social and political issue for the Chinese government. In addition, environmental protests involve post-material values.[18] Yet, studies of street protests over environmental

[12] 'China's environmental problems are grim, admits ministry report', *The Guardian*, (7 June 2013), available at: http://www.theguardian.com/environment/chinas-choice/2013/jun/07/chinas-environmental-problems-grim-ministry-report (accessed 25 January 2014).

[13] Kevin O'Brien, 'Introduction: studying contentious politics in contemporary China', in Kevin J. O'Brien, ed., *Popular Protest in China* (Cambridge, MA: Harvard University Press, 2008), pp. 11–25.

[14] Yanfei Sun and Dingxin Zhao, 'Environmental campaigns', in O'Brien, ed., *Popular Protest in China*, pp. 144–162.

[15] Guobin Yang, *The Power of the Internet in China: Citizen Activism Online* (New York: Columbia University Press, 2009).

[16] The most well-known cases were the cancellation of a planned PX chemical factory in Xiamen in 2007 and the shutdown of a PX chemical factory in Dalian in 2011 due to large-scale popular street protests.

[17] Xi Chen, *Social Protest and Contentious Authoritarianism in China* (Cambridge: Cambridge University Press, 2012); Yongshun Cai, *Collective Resistance in China: Why Popular Protests Succeed or Fail* (Stanford, CA: Stanford University Press, 2010).

[18] O'Brien, 'Introduction', pp. 21–22.

issues have not been sufficient. Third, differing from other research that focuses on contentious politics in rural China,[19] the focus of this article is exclusively on Chinese urban residents for the important role that cities and urban residents play in Chinese politics and political development.[20] The number of urban residents, for the first time in Chinese history, has surpassed that of rural residents.[21] Urban residents tend to be better educated and many of them are elites in various fields of Chinese society. They live in political, economic and social centers in China. Their trust and support are indispensable for the current regime in China. The 1989 protest events that shook up Chinese politics occurred primarily in China's urban areas. The final contribution is that this article adopts an empirical survey research technique in understanding why some people choose street protests as their first option with regard to the issue of environmental pollution. This article draws from large-scale updated cross-regional survey data from 34 Chinese cities, which is unprecedented in the literature of contentious politics in China. To analyze both individual and city-level factors, the authors employ a multilevel modeling with a Bayesian simulation method.

Understanding contentious politics in China

Contentious politics is not new in contemporary China. In fact, contemporary Chinese history is filled with revolutions, revolts, insurgencies and protests. The most serious and memorable mass protests in the reform era were the Tiananmen events that occurred in China in the summer of 1989.[22] There is no question that popular contentions with authorities have been on a dramatic rise in China since the 1990s even though official figures for popular collective social actions in China are hard to find.[23] According to Xi Chen, participants of collective petitioning per million increased by 13.59 times and 4.16 times in Hunan and Henan provinces respectively between 1991 and 2000 (p. 29).[24] According to another study, between 2000 and 2013 there were 871 street protests in China that involved over 100 participants. About 200 of them occurred in 2012 alone.[25]

Contentious politics in China has to be understood from a broader theoretical framework. There is extensive literature on why people decide to be involved in street protests. Classical theories explaining people's participation in protests are the grievance theories that contribute people's protesting activities to relative deprivation, frustration and perceived injustice.[26] Grievance theories, however, are not sufficient to explain why, among people who have the same or similar grievances, some people participate in protest activities while others do not. As a result, other theories have been developed focusing on resources, efficacy, opportunities, organization and personal traits such as emotion to explain people's engagement in protests.[27]

---

[19]O'Brien and Li, *Rightful Resistance in Rural China.*

[20]Urban residents in our survey include both permanent residents as well as temporary residents in the surveyed cities.

[21]According to China's National Bureau of Statistics, 51.27% of Chinese citizens lived in cities and towns by the end of 2011, as published on 17 January 2012, available at: http://www.nytimes.com/2012/01/18/world/asia/majority-of-chinese-now-live-in-cities.html (accessed 11 July 2015).

[22]Two book-length studies provide excellent analysis of the Tiananmen events in 1989. See Dengxin Zhao, *The Power of Tiananmen* (Chicago, IL: The University of Chicago Press, 2001); and Jeffrey N. Wasserstrom and Elizabeth Perry, eds, *Popular Protest and Political Culture in Modern China* (Boulder, CO: Westview Press, 1994).

[23]Cai, *Collective Resistance in China*, pp. 22–25.

[24]Xi Chen, *Social Protest and Contentious Authoritarianism in China*, p. 24.

[25]Lin Li and Tian He, *Zhongguo fazhif fazhan baogao 2014* (Beijing: Shehui kexue chubanshe, 2014), pp. 272–273.

[26]Walter G. Runciman, *Relative Deprivation and Social Justice* (London: Routledge, 1966); Ted Gurr, *Why Men Rebel* (Princeton, NJ: Princeton University Press, 1970); Leonard Berkowitz, 'Frustrations, comparisons, and other sources of emotion aroused as contributors to social unrest', *Journal of Social Issues* 28(1), (1972), pp. 77–91; Allen Lind and Tom Tyler, *The Social Psychology of Procedural Justice* (New York: Plenum Press, 1988).

[27]Bert Klandermans, 'Mobilization and participation: social–psychological expansions of resource mobilization theory', *American Sociological Review* 49(5), (1984), pp. 583–600; Doug McAdam, *Political Process and the Development of Black Insurgency, 1930–1970* (Chicago, IL: The University of Chicago Press, 1982); John D. McCarthy and Mayer N. Zeld, 'Resource mobilization and social movements: a partial theory', *American Journal of Sociology* 82(6), (1977), pp. 1212–1241; Martijn Van Zomeren, Russell Spears, Agneta Fischer and Colin W. Leach, 'Put your money where your mouth is! Explaining collective action tendencies through group-based anger and group efficacy', *Journal of Personality and Social Psychology* 87(5), (2004), pp. 649–664.

One scholar's work on social conflict is particularly useful for this study. Unsatisfied with both Marxism which puts too much emphasis on revolutions and Tarcott Parsons's general theory of social action that puts a great value on equilibrium, Lewis Coser in his seminal work, *The Functions of Social Conflict,* argues that social conflict is, first of all, the norm of every society and is not necessarily dysfunctional. He further argues that social conflict serves a number of positive functions, not the least of which is the function of a safety-valve in a given society.[28] Coser distinguishes two different types of internal social conflicts: realistic conflicts and unrealistic conflicts. Realistic conflicts involve specific objects and demands, while unrealistic conflicts are targeted at the fundamental values or interests of the existing structure or system.[29] While the former may stabilize the system and re-establish unity by releasing tension between antagonistic parties, the latter is likely to disrupt the existing structure and threaten the legitimacy of the social system. The key for a social system to prevent realistic conflicts from becoming unrealistic conflicts, according to Coser, is to reduce rigidity of the system to allow for conflict resolution in a tolerant fashion.[30]

Are street protests in China realistic or unrealistic social conflicts? Elizabeth Perry's analysis of Chinese protest activities is particularly enlightening. Perry traces Chinese conceptions of people's 'rights' from ancient Chinese philosopher Mencius to contemporary Chinese revolutionary leader Mao, and argues that the Chinese understanding of 'rights' is significantly different from that of the Anglo-American cultural tradition.[31] In the discourse of traditional Chinese philosophers and political leaders, according to Perry, the emphasis of 'rights' is on collective socioeconomic justice, while 'rights' from the Anglo-American perspective is more about individual rights and civil liberties. Chinese 'rights consciousness' is more concerned with livelihood issues than fundamental and abstract moral principles surrounding human rights. Perry believes that Chinese protesters are actually more 'rule conscious' than 'right conscious'.[32] In other words, people protest in China because their perceived rules are broken or policies are not properly carried out, not because they want to secure 'their naturally endowed protections against state intrusion'.[33] As a result, Perry concludes, 'widespread popular protest in China points neither to an indigenous moral vacuum nor toward an epochal clash with state authority'.[34] Differing from some other studies, Perry's analysis puts popular protests in China into the category of what Coser calls 'realistic social conflicts' and, therefore, they are not regime threatening.

Most studies on Chinese contentious politics seem to argue that Chinese contentious political activities are primarily issue-driven and, therefore, are not a serious threat to the current political regime in China. Following traditional approaches toward social movements that are under 'the assumption that social movement operated outside of politics, attacked political institutions, and followed different mechanisms and processes than did institutional groups',[35] however, the authors argue that what motivates people to participate in environment-related protests in China has to be broader than specific issues themselves and that institution-related factors such as support of the political regime and trust of the government are important factors in understanding why people choose to participate in environmental protests in China. In other words, the authors believe that people in China, as people elsewhere in the situation of a street protest, tend to perceive growing social issues such as pollution to be linked to institutional deficiencies such as lack of government transparency or lack of trust in government. People who are willing to participate in environmental protests may very well have institutional issues on their mind. As a result, environmental protests in China may be more regime threatening than some people think.

---

[28] This is a viewpoint that was initially proposed by German Sociologist Georg Simmel.
[29] Lewis Coser, *The Functions of Social Conflict* (Glencoe, IL: The Free Press, 1956), pp. 151–152, 156.
[30] *Ibid.*, p. 80.
[31] Perry, 'Chinese conceptions of "rights"'.
[32] Elizabeth Perry, 'Studying Chinese politics: farewell to revolution?', *China Journal* 51, (2007), pp. 1–22.
[33] Perry, 'Chinese conceptions of "rights"', p. 46.
[34] *Ibid.*, p. 47.
[35] Sidney Tarrow, 'Prologue: the new contentious politics in China: poor and blank or rich and complex', in O'Brien, ed., *Popular Protest in China*, p. 9.

Research design and data

This research is not a comprehensive study of why people participate in street protest in China. Rather it tests two hypotheses on likely participants of street protests over a potential environmental issue in urban China. Even though there have been a number of studies on protest activities in China, few have approached the issue of motivations for people's participation in street protest activities in a systematically empirical fashion. The main reason for the lack of such empirical studies rests in the difficulties with data collection. It is not feasible to conduct extensive interviews or surveys among protest participants while the protest is still going on. Even if it can be done, the interviews or survey would not include non-participants who face the same protesting issue but decide not to participate in the protest. It is also difficult to conduct surveys among participants and non-participants after the protest is over since it is almost impossible to identify the protest participants who would be reluctant to come forward for fear of reprisal. A substitute or proxy for surveying actual protest participants is an experimental survey study of likely protest participants and compares them with people who are less likely to participate in street protests. The main assumption in this article is that people who say they would choose to participate in street protest are more likely to do so, while those who say they would not opt for participating in street protests are unlikely to take part in such activities.

Data for this research were collected in a random telephone survey covering 34 large cities throughout China, most of which are provincial capital cities.[36] The cities represent different regions and different levels of economic development. The survey was carried out between April and May of 2013 by the Center for Public Opinion Research of Shanghai Jiao Tong University. The sample size for each city is 100 people, totaling 3,400 from all 34 cities. The sampling frame includes both landline and cell phone numbers in these cities. The Computer Assisted Telephone Interview (CATI) system generated random telephone numbers. Trained graduate and undergraduate students at Shanghai Jiao Tong University and several other surrounding universities in Shanghai conducted the anonymous survey. The dataset is truly unique in the sense that these kinds of large cross-regional scientific random surveys with political questions are not often carried out in mainland China.

Surveyees' responses can be influenced by city-level factors such as the level of economic development or the actual air pollution level as well as individual-level factors. To address this hierarchical structure of our data and explain variation across cities, this article employs a multilevel logit model with varying intercepts.

A related issue in this survey analysis is the potential social desirability bias. That is whether respondents in these types of surveys may freely express themselves in an authoritarian country like China. Survey experience in China tells us that if the questions are too sensitive in the Chinese context, it is problematic to judge whether Chinese respondents do indeed give truthful answers. However, the authors do not believe that our survey questions are too sensitive to be asked in the current political atmosphere in China. Moreover, the survey was conducted over the telephone (instead of face-to-face) in an anonymous fashion to ensure that respondents gave truthful answers. In addition, since this bias is associated with under-reporting of respondents' willingness to participate in street protests, we are likely to fail to find significant relationships between issue/institution-related factors and a respondent's probability of participating in street protest, not the other way around. Nevertheless, as the results show in the following sections, there are some institutional variables that reveal a strong positive impact on street protest, which implies that the real impact of these variables on the probability of street protest could be bigger than we observe in the results, if the social desirability bias exists. Therefore, even if this bias exists, the survey analysis still provides us with valuable information about contentious politics in China.[37]

---

[36]The following is the list of the surveyed cities: Beijing, Shanghai, Tianjin, Chongqing, Changchun, Changsha, Chengdu, Dalian, Fuzhou, Guangzhou, Guizhou, Harbin, Haikou, Hangzhou, Hefei, Huhhot, Jinan, Kunming, Lanzhou, Nanchang, Nanjing, Nanning, Ningbo, Qingdao, Shenyang, Shenzhen, Shijiazhuang, Taiyuan, Wuhan, Xian, Xining, Xiamen, Yinchuan and Zhengzhou.

[37]On survey research in China, see Melanie Manion, 'A survey of survey research on Chinese politics: what have we learned?', in Allen Carlson, Mary Gallagher, Kenneth Lieberthal and Melanie Manion, eds, *Contemporary Chinese Politics: New Sources, Methods and Field Strategies* (New York: Cambridge University Press, 2010), pp. 181–200.

Table 1. Willingness to participate in street protests (%).

	Do nothing	Contacting local people's congress deputies	Contacting local government officials	Mobilizing neighbors to contact local government officials	Participating in street protests	Other options
If a polluting accident happens in your area, what would be your first choice of action?	4.1	4.9	16.3	48.3	19.8	6.6

Note: *N*=3,400.

Willingness to take to the streets in environmental protests

The survey asks a straightforward question on people's willingness to take to the streets in protest: 'If a polluting accident happens in your living area, what would be your first choice of action to get the problem solved?'. The respondents were asked to choose one of the following six options: (1) no action; (2) personally contacting local people's congress representatives; (3) personally contacting local government officials; (4) mobilizing neighbors to contact local government officials; (5) participating directly in street protest to get the problem solved; or (6) other options. The authors fully realize that people in reality may pursue multiple venues and tactics to solve this problem. However, the central concern in this study is to find out how willing people are to participate in street protests. The authors feel that this question, in which our respondents were forced to choose just one option, can best capture their propensity or willingness to take part in street protests.

The survey finds that close to 20% of the respondents chose street protest as their first option while the rest preferred other options in dealing with a hypothetical polluting incident (see Table 1). Obviously it does not mean that people who say they would participate in street protests will actually do so in reality. However, it is logical to assume that those who say they would take part in street protests are more likely to do so in reality than those who do not choose street protests as their first option. Even though most people in our survey did not choose street protests as their first option to deal with a pollution problem, it is still significant that one fifth of our surveyed urban residents did. For a mega city like Shanghai with over 20 million residents, this means that 4 million of them are willing or have the propensity to participate in street protests. Even if a small fraction of those people do actually participate in real street demonstrations, the impact or consequence can be significant. It should be noted that, even though most street protests are tolerated by the Chinese authorities,[38] this form of contentious political activity is still considered unconventional and carries some political risk in China. For example, participants in street protests may be black-listed as 'trouble makers', which will affect their career, especially for those who work in the state sectors (government, universities, hospitals, state-owned enterprises, etc.). In addition, it is still possible that participants in street protests may be detained or arrested if the authorities decide to crackdown on the demonstration, especially when the protest turns less civil or even violent. Local government, which handles most street protests, is less tolerant than the central government in China.[39] Moreover, it is much harder for people in authoritarian countries to organize protest activities.[40] The sheer percentage of people who expressed their willingness to protest on the streets indicates that there is deep dissatisfaction with the official channels of interest articulation among Chinese urban residents. Willingness to participate in street protests

[38]Shaohua Lei, *Contentious Politics and Political Stability in China: An Institutional Explanation,* unpublished Ph.D. dissertation, The University of Utah, 2013, p. 155.

[39]Cai, *Collective Resistance in China*, p. 32.

[40]Ruth Kricheli, Yair Livne and Beatriz Magaloni, 'Taking to the streets: theory and evidence on protests under authoritarianism', paper presented at the annual meeting of the American Political Science Association, 2–5 September 2010, available at: http://ssrn.com/abstract=1642040 (accessed 12 July 2015).

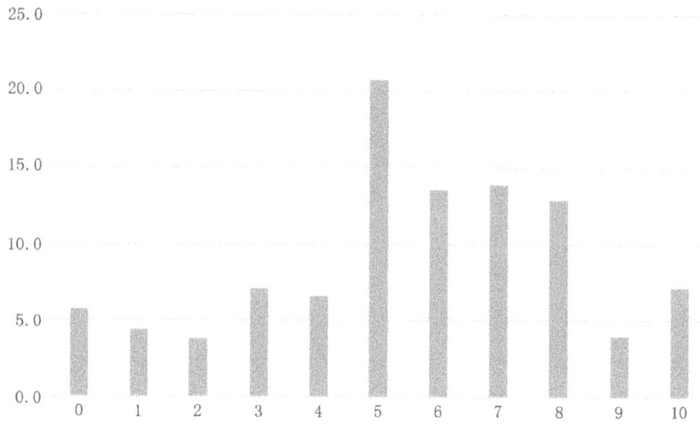

Figure 1. Subjective evaluation of city pollution level (%).

as the first option in dealing with a hypothetical pollution problem is used as the binary dependent variable in our multilevel logit analysis in this study.

Multivariate analysis

The central question to be answered in this study is why, facing the same or similar issues, some people choose street protests as their preferred option while others do not? Specifically, the authors are interested in the motivating factors behind people's intention to participate in environment-related street protests. This article designed three models to test the hypotheses. The first model consists of variables at the individual level, such as age, gender, education, communist party membership, personal wellbeing and level of political interest. The second model includes an additional cluster of environment-related issues. In the survey people were asked a number of questions concerning urban residents' feelings about environmental pollution and issues. First, the survey asked respondents to grade the pollution level in their city (from 0 to 10). More than half of Chinese urban residents in our surveyed cities graded the pollution level in their city above five (see Figure 1). When asked how pollution in their city affects their personal health, 16.6% believe the pollution in their city brings serious harm to their health, 51.4% claim it brings some harm, 28% say there is not much harm or no harm, and 4.1% do not know.

The survey next wanted to know how much knowledge our respondents have about environmental pollution. The authors presume that if people are concerned with the environment, they would like to know more about what leads to environmental pollution. Particular matters, especially particles less than 2.5 micrometers in diameter ($PM_{2.5}$), are extremely harmful to one's health.[41] Many Chinese cities have been plagued by $PM_{2.5}$ in recent years. When asked how familiar they are about $PM_{2.5}$, our respondents' answers are split in the middle. About half of them claimed they know a lot (2.2%) or some (42.9%) about $PM_{2.5}$, and the rest had basically no idea (45.1%) or absolutely no idea (4.2%) about it. More people in our survey claim that they know some or a lot about the general causes of pollution (78.1% and 5.5%, respectively).

The authors also believe that if one cares about the environment enough, he or she is willing to sacrifice material gains, time and money to protect and improve the environment. Development and environmental protection are often pitted against each other. China's double-digit economic growth in the last 30 years comes with a high cost in environmental degradation. Deng Xiaoping's famous saying 'development is the hard truth' is the central policy of the Chinese government in the reform era. How do Chinese urban residents feel about the trade-off between economic development and protection

[41]On the harmful effects of $PM_{2.5}$ see information provided by the US Environmental Protection Agency, available at: http://www.epa.gov/ttn/naaqs/pm/pm25_index.html (accessed 28 January 2014).

Table 2. Willingness to protect the environment (%).

	Very willing	Willing	Unwilling	Very unwilling	Hard to say
Willingness to sort garbage	15.5	76.9	3.7	0.3	3.6
Willingness to bring shopping bags to supermarket	16.1	71.0	8.6	0.3	4.0
Willingness to donate to environmental groups	2.7	60.8	18.2	1.3	17.0
Willingness to volunteer for environmental groups	4.5	72.8	13.3	0.4	9.2

Note: *N*=3,400.

of the environment? When asked what is more important: economic development or environmental protection, only 11.2% chose the former, while 77.2% preferred the latter, and the rest did not know how to answer the question. In the survey people were also asked about their willingness to help with the environment with some specific actions. Most of our respondents do express their willingness to protect the environment. The four items concerning willingness to improve the environment (see Table 2) are combined to form an additive index as the variable of environmental participation in the multivariate analysis.

If environment-related street protests in China are purely or mostly issue-driven, it would have to be assumed that people who are more concerned with pollution and the harm that pollution causes, who are more knowledgeable about pollution issues, who put environmental protection ahead of economic development and who are more willing to help in the endeavor to improve the environment, are more likely to participate in an environmental protest.

The third model adds some institutional factors. Traditional studies on why people participate in protests have focused on institution-related factors, such as lack of social justice and fairness, relative deprivation and distrust of authorities.[42] It is believed that, even though a protest activity may be triggered by an incident over a non-political issue, people who tend to participate in the protest are partially motivated by their feelings about the governing authorities and institutions. Specifically, this article hypothesizes that support for the political regime, trust of government, perceived governmental transparency and support for democracy are positively associated with Chinese urban residents' willingness to participate in street protests over an environmental issue.

This article measures urban residents' regime support by asking them a straightforward question on their attitudes toward system change. Respondents in the survey were provided with three general statements and were asked to choose one to describe their attitude toward the existing system in China. The three statements are: (1) We have many serious problems in our country, and we must fundamentally reform the current system; (2) We indeed have some problems in our country, and we should adopt gradual reform measures to improve the current system; and (3) Our country is basically good, and we should maintain the status quo so that destructive forces cannot harm the current system.

The authors believe that these three carefully designed statements can detect our Chinese urban residents' true attitudes and feelings toward the current political regime in China.[43] Around a quarter (25.6%) of respondents chose the first statement, indicating that they prefer fundamental change and lack of support for the current system in China. A plurality majority (43.7%) of respondents favored the second statement, indicating that they are moderates and prefer non-revolutionary change to the current system. A fraction (1.4%) of the surveyed opted for the *status quo* while the rest (29.2%) chose 'hard to say'. The authors coded preference for fundamental system change as '0' and coded all other responses as '1' for the *regime support* variable.

Another institutional factor used in the multivariate analysis is the trust of government. A number of surveys done in China over the last two decades have shown that levels of political trust among

[42]Tom R. Tyler and H. J. Smith, 'Social justice and social movements', in Daniel Gilbert, Susan Fiske and Gardner Lindzey, eds, *Handbook of Social Psychology* (New York: McGraw-Hill, 1998), pp. 595–629; Robert Folger, 'Rethinking equity theory: a referent cognitions model', in Hans Werner Bierhoff, Ronald Cohen and Jerald Greenberg, eds, *Justice in Social Relations* (New York: Plenum, 1986), pp. 145–162; Gurr, *Why Men Rebel*; Berkowitz, 'Frustrations, comparisons, and other sources of emotion aroused as contributors to social unrest', pp. 77–92.

[43]Yand Zhong and Yongguo Chen, 'Regime support in urban China', *Asian Survey* 53, (2013), pp. 369–392.

Table 3. Levels of political trust among Chinese urban residents (%).

	Strongly disagree	Disagree	Neutral	Agree	Strongly agree	Hard to say	*N*
The central government always tries to do the right things for the people	0.3	7.5	11.7	62.9	10.3	7.2	3,400
The municipal government in your city always tries to do the right things for the people	0.7	13.0	16.0	53.2	6.6	10.5	3,400

Chinese citizens toward the Chinese government and institutions are actually relatively high even though the questions asked in the surveys concerning political trust were phrased differently.[44] A survey conducted as far back as in 1993 shows that 70% of Chinese citizens trusted decisions made by their central government.[45] In fact, the World Value Survey shows that trust of political institutions among Chinese citizens is higher than the world averages.[46] However, anecdotal evidence seems to suggest that lack of trust on local government is a major factor in environmental protests in China. This article measures political trust of both the central government and local government among Chinese urban residents by asking them to agree or disagree with the following statements: 'The central government always tries to do the right things for the people' and 'The municipal government in your city always tries to do the right things for the people'. It is believed that these statements, which are based on a political trust question asked in the US National Election Studies (NES) survey,[47] are sufficient to capture the essence of political trust of the central government and the local government among Chinese urbanites. The majority of respondents agree that they trusted the central and local governments to do the right things for the people, even though the trust level of the central government is higher than that of the local government (see Table 3).

A third institutional factor is popular support for electoral democracy among Chinese urban residents. China currently is not a Western-style democracy and its national leaders are not directly elected by the population. Chinese intellectuals have long debated whether Chinese culture is suited for democracy, given China's long history of authoritarian tradition. Do Chinese people, especially the urban dwellers, support democracy? The survey examined respondents' attitudes toward democracy by asking them to agree or disagree with the statement regarding whether Chinese top leaders should be democratically elected directly by the people. More than half of our Chinese urban respondents either strongly favored (9.0%) or favored (47.7%) the direct election of Chinese top leaders, 17.2% were opposed to it, while the remaining 26.2% remained neutral.

The last institutional factor concerns perceived governmental transparency on environmental issues. Transparency in governmental affairs is believed to be associated with people's trust in government.[48] Lack of government transparency also seems to be a central theme in several large-scale environmental street protests in the last several years in China.[49] This article measured perceived governmental

[44]Lianjiang Li, 'The object and substance of trust in central leaders: preliminary evidence from a pilot survey', paper presented at the Annual Meeting of the American Political Science Association, Seattle, Washington, 1–4 September 2011.

[45]Tianjian Shi, 'Cultural values and political trust: a comparison of the People's Republic of China and Taiwan', *Comparative Politics* 33(3), (2001), pp. 401–419.

[46]Yang Qing and Wenfang Tang, 'Exploring the sources of institutional trust in China: culture, mobilization, or performance?', *Asian Politics and Policy* 2(3), (2010), pp. 415–436.

[47]The question asked in the National Election Studies survey is: 'How much of the time do you think you can trust the government in Washington to do what is right?' See Gabriela Catterberg and Alejandro Moreno, 'The individual bases of political trust: trends in new and established democracies', *International Journal of Public Opinion Research* 18(1), (2005), pp. 31–48.

[48]Yang Zhong, 'Do Chinese people trust their local government and why? An empirical study of political trust in urban China', *Problems of Post-Communism* 61(3), (2014), pp. 31–44.

[49]Lack of governmental transparency was a major cause for the large protests against the proposed and existing polluting chemical and power plants in Xiamen, Dalian and Kunming.

transparency by asking our respondents to assess whether the government is transparent with environmental issues and policies. The survey reveals that 31.3% of Chinese urban respondents did not think the government is transparent with regard to environmental issues, 31.4% remained neutral on this issue, and the remaining 37.4% did believe that the government is forthcoming with issues related to the environment.

Finally, this article included two control variables at the city level. One is level of economic development as represented by Gross Domestic Product per capita for the 34 cities included in our study.[50] It is anticipated that, since economic development fosters post-modern values such as concern with the environment,[51] people living in more economically developed cities are more likely to participate in environment-related street protests. Another city-level variable is the level of air pollution in the 34 cities between January and April before the survey was conducted.[52] It is logical to assume that a higher air pollution level is positively related to people's willingness to take part in environmental protests.

To perform a multilevel analysis with the binary dependent variable, this article employs a multilevel logit model. The multilevel logit model can be written in the general form $\pi_{ij} = f(X_{ij}\beta_j)$, where π_{ij} is the probability that the *i*-th individual in the *j*-th city is associated with willingness to participate in street protest; *f* is a nonlinear function (logit link function) of the linear predictor $X_{ij}\beta_j$. It is needed to specify a distribution for the observed response $Y_{ij}|\pi_{ij}$ The Y_{ij} are the observed (0,1) responses with the standard assumption that they are binomially distributed y_{ij}~$Binomial(n_{ij}, \pi_{ij})$ where n_{ij} is the denominator for the probability π_{ij}. It is also assumed that $\mathrm{var}(y_{ij}|\pi_{ij}) = \pi_{ij}(1-\pi_{ij})/n_{ij}$. The model including individual-level variations can be written as $y_{ij} = \pi_{ij} + \varepsilon_{ij}x_0$, where x_0 is used to specify the variation at the first level. With the assumptions that the n_{ij} are all equal to 1 and x_0 is also equal to 1, the variance of individual level random term ε_{ij} is $\pi_{ij}(1-\pi_{ij})$. Full details can be found in the works by Goldstein, Rodriguez and Goldman, and Rasbash *et al.*[53]

In the two-level logit model, the probability π_{ij} is defined as a function of the intercept and a series of individual-level predictors:

$$\mathrm{logit}(\pi_{ij}) = \beta_{oj} + \beta_1 * Trust_{ij} + ... + \varepsilon_{ij} \quad (1)$$

Additionally, the intercept is a function of city-level predictors, *GDP per capita* and *Air pollution* variables:

$$\beta_{oj} = \gamma_0 + \gamma_1 * GDPPC_j + \gamma_2 * AirPollution_j + \mu_{0j}. \quad (2)$$

This specification allows the intercept term, β_{0j}, to be a function of the city-level variables. That is, GDP per capita and the air pollution level measured in each city are assumed to affect the baseline probability of willingness to participate in street protests in different cities. To simplify the model, Equation (2) is substituted into Equation (1):

$$\mathrm{logit}(\pi_{ij}) = \gamma_o + \beta_1 * Trust_{ij} + \ldots + \gamma_1 * GDPPC_j + \gamma_2 * AirPollution_j + \mu_{0j} + \varepsilon_{ij}. \quad (3)$$

In this equation, γ_0 denotes the intercept. The multilevel disturbance term is composed of the two different components: μ_{0j} the city-level disturbance and ε_{ij} the individual-level disturbance. As a result, the multilevel disturbance term does not have constant variance. By testing whether μ_{0j} is statistically different from zero, which means that there are no remaining variances to be explained at the city level, it can be checked whether city-level predictors are good measures of explaining causal heterogeneity.

[50]Specifically, this variable is the annual GDP per capita of the 34 cities in 2012, obtained from the government websites of the 34 cities.

[51]Ronald Inglehart, *Modernization and Postmodernization: Cultural, Economic, and Political Change in 43 Societies* (Princeton, NJ: Princeton University Press, 1997).

[52]Data for this variable come from China National Environmental Monitor Center, available at: http://www.cnemc.cn/ (accessed 28 October 2013).

[53] Harvey Goldstein, *Multilevel Statistical Models* (New York: The Americas by Halsted Press, 1995); German Rodríguez and Noreen Goldman, 'An assessment of estimation procedures for multilevel models with binary responses', *Journal of Royal Statistical Society* 158(1), (1995), pp. 73–89; Jon Rasbash, William Browne, Harvey Goldstein, Min Yang, Ian Plewis, Michael Healy, Geoff Woodhouse, David Draper, Ian Langford and Toby Lewis, *A User's Guide to MLwiN* (Centre for Multilevel Modelling, Institute of Education, London: University of London, 2002).

Table 4. Pollution, institutions and street protestation in urban China (34 cities).

DV: street protestation	Model 1 (Individual-related)	Model 2 (Issue-related)	Model 3 (Institution-related)
Fixed effects			
Individual level			
Political interest	−0.063 (0.041)	−0.068 (0.058)	−0.058 (0.059)
Personal wellbeing	−0.184 (0.054)***	−0.167 (0.055)***	−0.113 (0.057)**
Male	0.127 (0.090)	0.119 (0.094)	0.097 (0.096)
Age	−0.063 (0.041)	−0.067 (0.043)	−0.060 (0.043)
Education	0.048 (0.074)	0.027 (0.077)	−0.029 (0.075)
Party membership	−0.110 (0.127)	−0.104 (0.128)	−0.086 (0.127)
Perceived pollution level		0.034 (0.018)*	0.019 (0.018)
Harm to personal health		0.061 (0.058)	0.025 (0.058)
Knowledge of causes of pollution		−0.016 (0.085)	−0.039 (0.086)
Knowledge of PM 2.5		0.039 (0.070)	0.010 (0.071)
Environmental protection over economic development		0.141 (0.106)	0.142 (0.110)
Environmental participation		−0.068 (0.047)	−0.058 (0.049)
Government transparency			−0.265 (0.052)***
Trust in the central government			−0.117 (0.067)*
Trust in the local government			−0.145 (0.064)***
Support for the system			−0.274 (0.097)***
Support for democracy			0.115 (0.121)
City level			
Constant	−0.867 (0.423)**	−1.055** (0.453)	0.940 (0.552)*
GDP per capita	0.050 (0.024)**	0.044 (0.023)**	0.037 (0.024)
Air pollution	−0.0005 (0.030)	−0.015 (0.030)	−0.002 (0.030)
Random effects			
City level	0.034 (0.028)	0.030 (0.027)	0.031 (0.027)
N	3,400	3,400	3,400
DIC	3,372.02	3,374.87	3,324.48

Notes: Multilevel analysis with MCMC estimation (50,000 iterations, 10,000 burn-in period). Standard errors are in parentheses. Significant credibility intervals: *** 99%, ** 95%, * 90%.

The individual-level disturbance variance is given as one, which means the model is fitted to have a binomial error distribution. To identify the multilevel model, this article assumes zero covariance between individual and city-level disturbances.

Estimation

Since the likelihood of the observed data in a binary dependent variable model does not have a closed-form expression in general, it is necessary to use approximate methods of estimation. Also, since quasi-likelihood methods tend to produce biased estimates, this article employs a Bayesian simulation method (i.e. Markov chain Monte Carlo estimation).[54] Specifically, the model is fit by the second-order penalized quasi-likelihood (PQL) procedure to obtain estimates. Then, using these estimates as starting values and vague prior distributional assumptions for the model parameters, this article simulates and generates parameter estimates with a burn-in period of 10,000 iterations followed by 50,000 iterations for the estimates. The *MLwiN* statistical package and its associated *Stata* program are used to obtain these estimates.[55]

Results

Table 4 reports test results in three different models in which different sets of variables at the individual level are included along with two city-level variables. In Model 1, this article includes only

[54]George Leckie and Chris Charlton, 'Runmlwin: a program to run the MLwiN multilevel modeling software from within Stata', *Journal of Statistical Software* 52(11), (2012), pp. 1–40.
[55]Rasbash *et al.*, *A User's Guide to MLwiN*; Leckie and Charlton, 'Runmlwin'.

individual-related variables, while pollution-related variables and institution-related variables are added to Model 2 and Model 3, respectively. With respect to individual-related variables, only *personal wellbeing* is statistically significant in all three models. As people feel happier, they are less likely to participate in street protests. Other than this variable, all other individual and issue-related variables (except for one) are not statistically significant at the 5% significance level. In the first two models, the GDP per capital variable is statistically significant. That is, as the level of economic development increases, cities have higher baseline chances to face pollution-related street protests. This result implies that people tend to pay more attention to the pollution issue when economic development becomes a less salient issue in the city.

The theoretical claim centers on the relationship between perceptions of institutions and willingness to participate in street protest. In Model 3, *transparency, trust in the central government, trust in the local government* and *support for the system* are all statistically significant and have their expected signs. However, *support for democracy* is not significantly related to people's propensity in taking part in street protests. As the perceived governmental transparency, trust in both local and central governments or regime support declines, people are more likely to participate in street protests. To measure the impact of these variables on willingness to participate in street protests, this article estimates predicted probabilities of street protestation at different levels of perceived government transparency, trust in both central and local governments, and regime support. To this end, the authors fix all other variables at their means (continuous or ordinal variables) or mode (binary variables) except *education* at three (two or four year college education) and *age* at three (30–39 years old).

This article reports four figures to effectively demonstrate the overall effects of these government-related variables on the predicted probability of people's participating in street protests. Figure 2 shows the predicted probabilities that those who trust in their local governments and support the current system are likely to participate in street protests at different levels of government transparency. Figure 3 shows the predicted probabilities that those who do not trust in their local government and do not

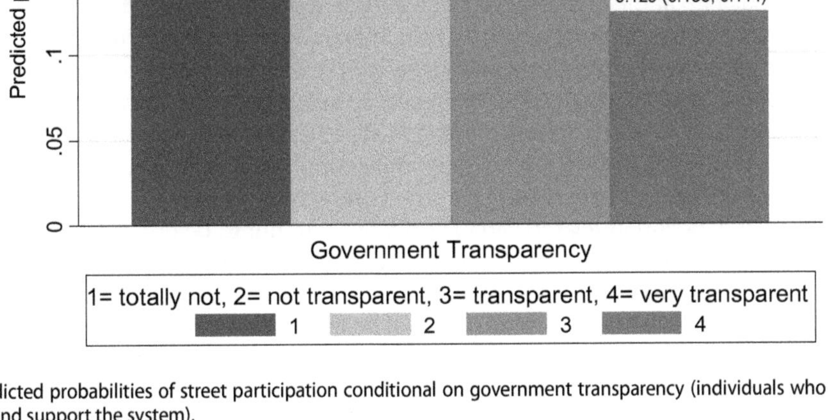

Figure 2. Predicted probabilities of street participation conditional on government transparency (individuals who trust the local government and support the system).
Notes: To estimate the predicted probabilities, we fix all other variables at their means or modes except 'Trust in the local government' at five (i.e. great trust) and 'Support for the system' at one (i.e. support the system); 95% CI in parentheses.

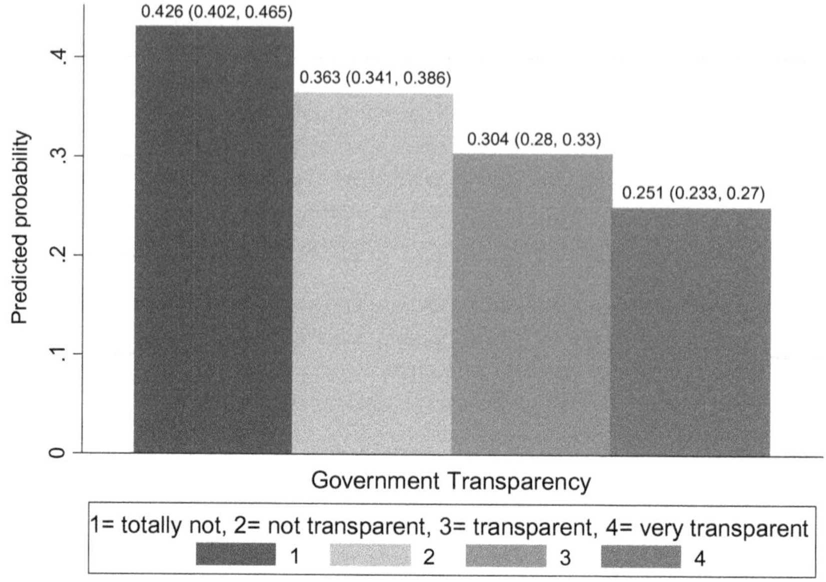

Figure 3. Predicted probabilities of street participation conditional on government transparency (individuals who do not trust the local government at all and do not support the system).
Notes: To estimate the predicted probabilities, we fix all other variables at their means or modes except 'Trust in the local governments' at one (i.e. do not trust at all) and 'Support for the system' at zero (i.e. do not support the system); 95% CI in parentheses.

support the current system are likely to participate in street protests at different levels of government transparency.

As seen in these figures, the difference is striking. When those who trust in their local government and support the current system perceive their government to be transparent, holding their trust in the central government at its mean value, the predicted probability of participation in a street protest is only about 12% in Figure 2. However, this probability increases up to 24% when the transparency level of the local government is minimal. Moreover, when those who do not trust in their local government and do not support the current system perceive their government to be not transparent at all, the predicted probability of participating in a street protest increases up to 42%, as shown in Figure 3. Figure 4 shows the predicted probabilities that those who strongly trust in both local and central governments and support the current system are likely to participate in street protests at different levels of government transparency (about 11% at the highest level of government transparency), while Figure 5 shows the same predicted probabilities for those who trust in neither government and do not support the system (about 51% at the lowest level of government transparency).[56] Between supporters and non-supporters of the political regime, there is about 4.5% difference in their probabilities of street protestation participation (19% and 23.5% for each group), holding trust in the local and central government variables at their mean values. Overall, these results highlight the importance of institution-related variables in explaining people's willingness to participate in street protests.

On the other hand, pollution-related variables did not turn out to be good predictors of people's willingness to participate in street protests in our multivariate analysis. *Perceived pollution level* has its expected positive sign and is only weakly statistically significant in Model 2 but very insignificant in Model 3. Even though perceived harm to personal health, favoring environmental protection and knowledge of $PM_{2.5}$ variables have positive signs, they do not have a statistically meaningful impact on willingness to participate in street protests. These results imply that it is not necessarily the actual

[56]It is likely that trust in the central government is highly correlated with trust in local governments. To see whether multicollinearity affects performance of these variables, the authors re-estimated Model 3 by including each variable separately as a robustness test. The results remain the same.

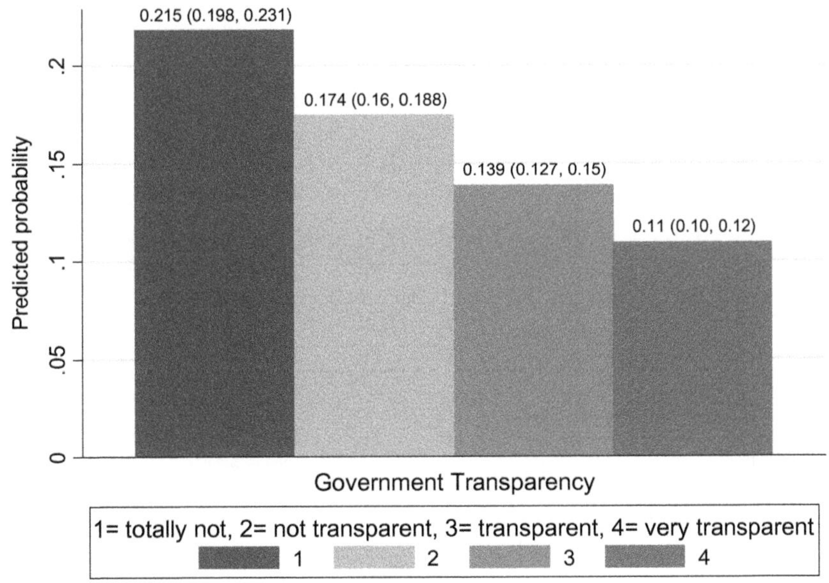

Figure 4. Predicted probabilities of street participation conditional on government transparency (individuals who trust both local and central governments and support the system).

Notes: To estimate the predicted probabilities, we fix all other variables at their means or modes except 'Trust in the central government' and 'Trust in the local government' at 5 (i.e. great trust) and 'Support for the system' at one (i.e. support the system); 95% CI in parentheses.

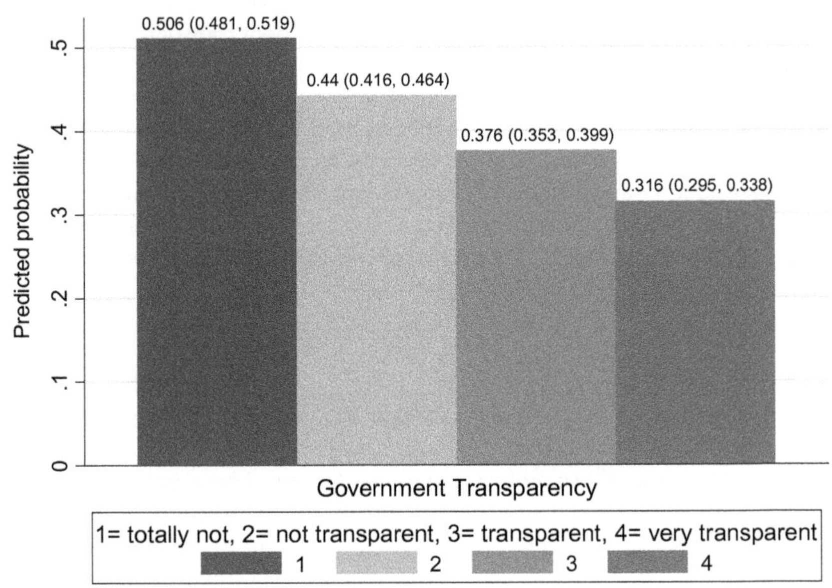

Figure 5. Predicted probabilities of street participation conditional on government transparency (individuals who do not trust the local and central governments at all and do not support the system).

Notes: To estimate the predicted probabilities, we fix all other variables at their means or modes except 'Trust in the central government' and 'Trust in the local government' at one (i.e. do not trust at all) and 'Support for the system' at zero (i.e. do not support the system); 95% CI in parentheses.

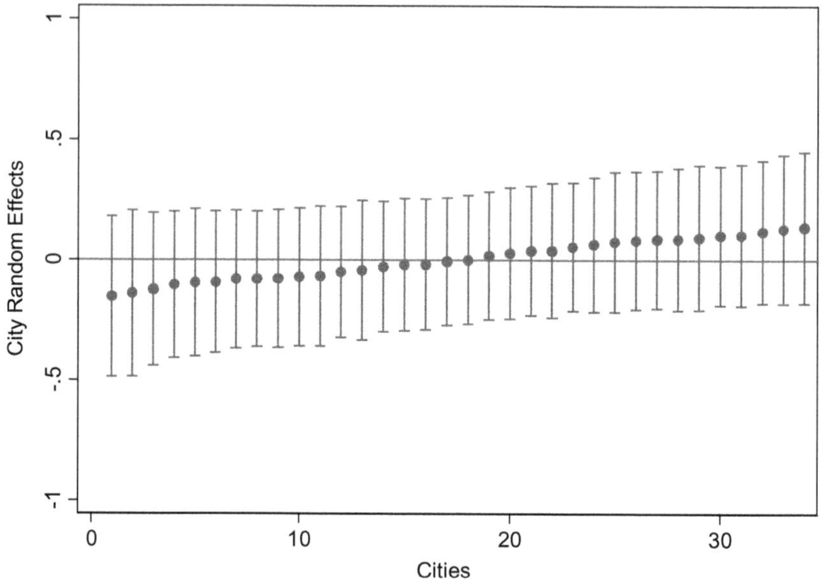

Figure 6. City random effects.
Note: This caterpillar plot shows 34 city level residuals (random effects), one for each city in the dataset. These residuals represent city departures from the overall average line predicted by the fixed parameters. Since the 95% credibility intervals for all residuals include zero, this means that all cities do not differ significantly from the average lines.

pollution issues or people's understanding of these issues that are associated with people's willingness to participate in street protests over pollution. Rather, it is their trust of the government, (dis)satisfaction with (or support for) the current system, and perceived government transparency that mostly explain their decision to take to the streets.

In all three models, random effects at the city level are not statistically significant. This implies that there is no remaining variance to be explained at the city level. To examine how random effects in each city differ significantly from the average city random effects, this article reports a caterpillar plot that shows 34 city-level residuals (random effects) using Model 3 (see Figure 6). These residuals represent city departures from the overall average line predicted by the fixed parameters. Since the 95% credibility intervals for all residuals include zero, this means that all the cities in this study do not differ significantly from the average lines, and also that the two-level model has a good fit to the data.

Conclusion

Contentious political activities have been on a dramatic rise in China. However, scholars differ on the nature of these activities. Some argue that these protesting activities are serious threats to stability in China, while others believe that these protests are primarily issue-driven and do not pose any serious threat to the Chinese political system. Unlike studies which try to explain the increase of protest activities in China, this article focuses on what motivates people to participate in street protest. In this study the authors try to differentiate between environmental street protests and other types of street protests that center on land issues or labor disputes. Using survey data from 34 Chinese cities, this article tries to explain why, facing environmental problems, some people choose to participate in street protests while others opt otherwise or who are more likely to participate in street protests in dealing with the same environmental issue.

Descriptive findings reveal that about 20% of surveyed urban residents choose street protests as their first option to deal with a hypothetical environmental problem in their area. This is not a comforting number for the Chinese government because it shows that a sizable portion of the Chinese urban population are potential street demonstrators or tend to use street protests to voice their concern. More importantly, findings from multilevel analysis show that institutional factors play a more important role in explaining the willingness of Chinese urban residents to take part in street protests. Specifically, people who prefer more fundamental change of the Chinese system, have less trust in the government and are more dissatisfied with government transparency, are more willing to take to the streets in protestation. In contrast, environment-related factors such as general concern with environmental degradation, knowledge of environmental problems and preference for environmental protection over economic development are not positively related to people's willingness to participate in a street protest in a hypothetical environmental accident.

Such multivariate analytical findings indicate that street protests in China are not purely issue-driven and they are related to institutional settings. What motivates people to participate in street protests has a lot to do with their feelings about the political system. In other words, these protests are not just what Coser calls 'realistic conflicts' which primarily involve specific issues and solutions. One implication from our study is that street protests in China may not be benign and as non-regime threatening as some scholars think. Since this study examines environmental issues only and their impact on street protests, there is a limitation in generalizing findings in this research into all different types of issues and protests. At the same time, however, it is also noticeable that, even though protest events are more often triggered by a specific issue or incident, they have the potential to spill over to other more general issues to become protestation against the regime if protesting participants are motivated by institutional factors. This may be particularly true for large-scale environmental protests. We should not forget that the massive demonstrations against the authoritarian regime in Tunisia in January 2011 were triggered by a small incident involving a policeman mistreating a young street vendor. This article also finds that people's willingness to participate in street protests is not associated with people's democratic value or preference for a democratic system, suggesting that social conflicts in China may not have become 'unrealistic conflicts' that involve fundamental ideological beliefs and values..

Pushing the Envelope for Representation and Participation: the case of homeowner activism in Beijing

YOUSUN CHUNG

This article discusses the evolution of urban homeowner activism in two senses: internally (growth through internal diversity) and externally (advancement in interaction with the state). The combination of these two aspects has directed the activism toward the expansion of its boundaries, as well as advanced representation and participation. Based on cumulative fieldwork carried out since 2007, I discuss two homeowner organizations in Beijing as core cases. Rights activism by homeowners has grown beyond the state-set boundaries of individual neighborhoods and has begun deploying innovative strategies and adapting existing institutions for its own use. Rights awareness and manifestation by social actors has evolved continuously. This evolution suggests the emergence of a complex interplay between state and society which goes beyond a confrontational or lopsided relationship.

Introduction

Housing commodification in China since the late 1990s has led to the emergence of a new social group of urban middle-class homeowners. Becoming aware of their rights as consumers, these homeowners started to form organizations that could uphold their property interests. According to the Regulations on Property Management (*wuye guanli tiaoli*), each neighborhood was permitted to elect representatives, based on the majority decision of individuals who own properties in that neighborhood. As bodies representing homeowners, homeowners' committees (*yezhu weiyuanhui*) organized various activities to defend homeowners' interests and rights over their properties, including petitions, litigation and even collective action.[1] To be brief, homeowner

1. For instance, see Benjamin L. Read, 'Democratizing the neighborhood? New private housing and homeowner self-organization in urban China', *The China Journal* 49, (2003), pp. 31–59; Fayong Shi and Yongshun Cai, 'Disaggregating the state: networks and collective resistance in Shanghai', *The China Quarterly* 186, (2006), pp. 314–332.

activism in its early phase was consumer activism in the newly built commodified residential compounds (*shangpinfang xiaoqu*).

The new empirical phenomenon highlighted in this article is the appearance of a kind of homeowner activism which has developed beyond the state-set boundaries of individual neighborhoods and pushed rights activism toward advanced representation and participation. Having started by organizing contentious activities against developers or management providers within individual neighborhoods, homeowners are now attempting to influence local governance. Behind this growth and expansion of activism lies the emergence of organizational linkages among homeowners across neighborhoods or even across different localities. In large Chinese cities, such as Beijing, Shanghai and Guangzhou, organizations have been set up that facilitate horizontal liaison among homeowners. These platforms have different formal titles and organizational forms: some take the form of research groups while others are consultancy firms or even very loose forums. Yet they commonly work to defend homeowners' interests in more effective ways.[2]

Considering that the Chinese state has always been extremely vigilant where the emergence of horizontal networks of social power is concerned,[3] the recent development of homeowner activism is particularly worthy of our attention. This prompts us to ask through what processes this breakthrough—the horizontal connection of social forces and their vertical engagement with the state in more skillful ways—has been possible, and what changes it brings to politics within neighborhoods and beyond. Understanding the evolution of homeowner activism will assist us to understand the diversified modes of interaction between state and society that are in constant flux. The evolution of social power—not as a finished outcome but as an ongoing process—reflects the complex interplay between the state and society, which transcends the dichotomous divisions of corporatism and civil society.

The remainder of this article is presented as follows. The next section proposes a framework for discussing two aspects of the growth and expansion of homeowner

2. In Guangzhou, one homeowner activist-led organization achieved formal legal status in 2010. 'NGO jiaoni jian yewei' ['NGO teaches you how to establish homeowners' committees'], *Nanfang Dushibao* [*Nanfang Metropolis Daily*], (29 August 2011), available at: http://gcontent.oeeee.com/4/4e/44ef2b50b3256d89/Blog/ef2/706e0a.html (accessed 14 October 2013); regarding the other entity which still does not have formal status, see Ngai-ming Yip and Yihong Jiang, 'Homeowners united: the attempt to create a lateral network of homeowners' associations in urban China', *Journal of Contemporary China* 20(72), (2011), pp. 735–750; Zhang Jingen and Zhuang Wenjia, 'Feizhengshi zhengzhi: yige caogen NGOde xingdong celue' ['Informal politics and action tactics of a grassroots NGO: a case study of the preparatory committee of Guangzhou proprietor committee's friendship association'], *Shehuixue Yanjiu* [*Sociology Studies*] 2, (2008), pp. 133–150. In Shanghai, there is an entity registered as a commercial company (consultancy firm) that has been developing horizontal linkages among homeowners in the city (interviews, Shanghai, 19 December 2007; 29 January 2010; 17 July 2012). Similar attempts are reported in many other cities including Xiamen, Wenzhou, Chengdu and Chongqing. For instance, see 'Woshi chengli yeweihuixiehui' ['Our city has established a Bidding Committee of the Association of Homeowners Committees'], *Wenzhou Dushibao* [*Wenzhou Metropolis Daily*], (5 January 2013), available at: http://dsb.66wz.com/html/2013-01/05/content_1371880.htm (accessed 14 October 2013).

3. Ching Kwan Lee and Yuan Shen, 'The paradox and possibility for a public sociology of labor in China', *Work and Occupations* 36(2), (2009), pp. 110–125. The development of homeowner activism contrasts starkly with an example mentioned in the work by Lee and Shen: a labor NGO in Shenzhen, which launched a joint signature campaign across the city, was soon banned. From this, we can surmise that the policy position of the Chinese leadership varies across different issue domains or different constituencies.

activism: (1) horizontal expansion accompanied by internal diversity; and (2) advanced strategic engagement with the state externally. The following section analyzes the evolution of homeowner activism in detail based on cumulative fieldwork carried out in Beijing between 2007 and 2012. Two representative organizations in Beijing are selected as core cases which demonstrate the growth and expansion of homeowner activism backed by internal diversity and external engagement. Empirical data have been gathered through in-depth interviews with core members of staff of these organizations and other relevant stakeholders. The article concludes with a summary of the implications of this study. The processes through which Beijing's homeowners have successfully repositioned themselves as active participants in local governance give us new insight into innovations in interaction between social actors and the state.

The evolving state–society relationship

That there is an uneasy balance between the socialist ideals ostensibly upheld by the state and the near-capitalism that is actually practiced in China is no surprise. As 'socialism with Chinese characteristics' continues to progress, more diversified actors from the market, such as urban middle-class consumers with purchasing power, must be included in our discussion of Chinese society. One question that follows from this is to what extent can these actors be independent of state power in their interest aggregation and articulation. The extent to which the economic autonomy of society can be transformed into political autonomy depends on the specific setting of the developing market. Especially in an environment such as China's, where the market is not completely independent from the influence of the state, it is questionable whether these new actors in the market can truly be autonomous.

Analysts of China have been interested in identifying social groups whose organizational activity is relatively independent of state power. More broadly, strenuous attempts have been made to discover a 'civil society' in China—a core feature of which is relative autonomy from the state. For instance, scholars have studied labor unions and business associations in an attempt to either prove or disprove such a possibility. Despite slight differences in the specific features of such organizations, on the whole they are found to have been more or less 'co-opted' by the state in one way or another.[4] It is also thought that associations and social organizations are more or less controlled through the mechanism of 'interest licensing'.[5]

4. Bruce J. Dickson, *Red Capitalists in China: The Party, Private Entrepreneurs, and Prospects for Political Change* (Cambridge: Cambridge University Press, 2003); Jude A. Howell, 'All-China Federation of Trades Unions beyond reform? The slow march of direct elections', *The China Quarterly* 196, (2008), pp. 845–863; Margaret M. Pearson, *China's New Business Elite: The Political Consequences of Economic Reform* (Berkeley, CA: University of California Press, 1997); Bill Taylor, Kai Chang and Qi Li, *Industrial Relations in China* (Cheltenham: Edward Elgar Publishing, 2003).

5. Qiusha Ma, *Non-governmental Organizations in Contemporary China: Paving the Way to Civil Society?* (London and New York: Routledge, 2006).

Other analysts have emphasized the ways in which Chinese society is different from that of the West.[6] These scholars argue that a semi-authoritarian setting does not merely restrict social activism, it is also conducive to a specific type of interest aggregation and articulation that avoids direct conflicts with the state. In addition, recent studies suggest that organizations in China manage to represent the interests of their constituents—albeit in a limited way—by skillfully maneuvering in the space between the party-state and society.[7]

As it is so difficult to draw a clear demarcation between state and society in China, and as we frequently observe interpenetration between the two, the traditional, dichotomous zero-sum formulations of state–society relations are gradually losing their persuasiveness.[8] On a related note, it is thought that the restrictive definition of civil society and social organizations, the core feature of which is opposition to the state, limits the scope of our discussions on state–society interaction.[9] While avoiding dichotomous views or putting an exclusive focus on autonomy, it is important for China scholars, and comparativists in general, to capture, conceptualize and explain the continuously changing modes of complex interaction between the state and society.[10]

Of the recent attempts to discuss the continuously changing modes of state–society interaction, one meaningful strand is concerned with dissecting the spaces between the state and society and examining the actors who maneuver in such spaces. Concepts such as 'institutional fields', 'organizational entrepreneurs'[11] and 'policy entrepreneurs'[12] suggest that there is a fragmented space not only between the state and society but also within these entities, and that there are actors who actively explore this kind of niche. Relational perspectives of state–society relations, which emphasize possible state–society partnerships or multi-faceted aspects of such relations, have also gained in persuasiveness.[13] In these recent studies, state–society relations are portrayed as mutually transformative and not necessarily lopsided.

6. Phillip Huang, '"Public sphere"/"civil society" in China? The third realm between state and society', *Modern China* 19, (1993), pp. 216–240; Thomas Heberer, 'Creating civil-society structures top-down?', in Jianxing Yu and Sujian Guo, eds, *Civil Society and Governance in China* (New York: Palgrave Macmillan, 2012), pp. 63–84.

7. Feng Chen, 'Legal mobilization by trade unions: the case of Shanghai', The China Journal 52, (2004), pp. 27–45; Xi Chen and Ping Xu, 'From resistance to advocacy: political representation for disabled people in China', *The China Quarterly* 207, (2011), pp. 649–667; Peter Ho, 'Introduction: embedded activism and political change in a semi-authoritarian context', in Peter Ho and Richard Edmonds, eds, *China's Embedded Activism: Opportunities and Constraints of a Social Movement* (London and New York: Routledge, 2008), pp. 1–19.

8. Richard Baum and Alexei Shevchenko, 'The "state of the state"', in Merle Goldman and Roderick MacFarquhar, eds, *The Paradox of China's Post-Mao Reforms* (Cambridge, MA: Harvard University Press, 1999), pp. 333–447; Timothy Brook and B. Michael Frolic, eds, *Civil Society in China* (Armonk, NY: M. E. Sharpe, 1997).

9. Jonathan Schwartz and Shawn Shieh, 'State and society responses to China's social welfare needs: an introduction to the debate', in Jonathan Schwartz and Shawn Shieh, eds, *State and Society Responses to Social Welfare Needs in China: Serving the People* (London and New York: Routledge, 2009), pp. 3–21.

10. Joel Samuel Migdal, Atul Kohli and Vivienne Shue, eds, *State Power and Social Forces: Domination and Transformation in the Third World* (Cambridge: Cambridge University Press, 1994); Joel Samuel Migdal, *State in Society: Studying How States and Societies Transform and Constitute One Another* (Cambridge: Cambridge University Press, 2001).

11. Yang Guobin, 'Environmental NGOs and institutional dynamics in China', *The China Quarterly* 181, (2005), pp. 46–66.

12. Andrew Mertha, '"Fragmented authoritarianism 2.0": political pluralization in the Chinese policy process', *The China Quarterly* 200, (2009), pp. 995–1012.

13. Baum and Shevchenko, 'The "state of the state"'; Yiyi Lu, *Non-governmental Organizations in China: The Rise of Dependent Autonomy* (London and New York: Routledge, 2009).

When discussing new social actors, such as urban homeowners or society in general, an exclusive focus on autonomy which posits a certain degree of secession of society from state power seems to limit our understanding of the incessant changes taking place in the transforming authoritarian system. Society should not always be seen as a counterweight to the state. Moreover, when we focus too much on the relationship between civil society on the one hand and the state on the other, we tend to overlook what is happening within each of these entities.[14] The process through which society is transformed is a reflection of the complex interplay between the state and society. Thus, internal evolution *within* either the state or society should not be disregarded in our discussion of state–society relations.

While resonating with recent attempts to discover the actual modes of interaction between state and society, this article aims to provide a nuanced understanding of the evolving process of state–society relations. The empirical study of urban homeowners and their organizations suggests that there are two aspects to their evolution: (1) the horizontal expansion of homeowner activism through internal heterogeneity; and (2) advanced external engagement with the state authority. These aspects are two sides of the same coin: internal diversity demonstrates that a spectrum of collective interest representation among homeowners has emerged, and this internal diversity undergirds rather than undermines the development of homeowner activism toward advanced representation and participation.

(1) Internal diversity

Just like the idea that the state is fragmented,[15] the idea that society is an organic entity with a variety of manifestations helps us understand the multi-faceted nature of its transformation. A certain social group is composed of diverse actors with heterogeneous perspectives and interests; thus, individuals belonging to the same social group do not all behave in the same way. This leads to our observation of many different interfaces between the state and society. State–society interaction is sometimes observed at a very specific level, even in formats which appear to be lacking in internal coherence, and at other times at a general, aggregated level. The complexity of this interaction, which is not in a clear-cut form, is a reflection of a state–society relationship in transition.

Social forces do not necessarily grow in a coherent way, and sometimes this is thought of as a weakness in representing the interests of their constituents.[16] However, coherence is not necessarily an absolute indicator of the vitality of a particular social group. Internal diversity is only to be expected in the evolution of social forces; it does not necessarily work against interest aggregation. From observing the development of homeowner activism over the past decade, the author

14. Heath B. Chamberlain, 'Civil society with Chinese characteristics?', *The China Journal* 39, (1998), pp. 69–81.

15. Kenneth G. Lieberthal and David M. Lampton, eds, *Bureaucracy, Politics, and Decision-Making in Post-Mao China* (Berkeley and Los Angeles, CA: University of California Press, 1992); Mertha, '"Fragmented authoritarianism 2.0"'.

16. Yip and Jiang, 'Homeowners united'.

finds that diversity within the social group of urban homeowners has been an important factor in the evolution of the relationship between the state and society. Through internal dialectical debate, this social group has developed a spectrum of stances in the pursuit of individual and common goals, and furthermore, a common important direction out of diversity.

In this sense, the internal dynamics of a social group are as important as external factors in deciding the group's direction and ultimate fate. And we need to keep in mind that endogenous evolution or diversification takes place even within a social group that is seen as homogenous from the outside. This is the case for urban homeowners. Homeowner activism had a relatively simple goal in the initial stage of housing reform: to contend with homeowners' collective enemies—housing entrepreneurs and relevant local government units. However, as time went on, the interests of homeowners became diversified and conflicts of interests among homeowners[17] and homeowner distrust of homeowner organizations also arose. In response, enthusiastic homeowner activists developed different stances regarding the direction in which activism should develop. All these seemingly incoherent facets of homeowner activism are part of a natural evolutionary process.

Despite many conceptual breakthroughs in delineating the changing state–society relationship, most scholarly discussions focus on the relationship between the state on the one hand and society on the other. Accordingly, changes and evolution that occur within society itself—for instance, internal conflicts or diversities within a particular social group and how this affects its relationships with external forces—are relatively neglected. Internal diversity, rather than hampering the formation of a solidified collective force, may be advantageous for the group's long-term viability, as a spectrum of different views concerning how collective interests should be represented gives the group more potential for growth. Internal evolution influences ongoing process and the future direction of the emerging social force. In particular, it may help with external negotiation or advance the activism to another level of representation and participation.

(2) External engagement

The other side—the external aspect—of the evolving state–society relationship is the social group's strategic interaction with the state. Discussing this aspect of state–society relations builds on discussion of autonomy in relational terms: an increase in society's autonomy is not necessarily equated with society's insulation from state power; such a situation would not favor the effective achievement of the social actors' goals.[18] For social actors to achieve their goals, it is better for them to be close to the state power than to be completely autonomous. Although this does not

17. Deborah S. Davis, 'Chinese homeowners as citizen-consumers', in Sheldon Garon and Patricia Maclachlan, eds, *The Ambivalent Consumer: Questioning Consumption in East Asia and the West* (Ithaca, NY: Cornell University Press, 2006), pp. 281–299.

18. Yang Guobin, 'Civil society in China: a dynamic field of study', *China Review International* 9(1), (2002), pp. 1–16; Lu, *Non-governmental Organizations in China.*

necessarily mean that such groups are co-opted, even co-opted groups can influence the state to pursue group interests.[19] The caveat is that even seemingly autonomous social groups strategically seek a certain kind of alliance or support from the state. 'Even for the most autonomous organizations, it would be foolish not to have strong party-state links.'[20]

Indeed, social groups need to be embedded to make an impact on local governance. For instance, when the group's ultimate goal is to influence local government, it is more efficient to have linkages with that government.[21] Civil society can only play a critical role by working within the political system, not outside of politics. What matters is whether social power can penetrate the state power; not necessarily whether it should pose a direct challenge to the state.[22] It would be helpful to remember that seemingly contentious activities such as protests do not necessarily pose a threat to the state authority.[23] More importantly, social actors' strategic engagement with the state contributes to changes in the state's perception of those social actors and their activism. Repeated encounters have some learning effect on the state's awareness of and responsiveness to voices of social actors.

As activities that cannot be grasped clearly by the absolute notion of autonomy are increasing, it is necessary for the conceptual containers for holding such empirical contents to go through some revision.[24] For instance, according to an earlier version of 'embeddedness', attempts to seek proximity to power were seen as a provisional strategy to be used in the initial stage of organizational development only;[25] thus, embeddedness was assumed to be incompatible with autonomy.[26] A more recent version of embeddedness is not so exclusive in its definition and application. For instance, in Peter Ho's study of environmental activism, embeddedness is seen less as a provisional survival strategy than as a continuously shifting development model: embeddedness, as part and parcel of state–society interaction, may induce incremental political change in China.[27]

Given the rapidly evolving dynamics of state–society interaction, our focus should be on the actual dynamics rather than on the ideal forms of civil society: that is, how social power utilizes existing limited institutional arrangements to make its voice heard by the state authority. Concepts such as 'policy entrepreneur',[28]

19. Tony Saich, 'Negotiating with the state: the development of social organizations in China', *The China Quarterly* 161, (2000), pp. 124–141.

20. *Ibid.*, p. 139.

21. Lily L. Tsai, *Accountability without Democracy: Solidarity Groups and Public Goods Provision* (Cambridge: Cambridge University Press, 2007).

22. David Da-Hua Yang, 'Civil society as an analytic lens for contemporary China', *China: An International Journal* 2(1), (2004), pp. 1–27.

23. Elizabeth J. Perry, 'Chinese conceptions of "right": from Mencius to Mao—and now', *Perspectives on Politics* 6(1), (2008), pp. 37–50.

24. It is not necessary for new concepts to be proposed, as our field is already flooded with concepts. However, critical reinterpretation of the existing concepts would help.

25. Kevin J. O'Brien, 'Chinese people's congresses and legislative embeddedness: understanding early organizational development', *Comparative Political Studies* 27(1), (1994), pp. 80–107.

26. Lu Yiyi, 'The autonomy of Chinese NGOs: a new perspective', *China: An International Journal* 5(2), (2007), pp. 173–203.

27. Ho, 'Introduction'.

28. Mertha, '"Fragmented authoritarianism 2.0"'.

'deliberate authoritarianism' and 'consultative authoritarianism'[29] suggest that the Chinese state authority has become more responsive to the demands of society and the space for citizens to influence public governance is gradually growing. Although it is highly unlikely that competitive elections will be adopted in China, citizens' political participation through other means—in the form of policy input—is on the rise. This is neither a completely new phenomenon nor an impending precursor of democratization, as authoritarian regimes are not devoid of political participation[30] and even encourage certain kinds of civic engagement.[31] Yet, with rapid diversification of socio-economic problems, newer forms of citizen interest representation with participatory nuance are noticeably increasing.

Against this backdrop, how 'political bargaining and contractual thinking'[32] emerge from state–society interaction based on utilizing limited input institutions needs further attention.[33] Although citizens in an authoritarian regime such as that of China cannot select their rulers through elections, they are keen to deliver their policy preferences to the state[34] in order to affect public policy.[35] Through such political communication, the terms of interest representation (albeit in a limited sense) and regime legitimacy are continuously renegotiated. The issue domain of private property rights is a good case from which to study such an evolving state–society relationship.

Expanding boundaries of homeowner activism

Over the past decade, relations between stakeholders in the commodified housing sector have developed significantly. There has been a gradual evolution toward further representation of homeowner interests—for example, homeowners' voices are being reflected in local legislation. Departing from its former stance, the local state now actively tackles disputes over private property rights. One recent progressive move by the Beijing municipal government has been its attempt to increase the legitimacy of the homeowners' assemblies (*yezhu dahui*) which represent all homeowners in a given residential compound.[36] Upgraded homeowner

29. Baogang He and Stig Thøgersen, 'Giving the people a voice? Experiments with consultative authoritarian institutions in China', *Journal of Contemporary China* 19(66), (2010), pp. 675–692.

30. Tianjian Shi, *Political Participation in Beijing* (Cambridge, MA: Harvard University Press, 1997).

31. Elizabeth J. Perry, 'Studying Chinese politics: farewell to revolution?', *The China Journal* 57, (2007), pp. 1–22; H. Gordon Skilling, 'Interest groups and communist politics', *World Politics* 18(3), (1966), pp. 435–451.

32. Thomas Herberer and Gunter Shubert, 'Political reform and regime legitimacy in contemporary China', *ASIEN* 99, (2006), pp. 9–28 (in particular, p. 22).

33. Although authoritarian institutions are regarded as mere window-dressing, recent studies suggest that even nominally democratic institutions have effects on policy outcomes and regime survival. Jennifer Gandhi and Adam Przeworski, 'Authoritarian institutions and the survival of autocrats', *Comparative Political Studies* 40(11), (2007), pp. 1279–1301; Jason Brownlee, *Authoritarianism in an Age of Democratization* (New York: Cambridge Press, 2007).

34. In particular, in times of crisis, institutions are secondary to the preferences of regime supporters. See Thomas B. Pepinsky, 'Capital mobility and coalitional politics: authoritarian regimes and economic adjustment in Southeast Asia', *World Politics* 60(3), (2008), pp. 438–474.

35. Shaoguang Wang, 'Changing models of China's policy agenda setting', *Modern China* 34(1), (2008), pp. 56–87; Steven J. Balla, 'Information technology, political participation, and the evolution of Chinese policymaking', *Journal of Contemporary China* 21(76), (2012), pp. 655–673.

36. Having acquired legal status, a homeowners' assembly may take part in litigation, manage funds and interact with the state. Currently, in Beijing, an experimental application in one district has been attempted and completed. The first case of a homeowners' assembly acquiring legal status was reported in Wenzhou. 'Wenzhou yixiaoqu

activism—advanced external engagement with the state backed up by internal diversity—has played a crucial role in bringing about such outcomes. The following comparisons of two representative homeowner organizations in Beijing[37] demonstrate how these two aspects of evolving homeowner activism—internal diversity and external engagement—have caused state–society interaction to rise to another level.

In terms of case selection, Beijing is a 'most likely case'. Homeowner activism in Beijing is far more broadly participatory, horizontally linked and mobilized than it is in other cities in China. First, in Beijing there are a number of organizations in operation that facilitate horizontal linkages between homeowners, whereas in some other cities establishing just one is tough. These organizations in Beijing take multiple forms—both formal and informal in terms of registration status—and the activities they engage in also differ. The existence of such a variety of organizations gives homeowners a multiplicity of ways in which they can aggregate and articulate their collective interests. Second, homeowner activism in Beijing strives to expand not only horizontal connections over different neighborhoods but also vertical connections with the state. Having already achieved tangible outcomes in political participation in the public sphere, homeowner activism in Beijing is becoming a role model for homeowner activists and organizations in other cities.[38] Considering that what has been institutionalized in Beijing is likely to be expanded to other areas, the Beijing case has enough future applicability.

Based on cumulative fieldwork conducted in Beijing since 2007, two representative homeowner organizations in the city are discussed below. Their most important features are summarized as follows: (1) while functioning as opinion leaders of homeowner activism, they provide necessary legal knowledge and enhance rights awareness for homeowners, and they work as platforms for training (*peixun*) homeowners as 'conscious citizens'; (2) the boundaries of these activities are not confined to individual neighborhoods but are expanded across neighborhoods (and even across cities), since many activities take the form of gatherings of homeowners and their representatives from different neighborhoods; and (3) they exhibit some differences in their choice of specific behavioral strategies for interaction with the state, yet both of them actively seek engagement with the state and have made

Footnote 36 continued
yezhudahui huofarenzige xiquanguo shouge' ['A homeowners assembly in a Wenzhou neighborhood acquires the status of a legal entity, the first such case in the nation'], *Zhongguo Pinglun Xinwenwang* [*China Review News*], (11 March 2013), available at: http://www.chinareviewnews.com/doc/1024/6/5/4/102465484.html?coluid=45&kindid = 0&docid = 102465484&mdate = 0311161232 (accessed 30 April 2013).

37. For convenience's sake, this article refers to umbrella organizations enabling horizontal liaison among homeowners briefly as homeowner organizations.

38. Homeowner activists in other regions have often commented that the Beijing government is far more attentive to the demands of society, and that in Beijing there is more space for social forces to voice their opinions to the state (interviews, Shanghai, 19 December 2007; 29 January 2010; 17 July 2012). This counter-intuitive outcome is the result of the governing structure of the capital, where power and responsibility are more concentrated than in other places. The Beijing municipal government faces pressure from two directions in its efforts to establish a property rights regime, from both ordinary citizens and from the central government. Paradoxically, these constraints on the local government offer greater political space for citizens to articulate their interests. The double-layered governing structure in Beijing is exploited as a resource by homeowner activists.

meaningful achievements in representation and participation, regardless of the different routes (*luxian*) they have chosen.

(1) Beijing Homeowner Organization A

One prominent feature of this organization is that it declares itself to be, and is publically recognized as, a research organization. A brief history of the organization supports this claim. It was set up in 2002 as a research group (*ketizu*) in a well-known university in Beijing, focusing on very practical issues related to community governance (*shequ zhili*). When the draft Regulations on Property Management[39] were released in that year, the research group began publicizing citizens' critical discussion of the Regulations. It organized numerous public meetings, and it came to the attention of the public when it introduced the controversial issue on a popular TV program. After its membership was swollen by enthusiastic homeowner activists and professionals, the research team was transformed into an independent, research-focused social organization. In 2005, it registered itself with the Bureau of Civil Affairs in Haidian district as a private, non-profit work unit (*minban feiqiye danwei*).[40] Having obtained *de jure* status, it started to expand the scope of its activities.

The outwardly academic appearance of this organization has been instrumental in facilitating connections between homeowners across the city and beyond. It carries out research-oriented activities, which it describes as forums, seminars and conferences. Since 2005, it has organized numerous conferences on various issues of neighborhood politics, such as how to interpret the draft Property Law and the Regulations on Property Management, and critical discussions of the 'harmonious society' (*hexie shehui*) and grassroots governance (*jiceng zhili*). By means of activities of this kind, the organization has assumed the role of an educator, disseminating essential information about rules and regulations among homeowners and introducing successful experiences of conflict resolution to other neighborhoods. Having previously been a university research team, the organization could call on many scholars and graduate students in Beijing, and now this academic-oriented network has been expanded to incorporate participants and supporters from other parts of Beijing and further afield.[41]

Organization A also sought to establish formal links with the state by acquiring formal legal status through registration. This has helped the organization to enjoy stable growth. Unless initiated by the government, social organizations in China find it difficult to gain legal legitimacy through registration. The 'two-tier registration system'

39. As previously mentioned, the Regulations on Property Management are the basic rules that define property rights and power relations in neighborhoods. They stipulate who qualifies as a homeowner, and under what circumstances a homeowners' committee can be established and reorganized.

40. Interview, Beijing, 23 August 2010; Hexie shequ fazhan zhongxin [Governance and Community Institute], *Rangsixiang gaishan xianshi yonghexie chujin fazhan* [*Idea Makes Reality Better, Harmony Facilitates Development*], (2010).

41. Scholars and professionals constitute the core membership of this organization. Because of the composition of its membership and the character its activities (purportedly, research-oriented), some think Organization A is not a direct representative of homeowner interests (interviews, Beijing, 27 August 2010; 31 August 2010); however, such seemingly neutral features have enabled it to expand the horizontal connections of homeowners more widely, and avoid manifest tension with the state authorities.

means they have to find a sponsor in an upper-level government organization outside of the civil affairs department. This adds to the difficulties encountered by many social groups.[42] The head of Organization A, who as a successful entrepreneur has a wide social network, was able to find a sponsor through his personal connections.[43] The resources and capacity of the leader are decisive factors in the growth and success of social organizations in China. On the flip side, some argue that this can hamper long-term stability because a change of leader can mean the loss of all the resources attached to him or her.[44] Yet, at least at the organization's initial stage of development, it is crucial to have an individual leader with abundant resources and capacity.

Registration is one of the ways in which social organizations seek so-called embeddedness, and this is a double-edged sword. On the one hand, a registered social organization can enjoy certain privileges. Legal legitimacy contributes to the organization's financial stability, for example. It enables the organization to obtain tax-free status or a tax rebate, and sometimes a financial subsidy from the government.[45] International donors that support social organizations in China often require recipients of funding to be legally registered. On the other hand, even registered social organizations do not necessarily enjoy unlimited stability. Registration—formal linkage with the state—can be cancelled at any time. And formal legal status gives the organization legitimacy among some audiences but not necessarily among others.[46] Thus, the advantages of embeddedness in terms of formal registration are uncertain. Nevertheless, in the case of Organization A, formal legal status has been useful.

Based on the reputation this organization has gained domestically and even outside of China, it has been able to expand the scope of its influence. Even though it is registered under a district office of the Beijing Civil Affairs Bureau, the actual boundaries and the ripple effect of its activities reach far beyond Beijing. A nationwide alliance of homeowners has yet to emerge in China, and for the time being such a network in any concrete form would be unthinkable, but this organization has managed to facilitate virtual connections among homeowners. Initially, it brought homeowners from different neighborhoods within Beijing together and provided them with opportunities to exchange ideas and experiences. Now the organization's staff visit other cities such as Shanghai, Guangzhou, Kunming and Wuhan at the invitation of local homeowners who want to learn from Beijing's experience. As the training of homeowners is a very meaningful project for them, the staff happily undertake the role of educators.[47] In this context, official registration has been utilized as a platform for pursuing more influential activities.[48]

42. Guosheng Deng, 'The hidden rules governing China's unregistered NGOs: management and consequences', *The China Review* 10(1), (2010), pp. 183–206.

43. Interview, Beijing, 23 August 2010.

44. Zhang and Zhuang, 'Feizhengshi zhengzhi'.

45. Deng, 'The hidden rules governing China's unregistered NGOs'.

46. For details on the different categories of legitimacy of social organizations, see Gao Bingzhong, 'Shehui tuanti de hefaxing' ['Problems related to the legitimization of associations in China'], *Zhongguo Shehui Kexue* [*China Social Science Journal*] 2, (2000), pp. 100–109.

47. Interviews, Beijing, 23 August 2010; 31 August 2010; 28 August 2012.

48. Once they are officially licensed and are no longer worried about their immediate survival, social organizations can start maneuvering between ambiguously defined dos and don'ts.

Finally, Organization A has developed itself into an active participant in local governance in various ways. From 2002 onwards, Organization A put forward numerous proposals regarding forthcoming laws and regulations on property management and grassroots governance. Its staff have delivered their proposals to people's congress delegates at various levels, and they have also invited delegates to attend their meetings. In 2006, the organization achieved a notable success when three of its proposals were included in a formal discussion of legislation in the National People's Congress (*quanguo renda lifa yicheng*).[49] Unlike experts such as the staff of Organization A, people's congress delegates often lack knowledge and experience of specific issues. This is because many of them are not professional politicians and they lack the time and energy to research important social issues. In these circumstances, experts who have a good grasp of what is going on in a specific issue domain can gain some leverage by advising legislators.[50]

Besides trying to exert direct influence on legislation by winning over legislators, the experts in Organization A have worked as direct consultants to the government regarding local legislation and its evaluation. For example, this group of ardent professionals has played an important role in the recently passed New Ordinance on Property Management in Beijing City (*Beijingshi wuye guanli banfa*).[51] Preparation of this new local ordinance was the responsibility of the city government's Construction Committee (*Beijingshi zhujianwei*), and as it carried out the work of revising the various drafts, the committee actively sought the opinions of experts. Members of staff of Organization A were frequently consulted by government officials either individually or through public hearings (*tingzhenghui*). Later, they were even asked to evaluate the implementation of the new ideas suggested in the Ordinance.[52] This kind of expert participation produced an Ordinance which contains many innovative clauses.[53]

Although they are inferior to government units in terms of actual power, groups of experts like Organization A have a wealth of resources for understanding what is really going on in neighborhoods, and this gives them a platform for their existence. Organizations such as this, led by neighborhood experts, gain their legitimacy through the recognition of homeowners in general,[54] and provide on-the-ground information that the government is lacking. Conflict resolution or the maintenance of social stability (*weiwen*) has become a priority for local governments these days. Official support for so-called grassroots self-governance (*jiceng zizhi*) from the

49. Feng Jinlei, 'Tansuo shequ minzhiyu hexie' ['Exploring community democracy and harmony'], *Xiandai Wuye* [*Modern Property Management*], (July 2006), pp. 15–17.

50. Feng Jinlei, 'Renda daibiao guanzhu shequ lifa' ['People's congress delegates pay attention to community legislation'], *Xiandai Wuye* [*Modern Property Management*], (April 2006), pp. 24–26; Zhang and Zhuang, 'Feizhengshi zhengzhi'.

51. It was announced by the Beijing municipal government in April 2010 and came into effect in October that year; see http://www.china.com.cn/policy/txt/2010-05/27/content_20129188.htm (accessed 7 May 2013).

52. Interview, Beijing, 28 August 2012.

53. For example, the new Ordinance clearly states that homeowners are the main actors who have the right to decide what happens within their neighborhoods; it also eased requirements for establishing homeowners' committees in neighborhoods and encouraged online voting by homeowners on important decisions. Another notable innovation contained in the Ordinance was that homeowners' assemblies (*yezhu dahui*) should become legal entities (*faren*), although that has yet to be fully implemented.

54. Gao Bingzhong, 'Shehui tuanti de hefaxing'.

center adds momentum to such moves.[55] Given the current situation, government agencies have begun to recognize that neighborhood experts can contribute to conflict resolution in commodified housing. As one official of the Beijing Construction Committee said, 'We encourage homeowners or neighborhood experts to actively express their thoughts. We also encourage them to resolve conflicts through legitimate channels. It may help to either decrease or prevent disputes regarding property management'.[56] Social groups rely on the state when they lack human and organizational resources and essential information in the field.[57] However, when this situation is to some extent reversed, especially in issue domains where it is inefficient or even risky for the state to take sole control and responsibility, social groups can find space to maneuver in the public sphere.

(2) Beijing Homeowner Organization B

Organization B claims to represent homeowner interests more directly, since all its working members are heads of homeowners' committees from different neighborhoods in Beijing. They share experience of a variety of conflicts with the business sector (such as developers and management providers) in their areas. Initially composed of leaders from four neighborhoods in 2006, at its peak, the organization recruited representatives from more than 100 neighborhoods. Based on its experience of having defended homeowner interests in numerous neighborhood disputes, this organization has established a contentious image which is both self-declared and publicly accepted. It adopts more direct and aggressive strategies in order to pressure the relevant stakeholders.[58]

Working as the *de facto* standing committee of all the homeowners' committees in Beijing,[59] Organization B elects its own representatives and holds a regular annual meeting and extraordinary meetings when necessary. At these meetings, the members discuss practical strategies for handling property disputes with the business sector. The organization also provides assistance to neighborhoods that lack sufficient resources to fight against the business sector themselves.[60] The organization has remained an informal entity with no office space of its own and it does not get any financial support from outside. Its members work in their spare time for the organization on a voluntary basis. Securing funds is a big problem that threatens the organization's existence and stable growth.[61] However, despite this comparatively unfavorable situation, the group has achieved a lot.

55. The promotion of self-governance for urban residents was discussed at the Chinese Communist Party's 17th National Congress; see http://www.china.com.cn/17da/2007-10/24/content_9119449_6.htm (accessed 7 May 2013).

56. Interview, Beijing, 1 September 2012.

57. Lu, *Non-governmental Organizations in China.*

58. Interviews, Beijing, 17 November 2007; 25 August 2010; 31 August 2012; 4 September 2012.

59. It could be said that this group aimed to be the 'representative of representatives' of homeowners. Some homeowner activists have criticized this move, saying that such *indirect representation* cannot truly reflect what general homeowners want. Yet, such debate itself shows that a spectrum of stances regarding homeowner interest representation has emerged.

60. Interviews, Beijing, 26 October 2007; 28 November 2007.

61. Interview, Beijing, 31 August 2012; 1 September 2012.

Organization B has built up its reputation by engaging in several important property disputes in the city, all of which emerged during the initial stage of housing commodification.[62] Since these disputes occurred around the time when the Property Law was promulgated in 2007, the disputes themselves and how they were resolved had great symbolic meaning and important repercussions. Several successful cases of defending homeowner interests contributed to Organization B's earning national fame. Even when it has not been so successful, this group has shown a strong presence, providing tangible support to homeowners in their struggles and inspiring them to defend their own rights. Since awareness of one's rights can only be gained through experience, the enthusiastic activists in this organization and their supporters believe that all experience is meaningful regardless of success or failure.[63]

Another feature of this organization is that it has made active attempts to advance into the public sphere—in particular, through existing institutional channels of representation. Based on their earlier experiences of standing for election to local people's congresses,[64] homeowner activists in Beijing have introduced an interesting twist into their practice of participation: despite the limited ability of the existing electoral system to truly represent the popular will, they believe that increased participation by independent candidates can change the nature of the system.[65] Elections to residents' committees are one such target. Residents' committee elections are usually just a formality, and Chinese citizens rarely pay serious attention to them. However, since residents' committees are the first institutional hurdle that homeowners have to jump when they begin to mobilize,[66] activists in Organization B have sought to capture the quasi-governmental organizations and change their nature.[67] Although still at an experimental stage, expanding civic participation by utilizing existing channels of limited representation is one direction in which this organization is advancing. In the same vein, seeking to influence legislation is another activity that has been pursued by this group. The joint signature movement of

62. Sun Long, 'Kuashequ jiti xingdong de yunzuo luojiji cicelüe: yi Beijing'yeshenwei' wei gean' ['The operational logic and strategies of cross-neighborhood collective actions: a case study of Beijing Association of Homeowners' Committees' Bidding Committee'], *Dangdai Zhongguo Yanjiu* [*Modern China Studies*] 17(3), (2010), pp. 91–127.

63. Interviews, Beijing, 26 October 2007; 28 November 2007; 31 August 2012; 1 September 2012.

64. A few founding members of Organization B felt that it was necessary to form a horizontal alliance of homeowners across neighborhoods, and in particular to expand homeowners' participation in the public sphere. This awareness stemmed from their direct and indirect experience of participating in grassroots people's congress elections in 2003. In that year, Beijing produced China's first homeowner activist-turned local people's congress delegate. To increase their fellow activist's chances of election, several homeowner activists initially registered as candidates, then withdrew at the last moment, thus concentrating support for the single most promising candidate. This strategy succeeded (interview, Beijing, 17 November 2007). However, after this symbolic achievement in 2003, it became more and more difficult for independent candidates to get elected to people's congresses as state interference increased (interview, Beijing, 4 September 2012).

65. On the development of independent candidates in local people's congress elections, see Junzhi He, 'Independent candidates in China's local people's congresses: a typology', *Journal of Contemporary China* 19(64), (2010), pp. 311–333.

66. In order to establish a homeowners' committee, it is necessary to gain the agreement, endorsement and a final stamp of approval of grassroots government organizations such as residents' committees and street offices.

67. Interviews, Beijing, 23 August 2010; 25 August 2010; Sun Long, 'Kuashequ jiti xingdong de yunzuo luojiji cicelüe'. As Tianjian Shi remarked, 'people choose to participate in these imperfect elections to facilitate desired changes in the election system itself, rather than wait for elections to become democratic to participate'. Shi, *Political Participation in Beijing*, p. 24.

early 2007 that brought about the partial revision of the Property Law is a representative achievement.[68] Organization B launched this movement requesting the revision of several ambiguous clauses of the law.[69] Starting with a press conference in Beijing, and through online mobilization, it attracted support not only in the capital but also from many other cities. Eventually, it gained more than 1.8 million signatures nationwide. As a result of this campaign some, though not all, of Organization B's suggestions were incorporated into the final version of the law. From this landmark event that helped make people aware of their rights, participants learned that they can ask for changes in policies, rather than passively accepting policies as they are.[70]

The group has attempted to influence other legislation at various levels by pressing people's congress delegates or government units. Through its online and offline activities, Organization B has brought the remaining controversial clauses of the Property Law to the attention of the public.[71] Some of the group's proposals were included in formal discussion of the legislation in the National People's Congress.[72] The group has also made a contribution to the New Ordinance on Property Management in Beijing. Along with other experts, core members of this group have been approached by government units and asked for their opinions. Because Organization B is not formally registered, its core members have been invited to participate not as representatives of the organization but as individuals. However, these experts still believe that their participation is meaningful, since it proves that they are at least informally recognized by the government.[73]

The final notable feature of this organization is that it has conducted all the above-mentioned activities without having any formal status. Strictly speaking, unlike the neighborhood homeowners' committees, this kind of horizontal alliance of homeowners has no legal grounds for existence. Therefore, some people are worried that it might soon be banned. So far, however, the Beijing City Government has maintained a very ambiguous attitude, and has refrained from pressuring it.[74] Because of its informal status, Organization B does not get any form of government subsidy or support. At the same time, it has not yet experienced any outright suppression, although it has been subject to intermittent indirect interference.

68. '"Yaoqiu wuquanfa diliuzhang baohu yezhu quanyi gongmin lianshu xingdong" qingkuang zongjie' ['The final settlement of "requesting revision of the sixth chapter of the Property Law"'], *Beijing Fangchanwang* [*Beijing Real Estate Network*], available at: http://www.focus.cn/msgview/4451/78214201.html (accessed 7 May 2013).

69. For instance, the draft did not draw a clear distinction between commonly owned space and individually owned space, leaving a lot of room for different interpretations.

70. Interviews, Beijing, 5 September 2007; 23 August 2010.

71. For instance, these issues include who owns common spaces, such as parking lots and conference rooms (clause 76), and whether a homeowners' assembly is qualified to pursue lawsuits (clause 78).

72. Interview, Beijing, 31 August 2012.

73. Interviews, Beijing, 25 August 2010; 31 August 2012.

74. Several years ago, when asked whether this group's request for formal status would be granted, the vice mayor of Beijing said, 'it can be considered (*keyi kaolü*)', which might be interpreted as tacit approval. 'Beijing fushizhang Chen Gang: kekaolü chengli yezhuweiyuanhui xiehui' ['Beijing vice mayor Chen Gang: can consider establishment of Beijing Association of Homeowners' Committees' Bidding Committee'], *Jinghaushibao* [*Beijing Times*], (26 January 2007), available at: http://news.sina.com.cn/c/2007-01-26/032312141156.shtml (accessed 9 May 2013).

Accordingly, Organization B is located at the borderline of *de facto* and *de jure*.[75] Being aware of how difficult it is to find a sponsor from an upper-level government organization and achieve registration, this group actually makes use of the current situation to some extent. On the one hand, it enjoys informal legitimacy as an unregistered social group.[76] In addition to its contentious image, not having official links with state power undergirds its externally claimed identity as an independent organization. Both the business sector and government recognize its reputation, and this is one reason why the group enjoys the *unofficial* recognition of important counterparts. On the other hand, although it maintains its contentious image, this organization does not necessarily seek a contentious relationship with the state. Since its establishment in 2006, it has attempted to acquire formal registration status; by doing so, it has sent a signal to the state that it respects the existing system (*tizhi*). Homeowner activists within the organization also know that the government will not ratify their group, for fear of a ripple effect. However, by continuously pursuing registration, it has knocked the ball of official recognition into the state's court.

Discussion and conclusion

The above discussion of two homeowner organizations in Beijing illustrates the evolution of homeowner activism in China: rights activism starts from within the neighborhood and develops beyond the boundaries of the neighborhood, while groups seek more representation and participation. Rights awareness and articulation has been continuously growing and evolving among Chinese citizens. What is notable in this process is that the state power is not necessarily seen as the target of contention, but as an object to utilize or cooperate with. Previously, the dynamics of state–society relations in this issue domain were more strained, and there was a lack of systematic support for the collective representation of homeowners' interests.[77] The state was quite uncertain and even suspicious of what homeowner activism was ultimately pursuing. Through frequent encounters of various kinds (even including confrontation), both the state and society either tested each other or came to understand more about each other's intentions. As a result, we now see meaningful changes not only in how social actors access the state but also in how the state treats social actors.

Well-known homeowner activists share the experience of having been under scrutiny in the past although they have received much less hostile treatment recently, which is a demonstration of how state–society interaction has evolved. As one activist testified,

> When I first started rights protection activities to propagate legal information which homeowners should know, the state authority may have thought that I was a dissident or a

75. Even with an ambiguous legal status, it retains informal legitimacy and recognition from relevant stakeholders. Strictly speaking, its continuous efforts to achieve formal registration status have not yielded the expected outcome—the response of the local government has been ambiguous—but that has not stopped it from making these efforts, so it can be said to be in the *process* of attempting to acquire formal legal status.

76. Sun Long, 'Kuashequ jiti xingdong de yunzuo luojiji cicelüe'.

77. In my earlier fieldwork, many homeowners expressed their frustration at how difficult it was to establish homeowners' committees in their neighborhoods or to keep an already established committee working.

> dangerous person. I noticed that I was under surveillance. Sometimes, I was warned about my activities, both directly and indirectly. I continued to do what I wanted to do anyway. What I did was to meet with homeowners and emphasize that they should have their own representative organizations. I helped them to establish homeowners' committees. After a few years, it seems that they found out that I was not a dangerous person who was attempting to subvert the state authority. I feel that the surveillance has greatly decreased. What is more, the relevant state agencies now invite me to come and advise them. They listen to my suggestions.[78]

Some other activists also testified that they or their colleagues have been under scrutiny, and have been occasionally invited to 'talk over tea' with someone dispatched from the public security department.[79] They also added that the state, through such uncomfortable encounters, gradually ascertained that homeowner activism does not aim to challenge the state authority and that actually it can help state governance. By its very nature, activism by urban middle-class citizens in China would be hard to turn into a dissident movement.[80] Moreover, as important constituents who undergird property-owning socialism, urban homeowners function in a way that keeps the reform from being reversed.[81] Rather than aiming to overthrow the existing system, through continuously raising complaints and requests to make better policies, homeowner activism actually complements an incompletely designed property rights system in a socialist country. The gradually changed state response to homeowner activism may be ascribed to such awareness.

To summarize, in this discussion of the evolution of homeowner activism, two points should be highlighted. First, homeowner activism has become more internally diverse. The internal mobilization of the social class that is 'urban homeowners' has not taken place in a uniform manner. In other words, homeowner activism has evolved through a process of dialectic interaction among its own constituents. Over the years, the homeowner organizations which facilitate horizontal connections among homeowners have multiplied. There are already more than three different streams of city-wide homeowner activism in Beijing. Differences of opinion regarding which strategic route these organizations should take, not to mention minor conflicts and criticisms of different stances, do exist. All the usual issues associated with the viability of social forces in China, such as autonomy, legitimacy and stability, are included in these internal debates.[82] Although they share the common goal of enhancing homeowners' interests, individual actors or organizations have chosen different behavioral strategies—for instance, some are more aggressive than others in seeking representation and participation.

Fierce internal debates have taken place within the social group of urban homeowners. Divided into doves (*hexiepai*) and hawks (*kangzhengpai*), they do not

78. Interview, Beijing, 4 September 2012.

79. Interviews, Beijing, 28 August 2012; 31 August 2012.

80. Yongshun Cai, 'China's moderate middle class: the case of homeowners' resistance', *Asian Survey* 45(5), (2005), pp. 777–799.

81. For the state's concerted efforts to create consumers (homeowners) in the initial stage of housing reform, see Neil Gibson, 'The privatization of urban housing in China and its contribution to financial system development', *Journal of Contemporary China* 18(58), (2009), pp. 175–184; Bill Adams, 'Macroeconomic implications of China urban housing privatization, 1998–1999', *Journal of Contemporary China* 18(62), (2009), pp. 881–888.

82. Interview, Beijing, 27 August 2010.

hesitate to criticize those who hold different opinions. In particular, there are active online debates through new media, such as the micro blog (*weibo*). But though they disagree as to what strategic direction they should take, they accept these differences, given that homeowners as a group include people from diverse backgrounds and age-groups. Some key leading homeowner activists belong to two or three different homeowner organizations, or they tend to change their affiliations.[83] The important thing is that a spectrum of collective interest representation has emerged, and this internal diversity undergirds the growth of homeowner activism as we see it today. The homeowner organizations discussed in this article are just two such examples.

Second, the flipside of internal diversity is the enhanced capacity of homeowner activism in general and its advanced strategic interaction with the state. Through expanded activities based on horizontal mobilization, homeowners have become a more organized social force and are seeking ways to expand their boundaries. Now they are actively looking for ways to get their interests represented in the public sphere. In order to do this, they choose to pursue and maintain connections with the state power. They are not seeking absolute independence or confrontation. Qualitative interviews with leading homeowner activists reveal how they perceive the current state–society relationship. They think they should remain somewhere *between* the state and society; in that way, they believe, they can induce incremental changes and narrow the state–society gap. As one leading homeowner activist said,

> If we stay too close to the government, people will not trust us; if we stay too close to the people only, we cannot move the government. We try to maintain an agreeable distance from the government. The important thing is that we work for society, and try to stay closer to society as far as we can.[84]

To a certain extent, the particular features of the issue (private property rights) have provided a niche for social power to infiltrate the state structure. Simply speaking, the state and its agencies are less confident about how they should handle middle-class homeowners than they are about handling, for instance, farmers or migrant workers. Many of my interviewees believe that the changes at grassroots level have been so rapid and huge that the government lacks the ability to keep up with them.[85] Moreover, experience of offering policy advice to government units which lack information about what is happening on the ground has added to these social actors' consciousness that they are experts who can help the state and its agencies in dealing with emerging issues in the commodified housing sector. For such people, the state is seen as a resource to be utilized to better represent their interests, and participation in the public sphere is the direction they want to pursue. This is a big change, considering their former status as passive recipients of policies.

83. Interviews, Beijing, 3 September 2012; 4 September 2012; 5 September 2012. Some activists choose to work independently without organizational affiliation. In general, most of the leading homeowner activists in Beijing have held or currently hold a position as head of the homeowners' committee in his or her own neighborhood. They have subsequently chosen to participate in expanded networks such as Organizations A and B. Such people include entrepreneurs, researchers, legal professionals and intellectuals from various backgrounds.

84. Interview, Beijing, 27 August 2010.

85. According to them, whereas urban homeowners are well equipped with essential information, legal knowledge, and even material resources, the corresponding government units at the grassroots level, such as street offices and residents' committees, are not competent enough to deal with citizens of this caliber.

All in all, these accounts indicate a repositioning of homeowners in a new social space, and a diversification of the ways in which the state and society interact. This article has discussed the evolution of homeowner activism in two senses: internally (growth through internal diversity) and externally (advancement in interaction with the state). Generally speaking, the activism is directed toward more representation and participation. Homeowners have started to go beyond the state-designated boundaries of their neighborhoods and are attempting to voice opinions about the rules and regulations that govern their lives and restrict their rights. At the same time, by emphasizing that they are not merely concerned about individual material interests but also stand for general civil rights (*gongminquan*), homeowners are building up the legitimacy of their own activism. For instance, as an extension of homeowner activism, recent anti-waste incinerator campaigns in large Chinese cities have successfully reframed waste disposal as an important public health issue.[86]

On the other hand, such advancement of homeowner activism does not mean that these social actors enjoy unlimited tolerance from the state. Although they have expanded over state-set boundaries in a physical sense, they are well aware of the ultimate boundary they should not cross—challenging the supremacy of the Party. Lest their activism be seen as a threat to state authority, homeowner activists keep to the basic codes, such as borrowing 'normative power' from state official rhetoric or policies[87] while raising claims and avoiding stepping into extreme situations that can be seen as riotous behavior (*naoshi*). Uncertainties do exist; the space they maneuver in today can shrink suddenly tomorrow. Yet, the state tolerates, accepts or even encourages civic engagement as long as it can gain more from cooperation than from suppression. Repression cannot be a universal tool over all different constituencies.[88] And to reconfirm its right to rule, the party-state needs to show its versatility—even without an effective representative body and competing parties—in dealing with the diverse interests of its constituencies.[89]

In this setting, the emerging mode of state–society interaction is more accurately portrayed as a complex interplay between the two, rather than a confrontational or lopsided relationship between state and society. Activism at the grassroots level has become more pragmatic and strategic, seeking cooperation with the state for more effective interest representation. Recent studies suggest emerging internal diversity among villagers, migrant workers and environmental activists, and ensuing advancement in their external engagement with the state: based on knowledge acquisition and rational calculation, social actors move from contention toward renegotiating interest alignment with different levels of governments,[90] navigating institutionalized channels of dispute resolution[91] and proposing alternative policy

86. Thomas Johnson, 'The health factor in anti-waste incinerator campaigns in Beijing and Guangzhou', *The China Quarterly* 214, (2013), pp. 356–375.
87. Shi, *Political Participation in Beijing*.
88. Gandhi and Przeworski, 'Authoritarian institutions and the survival of autocrats'.
89. Skilling, 'Interest groups and communist politics'.
90. Wooyeal Paik and Kihyun Lee, 'I want to be expropriated!: the politics of xiaochanquanfang land development in suburban China', *Journal of Contemporary China* 21(74), (2012), pp. 261–279.
91. Jeffrey Becker, 'The knowledge to act: Chinese migrant labor protests in comparative perspective', *Comparative Political Studies* 44(11), (2012), pp. 1379–1404.

solutions to government.[92] Future studies need to pay more attention to how rights awareness and manifestation in Chinese society is evolving, and in what ways and to what extent such input from society induces meaningful changes in state–society interaction.

92. Johnson, 'The health factor in anti-waste incinerator campaigns in Beijing and Guangzhou'.

Requests for Environmental Information Disclosure in China: an understanding from legal mobilization and citizen activism

Xinhong Wang

University of Turku, Finland

ABSTRACT
This article analyzes the fairly recent phenomenon of citizens and organizations requesting disclosure of environmental information in China. Chinese citizens and organizations are invoking the new open government information regulations to push government agencies, particularly environmental protection agencies, to fulfill their legal obligation of information disclosure. By requesting that government agencies disclose environmental information, citizens and organizations have turned themselves into active agents pushing forward the implementation of the new regulations. The findings of this article suggest that a bottom-up legal mobilization in the field of environmental information disclosure, though still with a limited scope, has been happening and endeavoring to make social and political changes in China. Furthermore, this legal mobilization can be seen as an important part of emerging civil society activities in contemporary China.

In October 2011, the US Embassy published on Twitter, via the account @BeijingAir, data on air quality with regard to PM2.5[1] in China, and also stated that the air quality in Beijing was 'hazardous'.[2] At that time PM2.5 was not included in air quality monitoring, and the Beijing Environmental Protection Bureau (EPB) said that the air quality was 'slightly polluted'. This sharp contrast aroused heated discussion and criticism on the Internet as well as citizen action requesting PM2.5 information disclosure. In November 2011, Beijing resident Yu Ping requested that the Beijing EPB disclose its daily inspection statistics

[1]PM2.5 refers to tiny particles in the air that are two and a half microns or less in width. It is an air pollutant that is of concern for people's health when levels in air are high. For detailed air pollutants and their health effects, please see, *The WHO Air Quality Guidelines for Particulate Matter, Ozone, Nitrogen Dioxide and Sulfur Dioxide Global Update 2005* (World Health Organization, 2006).

[2]The World Health Organization (WHO) guidelines set a PM2.5 annual mean average of 10 micrograms per cubic meter as the standard for the lowest risk for health. A statistical analysis shows an average annual PM2.5 concentration of approximately 100 micrograms per cubic meter for 2010–2011 in Beijing. This is nearly three times higher than the Chinese government's proposed annual standard of 35 micrograms per cubic meter, and ten times higher than the World Health Organization guidelines of 10 micrograms per cubic meter. See, Steven Q. Andrews, 'Beijing's hazardous blue sky', *China Dialogue*, (5 December 2011), available at: https://www.chinadialogue.net/article/show/single/en/4661?page=2 (accessed 28 May 2015).

regarding PM2.5 between 1 October 2011 and 18 November 2011.[3] In December 2011, Wang Xing, a journalist at the *Southern Metropolis Daily*, submitted information disclosure requests with regard to air quality and PM2.5 information to 31 provincial and autonomous regional-level Environmental Protection Departments (EPD) and municipality-level EPBs, and the Ministry of Environmental Protection (MEP).[4] By December 2011, the MEP had announced its plan with regard to PM2.5 inspection and information disclosure in China.[5] In early 2012, the central government passed revised air quality standards, which included an index for PM2.5, aiming to gradually establish a monitoring system of PM2.5 in major cities in China.[6]

It is not clear to what extent this citizen action of requesting information disclosure has contributed to the MEP taking measures to tackle the problem of air pollution. However, it is undeniable that the public has endeavored to use government information disclosure to impose pressure upon government agencies with regard to environmental issues. This could not have happened without China's establishment of its open government information mechanism.

In May 2008, both *Regulations of the People's Republic of China on Open Government Information* (*Zhengfu xinxi gongkai tiaoli*, ROGI)[7] and *Interim Measures on Open Environmental Information* (*Huanjing xinxi gongkai zanxing banfa*, MOEI) came into effect in China.[8] Aiming to guarantee public access to government information and enhance government transparency,[9] both the ROGI and the MOEI impose an obligation upon government agencies to disclose a broad scope of environmental information, both on their own initiative and upon request of disclosure by individuals, legal persons and other entities.

Studies on China's open environmental information have mostly focused on why the new mechanism of open government information has been implemented and whether it has been effective. Focusing on information disclosure for environmental risk management, while researchers have shown that the implementation of the MOEI in China is 'improving but far from widespread, full and effective',[10] the lack of enforcement and the ambiguity of some rules in the MOEI, as well as the 'longstanding closeness, secrecy and monopoly of information in China's political system' have made its implementation ineffective.[11] Moreover, although the open environmental information policy brings transparency in China, it does not mean that China is achieving full transparency and the policy is effectively implemented.[12] Concerns for economic growth and its relation to government officials' merits make it difficult for environmental protection policies to be strictly implemented by local governments.[13] While the new legislation created additional space for non-state actors, non-governmental organizations

[3]'Beijing EPB refused information disclosure due to PM2.5 not listed into state air quality standards' ['Beijingshi huanbaoju zhengshi huijue shenqing yin PM2.5 shangwei lieru guojia huanjing kongqi zhiliang biaozhun'], *Southern Metropolis Daily* [*Nanfang dushibao*], (3 December 2011), available at: http://www.360doc.com/content/11/1203/10/231981_169320798.shtml (accessed 24 June 2015).

[4]Wang Xing, 'Journalist requests PM2.5 information disclosure 31 provinces and municipalities 10 replies' ['Jizhe shenqing PM2.5 xinxi gongkai 31 shengqushi 10 ge dafu'], *Southern Metropolis Daily* [*Nanfang dushibao*], (11 January 2012), available at: http://www.ogichina.org/article/180/12880.html (accessed 7 July 2015).

[5]'Provincial level municipalities in China start PM2.5 monitoring from 2012' ['Zhongguo ge shenghui chengshi 2012nian qi jiance PM2.5'], *Caixin*, (22 December 2011), available at: http://china.caixin.com/2011-12-22/100341408.html (accessed 22 June 2015).

[6]'Monitoring of PM2.5 to be extended', *China Daily*, (29 February 2012), available at: http://www.chinadaily.com.cn/china/2012-02/29/content_14724821.htm (accessed 22 June 2015).

[7]*Regulations of the People's Republic of China on Open Government Information*, adopted at the 165th executive meeting of the State Council on 17 January 2007, effective 1 May 2008, Order of the State Council No. 492.

[8]*Interim Measures on Open Environmental Information*, adopted by the State Environmental Protection Administration (SEPA, predecessor of Ministry of Environmental Protection) of China on 8 February 2007, effective 1 May 2008, SEPA Order No. 35.

[9]*Regulations of the People's Republic of China on Open Government Information* (ROGI), Interim Measures on Open Environmental Information (MOEI), Article 1.

[10]Arthur O. J. Mol, Guizhen He and Lei Zhang, 'Information disclosure in environmental risk management: developments in China', *Journal of Current Chinese Affairs* 3, (2011), p. 163.

[11]*Ibid.*

[12]Yeling Tan, 'Transparency without democracy: the unexpected effects of China's environmental disclosure policy', *Governance* 27(1), (2014), pp. 37–62.

[13]*Ibid.*, p. 40.

(NGOs) were also constrained in acting on information to exert pressure upon polluting enterprises or make claims on the state due to political and institutional constraints.[14] Undoubtedly, the success of top-down open environmental information depended on the 'commitment, perception and resources' of local leaders and suggested that, concerning the new ROGI, active NGO engagement could apply pressure from the bottom up and help to establish a web of dialogue to further enable the public to participate in environmental decision-making.[15] In other words, both government commitment and public activism are crucial in realizing government information disclosure. However, with regard to environmental information disclosure in China, studies focusing on the agents–citizens and organizations are still lacking.

Underscoring the roles of citizens and organizations, this article argues that, while central government lays down the structure of open government information, it is in fact the public that has been mobilizing the law in order to push government agencies to implement the law, thus playing a vital role in the realization of government transparency, reflecting an important part of the emerging civil society in participating through legal channels in contemporary China. Moreover, it should also be noted that the legal mobilization of requesting government agencies to disclose environmental information is not a single and lone phenomenon of using the law to interact with the government. The 'rightful resistance' devised by O'Brien and Li,[16] the emerging rights-defense movement,[17] using legal procedures to seek social justice such as through public interest litigation[18] and initiating lawsuits against pollution enterprises,[19] have all shared similarities: citizens have been forming a bottom-up social activism in pushing forward the rule of law in China. While protests, demonstrations and other contentious methods of civil society activities are constrained and limited due to China's political environment, this has provided a new angle for the civil society to participate in China's political process. Moreover, through legal channels, citizens and organizations have formed a community; in the words of Yang, they have formed 'sites and agents of political change ... to push back political boundaries, and induce changes in the relationship between the state and citizens and between state and non-state organizations'.[20] Although environmental activism in China is rather apolitical, their actions have constituted citizen participation in China's political process, endeavoring to create political responses and political changes. This echoes Chen's argument about the transnational environmental movement in China that green activism is non-political or de-politicized but 'expands the public sphere and pluralises the political process'.[21] While it is a top-down process that has established the mechanism of open government information in China, it is the bottom-up activism of the public that makes it work. Citizens' and organizations' use of legal tactics has acted as not only a channel to access government information but also as a means of creating recursive pressure upon government agencies to be accountable to their legal obligations. This article argues that, no matter what the end result of information disclosure requests turns out to be, the process of requesting itself deserves our careful attention. During this process, law has played a pivotal role in enabling citizens' participation in the political process in China.

---

[14]Thomas Johnson, 'Environmental information disclosure in China: policy developments and NGO response', *Policy & Politics* 39(3), (2011), pp. 399–416.

[15]Wanxin Li, 'Self-motivated versus forced disclosure of environmental information in China: a comparative case study of the pilot disclosure programs', *The China Quarterly* 206, (2011), pp. 331–351.

[16]Kevin J. O'Brien and Lianjiang Li, *Rightful Resistance in Rural China* (Cambridge: Cambridge University Press, 2006); Kevin J. O'Brien, 'Neither transgressive nor contained: boundary-spanning contention in China', *Mobilization* 8(1), (2003), p. 53.

[17]See, e.g. Biao Teng, 'Rights defence (weiquan), microblogs (weibo), and the surrounding gaze (weiguan)', *China Perspectives* 3, (2012), pp. 29–41.

[18]Hualing Fu and Richard Cullen, 'The development of public interest litigation in China', in Po Jen Yap and Holning Lau, eds, *Public Interest Litigation in Asia* (London: Routledge, 2010), pp. 9–34.

[19]Benjamin van Rooij, 'The people vs. pollution: understanding citizen action against pollution in China', *Journal of Contemporary China* 19(63), (2010), pp. 55–77.

[20]Guobin Yang, 'Environmental NGOs and institutional dynamics in China', *The China Quarterly* 181, (2005), pp. 65–66.

[21]See, Jie Chen, 'Transnational environmental movement: impacts on the green civil society in China', *Journal of Contemporary China* 19(65), (2010), p. 523.

Table 1. List of cases of environmental information disclosure requests in the public interest.

Case no.	Information disclosure requester(s)	Information disclosure requestee(s)	Summary of information requested for disclosure	Result	Year
Requests submitted by individuals					
1	Yan Yiming	Henan EPD, Anhui EPD	List of polluting enterprises	Yes	2008
2	Mao Da	Beijing Industry & Commerce Bureau	Plastic bags usage fee	Yes	2009
3	Mao Da	Beijing EPB, Beijing Land & Resources Bureau	2006 report on Beijing Domestic Waste Landfill Risk Evaluation	No	2009
4	Sun Nong	Zhuhai EPB	Used battery disposal information	No	2009
5	Beijing netizen Yu Ping	Beijing EPB	PM2.5 inspection	No	2011
6	Mao Da	MEP	Result of the 2006–2008 National Survey on Persistent Organic Pollutants	No	2011
7	Tianjin blogger Wandering Sky	Wuqing District Government, Wuqing Forestry Bureau	Dahuangbao Wetland Nature Reserve plan maps	No	2011
8	Zhang Tao	Ministry of Oceans	Pollution situation of leaks in the Bohai oil field	Yes	2011
9	Ding Jinkun	Hangzhou Forest & Water Bureau	Qiandao Lake water diversion project proposal, etc.	No	2012
10	Hangzhou resident	Hangzhou Forest & Water Bureau	Qiandao Lake water diversion project proposal	No	2012
Requests submitted by organizations					
11	Greenpeace	Shanghai Environmental Protection & Hygiene Administration Bureau	BASF pollutants emission	No	2008
12	Greenpeace	Zhuzhou EPB	Zhuzhou polluting enterprises	No	2009
13	Friends of Nature	MEP, Ministry of Agriculture	Yangtse River upper reach fish preservation area readjustment	No	2011
14	Green Beagle	Beijing EPB	Sujiatuo Incinerator EIA public participation section	No	2011
15	Green Beagle	Hai'an EPB, Nantong EPB, Jiangsu EPD	Hai'an Incinerator EIA and pollutant emitting data	No	2011
16	All China Environmental Federation	Xiuwen EPB	Haoyiduo Dairy Co. daily inspection, EIA report and pollutants emission	Yes	2012
17	Green Beagle	MEP	2010 investigation result on PCB-containing electrical equipment and waste electricity equipment in eight key provinces	Yes	2012
18	Green Beagle	Beijing EPB	Emergency Plan for Heavy-polluted Day	No	2012
19	Green Watershed	Bank of China, Yunnan Banking Regulatory Bureau	Chromic slag pollution enterprises loan, regulations	No	2012
20	Tianxiagong (Justices for All)	Ministry of Housing & Construction	List of cities where water quality below required standard	Yes	2012

Table 2. List of cases of environmental information disclosure requests for private interest.

Case no.	Information disclosure requester(s)	Requestee(s)	Summary of information requested for disclosure	Result of disclosure	Year
21	Xu Taisheng	Shanghai Pudong EPB, Shanghai EPB	Bao Steel Plant approval and inspection record etc.	Yes	2008
22	Zhang Changjian etc.	Pingnan EPB	Houlong Village dumping site approval info etc.	No	2008
23	Huang Jianxin	Zhangjiagang EPB, Suzhou EPB	Sewage plant EIA report	False document	2009
24	Yang Zi	Beijing EPB	Gao'antun Incinerator annual inspection statistics	No	2009
25	Xie Yong	Hai'an EPB, Nantong EPB, Jiangsu EPD	Hai'an Incinerator approval and inspection information	No	2010–2012
26	Xu Yu *et al.*	Chuyang city & Jianping County government agencies	Water quality inspection report relating to chemical plant pollution	No	2010
27	Huai'an residents	Huai'an EPB	Huaigang Special Steel Co. EIA report	No	2011
28	Sun Bin	Hunan EPD	Neighboring telecommunications base approval information	Yes	2011

Sources and methodology

This article is a qualitative case study based on 28 cases and eight surveys of environmental information disclosure requests which occurred between May 2008, when the ROGI and the MOEI came into effect, and August 2012 when the case collection was completed.

The cases and surveys have been collected by the author through multiple sources, such as the Internet, news reports and her three tours of fieldwork in China between 2009 and 2012. The fieldwork is multi-sited, covering both cities and rural areas, where NGOs, lawyers and pollution victims were interviewed. In China, there are no official statistics available with regard to environmental information disclosure requests, nor is there a compilation of related court cases; these cases were mostly originally located by the author through the Internet search engines Google and Baidu, a Chinese search engine, and later numbered and documented by the author. This method of case collection has its own limits that make it incomplete. Analysis based on the data cannot represent the general situation in China. However, the processes of information disclosure requests, their successes or failures, do reflect how citizens and organizations interact with government agencies and how changes happen in today's China.

This study analyzes citizen information disclosure requests from the perspective of legal mobilization, and it particularly examines who are the agents, and why and how they have been invoking the law to request government agencies to disclose environmental information. According to Zemans, a legal mobilization happens when 'a desire or want is translated into a demand as an assertion of one's rights'.[22] This legal mobilization can be individually initiated or by collective action. A core understanding of legal mobilization, stated by political scientist McCann, is as follows:

> [L]aw is … understood to be a resource that citizens utilize to structure relations with others, to advance goals in social life, to formulate rightful claims, and to negotiate disputes where interests, wants, or principles collide. Legal knowledge thus can matter as both an end and means of action; law provides both normative principles and strategic resources for the conduct of social struggle.[23]

Studying legal mobilization can help us to understand public participation in the political process and how citizens can affect political changes through the language of law. From the perspective of legal

[22]Frances Kahn Zemans, 'Legal mobilization: the neglected role of the law in the political system', *The American Political Science Review* 77(3), (1983), p. 700.

[23]Michael McCann, 'Law and social movements', in Austin Sarat, ed., *The Blackwell Companion to Law and Society* (Marlden, Oxford, Carldon: Blackwell Publishing Ltd, 2007), pp. 506–522.

Table 3. List of surveys of environmental information disclosure requests.

Survey no.	Information requester(s)	Requestee(s)	Summary of information requested for disclosure	Result of disclosure	Year
1	Friends of Nature Shanghai members	Shanghai/ Shanghai districts EPBs	Water-related environmental information	Partly	2008
2	IPE&NRDC	113 EPBs	List of enterprises that have received an environmental penalty	Partly	2008–2011
3	Greenpeace	15 EPBs	Information of polluting enterprise	Partly	2009
4	Southern Weekend	29 EPBs	List of enterprises that have received an environmental penalty	Partly	2010
5	ARTICLE 19 & CLAPV	8 EPBs	17 types of government information as listed in Art. 11 of MOEI	Partly	2010
6	*Southern Metropolis Daily* journalist	29 EPBs	PM2.5 & Ozone inspection statistics	Partly	2011
7	Wuhu Ecology Centre	MEP, 4 EPBs, 26 EPDs	List of key enterprises that emit dioxin	Partly	2011–2012
8	Impact Law Firm	80 EPBs	Eight types of information as listed in Art. 11 of MOEI, i.e. pollutants emission	Partly	2012

mobilization, law is clearly not only about legislation and legal control, but also a resource for citizens to claim and defend their rights. Legal mobilization is about the strategic application of rules and taking actions based on law.[24] The processes of legal mobilization 'involve the strategic action of individuals and groups to promote or resist change in a given policy arena'.[25]

The agents of legal mobilization: citizen actors, environmental organizations and other entities

There are two general purposes of environmental information disclosure requests: in the public interest of environmental protection such as environmental information disclosure surveys, and for private interest such as victims of pollution obtaining information to support their environmental claims or to be aware of their surrounding environmental risks. A large majority of environmental information disclosure requests concern the public interest. Out of the 28 cases, ten individually-launched requests and ten organization-launched requests were in the public interest (Table 1),[26] which accounts for about 71% of the total cases.

Among the ten individually-submitted requests, four were submitted by lawyers,[27] three by an environmental activist (also a scholar on environmental history),[28] two by 'netizens',[29] and one by a resident of Hangzhou.[30] Lawyers rank the highest in requesting information disclosure for the public good, reflecting their capacity to utilize the new legal channel and their willingness to test it. Among the

[24]Lisa Vanhala, 'Legal mobilisation', *Political Science*, (2011), Oxford Bibliographies online, doi:10.1093/obo/9780199756223-0031.

[25]Rachel A. Cichowski, *The European Court and Civil Society: Litigation, Mobilization and Governance* (Cambridge: Cambridge University Press, 2007).

[26]The cases and surveys are listed chronologically and numbered by the author for the convenience of reference in this study. In this article, when Chinese names are used in the cases, the Chinese practice is followed in which the family name is placed before the given name. However, with regard to the name of an author in the footnote reference, the practice of academic English writing is followed.

[27]Cases 1, 4, 8 and 9.

[28]Cases 2, 3 and 6.

[29]Cases 5 and 7. Case 5 was launched by a person who works in media, but appears under the identity of a micro-blogger in reports about his information disclosure request; Case 7 was initiated by a blogger who has a blog entitled 流浪的天空 (Wandering sky), through which the author located the corresponding case.

[30]Case 10.

organization-submitted cases, a large majority, nine out of ten, were by environmental NGOs (ENGOs)[31] and only one[32] relates to an organization whose main focus is not environmental protection.

Eight individual cases were initiated for private interest (Table 2), which equals 29% of the 28 cases. They were all submitted by individuals, including city residents and villagers, and all of them were pollution victims.

All survey-related requests (Table 3) were public-interest related. Among the eight surveys of environmental information disclosures, four were conducted by environmental organizations,[33] two were media-related surveys,[34] Survey 5 was by an international organization focusing on freedom of information and a legal aid center, and Survey 8 was by a law firm. Clearly, ENGOs have been the most active in requesting government agencies to disclose environmental information.

Moreover, it appears that a few ENGOs, specifically Friends of Nature,[35] the Institute of Public and Environmental Affairs (IPE)[36] and Green Beagle,[37] have taken a leading and dedicated role in conducting environmental information disclosure requests since the coming into effect of the new legislation. The members of Friends of Nature were among the first to request information disclosure in China. IPE, a young Beijing-based ENGO, has used the Pollution Information Transparency Index (PITI) to conduct annual surveys on environmental information disclosures in 113 cities in China since 2008. Green Beagle has been involved in a total of four cases of information disclosure requests documented by the author.

International organizations have also been active in environmental information disclosure requests. Greenpeace is one of the international ENGOs that first started to carry out environmental information disclosure work after the MOEI came into effect in China.[38] It also published a report about enterprise information disclosure in 2009.[39] ARTICLE 19 is an international organization headquartered in London, focusing on 'defending freedom of expression and information';[40] it conducted joint investigative research with the Centre of Legal Aid for Pollution Victims (CLAPV), affiliated to the Chinese University of Political Science and Law, in 2010.[41] The Natural Resources Defense Council (NRDC),[42] an

[31]Cases 11–19.

[32]Case 20. Established in 2011, Justice for All is a policy advocacy NGO based in Nanjing. Its main focuses include: issues of discrimination against people with disabilities, hepatitis and HIV/AIDS; food and medication safety standards etc.

[33]Surveys 1, 2, 3 and 7.

[34]Surveys 4 and 6.

[35]Friends of Nature (*ziran zhiyou*) is the earliest and one of the most influential ENGOs in China. It was established in 1994 with approval from the Ministry of Civil Affairs. Since its creation, it has been active in promoting environmental education, organizing activities and conducting exchanges with foreign green NGOs.

[36]IPE (*gongzhong huanjing yanjiu zhongxin*) is a young environmental organization established in 2006. Besides many other achievements within its short history, such as its compilation of the water and air pollution databases for China and its promotion of the global green supply chain in China, it conducts an annual assessment of the situation regarding environmental information disclosure in China.

[37]Based in Beijing, Green Beagle (*daerwen ziran qiuzhishe*) was established in April 2009. This organization's Chinese name 达尔问 is partly after Charles Darwin; its English name is derived from the HMS Beagle, the sloop-of-war on which the great naturalist Darwin sailed. See, Sam Geall, 'China's environmental journalists: a rainbow confusion', in Sam Geall, ed., *China and the Environment: The Green Revolution* (London and New York: Zed Books, 2013), pp. 15–16. Green Beagle's work focuses on three aspects of environmental protection: urban environmental quality testing and research; China's environmental situation investigations; and environmental protection education.

[38]Greenpeace, 'Upgrading campaign against BASF, demand it for environmental information disclosure' ['Zhendui BASF de xingdong shengji, yaoqiu BASF gongkai huanjing xinxi'], Greenpeace website, available at: http://www.greenpeace.org/china/zh/news/basf (accessed 10 March 2014).

[39]Greenpeace, *Silent Giants: An Investigation into Corporate Environmental Information Disclosure in China* [*Chenmo de dadu-oshu, qiye wuranwu xinxi gongkai zhuangkuang diaocha*], Report 2009. The MOEI not only requires government agencies but also enterprises to disclose environmental information. Greenpeace's report focuses on enterprises' information disclosure.

[40]ARTICLE 19 was founded in 1987 in London, UK. Its mission is to promote freedom of expression and freedom of information, protected by international human rights law, such as Article 19 of the Universal Declaration of Human Rights.

[41]Survey 5.

[42]NRDC was founded in 1970 by a group of law students and attorneys. It currently has offices in New York, Washington, Chicago, Los Angeles, San Francisco and Beijing. The mission of NRDC is to 'safeguard the Earth: its people, its plants and animals and the natural systems on which all life depends'.

environmental organization headquartered in New York, jointly developed the PITI for environmental information disclosure assessment with IPE.[43]

Lastly, in addition to ENGOs, domestic media and law firms have also become part of the community requesting environmental information disclosures, reflecting the diversity of actors that have been working with this newly emerging mechanism of open government information. While the former has greater capacity to report the results of their requests and arouse more public debate, the latter has professionals who are rich in legal knowledge and ways of taking legal action. Both these factors play important roles in pushing legal mobilization forward in China.

Purposes of environmental information disclosure requests

Actions are made for purposes. Clearly whether it is for public or private interest, there are other specific purposes for citizens' and organizations' requests for environmental information disclosure: pushing government agencies to implement the new policy, raising public awareness of environmental issues and facilitating public participation in environmental decision-making, to collect evidence for legal claims, and for personal care about the environment.

When a few Shanghai members of Friends of Nature first started to request information disclosures in China, they put their reasons as follows:

> The reason why we want to request environmental information disclosures … is because the MOEI and the ROGI came into effect as of May 1, 2008, citizens have a duty and responsibility to coordinate with the government for the implementation of the new MOEI and ROGI and to request environmental information disclosure according to law.[44]

To push government agencies towards better performance also appears as the purpose of the IPE to 'systematically evaluate the first year of implementation for these regulations'[45] and the Impact Law Firm 'to push and help related government agencies to strengthen their information disclosure work and pollution sources monitoring; to know the achievements and weakness between the legislation and its practice, and make relevant proposals'[46] in conducting their surveys.

Moreover, to use the official channel to make the government fulfill its obligation and be more accountable is not only the aim of NGOs, but also of individuals. Yan Yiming, a Shanghai-based lawyer, was one of the earliest individuals to request an environmental information disclosure in China. Noticing that the Huai River was highly polluted, and Henan and Anhui provinces, both located on the upper reaches of the river, blamed each other for causing the pollution, Yan thought of requesting the disclosure of the related information in order to find out about the real situation. In May 2008, almost as soon as the regulations came into effect, Yan submitted his requests towards the Henan EPD and the Anhui EPD, asking for the disclosure of key polluting enterprises.[47] Yan wrote in his blog that:

> To request a government information disclosure is not my fundamental purpose. My purpose is to awake the consciousness of citizen participation, and make more people participate in all aspects of social life, to push the government to improve its governing capacity, and ultimately realize a stable and developing national politics, economy and culture.[48]

---

[43]For further studies about cooperation between international environmental organizations and their Chinese counterparts, please see Chen, 'Transnational environmental movement'.

[44]Friends of Nature, 'Introduction of Shanghai Friends of Nature group's environmental information disclosure requests' ['Shanghai xiaozu huangjing xinxi gongkai guocheng jieshao'], available at: http://www.fon.org.cn/content.php?aid=11200 (accessed 10 March 2014).

[45]IPE and NRDC, *Breaking the Ice on Environmental Open Information 2008 Pollution Information Transparency Index (PITI), First Annual Assessment of Environmental Transparency in 113 Chinese Cities*, Report, (2008), p. 2.

[46]Impact Law Firm, *The Highest Virtue is Like Water: 80 Chinese Pollution Source Monitoring Cities Environmental Information Disclosure Requests Public Interest Campaign Report* [*Shangshan ruoshui: zhongguo bashi chengshi wuranyuan jiankong zhengfu huanjing xinxi gongkai shenqing gongyi xingdong baogao*], (2012), p. 5.

[47]Interview with lawyer, 6 May 2011.

[48]Yiming Yan, 'Comments on the State Development and Reform Committee's reply' ['Guanyu guojia fagaiwei dafu de jidian pinglun'], (23 February 2009), available at: http://yan-yiming.blog.sohu.com/116885315.html (accessed 10 March 2014).

Besides pushing the government to fulfill its obligation, the purposes of Yan's requests clearly extend to other aspects: raising public awareness of social and political participation. This also appears in Beijing citizen Yu Ping's requests for the disclosure of PM2.5 related information.

> It is useless to merely criticize the government, [one should] make use of the available channels and methods, to push the government to take actions.[49]

A second goal of requesting government environmental information is to create public pressure on local governments. In 2011, Green Beagle, a Beijing-based environmental organization, submitted several information disclosure requests with regard to a local incinerator in Hai'an, Jiangsu Province.

> We need to communicate with the government in a proper process. It does not matter what the result will be, we want to take a legal procedure. When we choose to do so, we want to knock the door open and start a conversation; additionally, we want them to know, besides the complaints of local people, there is also the voice of outsiders that concern them.[50]

To discover more about environmental pollution incidents constitutes the third purpose of several information disclosure requests. Clearly, citizens and organizations do not want to stop at the stage of being informed but intend to know more through actively requesting related information. In 2011, 5,000 tons of chromic slag was disposed of on a hillside and later it was found that the same enterprise also disposed of tens of thousands of tons of chromic slag along the Nanjiang River in Yunnan Province. This directly aroused the attention of Green Watershed (*lüse liuyu*), an ENGO that has long been interested in Green Credit (*lüse xindai*), a policy that requires banks to assess the pollution situations of enterprises when granting loans. The NGO thus submitted information disclosure requests with regard to the bank regulations over the polluting enterprises.[51]

The information disclosure requests relating to PM2.5 disclosures, submitted by both Beijing netizen Yu Ping[52] and the journalist from *Southern Metropolitan Daily*,[53] also stemmed from public concern and public debate. Both requests relate to the heated discussions about PM2.5 on Internet forums and microblogs in late 2011.

To facilitate public participation in environmental decision-making is also one of the purposes of obtaining environmental information about projects. In 2011, the Beijing EPB published a notice concerning a new incinerator project that would be built in Sujiatuo, a town under the administration of the Haidian district of Beijing. Green Beagle conducted on-site investigations and found that many villagers in Sujiatuo did not know about the project. Questioning the accuracy of the content with regard to public participation in the project's environmental impact assessment (EIA) report, Green Beagle requested that the Beijing EPB disclose the chapter on public participation in the EIA report.[54]

It is not only environmental organizations that have shown their concern for environmental decision-making; individuals have done likewise. In 2012, when the lawyer Ding Jinkun noticed that the Hangzhou government planned to construct a new project diverting water from Qiandao Lake to Hangzhou city, he submitted his information disclosure requests to the Hangzhou Forest and Water Bureau (FWB). He asked the FWB to disclose the project proposal and project investigative report and related records.[55] Inevitably, concern has been increasing in China over government environmental

---

[49]Yang Yang, 'Learn to be angry, facing the government' ['Miandui zhengfu, yao xuehui shengqi'], *China Weekly* [*Zhongguo zhoukan*], (21 August 2012), available at: http://www.chinaweekly.cn/bencandy.php?fid=63&id=6189 (accessed 24 June 2015).

[50]Interview with NGO officer, 29 May 2010.

[51]Case 19; 'ENGO requested for Yunnan chromic pollution enterprise financing information but failed' ['Huanbao zuzhi shenqing gongkai Yunnan ge wuran qiye rongzi xinxi bei ju'], *China Youth Daily* [*Zhongguo qingnianbao*], (17 February 2012).

[52]Case 5.

[53]Survey 6.

[54]Case 14; 'ENGO requested for environmental information disclosure, doubting Sujiatuo Incinerator EIA' ['Huanbao zuzhi shenqing xinxi gongkai sujiatuo fenshao shou zhiyi'], *Legal Daily* [*Fazhi ribao*], (15 June 2011).

[55]Jinkun Ding, 'Qiandao Lake water diversion project information disclosure request letter' ['Shenqing qiandaohu yinshui gongcheng xinxi gongkaishu'], available at: http://blog.caijing.com.cn/expert_article-151570-35638.shtml (accessed 10 March 2014).

policies and environmental plans. To request related information constitutes the first step in participating in environmental decision-making. As noted by Friends of Nature members:

> We believe that environmental information disclosure cannot solve all environmental problems; however, solving environmental problems requires sufficient information disclosure.[56]

The fourth purpose of information disclosure requests is to obtain evidence to support other legal claims. In April 2011, Sun Bin, a resident in Changde, Hunan Province, requested that the Hunan EPD disclose its approval document for the establishment of a telecommunications base in his neighboring apartment. His request constituted part of his defense of his rights. In May 2011, he sued the telecommunications company, the housing company and the owner of the apartment for installing the base without informing other residents, and thus making them live in an environment of radiation pollution. Sun Bin asked for the removal of the base and also claimed for economic damages.[57] The same purpose was behind Xie Yong's environmental information disclosure request relating to a local incinerator. Xie wished to get evidence to support his civil litigation against the local incinerator whose pollution was thought to be causing his son's sickness.[58]

The fifth purpose for obtaining environmental information is simply for personal interests of loving nature or a general concern for environmental protection. In 2011, a blogger based in Tianjin requested the disclosure of maps of the wetland preservation area in Tianjin, as he loved lakes and wanted to know more about wetland protection.[59] Mao Da, a scholar of environmental history, submitted three information disclosure requests[60] over his concern for environmental protection.

While citizens and entities have been actively utilizing the new legislation to request that government agencies disclose information, they have also been imposing a demand upon government agencies and legal mobilization thus happens.[61] Inevitably, to obtain the information *per se* is not the single purpose of this legal mobilization. Instead, various and multiple purposes such as environmental concern, raising public awareness and putting pressure on government agencies to enforce their own policies and laws, are behind the actions. These purposes have clearly moved disclosure requests far beyond their original meaning of obtaining information. From another perspective, these purposes, probably even unknown to some requesters, have in fact turned them into an, in Frances Zemans' words, 'active, assertive participatory citizenry that is central to a democratic society'.[62] Besides carrying multiple purposes, citizens and organizations have also adopted various legal tactics.

From adopting legal tactics to the forming of a supporting structure

The process of utilizing the channel of information disclosure request has constituted a process of learning and the accumulation of experiences. Some citizens have self-studied Chinese law in order to assert their legal claims, and have changed themselves from environmental victims to quasi-legal experts. Xu Taisheng is an ordinary Shanghai resident. While getting involved in defending the rights of his residential area against Bao Steel Corporation for causing pollution, he was provided with legal aid by CLAPV. Nevertheless, he also studied law himself and drafted legal complaints. He even provided help to other pollution victims to communicate with Shanghai EPBs for solutions. Some information disclosure requesters such as Yang Zi and Xie Yong have been invited by ENGOs to give presentations

[56] Friends of Nature, 'Introduction of Shanghai Friends of Nature group's environmental information disclosure requests'.
[57] Case 28; 'Newly-weds neighbour "electron magnetic radiation", sues Hunan Province EPD' ['Xinhun yezhu yu "dianci fushe" weilin zhuanggao hunansheng huanbaoting'], *Hunan Broadcast & TV-Legal Weekly* [*Hunan guangbo dianshitai-Fazhi zhoubao*], (28 February 2012).
[58] Case 25; Interview, 23 June 2012.
[59] Case 7.
[60] Cases 2, 3 and 6.
[61] Zemans, 'Legal mobilization'.
[62] *Ibid.*, p. 701.

and share their experiences with concerned citizens at seminars and conferences. As for individual information disclosure requesters, it is clear that a growth of citizenship has been accompanying the development of environmental information disclosure requests.

With regards to organizations, it is also a process of experimenting, learning, practicing, experience-gaining and capacity-building. This can be seen with Friends of Nature's request for environmental information disclosures. When the ROGI and the MOEI came into effect in May 2008, a few members of Friends of Nature in Shanghai thought it a good opportunity to participate in environmental matters and proposed that they use the new legislation to request that government agencies disclose environmental information. However, others expressed their opposition, fearing it might be a challenge to the authorities and would affect the development of Friends of Nature.[63]

Facing this situation, four members in Shanghai decided to launch a project 'shangshanruoshui' (a Chinese idiom, literally meaning 'the highest virtue is like water') in the name of individuals but not members of Friends of Nature, and to request that the Shanghai EPBs disclose water-related environmental information.[64]

> We did not really have strategies for launching the project of information disclosure request. However, without knowing how government agencies would react to it, in order not to cause them to hold [bad] opinion towards Friends of Nature, we decided to use the form of 'performance art' and submit the requests as citizens.[65]
>
> For us, [information disclosure request] breaks the mystery and fear of interacting with government agencies. Although it is request according to law, at the very beginning, many felt worried and thought it was acting against the government and might cause retaliation; we hid the action under the cover of 'performance art' and felt it was something sneaky; we also did not dare to publicize our identity of members of Friends of Nature. Later we realized that it should not be like this. There was no retaliation. We can fulfill a citizen's duty without hiding anything and declare loudly that we are members of the Friends of Nature.[66]

The process of Friends of Nature's information disclosure requests has shown a trajectory of requesting government agencies to disclose environmental information: from hesitating to taking legal action through performance art, to final explicit and direct interaction with government agencies. Today, Friends of Nature is one of the leading organizations in requesting that government agencies disclose environmental information in China. They have in-house lawyers specializing in providing legal consultation and professional work for information disclosure requests. They have also extended their concern to people's living environments and natural protection.[67] Moreover, when failing to get the information requested, Friends of Nature also applied for administrative reconsideration to China's highest government administrative authority—the State Council (SC).[68] Inevitably, from some members hesitating to submit information disclosure requests to directly submitting administrative reconsideration to the highest executive authority in China shows that the attitude of Friends of Nature has changed sharply,

---

[63]Interview with NGO volunteer, 7 May 2011.

[64]Friends of Nature, 'Introduction of Shanghai Friends of Nature group's environmental information disclosure requests'.

[65]*Ibid.*

[66]*Ibid.*

[67]Case 13.

[68]In the administrative reconsideration application, Friends of Nature requested the SC to withdraw the Ministry of Agriculture (MoA)'s reply to Friends of Nature refusing to disclose the information and order the MoA to make new replies. It also asked the SC to review the legality of the *Opinions on Improving the Work of Disclosing Government Information upon Request*, issued by the General Office of the SC on 5 January 2010. It particularly requested a review of the opinion with regard to its explanation that internal management information made or obtained by administrative organs during their day-to-day work or in-process information under discussion, research or examination in general is not government information that should be disclosed as referred to in the Regulations. See, Friends of Nature, 'Fighting for Yangtze River protection, Friends of Nature requested the SC for final arbitration, letter of application to the SC for administrative reconsideration' ['Ziran zhiyou xiang guowuyuan shenqing zuizhong caijue, wei changjiang baohu qu zhengqu yixian shengji, guowuyuan xingzheng caijue shenqingshu'], (30 March 2011), available at: http://blog.sina.com.cn/s/blog_69a4de060100qjir.html (accessed 10 March 2014).

reflecting its increasing willingness, capacity and confidence to use the law to interact with the Chinese government.

Environmental information disclosure requests have also demonstrated that law has become a language for citizens and organizations to interact with government agencies. Although it is not required by law, clear legal basis has always been referred to from individuals to ENGOs, to make their requests more authoritative.[69]

In 2012, the Beijing-based Impact Law Firm conducted a survey of environmental information disclosure by requesting that 80 city EPBs disclose eight types of information. The requested information included pollutant emissions, a list of polluting enterprises, a list of polluting enterprises that had received an administrative penalty and enterprises that voluntarily disclosed their pollutant emissions. The types of information were chosen from the 17 types of information required to be disclosed voluntarily under Article 11 of the MOEI.[70]

Not only national laws and regulations are used as the basis for environmental information disclosures, but China's international obligation was also questioned by Green Beagle. In 2001, China signed the Stockholm Convention on Persistent Organic Pollutants (POPs). According to the Convention:

> Each Party shall report to the Conference of the Parties on the measures it has taken to implement the provisions of this Convention and on the effectiveness of such measures in meeting the objectives of the Convention.
>
> Each Party shall provide to the Secretariat: (a) Statistical data on its total quantities of production, import and export of each of the chemicals listed in Annex A and Annex B or a reasonable estimate of such data.[71]

PCBs are mixtures of some chemical substances and belong to POPs.[72] According to the *2010 Annual Report on the State of Environment*, the MEP completed an investigation with regard to PCB-containing electrical equipment and waste in eight key provinces.[73] In 2012, Green Beagle requested that the MEP disclose this investigation report based on the Stockholm Convention.[74]

Along with environmental information disclosure requests, a supporting network has started to emerge, linking organizations, lawyers, scholars, journalists and citizens through a common concern over environmental information disclosure.

This professional supporting structure can be seen in several cases. While cooperating with the international organization ARTICLE 19 in investigating environmental information disclosure in China, CLAPV provided direct legal assistance for three of the seven individual citizens' information disclosure requests that resulted in administrative lawsuits.[75] Furthermore, while the Impact Law Firm was conducting their survey covering 80 information disclosure requests, its lawyers also acted as legal representatives for both Green Beagle[76] and Friends of Nature[77] in their information disclosure requests.

An environmental community focusing on environmental information disclosure has also started to emerge. As incinerators and waste management have become controversial issues in China, both ENGOs and individuals have started to request information disclosure about this aspect, including Mao Da, as a scholar of environmental history, Xie Yong and Yang Zi as ordinary citizens, Friends of Nature and Green Beagle, based in Beijing, and Wuhu Ecology Centre in Anhui Province.

---

69 Yiming Yan, 'Request to Anhui Province to disclose information of 132 key provincial monitoring enterprises' ['Shenqing Anhuisheng gongkai 132jia shengji zhongdian jiankong qiye xiangguan xinxi'], (20 November 2009), available at: http://blog.sina.com.cn/s/blog_486261660100g71i.html (accessed 10 March 2014).

70 Impact Law Firm, *The Highest Virtue is Like Water*.

71 UNEP, *Stockholm Convention on Persistent Organic Pollutants*, Persistent Organic Pollutants Review Committee Fourth meeting, Geneva, (13–17 October 2008), UNEP/POPS/POPRC.4/14, Article 15.

72 PCBs refers to polychlorinated biphenyls. They are all persistent organic pollutants.

73 MEP, *2010 China Annual Report on the State of Environment*, (29 May 2011), p. 79.

74 Case 17; See also 'PCBs, an unforgettable ghost' ['Duolulianben buneng wangque de youling'], *China Science Daily* [*Zhongguo kexuebao*], (23 April 2012).

75 Cases 21, 23 and 25. For studies about environmental information disclosure lawsuits, please see, Xinhong Wang, 'Addressing failures of environmental information disclosure through administrative lawsuits in China: the paradox of legal mobilization', *China–EU Law Journal* 3, (2014), pp. 165–190.

76 Case 17.

77 Case 13.

Moreover, by attending meetings and seminars, citizens, lawyers, professors and ENGOs have worked together in exchanging experiences as well as making their voice stronger and more widely heard. In April 2012, Friends of Nature organized a seminar in Beijing, particularly focusing on the three-year implementation of the MOEI. The seminar attracted participants from all walks of life, from law professors, lawyers, NGO officials and environmental activists to journalists. At the seminar, people exchanged their experiences of seeking environmental information through disclosure requests, and discussed the problems and obstacles they encountered. In early 2012, the Impact Law Firm conducted a project, requesting EPBs to disclose information. A report based on its experience was also compiled and sent to interested parties, and a related seminar was held. At Green Beagle's weekend seminars,[78] environmental information disclosure was often a popular topic as well. These activities generally helped more people to understand the MOEI, and thus also become capable of using the law to request government information disclosures themselves.

Another important source of support comes from the media. First, there have been quite a few active journalists who have become directly involved themselves in environmental protection activities. The founders of two of the most active ENGOs in open environmental information, IPE and Green Beagle, are both journalists.[79] When Chinese journalists are pro-environmental protection,[80] environmental cases are more likely to be reported. Moreover, some journalists directly participated in the process of requesting government agencies disclose environmental information. Wang Xing, a senior journalist at the *Southern Metropolis Daily* [*Nanfang dushibao*], wrote his report on PM2.5 information disclosure based on his own experience of submitting requests under his own name.[81] Among other surveys, one was also conducted by the *Southern Weekend* [*Nanfang zhoumo*],[82] a leading open media in China.

Lastly, it must be emphasized that the Internet has been playing an unprecedented role in shaping the supporting structure and forming a community that has been pushing forward environmental information disclosure. The first information disclosure requests launched by Friends of Nature's Shanghai members were initiated and communicated through the Internet.[83] Whilst owning official websites, and some also having blogs, almost all ENGOs use microblogs to exchange information with each other, and also to inform and educate a wider online audience.[84]

The Internet has also been utilized by individual requesters and lawyers. The four lawyers who submitted information disclosure requests in the public interest all have microblog accounts and three of them also have blogs.[85] When netizen Yu Ping requested that the Beijing EPB disclose PM2.5 information, he updated his microblog[86] and posted his requests on his blog.[87] Yu Ping had 78,925 followers on the

---

[78]Between November 2009 and June 2012, Green Beagle organized more than 300 public seminars (*gongzhong huanbao ketang*) about environmental issues.

[79]Ma Jun, who used to be a media reporter, is now the director of IPE. Feng Yongfeng, the founder of Green Beagle, still acts as a journalist for *Guangming Daily* [*Guangming ribao*].

[80]A very active environmental NGO, Green Earth Volunteers (*lüjiayuan*), co-founded by journalist Wang Yongchen in 1996, organized the monthly Green Journalists Salon (*lüse jizhe shalong*) in Beijing. The salon is open to the public. It has been providing a platform for journalists and environmental activists to discuss environmental issues since 2007. The founder of Green Earth Volunteers, Wang Yongchen is a journalist with China National Radio, one of the 32 Heroes of the Environment in *Time* in 2008. Wang is also one of the main actors involved in the campaign to oppose the building of 13 dams along the Nu River in China.

[81]Survey 6.

[82]Survey 4.

[83]Survey 1; Interview with lawyer, 6 May 2011; see, also Friends of Nature's water information project blog, available at: http://shanghaiwater.blogbus.com/ (accessed 10 March 2014).

[84]Taking Sina microblog (*xinlang weibo*) as an example, as of 12 November 2012, Greenpeace had 85,366 followers and Friends of Nature 34,020. Additionally, ENGOs also have individual accounts updated by staff members who have hundreds to tens of thousands of followers. For example, the account of Li Bo, the director of Friends of Nature, had 38,204 followers, Ma Jun, the director of IPE, had 21,000, and Feng Yongfeng, the founder of Green Beagle, had 31,706.

[85]This online research was completed by 12 November 2012.

[86]In news media about Yu Ping's requests, he is mostly mentioned as *Qiyi de endian* [奇异的恩典], which is the ID of his NetEase microblog (*wangyi weibo*) account.

[87]Ping Yu, 'I submitted administrative reconsideration to the MEP on the Beijing EPB's refusal to disclose PM2.5 information' ['Jiu Beijing huanbaoju jujue wo de PM2.5 xinxi gongkai shenqing wo yi xiang huanbaobu tijiao xingzheng fuyi'], (9 December 2011), available at: http://goo.gl/j1W2x5 (accessed 10 March 2014).

NetEase microblog (*wangyi weibo*).[88] His blog post entitled 'Beijing EPB refused to disclose PM2.5 upon my request, I submitted administration reconsideration to MEP' got 13 recommendations, seven reposts, 8,879 readings and 50 comments.[89] Moreover, he was also invited to one NetEase online discussion where netizens were invited to ask him questions with regard to information disclosure requests. In total, 64 questions were posted and answered during the online interaction. He received support from many of the participants for requesting the PM2.5 information. For instance, one netizen commented:

> I support you. The public should be made aware of the environment they live in. To disclose the data can help the public to take appropriate safety measures. This is the duty of the EPB who shall not use research as an excuse to act irresponsibly to the public. Everyone should have the right to monitor the EPB.[90]

In another case where newly-weds sued the Hunan provincial-level EPD for not disclosing information about the telecommunications base which was installed next door to them,[91] their representative lawyer, Lei Zhifeng, an environmental protection volunteer particularly focusing on radiation pollution, posted the case, relevant laws and regulations, his administrative reconsideration application and government reply letters on his blog.[92]

Yang argues that, in a restrictive political environment, the Internet 'enables voluntary environmental activity with minimal financial resources' and 'plays a crucial role in providing environmental groups with a presence and creating public visibility'.[93] Inevitably, the Internet has made environmental information disclosure requests not only visible, but also cost-effective in raising public awareness and garnering public debate and support.

Discussion

According to Zemans, a dependence relationship exists between law enforcement and how citizens use the law; individual citizens, although acting largely in their own interest, in an aggregation can strongly influence the implementation of public policy.[94] However it suggests that this aggregation has not been forming in China at present due to the fact that most people still have not got used to challenging government authorities. Generally, Chinese citizens and environmental organizations are mostly reactive rather than proactive in taking action. In the words of a Chinese lawyer:

> [There is] a psychological barrier, that to request an information disclosure is to challenge the government and act against the government. … This request is a legal right and we did not see anyone detained for an information disclosure request. There is no need to worry about it. However, it has been an old habit to think that to challenge the government is risky. Many people do not really understand the law, thus this customary concept exists.[95]

Nevertheless, a legal channel has been established and has enabled Chinese citizens and organizations to participate in environmental matters. Along with the development of requesting government agencies to disclose information, visible changes have also been happening in both the social and political system. First, citizens' activism in environmental information disclosure requests has clearly made government agencies become aware of their legal obligations. Before citizens' requests, many government agencies did not know the new regulations well or did not have officials to deal with environmental information disclosure. When members of Friends of Nature first went to the Shanghai EPB with an

[88] Data collected 24 October 2012.
[89] Data collected 27 November 2012.
[90] NetEase online discussion dated 6 December 2011.
[91] Case 28.
[92] Zhifeng Lei, 'About request Hunan EPD to comply its obligation of electromagnetic monitoring' ['Guanyu shenqing hunansheng huanbaoting lüxing dianci jianguan fading zhize de shenqing'], (25 May 2012), available at: http://blog.sina.com.cn/s/blog_4ed8b93b010165jf.html (accessed 10 March 2014).
[93] Guobin Yang, *Weaving a Green Web: The Internet and Environmental Activism in China*, China Government Series Issue 6, Environmental Change and Security Program (ECSP) (Washington DC, United States, 2003), p. 91.
[94] Zemans, 'Legal mobilization', p. 690.
[95] Interview with lawyer, 6 May 2011.

information disclosure request, they were mistakenly regarded as 'petitioners' (*shangfang renyuan*);[96] however, later they started to cooperate with each other. When they first went to the Jiading District EPB, nobody in the EPB knew about environmental information disclosure but, later, the Jiading EPB did disclose all the information as requested.[97]

It is argued here that the attitude of government agencies plays an important role in encouraging more public requests for environmental information disclosures; a positive attitude by the government agencies towards public requests makes people feel that there is no need to fear challenging the government. Nevertheless, it is more important to understand that this changing of attitude is in fact facilitated by the public, and not delivered automatically by the government agencies. It is clear that the core argument in the approach to opportunity structures is that the opportunity, either in its constraints, possibilities or threats, matters in collective actions.[98] However, it must also be emphasized that public action can cause the opportunity structure to change towards providing more possibilities. Accordingly, the positive responsiveness of government agencies will thus encourage more citizens to take action. This development could be gradual and slow; nonetheless, in the field of environmental information disclosure and in terms of the cycle of requesting and responding, more requesting and more responding has been happening in China. And more importantly, this cycle is evolving around utilizing legal rules and legal tactics, making it difficult for the government to directly reject this new type of public participation.

Second, environmental information disclosure can also result in specific policy changes. Undoubtedly, the pressure imposed by public opinion and environmental information disclosure requests has helped to force the Chinese government to begin to monitor PM2.5 as one standard of air quality. Thus, it can be predicted that, if more requests for environmental information disclosures are made, more pressure will be imposed upon government agencies and more changes will be initiated.

Conclusion

To sum up, the changes in the legal system have shaped and disseminated a new concept of access to government information in Chinese society. Moreover, during this process, empowered by law, the public has been gaining more capacity to interact with and push government agencies to fulfill their legal obligation. This has successfully pushed citizens' requests for information disclosure beyond their initial target of obtaining the information *per se*; instead, the legal mobilization of environmental information disclosure requests turns the requesters into active players in the political process.

Although it is too early to say that citizens' actions have created a measurable effect already, cumulatively they will raise public awareness and create political change, thus forming part of the emerging civil society activities. Law, even not fully implemented, has a serious role to play in Chinese politics.

Acknowledgements

The author would like to express her deep gratitude to Lauri Paltemaa, and the two anonymous reviewers for their constructive comments on this article. She is also very grateful to all the citizens and organizations who kindly offered help for her interviews and fieldwork.

[96] Friends of Nature, 'Introduction of Shanghai Friends of Nature Group's environmental information disclosure requests'.
[97] *Ibid.*
[98] Lisa Vanhala, *Making Rights a Reality?: Disability Rights Activists and Legal Mobilization* (Cambridge: Cambridge University Press, 2011), p. 10.

Grand Mediation and Legitimacy Enhancement in Contemporary China—the Guang'an model

JIEREN HU and LINGJIAN ZENG

China has seen numerous instances of collective resistance in recent years. Suppression cannot stop popular resistance. It is also hard to solve all problems through the existing judicial system, administrative method or by social means. Based on a case study in Sichuan, this article studies the Grand Mediation (GM) mechanism in Guang'an as one of the ways in which the Chinese government chooses to build institutions and channel social grievances. GM is successful in containing social conflicts and helping the state to garner legitimacy by reducing people's hostility towards local government, which could enhance the CCP's legitimacy, whose paramount goal is to maintain political stability and social harmony.

More than 30 years have passed since China's reform and opening policies of the late 1970s. The continuous economic transformation, cultural innovations and legal reforms in China reflect an on-going effort by the ruling Chinese Communist Party (CCP) to enhance its ruling legitimacy and reach a harmonious society under pressure from a large number of domestic social conflicts, the grievous surrounding territorial disputes and the ever changing international environment. The new generation of scholarship has born witness to the great variety and increasing intensity of contentious politics in contemporary China. Since 1994, when a total of 10,000 incidents of 'public order disturbance' were recorded, the frequency and scale of mass protests have increased significantly each year.[1] The Ministry of Public Security reported that in 2005 police dealt with a total of 87,000 cases of 'public order

1. See Immigration and Refugee Board of Canada, 'China: civil unrest involving farmers, workers, homeowners and tenants, particularly in rural areas of Guangdong; conditions causing the unrest; government response; reports of arrests, beatings and detention (2004–2006)', available at: http://www.refworld.org/docid/45f147e22f.html (accessed 23 September 2013).

disturbance', or an average of 240 incidents per day across China, many of which involved disruptive tactics or even violence.[2]

Although these Chinese contention repertoires still draw on traditional forms of resistance like tax protests, labor conflicts or petitions, they have expanded to involve new forms such as Internet-based mobilization and online protests.[3] Moreover, most reported protests, triggered by official unresponsiveness, corruption, violation of citizens' rights and laws, or repressive tactics by authorities, began peacefully but were further fueled by citizens' growing awareness and understanding of their legal rights. And, unlike other social movements in the post-Mao era that were led by urban intellectuals focusing on national politics such as the Democracy Wall movement of 1979, the student protests of 1986, the Tiananmen democracy movement of 1989 and the China Democracy Party of 1997–1998, the recent social unrest reflects local economic grievances and lacks political goals and organizational strength. This is because the state monopoly of the public sphere fosters and reproduces large numbers of individual behaviors with similar claims, patterns and targets. The state bureaucratic apparatus in the workplace also generates similar discontents and links them with national politics.[4] If handled improperly, social grievances could have great potential to help undermine the CCP's power and the ruling legitimacy of the Party leadership, making the state intrinsically unstable.[5]

With the paramount goal of maintaining political stability and social harmony, the Party-state has never stopped seeking new mechanisms to defuse and resolve social problems as the Party leadership is concerned about the potential crises brought about by popular resistances, mainly fearing the danger of collapse. The Party-state is always struggling with effective methods of handling social disputes motivated by urbanization and social transformation. For example, in order to resolve labor conflicts, it has attempted to promote the 'tripartite mechanism', and in particular to enforce collective contracts.[6]

Authoritarian regimes such as China are characterized by the lack of an independent judicial system and a failure to provide adequate legal remedies for the people who seek justice.[7] Although state power always tries to prevent regime-threatening actions

2. The collective incidents include labor strikes, disruptive collective petitions, sit-in demonstrations, fasting, posting slogans, attacking governmental agencies, surrounding leaders, blocking public traffic and damaging public property, etc. For the increased frequency and size of these incidents, see Jae Ho Chung, Hongyi Lai and Ming Xia, 'Mounting challenges to governance in China: surveying collective protestors, religious sects and criminal organizations', *The China Journal* no. 56, (2006), p. 7.

3. Nowadays citizens seek more support from the media or from sympathetic social organizations to gain resources and access to formal institutions. In particular, the Internet provides people with access to news from a variety of sources, up-to-the-minute information on events and processes, and different points of view. It also allows unprecedented interactivity on rapidly growing social networks such as Twitter, YouTube, Facebook and MySpace. The Internet has introduced new forms and dynamics into popular protest; see Guobin Yang, 'The Internet and civil society in China: a preliminary assessment', *Journal of Contemporary China* 12(36), (2003), p. 458.

4. Xueguang Zhou, 'Unorganized interests and collective action in Communist China', *American Sociological Review* 58(1), (1993), pp. 54–73.

5. Dingxin Zhao, 'China's prolonged stability and political future: same political system, different policies and methods', *Journal of Contemporary China* 10(28), (2001), pp. 427–444.

6. Feng Chen, 'Labor conflicts in China: typologies and their implications', *Asian Survey* 53(3), (2013), p. 481.

7. Randall Peerenboom and Xin He, 'Dispute resolution in China: patterns, causes, and prognosis', *East Asia Law Review* 4, (2009), p. 9, available at: https://www.law.upenn.edu/journals/ealr/articles/Volume4/issue1/PeerenboomHe4E.AsiaL.Rev.1%282009%29.pdf (accessed 10 August 2013).

and to maintain social order amid a legion of social conflicts, this does not mean that ways of dispute resolution are absent in China even if they are not so effective.[8] One recently implemented mechanism—GM (*datiaojie*)—has been practiced to manage intractable disputes in political, economic or ideological areas during China's dramatic social change.[9]

GM was started in Nantong, Jiangsu Province in 2003, which was identified as a 'linked mechanism' (*datiaojie liandong jizhi*) with the integration of civil mediation (*minjian tiaojie*), administrative mediation (*xingzheng tiaojie*) and judicial mediation (*sifa tiaojie*). It was implemented with a combination of all kinds of political and administrative resources from different levels of government agencies to resolve social disputes at the grassroots level.[10] In fact, it is a macro-control system aimed at detecting any potential danger the government may face, preventing the escalation of conflict, and reducing the magnitude of social resistance and easing the tensions between the people and local government.

Given that the Chinese courts bear the heavy burden of addressing social disputes and maintaining stability, at the local level courts and government have been actively involved in conflict resolution and have tried some innovative practices and alternative ways of dispute resolution (ADR) to fulfill political tasks, such as promoting 'active judiciary' (*nengsong sifa*) and requiring that judges go to the local communities to mediate disputes and solve people's complaints towards the government.[11] The People's Courts in China, as subordinate organizations of the state apparatus, have to take the state's priority of maintaining social stability seriously and are strongly responsible for preventing and defusing social conflicts, which are perceived by the state as great threats to the social order. Therefore, notwithstanding the Chinese Constitution's stipulation that 'the people's court should exercise its independent judicial power without any interference from administrative organizations, social groups, or individuals',[12] the courts are actually greatly dependent upon the political authorities and work closely with administrative organs like the Office of Letters and Visits (*xinfangban*), particularly for funds and support. Moreover, judges in such a judicial system share a dual identity: representing adjudicators as well as government officials. They also bear 'potential hazards' when dealing with collective disputes largely because of how they settle these cases is related to the evaluation of their work and future promotion. This leads to public worries about the Party/government's interference in managing disputes and may lead to

8. See for example, Xiaohua Di and YuningWu, 'The developing trend of the people's mediation in China', *Sociological Focus* 42(3), (2009), pp. 228–245.

9. Jieren Hu, 'Grand mediation: mechanism and application', *Asian Survey* 51, (2011), pp. 1065–1089; Keith J. Hand, 'Resolving constitutional disputes in contemporary China', *University of Pennsylvania East Asia Law Review* 7(1), (2011), p. 143.

10. Hu, 'Grand mediation', p. 1070; for the implementation of GM in different places in China, see Lamei Song, 'Nantong dengdi de datiaojie tansuo jiqi qishi' ['The exploration and implications of grand mediation in Nantong and other places'], available at: http://www.szps.gov.cn/shenzhen/cms/article.jsp?articleId=2c9084c7260783b501263fa39e4102da (accessed 22 July 2013).

11. Suli Zhu, 'Guanyu mengdong sifa yu datiaojie' ['On active judiciary and grand mediation'], *Zhongguo Faxue* [*China Legal Science*] no. 1, (2010), available at: http://article.chinalawinfo.com/Article_Detail.asp?ArticleId=53760 (accessed 29 July 2013); Yingzi Wu, 'Shenme shi nengdong sifa? weishenme yao mengdong sifa' ['What is active judiciary? Why it needs active judiciary?'], available at: http://www.gmw.cn/01gmrb/2010-05/13/content_1119469_3.htm (accessed 29 July 2013).

12. *Constitution of China*, Article 126.

a lack of impartiality during the mediation process, especially when the amount at stake is high or the legal issues *ad hoc* significant to local or national interests, or when the outcome of the case might affect a particular government official, who, for example, might have been involved in corrupt behavior or responsible for decisions that would lead to losses for the defendant organization. Putting it another way, the lack of rule of law and judicial independence has reduced people's confidence in the court/judicial system, diverted their preferences for choosing non-litigation paths to settle disputes, and even damaged the central government's legitimacy.

Lipset emphasized that legitimacy is a long-term, historical process by which a regime overcomes crises and evolves into a political system whose governance is broadly accepted and seldom challenged, except by fringe groups or after protracted crises of performance.[13] Therefore, legitimacy is about the worthiness of a regime's political system being recognized by its people under governance.[14] All political regimes have to make sure that their authorities are accepted without resorting to overt coercion.[15] Legitimacy is a concept that encompasses different criteria relating to the nature of dispute resolution: is a form of dispute resolution properly embedded in a reliable institutional environment? Are its outcomes properly underpinned? What strategies does the Chinese government use now to build institutions and channel energies for social conflicts? How can the Chinese government maintain and consolidate the regime's legitimacy while facing great pressures from egregious popular protests and the constraints in controlling the situation of non-institutionalized or illegal modes of collective action?[16] Scholars have mostly focused on the motivation, forms, discourse and organization of GM at different places in China; they have also investigated the factors pushing the Chinese government to promote this mechanism as a response to severe social movements with the aim of defusing collective incidents.[17] However, very few of them have clearly addressed the political concern for GM as a form of institutional building and conflict containment, and how it could help to consolidate state legitimacy by resolving disputes effectively.

This article examines the link between the institutional background and practice of GM and the legitimacy problem in China. After operationalizing the use of 'legitimacy' as an evaluative concept, it explores how GM works as a form of

13. Seymour M. Lipset, *Political Man* (New York: Doubleday and Company, 1960).

14. Yongshun Cai, 'Power structure and regime resilience: contentious politics in China', *British Journal of Political Science* 38(3), (2008), p. 417.

15. William Connolly, ed., *Legitimacy and the State* (Oxford: Basil Blackwell, 1984).

16. The 'non-institutionalized collective action' refers to the protests and displays of open defiance that are not initiated by the state—they bypass legitimate institutional channels to directly challenge the state; see Zhou, 'Unorganized interests and collective action in Communist China', p. 62.

17. See, for example, Lusheng Wang, 'Diwei yu celue: "datiaojie" zhong de renmin fayuan' ['Status and strategy: people's courts in the "grand mediation"'], *Fazhi yu Shehui Fazhan* [*Law and Social Development*] 6, (2011), available at: http://www.civilprocedurelaw.cn/item/Print.asp?m=1&ID = 2241 (accessed 10 August 2013); Jiahui Ai, '"Datiaojie" de yunzuo moshi yu shiyong bianjie' ['The operation pattern and boundary suited for grand mediation'], *Fashang Yanjiu* [*Studies in Law and Business*] no. 1, (2011), available at: http://www.civillaw.com.cn/article/default.asp?id=52598 (accessed 10 August 2013); Weiming Zuo, 'Tanxun jiufen jiejue de xin moshi—yi Sichuan "datiaojie" moshi wei guanzhudian' ['Exploring the new mode of dispute resolution: focusing on "grand mediation" in Sichuan'], *Falv Shiyong* [*Journal of Law Application*] 2(3), (2010); Hu, 'Grand mediation', pp. 1065–1089.

institutional building and conflict containment to resolve collective disputes so that it could serve as an effective method to mitigate social anger and consolidate the government's legitimacy, i.e. to ease social tension, maintain state power while minimizing political costs? We argue that the enhancement of an authoritarian regime's legitimacy should be balanced against the need for social conflict resolution: the lack of an effective method of defusing social unrest from the grassroots level is of no avail to strengthen state resilience. And, in essence, collective action in China is actually an aggregation of large numbers of spontaneous individual behaviors produced by the particular state–society relationship. GM, as a special way of managing social disputes by uniting judicial, administrative and social forces, can, to a large extent, more effectively resolve disputes by reconciling the relationship between state and society, i.e. request the government to make more concessions and satisfy citizens' needs according to their requests while balancing the interests of different parties.

In the following sections, we will first analyze and compare the basic modes of conflict resolution in contemporary China that are now used to defuse social disputes between the state and the people. Then, we will examine how GM could enhance legitimacy by defusing social disputes and collective incidents in China. Based on the case study of the 'Guang'an model' (*Guang'an moshi*) in Sichuan, China, where the traditional people's mediation has been practiced for years and with quite notable achievements of conflict resolution after GM was established on 20 August 2008,[18] it verifies GM's effectiveness in helping restore rapprochement between the local people and the government according to law. This article argues that GM could grant: (1) more concessions by the party who should pay compensation to the other after the reconciliation is achieved by local government and the mediators; and (2) fewer chances for collective protests to escalate into a situation that is out of the state's control. It concludes that the Chinese central government would be able to enhance its legitimacy through the successful practice of GM at the local level—using GM to defuse collective resistance and social grievances and regain acceptance from the people.

GM and the modes of conflict resolution

Many a paper has analyzed the nature, development, roles and effects of different means of dispute resolution in China.[19] Diamant argued that there was diversity among Chinese in their choices of dispute settlement, but mediation, together with 'adjudication, appeal to higher level political institutions, and violence' were all 'often used methods'.[20] No matter what methods the government chooses, it has been attempting to adopt a pragmatic and problem-solving approach to balance justice and

18. From the internal document, Justice Bureau of Guang'an, *Guang'an shi renmin tiaojie weiyuanhui lianhehui gongzuo qingkuang huibao* [*The Work Report on the Municipal Federation of People's Mediation Committee in Guang'an*], (15 October 2009).

19. For example, Kevin O'Brien and Lianjiang Li, 'Suing the local state: administrative litigation in rural China', *The China Journal* 51, (2004), pp. 75–96; Ethan Michelson, 'Climbing the dispute pagoda: grievances and appeals to official justice system in rural China', *American Sociological Review* 72(3), (2007), pp. 459–485.

20. Neil Diamant, 'Conflict and conflict resolution in China: beyond mediation-centered approaches', *Journal of Conflict Resolution* 44(4), (2000), p. 543.

efficiency while maintaining socio-political stability and rapid economic growth. The outcome is continuous experimentation leading to the creation of new mechanisms.[21] GM is one typical example designed to achieve this goal.

Studies of Chinese polity have found the unique dual institutional structure of the state–society relationship: the state's strong organizational control over society and the systematic positive incentives for compliance offered by the socialist economic institutions.[22] Andrew Walder has deeply studied the 'unit-ownership system' (*danwei suoyouzhi*) in Communist China which ties workers to their workplaces, peasants to their villages and individuals to their work units.[23] The Chinese state has effectively monopolized the resources for social mobilization and denied the legitimacy of any organized interests outside its control. As a matter of fact, the creation and promotion of a GM mechanism can be interpreted as a strategy mobilizing all kinds of political and administrative resources and coordinating the judicial system, local government and other public departments such as the Police, the Bureau of Civil Affairs, the Urban Construction, the Environmental Protection and so on, to resolve disputes more effectively, and to increase political support from the people and thereby try to avert threats to social stability and consolidate the state power. GM, as a mechanism devised by the state, could produce more conformity among officials, develop a higher level of technical skills in mediation and problem solving, and encourage officials to devote to the regime's stability maintenance as their own interests and political chances are related to their performance on defusing collective resistance.

Before talking about the advantages and special role of the GM mechanism in legitimacy enhancement, a comparison of GM and the three most popular modes of dispute resolution will be made to illustrate their characteristics and limitations. From Table 1 we can see that judicial, administrative and the traditional people's mediation are the most common ways chosen by Chinese people to manage disputes. The People's Courts can attempt mediation provided by the courts on the premise of voluntariness by the disputing parties. As long as they achieve consensus, the 'mediation agreement' (*tiaojie xieyishu*), which needs to be signed by both parties, carries the same legally binding power as court decisions. Critics of judicial litigation/court mediation point out that courts and judges lack independence and have to submit to the will of political power rather than to the law, particularly when dealing with politically relevant cases. Lawyers and judges still face social and political constraints. The outcomes of a number of high-profile cases tried in the past few years, involving political dissidents or rights activists, indicate that courts are showing a continuing commitment to the primacy of state power and have come close to being the 'lieutenant of the local government'.[24] Besides, the high cost of litigation, the long legal proceedings and uncertain results lead people to seek alternative forms as substitutions.

21. Peerenboom and He, 'Dispute resolution in China', p. 2.
22. Zhou, 'Unorganized interest', p. 55.
23. Andew Walder, *Communist Neo-Traditionalism* (Berkeley, CA: University of California Press, 1986), p. 6.
24. Solomon argues that judges in authoritarian states understand the limits of what is possible and do not challenge the regime's core interests unless the regime is losing or leaving power; see Peter Solomon, 'Courts and judges in the authoritarian regimes', *World Politics* 60(1), (2007), p. 136; also see Qianfan Zhang, 'The people's court in transition: the prospect of Chinese judicial reform', *Journal of Contemporary China* 12(34), (2003), p. 71.

Table 1. GM and modes of conflict resolution

Modes of conflict resolution	Organization(s) taking the corresponding responsibility	Functions	Limitations
Judicial way	The People's Court	To provide litigation/ adjudication and court-based mediation (*fayuan tiaojie*); ensure legally binding agreements between disputing parties	Courts and judges remain fully embedded in the state apparatus so that judiciary becomes the last line of defense for social justice
Administrative way	Governmental organizations/ *xinfangban* or trade unions (*gonghui*)	Administrative mediation provided by officials from the government	Conflicting parties may violate the administrative mediation agreements and may bring the disputes to the court again. The core weakness is that it lacks effectiveness in conflict resolution
The traditional people's mediation	People's mediation committees (*renmin tiaojie weiyuanhui*)/ mediation workrooms	An informal, non-judicial type of dispute settlement conducted by mediation organizations with legally binding protocol signed by the conflicting parties	Although people's mediation is free and based on the mutual agreement of the disputing parties, the mediation organizations' close links with the government reduce their flexibility and autonomy when managing disputes and may even create bureaucratic inclinations
Grand mediation	Operating by various governmental organs at different levels from provincial to county, under the leadership of Party Committee (*dangwei*), the government, and the Judicial and Administrative Departments (*sifa xing zheng bumen*), coordinated by the Comprehensive Control Department (*zonghe zhili bumen*) of the Politics and Law Committee (*zhengfawei*)	A united mechanism linking civil mediation, administrative mediation and judicial mediation together to settle disputes	Governmental interference is still strong, courts are unable to play an independent role in GM; high cost to unite different organizations together therefore it creates great financial burdens for the government; great submission to the Party Committee and the government may easily cause unfairness and opacity for citizens during the process of dispute settlement

Source: designed by the author.

An administrative method of dispute resolution is a form of mediation conducted by officials from local governments at different levels or state administrative organs like *Xinfangban* or trade unions according to administrative laws and civil laws. In the case when the parties do not conform to the administrative mediation agreements and bring their disputes to the people's court, the court will reinvestigate the disputes regardless of the previous agreement. This means that the agreements made by administrative mediation lack legally binding power and effectiveness in dispute resolution. It could hardly reach a win–win situation if both parties are not satisfied with the outcome and definitely would waste their time and energy during the repetitive process of litigation.

People's mediation is under the guidance of the People's Courts and local governments. The *People's Mediation Law* in China, which came into effect in August 2010, prescribes that people's mediation committees are local residents' self-governed organizations with a specific function to solve civil disputes.[25] Due to the principle of free will and free of charge, as long as both parties agree, they can go to the people's committee or the People's Mediation Workroom (*renmin tiaojie gongzuoshi*) to negotiate and solve their problems.[26] However, the claim that the people's mediation committee works as a 'self-governed' one is often criticized as being part of the local state in that the strong intervention of state power ruined its independence and impartiality during the mediation process. The fact is that the Chinese government, even by revitalizing the people's mediation organization, has the intention of regaining its organizational grip over grassroots society so that the Party's political control over the larger Chinese society could be consolidated.[27]

GM is *de facto* the product of the mixed non-litigation culture and authoritarian governance in China. It operates from the provincial to the county level under the leadership of the Party Committee and various governmental organs. Previous research has shown that the main problem with this united mechanism is that the strong governmental interference leads to courts' incapability of playing an independent role and lack of transparency during the dispute settling process.[28] However, the question remains whether GM can perform such a role of enhancing the regime's legitimacy? If yes, in what ways? The following section will discuss the rationale behind the implementation and deepening of GM by the Party-state and the degree to which it could fulfill the political task while settling social conflicts.

25. See *Zhonghua Renmin Gongheguo Renmin Tiaojiefa Quanwen* [*The People's Mediation Law in the People's Republic of China*], available at: http://www.chinanews.com/fz/2010/08-28/2497656.shtml (accessed 20 March 2013).

26. For the newly practiced People's Mediation Workroom and its operation at the grassroots level to settle disputes, see Jieren Hu, 'Weiquan Zhengti Xia de Chongtu Jiejue—Shanghai Shequ Quntixing Chongtu de JingyanYanjiu' ['Conflict resolution in the authoritarian regime: empirical study of collective conflicts settlement in Shanghai communities'], *Zhongguo Xingzheng Pinglun* [*The Chinese Public Administration Review*] 18(2), (2011), p. 125.

27. Jieli Li, 'A response to "The developing trend of the people's mediation in China": an institutional transformation of grassroots mediation in conflict resolution: where is China headed?', *Sociological Focus* 42(3), (2009), p. 248.

28. Hu, 'Grand mediation', pp. 1069, 1086.

GM as a form of conflict resolution and legitimacy enhancement

Scholars studying the regime's legitimacy and contentious politics in China argue that the state's response to popular resistance depends on its political arrangements that can help the state address the concession–repression dilemma and enhance the regime's resilience.[29] GM could be viewed as another kind of 'political arrangement' from the top-level government to allow lower-level authorities a certain degree of autonomy in dealing with collective incidents. The most recent document from the Central Comprehensive Control Committee of Social Management (*zhongyang shehui guanli zonghe zhili weiyuanhui*) makes a strong request for promoting the *People's Mediation Law of PRC*, reinforcing the GM system in resolving social disputes.[30] The aim is to strengthen the state power and prevent potentials that threaten the ruling legitimacy.

Firstly, to smooth cooperation and promote grand integration. The ten-year practice of GM since 2003 shows a loose cooperation among various departments when managing social disputes. This is against the original intention of making an integrated system to unite administrative, judicial and people's mediation together. Given that the court is endowed with the central position and acts as the final decision-maker to ensure the effectiveness of people's mediation in GM,[31] it should enjoy more independence in the dispute resolution process and take the leading role in coordinating the whole GM system. Moreover, other organizations like the trade unions, Women's Federations and Communist Youth League should also participate actively in the mediation of labor disputes, marriage and family problems, and disputes among adolescents, respectively. With all functional departments involved in the GM mechanism, the process of managing disputes and preventing severe collective resistance could be shortened so that the efficiency of managing disputes and citizens' trust toward the government could be increased.

Secondly, well-defined power and responsibility. Each department involved in GM should have a clearer division of labor and make different responses based on the nature and magnitude of the conflict *per se*. Past experience shows that some officials would pass the buck if their higher leaders gave harsh directions on the dispute settlement. However, in our study of the Guang'an model, few officials working in the GM system would complain or say no to the work due to the balance and coordination between the lower-level government and other functional departments involved. The appraising and rewarding standards for the officials and mediators' performance are also based on their achievements in dispute resolution. Officials who make contributions and provide efficient and effective advice on dispute resolution should be granted high praise and awards. On the contrary, those who shirk their responsibilities and cause severe outcomes would be seriously criticized and

29. Cai, 'Power structure and regime resilience', pp. 414–415.

30. See 'Guanyu shenru tuijin maodun jiufen datiaojie gongzuo de zhidao yijian' ['Guidelines on further deepening the grand mediation for social disputes and conflicts'], available at: http://www.legaldaily.com.cn/index_article/content/2011-05/17/content_2663226.htm?node=5954 (accessed 7 August 2013).

31. Li Su, 'Guanyu nengdong sifa yu datiaojie' ['On judicial activism and grand mediation'], *Zhongguo Faxue* [*China Legal Science*] no. 1, (2010), p. 14.

punished or even dismissed from their current position. Therefore, the authority and credibility of government agencies and officials could be guaranteed.

Thirdly, to encourage social organizations and greater autonomy. Quite a lot of social organizations and quasi-administrative units in China are allowed by the state as the state's top-down political arrangement to improve its relationship with the society. But it is a 'state-led civil society' in that social organizations are affiliated with government departments and lack independence compared with their counterparts in Western countries which are self-governed, full of freedom and have an active participation in social affairs.[32] However, we could view the support for social organizations from the central government as a reconstruction of state power and civil society: it shows a decline in state power giving rise to rights consciousness and civil society development because the leaders have become aware of the advantages of social organizations in reducing mediation costs and sharing government's or court's burdens in defusing social grievances. The role of social organizations in connecting laborers, residents and all walks of society to the government has been confirmed and stressed in the implementation of GM.[33]

Hence, GM is designed to resolve conflicts and defuse social grievances more effectively. As a mechanism promoted by the government, it hopes to control and manage social crises and emergencies, alleviate social tensions, and prevent instability brought about by social conflicts; and, most importantly, to enhance its legitimacy.

The central government would enjoy legitimacy as far as society expects it to fulfill its end of the deal.[34] In practice, how does GM work to fulfill the task of reducing the confrontation between the state and the people and enhancing legitimacy? The empirical study in Guang'an in Sichuan Province is selected to illustrate the special functions of GM in reconciling conflict and increasing people's trust and acceptance of local government by resolving collective disputes. The implementation and limitations of GM will also be critically analyzed.

The Guang'an model and its implications

Guang'an is the hometown of the previous President of China, Deng Xiaoping, and is located in the eastern Sichuan Province with a population of 4.6 million. It has become famous for the long-term strategy and policy of implementing people's mediation and promoting diversified dispute resolution methods. The *Guang'an model* is defined as the GM mechanism in Guang'an with a collaborative mediation network—the Federation of People's Mediation Committee (FPMC) (*renmin tiaojie weiyuanhui lianhehui*)—which is comprised of five-level mediation committees and

32. Michael Frolic, 'State-led civil society', in Timothy Brook and Michael Frolic, eds, *Civil Society in China* (New York: M.E. Sharpe,1997), p. 48.

33. The role of social organizations has been recognized by Chinese government and society during recent years, especially their advantages in settling social disputes; see Yue Pan, 'Shehui zuzhi guanli tizhi gaige: rang "wendingqi" fahui gengda zuoyong' ['Reform on the management system of social organizations: bringing the "social stabilizer" into full play'], available at: http://politics.people.com.cn/GB/1026/15908392.html (accessed 20 August 2013).

34. Yanqi Tong, 'Morality, benevolence, and responsibility: regime legitimacy in China from past to the present', *Journal of Chinese Political Science* 16(2), (2011), p. 152.

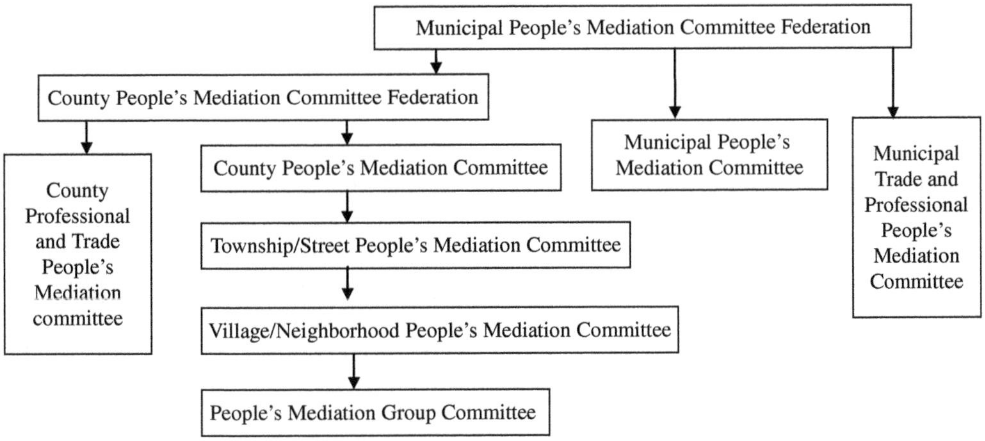

Figure 1. The structure of the Guang'an model.
Source: Authors' survey, Guang'an, Sichuan Province, 2009.

the specialized mediation committees working together to handle various kinds of social disputes and collective resistance. It was stipulated by the Justice Bureau of Guang'an in 2008 that the legal nature of the FPMC is that it is a non-profit and voluntary organization comprised of mediation committees and mediators at municipal and county level. The funds are mainly from the government, interest accumulation and other legitimate income.

Figure 1 shows the structure of the Guang'an model: vertically, from Municipal, District/County, Township/Street, Village/Neighborhood, to Building;[35] horizontally, it has professional and trade mediation committees, aiming to unite people's mediation with judicial mediation, administrative mediation and Letters and Visits mediation (*xinfang tiaojie*), etc.[36] The federation council of FPMC is composed of one chairman, six vice-chairmen and one secretary-general.[37] In 2010, Guang'an started to employ 'persuader and mediator' (*quantiaoyuan*) at the grassroots level and hence now forms a six-level mediation web besides the implementation of the five-level mediation system network from Municipal to Building. It is worthwhile investigating the characteristics of this model and how it works to help enhance state legitimacy. In-depth interviews and participatory observation were conducted in August and December 2009 to study

35. There have been 25,161 mediation groups, 2,974 Village/Neighborhood mediation committees, 181 Township/Street mediation committees, five District/County mediation committees and one municipal mediation committee up to July 2009 in Guang'an. Data are from *Guang'an shi renmin tiaojie zuzhi jianshe qingkuang biao* [*Table of Organizations Building in Guang'an*], (July 2009).

36. There have been 127 professional mediation committees including enterprises and institutions, administrative departments, transportation, health, markets, properties, consumer's associations, etc. up to July 2009. Data are from *Guang'an shi renmin tiaojie zhidu chuangxin yu fazhan* [*The Institutional Innovation and Development of People's Mediation in Guang'an*], (September 2009), p. 21.

37. Details can be found in Judicial Bureau of Guang'an, ed., *Guang'an shi xian renmin tiaojie weiyuanhui lianhehui ziliao ji* [*Data Set of Municipal and County People's Mediation Committee Federation in Guang'an*], (2009), p. 23.

the characteristics of the Guang'an model and to pursue the empirical cases resolved through the GM mechanism there. We also returned to the field in October 2010 so that the role of the FPMC and the GM's reconciling relationship between the government and local people could be further explored.

The people's courts in Guang'an also faced mushrooming civil and commercial disputes and were incapable of resolving all the disputes at the grassroots during the social transformation. Table 2 illustrates that from 2005 to 2008, especially after 2007, the number of cases the people's courts had to manage kept rising, with a dramatic increase in civil and criminal cases in particular. This is due to the failure of mediation by the traditional people's mediation committees with part-time and unprofessional mediators—most of whom were actually Party leaders at different levels—and shortages of resources for coordination. Tables 3 and 4 showthat the allocation of mediators in Guang'an at Township/Street and Village/Neighborhood level demonstrates the insufficiency of specialized mediators in various areas and, particularly, for mediating medical disputes and provincial border issues which are actually should be resolved with great urgency.

These limitations, plus the situation of the intensification and greater magnitude of conflicts between the people and the local government, make it hard to control collective protests and riots and to defuse the grievances from the people for the local state. Hence, the Guang'an model was established to overcome these problems by

Table 2. Cases dealt with by the courts at two levels in Guang'an

Year	Total (case)	Criminal (case)	Civil and commercial (case)	Administrative (case)	Judges (people)	Average cases/ per judge	Rate of increase (percentage)
2005	9,743	2,008	7,515	220	336	29	/
2006	8,179	1,692	6,330	157	339	24.1	− 16
2007	8,822	1,689	6,951	182	352	25	7.86
2008	13,267	1,847	11,130	290	340	39	50.39

Source: *Guang'an shi renmin tiaojie weiyuanhui lianhehui de wanshan yu fazhan* [*Perfection and Development of the Federation of People's Mediation Committee in Guang'an*], (December 2009), p. 4.

Table 3. The allocation of mediators at Township/Street and Village/Neighborhood level

	Mediators total (people)	Members of mediation committee (people)	Mediators (people)	Full-time mediators (people)
Township	2,236	516	860	860
Street	117	27	45	45
Village	20,804	5,944	14,860	0
Neighborhood	324	108	180	36
Total	23,481	6,595	15,945	941

Source: Justice Bureau in Guang'an, ed., *Guang'an shi renmin tiaojie zhuanxiang diaoyan tongjibiao* [*Statistics of specialized people's mediation in Guang'an*], (2009), p. 1.

Table 4. The allocation of mediators in professional and trade mediation committees

Types of mediation committees	Mediators total (people)	Full-time mediators (people)
Corporations	314	138
Traffic accidents	45	15
Medical disputes	9	0
Academic areas	15	6
Labor disputes	24	12
The protection of the rights and interests of consumer associations	21	13
Property management disputes	21	18
The provincial border	7	0
Others	12	10
Total	468	212

Source: Justice Bureau in Guang'an, ed., *Guang'an shi renmin tiaojie zhuanxiang diaoyan tongjibiao* [*Statistics of specialized people's mediation in Guang'an*], (2009), p. 1.

getting full support from the government for resources and mobilizing functional departments to join the FPMC.

Firstly, the Guang'an municipal government has ensured adequate funds for the implementation of the Guang'an model including hiring professional mediators as specialists for settling disputes and other related expenses.

Secondly, mediators are required to have professional qualifications and a university degree, preferably B.A. of Laws or above. They should have a certain amount of experience of mediating disputes in the field and after being recruited they should be appraised through a professional titles evaluation system. Opportunities for further training and skills promotion will also be provided by the Guang'an municipal government.

Thirdly, by learning lessons from the 'Li Qin People's Mediation Workroom' in Shanghai, the Guang'an model would establish its own mediation platform like workrooms and specialized mediation teams.[38]

When dealing with conflicts of only a small scale, a few people or daily disputes, such as family and marriage disputes, lending disputes and so on, there is no big difference between the Guang'an model and the other forms of dispute resolution regarding the method of management and settlement and the resulting outcomes. However, in cases of serious disputes with a wide range, a large number of people or with violence, the Guang'an model has its advantages with regards to effectively reducing grievances and resistance towards the local government. Table 5 listed a string of large-scale incidents involving death from 2008 to 2010 in Guang'an, all of which have been mediated and settled by the FPMC in a short period of no more than 20 days, and some were resolved in only one day. This is due to the united force from Party and government, Bureau of Justice and other social forces to prevent severe

38. For the study of 'Li Qin People's Mediation Workroom' in Shanghai, see Jieren Hu, 'Tiaojie, zai xinfang he falv zhiwai—duoyuanhua shequ jiufen jiejue jizhi yanjiu' ['Mediation, beyond law and petition—a study on diversified conflict resolution mechanism in communities'], *Zhongda zhengzhixue pinglun* [*Sun Yat-Sen University Political Review*] no. 5, (2011), pp. 34–59.

Table 5. Collective dispute resolution from 2008 to 2010 in Guang'an

No.	Date	Case	Agency responsible for resolving the disputes	Results	Duration (days)
1	3 September 2008	A high school student—Mr Tan—died of some illness on campus in Wusheng County. His parents and relatives prepared to petition the local government, asking for 500,000 yuan as compensation	The FPMC in Wusheng County mediated this dispute until consensus was reached	The village health center paid 36,000 yuan as compensation and the high school provided 19,000 yuan as financial aid for the students' family	9
2	19 December 2008	A teacher—Mr Zhang—died after receiving treatment in a clinic in his factory	The FPMC in Huaying mediated the dispute	The clinic provided 5,000 yuan as humanitarian aid for Mr Zhang	5
3	5 January 2009	A villager of Wusheng County—Mr Chen—got injured when working on the construction site; he died after first aid in the hospital	The FPMC in Wusheng County mediated the dispute	The construction company paid 205,000 yuan for all kinds of expenses, on the condition that Chen's relatives were to help the company claim compensation from the insurance company	5
4	30 August 2009	One student in Linshui County died when swimming in the reservoir	The FPMC in Linshui County mediated the dispute	The school failed to supervise the student and paid 36,000 yuan as compensation to the family	18
5	23 May 2010	One villager in Wusheng County—Mr He—was drowned when he was swimming with his friend—Mr Chen	The FPMC in Wusheng County mediated the dispute	Mr Chen paid 19,000 yuan as compensation for He's death, funeral expenses and other expenditures	1
6	9 June 2010	A madman—Mr Li—in Yuechi County suddenly beat Mr Feng, causing Feng's son huge anger who then hit Li. Li was assailed with fierce blows to the head by Feng's son and was pronounced dead after first aid in the hospital	The FPMC in Yuechi County mediated the dispute	Mr Feng paid 50,000 yuan to Li and his sister as compensation for medical expenses, funeral expenses and other expenditures	10

Source: from authors' survey in Guang'an, Sichuan Province, 2010.

conflicts with the potential for escalation. During the process of dispute resolution, the governance legitimacy of the local government has been enhanced. By analyzing a typical case of one citizen's unnatural death in a county of Guang'an, this article will illustrate how the Guang'an model functions to resolve collective disputes and work as the stabilizer to improve the people's trust towards the local government.

This collective dispute was caused by the death of a college student—Mr Chen—in Guang'an F College. On 22 March 2009, Mr Chen was bathing in the dorm on campus but was then found dead later that night. Chen was only 21 years old and his parents and relatives could not believe the fact of his passing away. After the police investigation, the medical report showed that Mr Chen took his bath after drinking two bottles of wine (1L) and slipped while having a thermos in hand, injuring his brain and chest with the fragments of the broken thermos. The doctors failed to bring him back to life despite treatment in the hospital. Mr Chen's father could not accept this explanation and insisted that it was an unnatural death. On 27 March, Mr Chen's parents and 20 more relatives went to F College and demanded the college pay 800,000 yuan as compensation for their son's accidental death. They insisted that the College should take responsibility for their son's death. After negotiations, the College only agreed to pay 85,000 yuan as compensation for Chen's tuition fee and other expenses on campus, with another 65,000 yuan as financial aid to his family. There was still a huge distance between the expectations of Chen's parents and the total amount willing to be paid by the College. No consensus was reached in the first round. This result aggravated Chen's parents and drove them to turn to the government and society in order to seek justice and help. The death of Mr Chen also caught the media's attention and was reported continuously after it happened. It also aroused a strong sense of sympathy and unfairness among the people in Guang'an and other provinces in China.

In the Chinese institutional setting, citizens involved in collective action may have diverse targets and demands at the beginning, but they would tend to converge in a common direction owing to the centralized goal and opportunity structure. Chen's relatives' refusal of the compensation offered would drive Chen's family to seek help from higher level agencies. This, as a result, would bring great pressure on the College to control the situation and settle the dispute, and make the local government worried about violent resistance and petitions to the central government. Hence, on 28 March, as soon as the FPMC in Guang'an received the information, they called on several departments in charge of dispute resolution and stability maintenance together to work out a way of defusing the grievances of Chen's relatives and tried to prevent collective actions, which included the Municipal Office of Stability Maintenance (*weiwenban*), the intermediate people's court, the Police, the Bureau of Justice, the Education Bureau, the Politics and Law Committee of Yue chi County, and the officials in the Township government and Party Committee. These administrative agencies formed a dispute resolution team on the spot.

After studying Chen's case, the FPMC organized six work groups with clear division of labor to control the situation and settle the conflict. These groups included the Investigation Group, the Emotion Pacification Group, the Social Order Maintenance Group, the Public Feeling Management Group, the Legal Advice Group and the Mediating Work Group, as shown in Table 6. The Guang'an Municipal Government and Party Committee (*shiwei shizhengfu*) led the other agencies to

Table 6. Six work groups organized by the FPMC to handle the case

Order number	Work group	Responsible agency	Specific task in mediating the dispute
1	Investigation Group	The Police	To investigate the cause of death by the autopsy and elicit the truth of the case
2	Emotion Pacification Group	The officials in the Township government and Party Committee	To avoid the exacerbation of the conflict and try to pacify the emotions of Chen's parents and relatives
3	Social Order Maintenance Group	Led by the Police, coordinated by Education Bureau and the Street Office/Township Government	To keep social order and ensure liaison between the school and parents
4	Public Feeling Management Group	Led by the Police, coordinated by Education Bureau and the Street Office/Township Government	To pay attention to the media and news reports on this case especially the information on the Internet, especially to prevent rumors on the case
5	Legal Advice Group	Led by the Politics and Law Committee and in the charge of the courts, the Police, the Bureau of Justice and the Education Bureau	To provide legal advice for the mediation committee and both parties based on law and policy; to make clear each party's rights and responsibility (the student vs. the College) and prevent the exacerbation of the dispute
6	Mediating Work Group	Experts in the FPMC working as the mediators	To provide professional mediation and try to reconcile the two parties and reach a consensus on the compensation

manage the case as coordinated by FPMC. Mr Chen's father accepted the facts of his son's natural death rather than a murder after the explanation from the Investigation Group. He accepted further concessions and claimed that the compensation should be no less than 300,000 yuan after being comforted by officials from the Emotion Pacification Group.[39] Meanwhile, the work teams also contacted the F College and made the College heads agree to pay 170,000 yuan for compensation. However, the gap between the two party's expectations was still very big. On 30 March, the angry relatives from Chen's family came to F College again, shouting that if they refused to pay 300,000 yuan they would gather at the gate of the Municipal government and ask for justice from the leaders.

Given the dominant role of the Chinese government in managing social affairs, the effectiveness of dispute resolution in the country—how the government exercises its power—has a significant impact on citizens' rights protection. As is often the case, collective disputes between citizens and companies, factories, developers or other related parties at first would later turn to target the local government. This would lead to an escalation of society's hostility toward the government and even harm the legitimacy. As demonstrated in cases in both rural and urban China cities, lack of an efficient and effective way of defusing the collective disputes would worsen the relationship between the local citizens and the government, and this would threaten social stability and in turn lead to bad impact on economic development and human security. The officials in Guang'an detected the tension between Chen's family and the government and thought of inviting lawyers and professional mediators to the mediation meeting held on 31 March. The specialists from the Social Order Maintenance Group and the Mediating Work Group explained the civil law to Chen's relatives and the possible result if they went to court, and calculated the compensation fee F College should pay by law. One of Chen's relatives—Ms Wang—told us that they could accept the explanation from the lawyers and leaders because they presented the facts and persuaded by reasoning: 'We are grateful that the leaders from the government took this case seriously. We just hope that my cousin did not die without a clear explanation'.[40]

After four days' mediation, in addition to the previous amount of compensation, i. e. 85,000 yuan for Chen's tuition fees and other expenses on campus and 65,000 yuan as financial aid to his family, F College accepted to pay another 30,000 yuan as the mental injury solatium for Chen's parents and their family. Hence, a potential collective petition towards the government has been defused and settled within a short period of time. The advantage of FPMC is reflected in the government's leading role and the work teams' efficient resolution with clear division of labor. In particular, the Party Committee and the local government directly contacted Chen's family members and comforted them. The people hereby have self-identification with the local government and their grievances caused by the death of their son are reduced. During this process, the local government's ability to handle disputes is appreciated and accepted by the people and the legitimacy has been enhanced. The central government of China also confirmed the successful practice of the Guang'an model

39. From the interview with Mr Chen's father conducted during the field work.
40. From the interview with Mr Chen's auntie, Ms Wang, conducted during the field work.

in controlling social unrest as protection of civilian interests and preservation of social stability are essential sources of the regime's legitimacy.

Discussion

Although the GM is encouraged and promoted by the central government, real cases show the effect of its practice on resolving disputes and the degree to which it enhances legitimacy and people's acceptance of the government by reducing citizens' grievances in collective incidents. Moreover, it could be seen that the local government contributes most significantly to dispute resolution vis-à-vis the central government and hereby succeeded in enhancing legitimacy by reconciling conflicts and preventing serious collective actions towards the government.

The FPMC is the specific organization in the Guang'an model which plays a key role in coordination and implementation and keeping efficiency and effectiveness in dispute detection and resolution. The positive feedback on the dispute management by FPMC could be viewed through three aspects, i.e. the citizens, including the parties involved in the disputes and the public; the media reports and news on this issue; and the higher level government.

The evaluation by the public is of great value to judge the feasibility and validity of promoting GM in the long run. A single party could only provide critics or comments based on their typical case. In the GM mechanism, when collective disputes occur, extrajudicial means are applied first. The local government has developed a set of mechanisms that assigns different agencies, township governments and social organizations to defuse citizens' collective actions. In the case of Mr Chen's death, Chen's parents agreed to sign the mediation agreement because they realized that their original request was unrealistic after explanations from experts and officials so that mutual considerations from both parties could be reached. Mr Chen's parents made a silk banner for the staffs in FPMC and the local officials to express their gratitude. In other cases in Guang'an, the villagers told us that after they obtained satisfactory compensation, they usually gave high appraisals to the officials in the government as they put problem solving and reasonable explanations forward to help them understand the law and find the best choice for settling the disputes.[41] The real case convinced the people that the government is responsible for resolving their problems within a reasonable timeframe and for trying to meet their expectations. In this way, GM exemplifies the advantages of this mechanism uniting various administrative agencies in making both parties reach consensus by concession and compliance. Hence, it is successful in gaining support and acceptance from its people and enhancing the government's reputation in people's hearts and to a certain degree working to reduce the governance challenges faced by the government.

Media in the Mainland reports that the general mechanism functions effectively in that it can play a special role in reconciling the relationship between the citizen and the leaders by efficient dispute resolution. For example, the popular newspaper in Sichuan, the *Sichuan Daily*, argued that the FPMC in Guang'an has been successful in coordinating five-level government to detect, defuse, mange and resolve

41. From the interview conducted during the field work in Guang'an in 2010.

complicated and large-scale conflicts. It also claimed that a smoother cooperation and greater funds would be needed for the further development of this model.[42]

The role of the FPMC in the mediation process is given adequate credit by the higher level government. FPMC is known as a quick 'clean-up' as soon as a collective dispute starts for its timely control of the situation and prevention of escalation which serves the government's purpose of minimizing risks and costs involved in defusing collective incidents. At the Conference of Administration and Justice in January 2010, it was decided to spread and implement the Guang'an model over the whole province from Municipal, District to Street/Township and across various areas and industries.[43] The following November, the GM investigation working team from the central government went to Guang'an to inspect the work and evaluate the pros and cons from its practice. The investigation team gave high praise for the Guang'an model and planned to let the whole country take it as a reference for settling collective disputes.[44] The central government recognized the practice of the Guang'an model and stressed its role in improving the relationship between officials and citizens as well as the success in maintaining social stability by defusing conflicts effectively.

Given the special attention from the higher-level government in China, citizens would prefer to choose GM as a way of addressing their grievances because the top-down intervention if any could increase their chances of getting problems resolved. Ceteris paribus, the more support from the higher-level government, the greater the chances for people to be successful in their petition. This is because the central government is more concerned about regime legitimacy than the local government.[45] One special characteristic of GM compared with the simple format of conflict resolution is that the administrative, judicial and people's mediation could be applied independently or combined together in different conditions. This more integrated method could, on the one hand, save public resources, and make it easier for the government to devise flexible measures to resolve conflicts on the other. However, it is not uncommon for administrative departments at different levels in China to pass the buck, postpone the issue or direct it to other organizations. This is what Chinese citizens call *tuiwei* (shifting responsibility) which would bring great damage to the government's reputation and arouse great rage among the citizens if they failed to address their problems. To address this problem, the Guang'an model stipulates that government at all levels must further define their specific functions to prevent shifting responsibilities or breach of duty.[46] Since administrative power is checked and

42. Hongping Zhang and Qingshan Wang, '"Dongfang jingyan" kai Xinhua—wo sheng goujian "datiaojie" gongzuo tixi youli weihu shehui hexie wending' ['The few flowers of "the oriental experience"—the construction of GM would effectively keep social stability and harmony in our Province'], *Sichuan Ribao* [*Sichuan Daily*] no. 3, (2010).

43. Ke Chen, 'Jinnian Sichuan gedi jiang jian xianji renmin tiaojie zuzhi' ['All counties would establish people's mediation organizations this year'], *Sichuan Ribao* [*Sichuan Daily*], (10 January 2010).

44. Mao Yang, 'Zhongyang "datiaojie" diaoyan gongzuozu dao woshi diaoyan' ['The GM investigation working team came to our city to inspect'], *Guang'an Ribao* [*Guang'an Daily*], (14 November 2010).

45. Yongshun Cai, *Collective Resistance in China: Why Popular Protests Succeed or Fail* (Stanford, CA: Stanford University Press, 2010), p. 32.

46. See 'Wen Jiabao zhuchi zhengfu baogao fengong yaoqiu kefu tuiwei chepi' ['Wen Jiabao held the government reports on division of labor, requiring overcoming shifting responsibility and buck-passing'], available at: http://news.qq.com/a/20100318/000075.htm (accessed 10 August 2013).

balanced by the judicial power to guarantee justice during the mediation process, the Guang'an model could enhance public accountability and prevent passing the buck to other department. Citizens' trust toward the government could be increased through the effective problem solving strategies and united work by various parties in the GM.

Most people in China are driven to protest and violent responses are not anti-government or with the purpose of destroying society; rather, their sense of injustice triggered by the local state agencies that infringe upon people's interests is at the root of many disputes.[47] We call their protests the 'resistance of the weak', which is allowed by law but prohibited by Chinese politics. As both parties have rational calculations on the specific issues and want to gain what they want through bargaining, the result is a non-judicial method of dispute settlement—GM as an example—to meet the citizens' requests to seek compensation and justice while meeting the government's need to defuse protests and reduce social threats.

Conclusion

Facing serious social conflicts and intractable problems during China's socio-economic transformation and urbanization, the Chinese government has kept up an on-going effort to create and implement more effective forms of dispute settlement. Although unorganized and spontaneous, collective action in China is systematically structured by the particular type of state–society relationship. The motivation for addressing the people's requests is the government's strong concern to prevent social unrest triggered by collective incidents and to enhance the regime's legitimacy rather than to build up some institutionalized modes of conflict resolution.[48] The GM mechanism, as a way of defusing social stress in nature, is aimed at rescuing the government from losing acceptance from the people, preventing the country from disintegrating, and enhancing the authority and legitimacy of the Party/state. It could be seen as one form of state arrangement to foster the interconnections among the otherwise unorganized functional departments by uniting them together in a dispute resolution mechanism, by lining local agencies with central government, and by a mobilization policy that incorporates governmental and social groups.

The Guang'an model is a typical mode of GM and has played a major role in easing social tensions and defusing popular grievances in the collective disputes by integrating judicial professionalism in mediation and law with their political functions. It demonstrates a state-led mechanism for resolving social contentions and reducing challenges for the local government. The political implication from the Guang'an model is the acceptance and praise from the higher-level government and particularly the central government in China to improve its relationship with the local society through effective problem solving. It is undeniable that this 'pragmatic solution' for preventing threats toward the government allows a diversified form of

47. Ray Yep, 'Containing land grabs: a misguided response to rural conflicts over land', *Journal of Contemporary China* 22(80), (2013), p. 281.

48. Cai also stressed in his article that the recurrence of social protests suggests that conflict resolution in China is far from being fully institutionalized; particularly, the state–citizen disputes; see Yongshun Cai, 'Social conflicts and modes of action in China', *The China Journal* 59, (2008), p. 108.

dispute management in the grassroots level. GM has reduced direct confrontations between citizens and the local government as well as the parties in conflict. Even if we are unable now to predict what would happen without the FPMC's intervention in disputes, it would be too naïve to draw the conclusion that people's collective legal protests would necessarily lead to largely organized action towards the central government.

Whether GM, and particularly social organizations in GM, could have a greater developing space still remains to be seen, but up to now, the local practice of GM demonstrates a positive outcome of improving the relationship between the Chinese government and the society. The local citizens' trust and acceptance of the local government are also increased during this process and therefore this enhances the legitimacy for the central government, albeit indirectly. It also verifies Cai's argument that China's legitimacy gains from its political structure within the Chinese political system (divided state power) adds significant resilience to the regime in addressing social conflicts by granting conditional autonomy to local governments.[49]

However, we must be clear that legitimacy is gained from stable and fundamental reforms of a political system rather than from instrumental mechanisms without 'judicial independence' and GM *per se* is unable to thoroughly resolve the collective disputes and social unrests with the increasing conscientization of both peasants and urbanites in China to pursue their entitlements and rights. As a result, the challenge facing the Party-state of China is the institutional building which could resolve problems from the roots. It is also worth noting that the current situation of social problems in China has drawn the central government's attention on social stability and regime legitimacy enhancement, which in turn, could be an important driving force for democratic development and social changes in China, to encourage social organizations to help defuse contentions in particular.

49. Cai, 'Power structure and regime resilience', p. 415.

Performance Legitimacy, State Autonomy and China's Economic Miracle

HONGXING YANG and DINGXIN ZHAO

Theories that explain post-Mao China's economic success tend to attribute it to one or several 'successful' policies or institutions of the Chinese government, or to account for the success from economic perspectives. This article argues that the success of the Chinese economy relies not just on the Chinese state's economic policy but also on its social policies. Moreover, China's economic success does not merely lie in the effectiveness of any single economic or social policy or institution, but also in the state's capacity to make a policy shift when it faces the negative unintended consequences of its earlier policies. The Chinese state is compelled to make policy shifts quickly because performance constitutes the primary base of its legitimacy, and the Chinese state is able to make policy shifts because it enjoys a high level of autonomy inherited from China's past. China's economic development follows no fixed policies and relies on no stable institutions, and there is no 'China model' or 'Beijing consensus' that can be constructed to explain its success.

The Chinese economy has grown 9.7% annually since 1978,[1] and the size of China's GDP has jumped from eighth place in the world in 1980 to second place in 2010. After the Second World War, no other states except for the East Asian 'four small dragons' have sustained such a high speed of development for so long. In comparison with the four small dragons, China has a much larger population and huge regional disparity in geography, resources and human capital. We would think that, in comparison with the four small dragons, it would be much harder for China to achieve a durable development, but China did. As of today, the living standard of the Chinese in coastal regions has already reached or even surpassed the level of many

1. National Bureau of Statistics of China, *Statistics Bulletin*, see also: http://www.stats.gov.cn.

developed nations, and China is also predicted to be able to maintain high-speed development for many years to come.[2] Back in the early 1990s, many countries adopted neoliberal policies, but today their experiences have all become hard lessons. Yet, the Chinese economy has developed quickly under an authoritarian regime with a strong capacity in directing economic activities. The Chinese way of achieving economic success has, thus, been labeled as the 'China model' or 'Beijing consensus', and has attracted great attention from both intellectuals and policymakers and inspired heated debates.[3]

Theories that explain China's successful development vary greatly, but they attribute the success to good government policies and institutional designs. They differ only in identifying specific government policies or institutional designs that have actually contributed to China's success. Scholars who favor neoliberal economic policies believe that China's success is largely thanks to the market-oriented reform policies, especially the establishment of a price mechanism and promotion of property rights. Yet, state-centered theorists argue that China has had a successful economic development because of the autonomy that the Chinese state has enjoyed, which allows Chinese leaders to adopt policies that may not be in line with market principles but are conducive to sustainable development.

This article argues that, while the Chinese government has adopted many policies aimed at improving its economic performance, these policies have at the same time also generated significant unintended consequences inimical to the economy's long-term performance. What is behind China's economic success is not specific state policies, but the autonomy of the Chinese state as well as the existence of societal pressure that has effectively checked the state power. The autonomy allows the state to adjust its policies and implement new policies and institutional designs once the economy faces problems, while the societal pressure compels the state to use its autonomy prudently, so as not to make the disastrous mistakes that the Chinese state repeatedly made during Mao's time. The Chinese state derives its autonomy from China's historical legacies, and the autonomy is constrained by the state's performance-based legitimacy. We refer to this particular kind of autonomy as 'bounded autonomy' and argue that the combination of state autonomy and performance legitimacy is the key to China's economic success.

2. Robert Fogel, 'Why China's economy will grow to $123 trillion by 2040?', *Foreign Policy*, (4 January 2010); Justin Yifu Lin, 'Zhongguo Jingji Baochi 20 Nian Gaosu Zengzhang Mei Wenti' ['China has no problem to keep high-speed economic growth in the coming 20 years'], Special Article in Phoenix Website, (18 July 2011).

3. Joshua Cooper Ramo, *The Beijing Consensus: Notes on the New Physics of Chinese Power* (London: The Foreign Policy Centre, 2004); Minglu Chen and David S. G. Goodman, 'The China model: one country, six authors', *Journal of Contemporary China* 21(73), (2012), pp. 169–185; Suisheng Zhao, 'The China model: can it replace the Western model of modernization?', *Journal of Contemporary China* 19(65), (2010), pp. 419–436; Barry Naughton, 'China's distinctive system: can it be a model for others?', *Journal of Contemporary China* 19(65), (2010), pp. 437–460; Scott Kennedy, 'The myth of the Beijing consensus', *Journal of Contemporary China* 19(65), (2010), pp. 461–477; Shaoguang Wang, 'Xuexi Jizhi, Shiying Nengli yu Zhongguo Moshi' ['Learning mechanism, adaptation capability and "China model"'], *Kaifang Shidai* [*Open Times*] 7, (2009), pp. 36–40; Yongnian Zheng, *Zhongguo Moshi: Jingyan yu Kunju* [*The China Model: Experience and Dilemma*] (Hongzhou: Zhejiang People's Press, 2010); Xueliang Ding, *Bianlun 'Zhongguo Moshi'* [*Debates on 'The China Model'*] (Beijing: Social Sciences Academic Press, 2011); Yasheng Huang, *'Zhongguo Moshi' Daodi You Duo Dute* [*How Unique is the 'China Model' in the End?*] (Beijing: Zhongxin Press, 2011).

This article first provides a critical assessment on the current theories that explain China's success and summarizes our major argument. It then elaborates two key terms used in this article—state legitimacy and bounded autonomy. Finally, after a brief discussion of China's positive legacies conducive to current economic success, we present an account on the actual process of China's reform based on the theoretical framework of this article.

Theoretical background

Theories that explain China's economic success fall between two opposite traditions—the neoliberal and the state-centered argument. Neoliberals contend that China has had a successful economic development because it has embraced market-oriented reforms,[4] and established institutions (i.e. property rights, rule of law and the freedom of contract) vital for a healthy economy.[5] It is worth noting that neoliberals also call for a strong state, which is needed to install the price mechanism, property rights and the rule of law in places where such institutions are absent. A strong state is also needed to push forward reforms against the interest of powerful social groups.[6]

The state-centered theorists are not necessarily against the market. Yet, to them, the key to economic success lies in the existence of a 'developmental state', that is, a state with a strong capacity to penetrate society and great autonomy to free itself from powerful social groups.[7] Along these lines, Yao argues that China has successful development because the government can free itself from the control of the major interest groups.[8] Oi and Walder develop the concepts of 'local state corporatism' and 'local governments as industrial firms', and argue that Chinese local governments' all-round support to local industries is the key to economic success.[9] Zhou argues that the central government's GDP-centered evaluation of official performance has compelled its cadres to develop the local economy, and that China's success is attributable not to economic incentive but to political incentive.[10]

4. Jinglian Wu, *Understanding and Interpreting Chinese Economic Reform* (Mason, OH: Thomson/South-Western, 2005).

5. Yushi Mao, 'Zhongguo Gaige de Zhiduguan' ['The institutional perspective of China's reform'], *Gaige yu Zhanlve* [*Reform & Strategy*] 6, (1994), pp. 13–17; Hong Sheng, 'Guanyu Zhongguo Shichanghua Gaige de Guodu Guocheng de Yanjiu' ['Research on the transitional process of China's market-oriented reform'], *Jingji Yanjiu* [*Economic Research Journal*] 1, (1996), pp. 69–81; Weiying Zhang, 'Cong Xiandai Qiye Lilun Kan Zhongguo Guoyou Qiye de Gaige' ['China's state-owned enterprises' reform from the perspective of theories of the firm'], *Gaige yu Zhanlve* [*Reform & Strategy*] 6, (1994), pp. 18–20.

6. Douglass North, *Structure and Change in Economic History* (New York: Norton, 1981).

7. Chalmers A. Johnson, *MITI and the Japanese Miracle: The Growth of Industrial Policy, 1925–1975* (Stanford, CA: Stanford University Press, 1982); Alice H. Amsden, *Asia's Next Giant South Korea and Late Industrialization* (Oxford and New York: Oxford University Press, 1989); Robert Wade, *Governing the Market: Economic Theory and the Role of Government in East Asian Industrialization* (Princeton, NJ: Princeton University Press, 1990); Peter Evans, *Embedded Autonomy: States and Industrial Transformation* (Princeton, NJ: Princeton University Press, 1995).

8. Yang Yao, 'Zhongxing Zhengfu yu Zhongguo de Jingji Qiji' ['The neutral state and China's economic miracle'], *Twenty-First Century Review* 107, (June 2008), pp. 15–25.

9. Jean C. Oi, *Rural China Takes Off: Institutional Foundations of Economic Reform* (Berkeley, CA: University of California Press, 1999); Andrew Walder, 'Local governments as industrial firms: an organizational analysis of China's transitional economy', *American Journal of Sociology* 101(2), (1995), pp. 263–301.

Scholars also explain China's economic development by combining both the neoliberal and state-centered perspectives. Qian and Shirk attribute China's economic success to an institutional arrangement that they label as 'fiscal federation'. They argue: the fiscal responsibility system installed in the 1980s allowed local governments to retain the revenues beyond a predetermined quota; the local officials thus became strongly motivated in promoting the local economy.[11] Cheung argues that the competition among county-level governments is an important feature in China, and the key to China's success.[12]

The above theories have one thing in common, that is, they all attribute China's economic success to state policies or institutional designs. They differ only on the issue of which state policy or intervention is the key. I must stress that each of the above theories has certain validity. Who can deny that a price mechanism and institutions that support it have been crucial for a sustainable economic development? Yet, once we hold too strong a faith on this neoliberal logic, we would find it hard to explain the following reality: in China, government manipulation of the market is commonplace, and transaction costs are always high. China's market-oriented reform does not weaken the state intervention into the economy but only change the forms of intervention. What makes it ironic is the co-existence of a high-speed growth rate and a high level of state intervention, which is contradictory to the neoliberal principles. Those theories that stress the role of the Chinese state in economic development also have their strengths. Who can deny the significant roles that some government policies (e.g. the open-door for foreign ideas and investment, the establishment of a price mechanism) and the government's capacity to implement these policies have played in China's economic success? Who can say no to the argument that some institutions that have been put in place by China's central government (such as the fiscal responsibility system, cadre assessment system and leadership responsibility system) have encouraged or compelled China's local governments to promote the economy, and are playing or have played certain positive roles in development? On the other hand, these scholars have neglected to note that most reform measures in China have ended in failure, and even the successful ones have given rise to serious unintended consequences detrimental to further economic success.[13] The question, then, is: why can the Chinese economy still grow at a high speed after a certain policy that some scholars have identified as the key to the economic success is abandoned by the Chinese government?

Footnote 9 continued

10. Li-An Zhou, 'Zhongguo Difang Guanyuan de Jinsheng Jinbiaosai Moshi Yanjiu' ['Governing China's local officials: an analysis of promotion tournament model'], *Economic Research Journal* 7, (2007), pp. 36–50.

11. Yingyi Qian, Gabriella Montinola and Barry Weingast, 'Federalism, Chinese style: the political basis for economic success in China', *World Politics* 48, (1995), pp. 50–81; Susan L. Shirk, *The Political Logic of Economic Reform in China* (Berkeley, CA: University of California Press, 1993).

12. Steven N. S. Cheung, *Zhongguo de Jingji Zhidu* [*The Economic System of China*] (Beijing: Zhongxin Press, 2009).

13. For instance, in the 1980s and 1990s, labor intensive foreign companies in Guangdong, Fujian and Zhejiang absorbed a huge amount of surplus labor and contributed to China's economic development, but now these industries are the source of pollution, unemployment, China's trade war with the US and frequent workers' protests. Also, when the Chinese government pushed forward the housing reform in 1998, its original intention was to improve urban Chinese's living conditions. Yet, in a few years, while housing conditions have indeed hugely improved, Chinese can no longer buy an apartment at affordable prices.

We argue that China's economic success never lies in *any* of the policies that many scholars regard as key to economic success, but in the government's autonomy and capacity to free itself from the ideological restrictions and interest group politics and to implement new policies when negative consequences of earlier policies loom large. Our argument is close to Yang Yao's theory because we both stress the role of state autonomy in economic development.[14] Yet, Yao's theory places no importance on the frequent changes of government policies in China's economic success. It also gives no clue as to why the Chinese government is able to maintain such autonomy, and why the Chinese state has not used the autonomy to bring disaster to the country. The latter question is particularly important because history has presented ample examples that when a regime possesses great autonomy, it is very likely to use that autonomy in detrimental ways. The disasters that the Maoist regime brought to China are examples of this point.

Our argument bears similarities with the Chinese government's own explanation of China's economic success: namely, that the experimental/piecemeal nature of the Chinese reform (e.g. 'crossing the river by feeling for stones') is the key of China's success. Yet, our argument and the Chinese government propaganda differ in three crucial aspects. First, the government propaganda emphasizes only the 'state autonomy' aspect of China's success, while we stress how China's state–society relationships have constrained the state's policy choices so much so that many factors that have contributed to the economic success cannot be credited to any specific state policies. Second, the government propaganda sees much of China's economic success as intended consequences of the state policy, but our article stresses unintended consequences. Third, in our article, we stress that many historical events that led China to success (such as the rise of the household responsibility system and the rise of rural collective industry in the 1980s) were not even the targeted state policies of the time, but the positive unintended consequences unleashed by some state policies for other purposes. In other words, we are arguing that the Chinese government often touches the wrong stones, but the societal energy generated by the government's moves has led to positive consequences that the government was compelled to accept and later even motivated to take credit for it.

In explaining China's economic success, the earlier theories have also neglected the crucial roles that China's 'historical dividend' and societal forces have played in the success. By 'historical dividend', we mean some positive unintended consequences derived from China's past. More specifically, China has a strong state tradition, a tradition to base state legitimacy on good performance, and a culture that facilitates the forging of a national identity.[15] In other words, while most developing countries needed to pass the hurdles of nation-building and state-building before successful economic development becomes even possible, China has only economic development as its main task. Moreover, the ultra-leftist Maoist policies, in particular the calamitous Great Leap Forward (1958–1960) and the Cultural Revolution

14. Yao, 'Zhongxing Zhengfu yu Zhongguo de Jingji Qiji'.

15. Performance has always been a major source of state legitimacy in China ever since the Western Zhou Dynasty (ca. 1066–771 BCE). See Dingxin Zhao, 'The mandate of heaven and performance legitimation in historical and contemporary China', *American Behavioral Scientist* 53(3), (2009), pp. 416–433.

(1966–1976), led to a quick erosion of the regime's ideological legitimacy within the period of a single generation. By the late 1970s, while most communist veterans were still alive, the government had to resort to market-oriented reform to survive. When the reform started, the Chinese government still possessed a high level of autonomy and infrastructural capacity typical of a revolutionary regime, even though it was compelled to use its autonomy and capacity cautiously in order to retain the regime's eroded legitimacy.

Yet, performance-based legitimacy has the following characteristic: its promises are too concrete and it will continuously raise the people' expectations. In the case of China, unsuccessful reform measures induce massive grievances, whereas successful reforms are always accompanied by significant negative unintended consequences. Successful reforms not only improve people's lives, but also change how people think and raise people's demands. Therefore, although China has a successful economy and Chinese lives have been improving tremendously, the pressure faced by the Chinese government has never eased. Such pressure forces the Chinese government to use the autonomy it possesses to implement ever newer reforms to enhance its performance. These reforms may have fostered economic development, but they also induce more pressure from society. The social mechanisms associated with performance legitimacy and bounded autonomy have thus propelled a quick economic development.

State legitimacy and autonomy

Legitimacy and autonomy are two key concepts of this article. Any state has a certain amount of autonomy in decision making. State autonomy is first derived from some functions (e.g. territorial defense and lawmaking) that other types of organizations cannot effectively provide.[16] Modern states also derive their autonomy from many elements that constitute a state, such as the bureaucracy, army and police, and the state's capacity to monopolize certain information, materials and resources. Autonomy is crucial for a state to adopt policies against societal interest.

However, there is no guarantee that a state will use its autonomy to benefit the people. The Maoist state had an extremely high autonomy, but it was exactly in that period that the state adopted policies that brought the Chinese decades of hardship. To ensure that a state would use its autonomous power to good ends, such power must be balanced by societal forces. Therefore, Zhao and Hall have proposed the concept of 'bounded autonomy' and argued that it is most crucial for a successful economic development.[17] A state's autonomous power can be constrained by multiple forces. Competitive elections, separation of executive and legislative branches of the government, elite factionalism, interest group politics, procedure-based decision making and media freedom are the usual candidates. This article argues that the state's autonomous power can also be effectively constrained by the sources of state legitimacy. The reason behind China's success is actually a very simple one: the

16. Michael Mann, *States, War and Capitalism* (Oxford: Basil Blackwell, 1988).

17. Dingxin Zhao and John A. Hall, 'State power and patterns of late development', *Sociology* 28(1), (1994), pp. 211–229.

Chinese state enjoys strong autonomy and its autonomy is seriously constrained not by various local interests but by the regime's performance-based legitimacy.

To rule effectively, state power must be seen as legitimate by both rulers and the ruled. Following Linz, this article defines legitimacy as 'the belief that in spite of shortcomings and failures, the political institutions are better than others that might be established and therefore can demand obedience'.[18] Legitimacy became a central concept after Weber's formulation.[19] Weber believes that habit, affection and rational calculation are three bases of human compliance. Accordingly, he proposes three ideal-typical aspects of state legitimacy: a state enjoys traditional legitimacy when its power is seen by the people as being inherited or always existent; a state has charismatic legitimacy when the head of the state is perceived by the people as having exceptional quality by virtue of some kinds of mystical experiences and personal qualities; and finally, a state possesses legal legitimacy when its power is derived from a set of judicial and administrative principles that bind all members of a society.[20] Weber's classification is illuminating. However, when we apply it to understand state power, it leads to two problems. First, Weber's classification is static, while any authority relationships in real life are dynamic and interactive.[21] People's understanding of state legitimacy shapes the way people interact with the state, and such patterns of interaction will in turn shape people's perception of the nature and sources of state legitimacy. Second, Weber's ideal type separates the emotional and rational aspects of human perception, but in real life people's perception of state legitimacy is always a mixture of the two. For instance, in Chinese history, the emperor was legitimized as the 'Son of Heaven', but if he was unable to deliver some basic public goods such as natural disaster prevention and local security, his rule would be seriously challenged. The same is also true for a charismatic leader. People follow him usually out of a mix of two purposes: adoration and a hope to be better awarded. Since Weber's classification has neglected the dynamic aspect of authoritative relations and isolated emotional and rational bases of authoritative relations, it is hard to be applied in empirical analysis.

In this article, the sources of state legitimacy are not classified according to people's perception of state power, but by the ways in which state power can be justified: by a commonly accepted leader selection procedure; by services that a state provides; and by a promise to bring a better future. Accordingly, we identify legal-electoral, ideological and performance as three bases of state legitimacy.[22]

A state is based on legal-electoral legitimacy when it takes laws as binding principles for all social groups including the state elite, and when top leaders are

18. Juan J. Linz, 'Legitimacy of democracy and socioeconomic systems', in Mattei Dogan Boulder, ed., *Comparing Pluralist Democracies: Strains on Legitimacy* (Boulder, CO: Westview Press, 1988), p. 65.

19. John H. Schaar, *Legitimacy in the Modern State* (New Brunswick: Transaction Books, 1981); William Connolly, ed., *Legitimacy and the State* (New York: New York University Press, 1984); Samuel P. Huntington, *The Third Wave: Democratization in the Late Twentieth Century* (Norman, OK: University of Oklahoma Press, 1991).

20. Max Weber, 'The nature of social action', in W. G. Runciman and E. Mathews, eds, *Max Weber: Selections in Translation* (Cambridge: Cambridge University Press, 1978), p. 28.

21. Randall Collins, 'Prediction in macro-sociology: the case of the Soviet collapse', *American Journal of Sociology* 100, (1995), pp. 1552–1593.

22. For more detailed discussion, see Zhao, 'The mandate of heaven and performance legitimation in historical and contemporary China'.

popularly elected on a regular basis. Ideological legitimacy means that a state's right to rule is justified by a certain value system in the form of tradition, religion and philosophy. Performance legitimacy means that a state's right to rule is justified by its economic and/or moral performance, and by the state's capacity of territorial defense.

Weber's original formulation did not include performance legitimacy. Among Weberians, Lipset has singularly emphasized the importance of state performance to a regime's stability.[23] Yet, he also believes that state performance should not be seen in legitimacy terms because 'effectiveness is primarily instrumental, legitimacy is evaluative'. To us, evaluative process is an essential part of performance legitimacy because people naturally judge a state's performance in ways similar to their assessment of state legitimacy based on the other criteria. The only difference lies in the basis of such an evaluation. Performance legitimacy is irreducible to the other two sources of state legitimacy.

It should be stressed that all three sources of state legitimacy that we have defined are ideal types. No state will base its survival only on a single source. Nevertheless, in one country at a particular time, one source of legitimacy tends to dominate, which defines the nature of a state. This article argues that ever since the late 1970s, performance has increasingly become the primary basis of state legitimacy, and this nature of the Chinese state is crucial for us to understand not only China's economic success, but also many other aspects of Chinese society.[24]

Historical 'dividend'

The rise of the nation state and capitalism defines the age of modernity.[25] These two historical processes are related in the sense that the solid foundation of the nation state (i.e. a widely shared national identity, a modern bureaucracy and a high capacity for the state to penetrate the society) holds the key to sustainable economic development. If the major identities of a country are local rather than national or if the major identity groups in a country are engaged in an uncompromising struggle, this country will be plagued with wars and other types of conflicts. Likewise, if a state does not have an effective bureaucracy, the policies of that state will lack consistency and the officials will be prone to corruption. No economy is going to be successful in this kind of situation either. In the twentieth century, when a state was unable to develop a successful economy, it was often because that state was unable to launch a successful nation-building project.

23. Seymour Martin Lipset, *Political Man: The Social Bases of Politics* (New York: Anchor Books, 1963), pp. 64–69.

24. For the most recent debates on state legitimacy in contemporary China, see Florian Schneider and Yih-Jye Hwang, 'The Sichuan earthquake and the heavenly mandate: legitimizing Chinese rule through disaster discourse', *Journal of Contemporary China* 23(88), (2014), DOI: 10.1080/10670564.2013.861145; Jinghan Zeng, 'The debate on regime legitimacy in China: bridging the wide gulf between Western and Chinese scholarship', *Journal of Contemporary China* 23(88), (2014), DOI: 10.1080/10670564.2013.861141.

25. Charles Tilly, 'Reflections on the history of European state-making', in Charles Tilly, ed., *The Formation of National States in Western Europe* (Princeton, NJ: Princeton University Press, 1975), pp. 3–83; Rudolf Braun, 'Taxation, sociopolitical structure, and state-building: Great Britain and Brandenburg-Prussia', in Tilly, ed., *The Formation of National States in Western Europe*, pp. 243–327.

China, however, is more blessed among the developing countries. During late imperial China, neo-Confucian philosophy and organizations started to penetrate Chinese society. The process homogenized the Chinese culture, which allowed modern nationalists to construct a Han ethnicity with which most Chinese (over 92%) identify.[26] Moreover, China has a long bureaucratic tradition. In comparison with most developing countries, the task for China to build a modern nation state is considerably easier, or in other words, economic development is the major obstacle in China's modernization process. It is still not an easy task, however. Facing Japanese aggression, China never had a real chance to focus on the economy before the end of the Second World War. Subsequently, Mao's radical policies led China into another kind of disaster. It was not until after the death of Mao that China got a real chance to launch a sustained market-oriented economic development.

Yet, even though the Maoist policies brought hardships to the Chinese, they at the same time left several unintended consequences quite crucial for China's recent economic success. For instance, the Maoist self-reliance (import substitute) economic model gave rise to an industrial system that can produce almost everything, albeit with very poor quality; the Maoist education system failed to produce first-rate scientists and engineers, but it prepared for China a high-quality labor force; Mao's village industries were totally infeasible economically, but Chinese farmers gained firsthand knowledge of industrial technologies through practice; millions of urban youths were sent to the countryside during the Cultural Revolution, but these miserable souls brought new ideas and ways of life to rural China. The Cultural Revolution, exactly because it was an outright disaster for the Chinese, accelerated the decline of the Maoist ideology, fostered a shift of the primary basis of state legitimacy from the communist ideology to economic and moral performance, and compelled the Chinese state to embark on reform immediately after the death of Mao, in a time when many communist veterans were still alive and the state still retained many characteristics of a revolutionary regime. These conditions have all decisively contributed to the regime's political stability and have positively affected post-Mao China's economic development.

Recently, some Chinese neo-leftists have argued that China could have a successful economic development largely because the sociopolitical development of the Maoist era had laid the groundwork.[27] This argument is not completely senseless. As mentioned, many policies and practices from the Maoist era had some positive effects on the post-Mao economic success. Nevertheless, we must be absolutely clear that the Maoist economic model had brought hardships to the Chinese and has no future. While some of the Maoist policies and practices had positive effects on the current economic success, they are unintended consequences rather than goals of the Maoist policies and practices.

26. In comparison, Russians constituted only 44% of the population in the former Soviet Union.

27. Yang Gan, 'Zhongguo Daolu: Sanshinian yu Liushinian' ['The road of China, thirty years and sixty years'], *Dushu* [*Reading*] 6, (2007), pp. 3–13.

Road toward economic success—an empirical account

Rise of performance legitimacy: 1978–1984

During the Maoist era, the planned-economy model was unable to provide effective incentives for people to work harder, and the government-initiated social movements, especially the Great Leap Forward and the Cultural Revolution, brought the Chinese economy to the verge of collapse. At the time of Mao's death in 1976, the Chinese were very unhappy and the government faced monumental pressures, especially from people in urban areas.[28] It is not that the rural Chinese endured less hardship during the Cultural Revolution. Rather, in comparison with people in urban areas, especially the costal urban Chinese, the rural Chinese at the time had much less education, lived in scattered villages away from the political center, and knew much less of what was happening elsewhere. They had less potential to articulate politicized grievances and make their voices heard by the government. Before the reform started in 1978, the urban employment situation was grim and wages had stagnated for over 20 years; 20 million urban youths who had been sent by the state to the countryside during the Cultural Revolution desperately wanted to return home; many intellectuals and communist veterans who had been persecuted during and before the Cultural Revolution demanded rehabilitation.

Facing these pressures, the state restored the college entrance examination, rehabilitated the persecuted cadres and intellectuals, loosened its control over the media and publications, and launched the reform and open-door policy. While these policies were embraced by the Chinese, the new problems that these policies generated added more pressure onto the Chinese government. Briefly, once the people got more freedom, they started to criticize the ultra-leftist policies of the Cultural Revolution. People's grievances were not alleviated but intensified as a result. The open-door policy attracted a large number of overseas Chinese from Taiwan, Hong Kong and other parts of the world. These people not only brought into China new ways of life and ideas, but shocked their mainland relatives by their affluence. The old state propaganda on the superiority of socialism over capitalism, that the Chinese had tried to believe, was invalidated. By and by, more and more Chinese lost their faith in the communist ideology, and the state was forced to increasingly rely on performance, especially economic performance, as the fundamental basis for its legitimacy.[29]

In short, while most Chinese welcomed the new policies, what the Chinese government received in return was not praise but more and different kinds of pressure. In late 1978, the sent-down urban youths in many parts of China put on large-scale and sometimes violent protests demanding to return home. In 1979, some Beijing youths and intellectuals staged the 'Xidan Democracy Wall' movement, and the big-character posters that appeared on the walls turned increasingly critical toward the regime.[30] In the late 1970s and early 1980s, young writers who had

28. Maurice Meisner, *Mao's China and After: A History of the People's Republic* (New York: Free Press, 1986).
29. Dingxin Zhao, *The Power of Tiananmen: State–Society Relations and the 1989 Movement* (Chicago, IL: University of Chicago Press, 2001).
30. Jianying Zha, *Bashi Niandai Fangtanlu* [*Interview Records of 1980s*] (Beijing: Sanlian Publishing House, 2006).

suffered during the Cultural Revolution initiated a highly critical 'scar literature' movement. Finally, in Guangdong, Chinese crossed the border and escaped to Hong Kong on a massive scale.

Facing this situation, the Chinese state's response was to repress the radicals (i.e. the key leaders of the Xidan Democracy Wall movement) and placate the rest. Yet, the state's main thrust was on the economic reform. In this period, the Chinese government implemented the following reforms: (1) readjusting the industrial structure and introducing an incentive system to reward better workers; (2) introducing various kinds of management responsibility systems to enhance the decision-making power of the leaders in factories, universities and research institutes;[31] (3) installing the fiscal responsibility system to boost the local government's interest in economic development; (4) establishing four special economic zones to experiment with a market economy; (5) legalizing small-scale private businesses; and (6) promoting the household responsibility system in rural areas.

In China's official and scholarly circles, most people now believe that China's reform started in rural areas (i.e. the household responsibility system), and was initiated by the farmers in the poorest regions and then accepted by the government.[32] This is, however, a wrong consensus. Coase and Wang's recent study shows that, while the household responsibility system was indeed initiated by farmers and later legalized and promoted by the government, the Chinese reform started in the cities.[33] Yet, while most early urban reform measures ended in failure, the household responsibility system in rural areas was a great success. The success of the household responsibility system made the Chinese government silent about China's other early reforms and it accepted the claim that China's reform started in rural areas. Coase and Wang's finding fits our argument well: the Chinese government had to start the reform in the cities and coastal areas because these were the regions where the government faced increasingly serious challenges.

We would also point out that leftism still had a strong imprint on both Chinese officials and the people in the 1980s. Among the top officials, although most of them firmly believed that reform was the only future for China, they also inherited ways of thinking belonging to the Maoist era. Most importantly, these officials all maintained their faith in communism and saw the communist ideology as the foundation of state legitimacy. In other words, the primacy of performance legitimacy was not yet firmly established in this period. Therefore, when the top state leaders believed that their power was seriously challenged, they always launched retaliative political campaigns, even though those campaigns never lasted long under the reform environment.[34]

31. Han Zong, *Guoqi Gaige Sanshinian Qingliji* [*Personal Experience of Thirty Years of State-Owned Enterprises Reform*] (Shanghai: Shanghai People's Press, 2008).

32. Kate Xiao Zhou, *How the Farmers Changed China: Power of the People* (Boulder, CO: Westview Press, 1996).

33. Ronald Coase and Wang Ning, *How China Became Capitalist* (London: Palgrave Macmillan, 2012).

34. The anti-spiritual pollution campaign in late 1983 and the anti-bourgeoisie liberalization campaign in early 1987 are two prominent examples.

The urban reform: 1984–1989

China's agricultural productivity was greatly increased under the household responsibility system. Yet, this success carried several unintended consequences. Most importantly, when the farmers started to work hard, agricultural labor surplus immediately became an issue. Beginning in the early 1980s, more and more farmers migrated into cities to find jobs. These rural migrants competed with the urban youths and millions of sent-down youths who had just returned home, but China's state-owned industry at the time faced over-employment and new industries popularized in the 1990s, such as private companies, foreign companies, joint-venture companies and service sectors, were just emerging. The rural to urban migration and the associated unemployment became a serious problem.[35]

Meanwhile, the introduction of the fiscal responsibility system weakened the central state's taxation capacity. The market-oriented reforms induced inflation to the Chinese who had been accustomed to a life with little inflation. On top of these, more and more intellectuals stood up to criticize the wrong doings of the CCP (Chinese Communist Party) during the Cultural Revolution, and the whole process induced the rise of humanitarianism and liberalism (Chinese style) at odds with the state's ideological stance.

The Chinese government implemented more reforms to tackle these problems. In 1984, the state launched a series of more aggressive reforms aimed at enhancing the productivity of the state-owned industry, which included: (1) further expanding the managerial autonomy; (2) installing the contract worker system to break up the 'iron rice bowl'; (3) strengthening the fiscal responsibility system; (4) establishing a 'dual price system'; and (5) establishing more special economic zones in coastal regions (14 in 1984, and Hainan Province, Zhujiang Delta and Yangtze Delta were added in 1988).

These reform measures opened people's minds, imbued the price mechanism in an otherwise rigid planned economy, built up new institutions, and accumulated experiences for the later full-scale market-oriented reforms in the 1990s. From today's point of view, none of these reform measures should be regarded as failures. Back in the late 1980s, however, these reforms not only did not reach their targeted goals, but also brought a new round of social problems. Briefly put, the dual price system in conjunction with the greatly expanded power of the managers induced serious official corruption, which in part triggered the outbreak of the 1989 Student Movement and subsequently compelled the state to place 'anti-corruption' and 'rule of virtue' at the center of the state's legitimacy. The freer economic policies that the special economic zones had enjoyed allowed the local people to smuggle everything they could and sell illegally in China. Together with the rise of private business, they allowed some poorly educated Chinese to get rich almost overnight. This aroused widespread jealousy, especially among the intellectuals and college students who otherwise regarded themselves as the elite and backbone of the society. Such grievances constituted another major cause behind the 1989 Student Movement.

35. For more discussion on problems associated with the rural to urban migration, see Deng Quheng and Bjorn Gustafsson, 'The hukou converters—China's lesser known rural to urban migrants', *Journal of Contemporary China*, 23(88), (2014), pp. 657–679.

Most importantly, once the government no longer controlled the price of the goods that were in severe shortage, inflation ensued. High inflation was yet another major cause of the 1989 Student Movement.[36]

China's economy did have one shining spot, namely, the rise of rural collective industry. Yet, this was not the result of state reform, but the unintended consequence of the dual price system and fiscal responsibility system. When the Chinese government implemented the dual price system, its initial intention was to allow those state-owned industries that were able to produce more than their quotas to buy raw materials at a higher market price. What the policymakers did not expect was that the policy also allowed rural collective enterprises to buy market-priced raw materials to expand their production.[37] The rural collective industry expansion was also heavily supported by the local governments because it was then the local governments' cash cow under the fiscal responsibility system.

The rise of rural industry has been regarded by some scholars as crucial to China's economic success. Yet, China as a whole was in deep crisis. By the late 1980s, 'liberal' ideas started to take root among more intellectuals and students. These 'liberals' shared a belief that successful economic development was impossible in a country without democracy. They also condemned Deng Xiaoping's 'crossing the river by feeling for stones' style of reform and enthusiastically praised Gorbachev's 'new thinking'. They, thus, advocated political reforms and tried to expand their influence in universities, and the students who were under their influence embraced street politics. Most importantly, the grievances of different urban groups started to converge in the late 1980s on the issues of inflation, corruption and income disparity. Together, they triggered the rise of the 1989 Student Movement.[38]

The 1989 Student Movement was ended by bloody repression. Many reasons were behind this tragic ending, but the one that was most relevant to the argument of this article is the nature of the Chinese state. In the 1980s, those who held the highest power in the CCP were veterans who were fighting for the revolution and still had a deep faith in communism. Yet, these people had also suffered greatly during the Cultural Revolution and knew that reform and open-door was the only solution for China. From the perspective of this article, we see a great tension in the minds of these veterans: they insisted that the regime possessed ideological legitimation, but they all knew that only through enhancing the state's performance, especially its economic performance, could the regime survive. Therefore, these veterans all supported the reform to a varying degree, but when they felt that their power was seriously threatened, they resorted to the use of force in dealing with opposition.[39] This is why the 1989 Student Movement did not end up with a regime change as had happened in the former Soviet Union, but with a military crackdown. This is also why the crackdown not only did not end China's open-door policy, but also forced the state to stage more rigorous reforms after 1992.

---

36. Zhao, *The Power of Tiananmen*, pp. 126–128.

37. Yao Yang, 'Zhongxing Zhengfu: Dui Zhuanxingqi Zhongguo Jingji Chenggong de Yige Jieshi' ['The neutral state: an explanation of China's economic success in the transformation period'], *Economic Research Journal* 3, (2009), pp. 3–13.

38. Zhao, *The Power of Tiananmen*.

39. *Ibid.*, ch. 7.

Hesitation and determination: 1989–1992

China faced tremendous pressure after 1989. Internationally, the bloody repression was widely condemned and the Chinese government's image hit rock bottom. Domestically, although the repression ended the protest, the regime's legitimacy was also greatly eroded. China's top leaders were caught in a dilemma: they knew that China had to reform, but they were very afraid of losing control over the society.

To get out of the repression-induced legitimacy crisis, the state introduced military education to university students and staged a patriotic education campaign, but such actions only intensified the people's fear that the state was going to bring China back to the ultra-leftist past. In 1990, Beijing students jammed the door of TOEFL testing centers and waited overnight just in order to register for the examination.[40] The students were worried that the state was going to end the open-door policy and that they might no longer have the chance to leave China. They became desperate.

The top echelon of the CCP, particularly Deng Xiaoping, obviously knew the mood of the Chinese. On 31 May 1989, or a few days before the bloody repression, when Deng met with Li Peng and Yao Yilin, he told them that 'The new leaders should be new faces and give people a clear impression that they are reformers and China has hopes under their leadership'.[41] Obviously, even when the bloody repression was about to start, Deng sill held firmly to the view that the future of the CCP and China hinged on whether or not China would stick to the reform and open-door policy. Therefore, even though China's propaganda machine turned left after 1989, several important reform measures were implemented in this period, most prominent ones being the establishment of Shanghai's Pudong Development District in 1990 and Shanghai and Shenzhen stock exchanges in 1991, and the acquisition of membership in the Asian Pacific Economic Cooperation (APEC) in 1991.

Neoliberal development: 1992–2003

In 1992, annoyed by the leftist propaganda and slow pace of reforms, Deng started his southern China tour and made several famous speeches to call for more radical economic reforms. Deng's southern China tour was decisive. After the tour, top Chinese leaders all stepped out to show support, leftist propaganda disappeared from mainstream media, and the state seemed to have quietly abandoned the communist ideology as the basis of state legitimacy.

Before 1992, most Chinese still had keen memories of what they had gone through during the Cultural Revolution, and were greatly concerned that the state was going to restore the leftist policy. Therefore, in the 1980s, whenever the Chinese detected leftist voices in the CCP, they became very nervous. Deng's southern China tour brought a positive unintended consequence: seeing that the state was promoting reforms after the 1989 Student Movement, the Chinese people somehow realized that boosting economic performance through reform was the only viable policy choice for the state. In a sense, Deng's southern China tour in conjunction with the 1989 bloody

40. *Ibid.*, p. 131.

41. Mouren Wu, Minghui Bao, Peihua Ni, Peimin Ni and Qingjia Wang, eds, *Bajiu zhongguo minyun jishi* [*Daily Accounts on the 1989 Democracy Movement in China*], (no publisher, 1989).

repression, had actually enhanced people's trust in the state, and such trust also increased the state autonomy.

Economic reform was sped up. In 1992, China ended its tight monetary control, deregulated most prices except for 89 products of strategic importance, and implemented policies to encourage the development of foreign and joint venture companies. In 1994, the state recentralized taxation by installing a new tax sharing system. In 1995, the state legalized the bankruptcy and selling of state-owned industries (with the exception of 500 largest enterprises of strategic importance). At the Fourteenth Congress of the CCP held in 1992, the Chinese government announced that the establishment of a market economy was the goal of the reform. These policy changes triggered a wave in the early and mid-1990s, during which over 20 million government officials, professors, researchers and workers quit their state jobs and went into private business.[42]

Of the new reform measures, the replacement of the fiscal responsibility system with a tax sharing system deserves special attention. The fiscal responsibility system in the 1980s motivated local governments to promote businesses and stimulated the rise of rural collective industry. At the same time, it also carried negative unintended consequences. Namely, as the local economy quickly developed, the fixed tax deals under the fiscal responsibility system allowed the local governments to retain an increasingly larger portion of the revenues, and the central state became increasingly poor and had to borrow money from local governments to function. This problem eventually prompted the central state to abolish the fiscal responsibility system and replace it with a tax sharing system, which allowed the central state to take a much bigger share of the local revenue.

Some scholars argue that the fiscal responsibility system was crucial to China's economic success. Yet, the Chinese economy has gained greater momentum after the fiscal responsibility system was ended in 1994. We argue that the fiscal responsibility system had its positive side and unintended consequences, as does the new tax sharing system. China's economic success never hinges on any *one* of the state policies, but on the state's autonomy to free itself from the control of vested interests to implement new reforms when the side effects of old policies loom large. With regard to the change of fiscal policy, the Chinese state derived its autonomy largely from the 'historical dividend'—China's long centralized state tradition had given local governments little basis or means to resist a policy change even when the change would definitely hurt their interests. This, of course, is not to say that the local governments were completely passive vis-à-vis the central state's decision. After the installation of the tax sharing system, many local governments, especially those in the poor regions, faced serious financial difficulties. This compelled local officials to tax farmers more heavily, and to attract outside investment and generate income from land sales. The new tax sharing system, therefore, greatly boosted the development of foreign and joint venture companies and the rise of China's housing market. At the same time, it also created environmental problems, induced frequent land disputes and gave rise to countless protests provoked by these developments.

42. Coase and Wang, *How China Became Capitalist*.

The privatization of the state-owned industry was another reform of great consequence in this period.[43] The reform altogether removed the state's burden to subsidize a huge amount of small- and medium-size state-owned companies that could no longer be saved. In the process, most of the state property was siphoned away by those Chinese who had power and connections or even by foreign companies. Yet, the whole process, as wicked as it was, did no harm to the overall performance of the economy because those who had taken over the state-owned enterprises were often able to use them to produce better products at lower cost. The process did, however, create a moral outcry and triggered the re-emergence of leftist ideologies in China. Most importantly, millions of workers in state-owned industries lost their jobs in the process. Very frequent and sometimes violent protests by the laid-off workers and military veterans (who were assigned jobs in state-owned factories after demobilization but soon lost those jobs as the factories closed down) became headaches that the Chinese government had to face for many years to come.

In this period, the rural collective industry, which has been regarded by some scholars as the key to economic success, declined and then disappeared. The age of rural collective industry had passed, but China's economy gathered greater momentum. This again proves our argument that 'the success of China's economy never hinges on any one of the state policies'. Wei Pan, a leftist scholar, argues that the rural collective industry collapsed largely because China's neoliberal policymakers saw it as an obstacle to privatization and, therefore, were determined to end its existence.[44] We argue that, while ideology was indeed somehow behind the disappearance of the rural collective industry, it was not the main reason. Back in the 1980s, the rural collective industry was very positively regarded because it exhibited a vitality that state-owned industries did not have. Yet, in the mid-1990s, the rural collective industry, due to its low value-added technology and traditional styles of management, became increasingly unable to compete with foreign or joint ventures or even with burgeoning private companies. Another state policy was also instrumental to the disappearance of the rural collective industry: as China's state-owned banks started market-oriented reforms in 1993, it became increasingly harder for the rural collective industries to obtain cheap loans from the banks through the local governments that no longer relied as much on the revenue from the rural collective industries as before due to the rise of alternative revenue sources from foreign companies, joint ventures, private businesses and even land sales. Many rural collective enterprises were bankrupted because their capital flows discontinued. What we want to stress here is that no 'anti-rural collective industry conspiracy' existed among China's top policymakers at the time. China's reform policies were never as coherent as Pan imagined.

The reform in the 1990s was also carried out in a more 'friendly' sociopolitical context: (1) the 1989 repression forced many dissidents out of China and silenced the voices of 'liberal' intellectuals; (2) the shift of political winds after Deng's southern

43. Yang Yao, 'Privatizing the small SOEs', in Ross Garnaut and Ligang Song, eds, *China's Third Economic Transformation: The Rise of the Private Economy* (London and New York: Routledge Curzon, 2004), ch. 7.

44. Wei Pan, *Nongmin yu Shichang: Zhongguo Jiceng Zhengquan yu Xiangzheng Qiye* [*Farmers and Market—China's Grassroots Political Authority and the Township and Village Enterprises*] (Beijing: Commercial Press, 2003).

China tour silenced leftists, which meant that the forces that could potentially give support to China's underprivileged population were also silenced; (3) with the rise of the market, the lives of the Chinese people became much less determined by the policy of the central state. In other words, the social problems and people's grievances to a certain degree were localized and depoliticized; and (4) the Chinese people were still enjoying the newly achieved affluence and had not yet developed a very strong sense of rights and entitlement as they have now. Together, these structural conditions granted the state great autonomy, minimized the 'collective action problems' induced by interest group politics or/and social protests, and contributed to the 'ten golden years' of the Chinese economy.

Social policy-oriented development: 2003

Yet, while the reform in the 1990s brought a booming economy and greatly improved the living standard of the Chinese as a whole, the negative unintended consequences of the reform (including income disparities, official corruption, the collapse of the public welfare and health system, massive layoff of workers, tax burden of farmers, land appropriation and forced relocation, environmental degradation) also developed quickly. According to state statistics, incidents that can be regarded as collective actions reached 10,000 in 1994, 20,000 in 1998 and 40,000 in 2000. In 2005, collective action incidents had reached 87,000 occurrences.[45] By 2002, when Hu Jingtao and Wen Jiabao became China's new leaders, the negative unintended consequences of the neoliberal reforms of the 1990s had become very serious.

It is without doubt that the kind of protests mentioned above will create serious 'collective action problems', increase production costs and prevent further economic development. Yet, against all these odds, the Chinese economy has still maintained a high-speed development in a time when the world economy has experienced a prolonged downturn. We argue that what is behind China's current high-speed development is not the economic policy but the social policy. Confronted with these problems, the Hu–Wen administration turned its attention to social policies to ease the tensions caused by earlier reform policies. This is the so-called 'Hu–Wen New Deal'. The 'New Deal' has, to a certain degree, lowered the occupational and regional income disparities and alleviated social tension, and created a stable environment for further economic growth. On the other hand, the 'New Deal' has created its own unintended consequences that are now looming large.

The Hu–Wen New Deal has two legs—social policies and government spending on infrastructural projects. While the social policies have provided the 'changing society' with a 'political stability',[46] the government spending, together with a favorable environment created by China's entry into the WTO in 2001, has sustained China's high-speed development in the last ten years.

Among the social policies that have been implemented by the Chinese government, the following are particularly significant: (1) in 2003, the government began to establish a rural cooperative medical system that has by now covered most

45. Andrew C. Mertha, 'Society in the state: China's nondemocratic political pluralization', in Stanley Rosen and Peter Hays Gries, eds, *State and Society in 21st Century China* (London: Routledge, 2009), pp. 2–3.

46. Samuel P. Huntington, *Political Order in Changing Societies* (New Haven, CT: Yale University Press, 1968).

rural areas; (2) in 2004, the government significantly lowered the agricultural tax and started to provide subsidies for agricultural production. Farming is no longer an unattractive business as it was before; (3) in 2005, the government initiated an appliance subsidy program in rural areas. By now, big screen TVs, refrigerators and microwaves are commonplace even in remote rural areas; (4) since 2005, the government has spent heavily to construct paved roads in villages; (5) in 2006, the government passed legislation to enforce nine-years of free education, which has since then been rigorously implemented; and (6) in 2007, the government passed the labor contract law, which has played a decisive role in pushing up the wages of China's lowest income sectors several times since then.

Government spending has also become a major engine of economic growth. The infrastructural projects, such as airports and train stations, highways, and high-speed trains, have not only facilitated the travel of the Chinese people, but have also greatly lowered the transaction costs of business activities and stimulated the development of many industries. The government's appliance subsidy programs have for many years sustained the development of several related industries while world demands have sharply declined. Finally, capital from various state sectors has continuously found its way into China's booming housing market over the last ten years. Together with the money from China's ever expanding middle class, the money has significantly boosted China's housing market.

Yet, these new policies and developments carry their own unintended consequences as well. The 'New Deal' made people increasingly reliant upon the government. Consequently, Chinese interest, rather than being expressed in the form of interest group politics, is developed into a kind of poorly organized and emotionally charged populist politics. In the presence of the rising tide of protests, the Chinese government has only one effective method of containment, that is, to appease people with money.[47] This strategy channels social grievances in a direction that is impossible to institutionalize. Riots and protests have increased at a time when people's lives have actually undergone huge and general improvement.

The rise of populist politics has also created conditions for a quick re-emergence of leftist ideologies, and allowed some ambitious politicians and ideologues to tap into people's populist mentality for personal political gain, which not only undermines the autonomy of the central state but also adds uncertainties to Chinese politics. What Bo Xilai and his intellectual followers were doing in Chongqing for the past few years, and the huge impact they have created, is very much facilitated by the populist nature of the 'New Deal'.

The government-spending driven economic development has also created its own problems. In the past ten years, such a proactive fiscal policy has greatly raised the status of large-scale state-owned firms, weakened the roles of the market and private businesses in the economy, and induced massive poor-return investment. The rising state power and the power of those people who have benefited from the recent state policies have invited criticisms from liberal-minded intellectuals and created massive grievances against the privileged people. Moreover, the development of

47. Dingxin Zhao, 'Mincui Zhengzhi—Zhongguo Chongtu Zhengzhi de Zouxiang' ['Populism politics—the trend of China's contentious politics'], *Lingdaozhe* [*Leader*] 20, (February 2008), pp. 42–49.

infrastructural projects has passed its peak and cannot contribute as much to the GDP as before. China's further development depends increasingly on whether or not China is able to have a successful transition from the labor intensive, environment unfriendly development model to a capital intensive, technology-driven model.

China's state revenue has increased very quickly thanks to the superb economic performance. However, the state has started to run small budget deficits in recent years due to its huge spending on welfare provision and infrastructural projects. The Chinese government will surely face a hard time if the economy hits a major crisis. We, however, do not want to predict 'the coming collapse of China'. Scholars have frequently made this kind of 'prediction' based on different logics ever since the 1980s, but the CCP has been able to retain its power and the economy has grown continuously. China has not developed according to those ominous predictions largely thanks to the nature of the Chinese state: the state's performance-based legitimacy compels the government to keep its focus on promoting economic development and makes the government very cautious in dealing with grievances and protests, and the Chinese state's autonomy has given the government a great capacity to launch new reforms when the negative unintended consequences of old reform measures become apparent.

We are certain that China's new leaders will implement different policies. The problem, however, is that good government policies will raise people's desire and demand and bad policies will induce state-centered grievances. Regardless of how the state actually performs, it is going to face increasingly difficult challenges. Yet, it might be hard for a linear thinker to understand that such challenges are also the very secret behind China's economic success.

Conclusion

S. E. Finer has attributed the rise of the West to the existence of an unstable institutional arrangement in pre-modern Europe. He argues that while the great Asian civilizations all 'had reached the condition with which they were quite consciously satisfied and from which they did not wish to move', Europe 'from the fall of the Western Roman Empire' 'was always restless, uncomfortable with itself'.[48] What Finer means is that the medieval European elite—kings, aristocracies, priests and later the bourgeois—could never reach a stabilized power balance and were always in a state of conflict and restlessness. By the eighteenth century, the restlessness had spread to all spheres of European society as never before. Modern industrial capitalism and the nation state stumbled upon us exactly because of this never stabilized institutional arrangement. Applying this Finerian insight to understand modern China, we can immediately see that China's economic success lies also in the restlessness of the Chinese society partly induced by the Chinese state's performance-based legitimacy. Performance-based legitimacy gives the Chinese government and people a perpetual sense of crisis, on the one hand, and the Chinese society a great tension and rare kind of energy, on the other hand. This tension can lead to economic breakthrough as well as state breakdown.

48. Samuel E. Finer, *The History of Government from the Earliest Times (vols 1–3)* (Oxford: Oxford University Press, 1997), pp. 1473–1475.

The Sichuan Earthquake and the Heavenly Mandate: legitimizing Chinese rule through disaster discourse

FLORIAN SCHNEIDER and YIH-JYE HWANG

In the aftermath of the 2008 Sichuan earthquake, the Chinese authorities launched a major public relations campaign to relay positive images of their relief effort and strengthen their political legitimacy. The effect has been a proliferation of symbols and political statements related to the disaster, not only in the official media, but also in cultural products such as movies or mass-media events. The earthquake has become part of the discourse of suffering, struggle, solidarity and ultimately victory. This article examines the ways in which various cultural products present the Sichuan earthquake and asks what meanings national crises have in the Chinese discourse on political legitimacy. The article analyses two cases: Chinese film, here in the form of Feng Xiaogang's blockbuster Aftershock, and performance-based discourses during the Beijing Olympics, the PRC's 60-Year Anniversary and the Shanghai Expo. By conducting a discourse analysis, we show how the earthquake has become part of a recurring discursive formation that is used by state and non-state actors alike to legitimate China's developmental model. Within this discourse, the leadership of the Party, the mastery of free markets and a revamped version of the Confucian idea of benevolent rule are marshaled as the decisive factors for winning any 'battle'.

I. Introduction[1]

On 12 May 2008, three months prior to the Beijing Olympics, Sichuan province was hit by an earthquake measuring eight on the Richter scale. The central authorities were quick to respond, dispatching rescue teams and tens of thousands of People's Liberation Army (PLA) troops to disaster-hit areas just hours after the impact. Ninety

1. If not noted otherwise, all translations throughout are by the authors.

minutes after the earthquake occurred, Chinese Premier Wen Jiabao flew to the affected area to oversee relief efforts in person. Over the course of the following days, Chinese media outlets, such as China's state-owned national TV service China Central Television (CCTV), provided round-the-clock coverage of the earthquake aftermath, transmitting iconic images of disaster relief work and statements by Chinese leaders into homes across the nation.

For the Chinese state, this natural disaster posed a crisis, albeit in the Chinese sense of the word *weiji* (危机), which consists of the characters for both 'danger' and 'chance'. As other studies have shown, a natural disaster creates not only challenges that can destabilize the existing political order, for instance by highlighting instances of corruption, social inequalities, discrimination, etc.,[2] but a disaster also provides opportunities for a government to bolster its performance-based legitimacy if it properly manages the natural calamity and is able to guarantee the livelihood of its people.[3] What is more, at a moment of national crisis, citizens are supposed to depend even more on the state, expecting the government to lead them out of the calamity. In other words, disasters are not merely natural phenomena, but political events in and of themselves. They are symbols which can be used by various actors in order to serve their respective interests.[4]

In the Chinese case, a disaster like the Sichuan/Wenchuan earthquake provides an opportunity for the Chinese Communist Party (CCP) to retain and even enhance its legitimacy. Legitimacy here means creating acceptance for a political system and its policy outcomes among its subjects.[5] It is 'a very particular form of consensus, which revolves around the question of the right or title to rule'.[6] As a number of scholars have shown, the CCP's legitimation strategy consists of a complex mix of factors, including economic performance,[7] structural reforms of Party and state institutions,[8] a broader ideological foundation for China's political system,[9] and attempts to facilitate a sense of national unity through patriotic education and cultural

2. See for instance, A. Cooper Drury and Richard Stuart Olson, 'Disasters and political unrest: an empirical investigation', *Journal of Contingencies and Crisis Management* 6, (1998), pp. 153–161, as well as Philip Nel and Marjolein Righarts, 'Natural disasters and the risk of violent civil conflict', *International Studies Quarterly* 52(1), (2008), pp. 159–185. For the Chinese case, see Heike Holbig and Bruce Gilley, 'Reclaiming legitimacy in China', *Politics & Policy* 38(3), (2010), p. 412.

3. See Jonathan Schwartz and R. Gregory Evans, 'Causes of effective policy implementation: China's public health response to SARS', *Journal of Contemporary China* 16(51), (2007), pp. 195–213, as well as Beatrice Chen, 'Resist the earthquake and rescue ourselves', in Lawrence J. Vale and Thomas J. Campanella, eds, *The Resilient City: How Modern Cities Recover from Disaster* (Oxford: Oxford University Press, 2004), pp. 235–253.

4. Susanne M. Hoffman, 'The monster and the mother: the symbolism of disaster', in Susanne M. Hoffman and Anthony Oliver-Smith, eds, *Catastrophe and Culture: The Anthropology of Disaster* (Santa Fe, NM and Oxford: School of American Research Press and James Currey Ltd, 2002), pp. 113–141.

5. Cf. Max Weber, *Wirtschaft und Gesellschaft* [*Economy and Society*] (Tübingen: Mohr Siebeck, 1980).

6. Carl J. Friedrich, *Man and His Government: An Empirical Theory of Politics* (New York: McGraw-Hill, 1963), p. 233.

7. Dingxin Zhao, 'The mandate of heaven and performance legitimation in historical and contemporary China', *American Behavioral Scientist* 53(3), (2009), pp. 416–433.

8. Andrew Nathan, 'Authoritarian resilience', *Journal of Democracy* 14(1), (2003), pp. 6–17; Gunter Schubert, 'One-party rule and the question of legitimacy in contemporary China', *Journal of Contemporary China* 17(54), (February 2008), pp. 191–204; David Shambaugh, *China's Communist Party—Atrophy and Adaptation* (Berkeley, CA: University of California Press, 2008).

9. Anne-Marie Brady, 'Mass persuasion as a means of legitimation and China's popular authoritarianism', *American Behavioral Scientist* 53, (2009), pp. 434–457.

production.[10] Our argument is that the Wenchuan disaster discourse has become a central part of this mix, not only because of the opportunity that the event offered to further increase performance-based legitimacy, but also because the event ties into a broader disaster discourse that draws from pre-modern Chinese ideals of legitimate rule.

In this article, we look at various ways in which the Wenchuan earthquake has been presented and represented in official propaganda and mass cultural products alike, and how the event is used in such instances to evoke the idea that political unity and harmony can only be achieved under the virtuous rule of the CCP. In other words, we are concerned with legitimation practices and with the question of how these practices influence political discourse, i.e. the communication practices that shape what societies consider to be true regarding a specific political issue at a given point in time.[11] Our research is concerned with the kinds of processes that Sandby-Thomas examines in his study of the CCP's 'stability' discourse in this special section.[12] We are interested in the way in which the authorities legitimize their actions and the political system they are embedded in through discursive practices. This is not to say that our agenda is at odds with the *legitimacy* research that Schubert advocates in this same issue.[13] As Schubert points out, the legitimacy research project he has in mind includes legitimation, even if his own empirical work focuses on other pieces of the larger legitimacy mix. We will return in our conclusion to what we think the implications might be of integrating studies of legitimation with research on legitimacy.

Our key research questions are: how are the meanings of the natural disaster that hit Sichuan in 2008 tied to the Chinese discourse on legitimacy, and to what extent do cultural representations of this disaster relay the government's official disaster discourse? To answer these questions, we focus on both the official discourse and on products of *mass* culture, i.e. on cultural products that utilize technical systems of mass production to engage as broad an audience as possible.[14] In China, such products are always created within the constraints of state censorship and Party politics,[15] but should not themselves be confused with straight-forward propaganda (宣传 *xuanchuan*):[16] they are often created in cooperation with non-governmental, commercial agents precisely to add mass appeal. They are a compromise between commercial viabilities and political interests, and thus a perfect testing ground to explore what happens to official Chinese discourse as it is reworked for broad mass

10. Peter Hays Gries, *China's New Nationalism: Pride, Politics, and Diplomacy* (Berkeley, CA: University of California Press, 2004); Suisheng Zhao, *A Nation-State by Construction: Dynamics of Modern Chinese Nationalism* (Stanford, CA: Stanford University Press, 2004); Xiaoping Cong, '*Road to Revival*: a new move in the making of legitimacy for the ruling party in China, 2009', *Journal of Contemporary China* 22(83), (2013), pp. 905–922.

11. Cf. Michel Foucault, *Discipline and Punish: The Birth of the Prison* (New York: Vintage Books, 1975/1995).

12. Peter Sandby-Thomas, 'How do you solve a problem like legitimacy?: contributing to a new research agenda', *Journal of Contemporary China* 23(88), (2014), doi: 10.1080/10670564.2013.861138.

13. Gunter Schubert, 'Political legitimacy in contemporary China revisited: theoretical refinement and empirical operationalization', *Journal of Contemporary China* 23(88), (2014), doi: 10.1080/10670564.2013.861139.

14. Cf. Noël Carroll, *A Philosophy of Mass Art* (Oxford: Oxford University Press, 1998).

15. Cf. Anne-Marie Brady, *Marketing Dictatorship—Propaganda and Thought Work in Contemporary China* (Plymouth: Rowman and Littlefield, 2008).

16. Alex Chan, 'From propaganda to hegemony: Jiaodian Fangtan and China's media policy', *Journal of Contemporary China* 11(30), (2002), pp. 35–51.

consumption.[17] For our study, we have therefore selected the earthquake representations in the recent series of Chinese mass-media events that followed the earthquake (the Beijing Olympics, the PRC's 60-Year Anniversary parade and the Shanghai Expo), as well as one of the most popular films in Chinese cinema history: Feng Xiaogang's 2010 blockbuster *Aftershock*.

Methodologically, we have subjected these cases to a multi-modal discourse analysis.[18] Such an analysis shares common conceptual ground with other approaches to discourse, but is less focused on linguistics. Instead, multi-modal analyses combine written texts with verbal, acoustic and visual elements, arguing that all of these 'modes' contribute to relaying discursive content. To conduct this analysis, we have collected multi-media data on the various cases (e.g. DVD recordings, photographs, maps, etc.) and have then compiled these data in protocols that break down the dynamic communication units (such as scenes, sequences, exhibit halls, etc.) into their visual, acoustic, verbal and written elements. We then coded these elements and compared them across the different products.

In what follows, we first explain the role that natural disasters play in Chinese political thought, and how in particular pre-modern concepts of a heavenly mandate are connected to the contemporary discourse of managing disasters. We then briefly examine the mechanisms that govern the construction of such discourse, arguing that these processes are best understood as cultural governance, and offer a visualization of how the cultural governance of disasters could be conceptualized. Next, we summarize the building blocks of the official earthquake discourse as presented in China's state media, which revolves around the slogan 'putting people first' (以人为本 *yi ren wei ben*). We then investigate the selected cultural products that deal with the Wenchuan event to check whether they relay or challenge this official narrative. Our qualitative analysis confirms that the Chinese authorities are engaged in complex processes of cultural governance, but also suggests that the earlier theoretical considerations need to be expanded to incorporate the fact that these processes demand the emotional investment of audiences. Based on these findings, we conclude that the Wenchuan earthquake has indeed afforded the leadership with the opportunity to strengthen its legitimacy by indirectly controlling the proliferation of meanings and, in the words of Edelman, by 'defining the geography and topography of everyone's political world'.[19]

II. The heavenly mandate discourse

The Chinese notion of legitimacy is originally grounded in the pre-modern political idea that the right to rule derives from a divine source: the heavenly mandate (天命 *tianming*).[20] Originally invented in the Western Zhou Dynasty (ca. 1045–771

17. Anne-Marie Brady and Wang Juntao, 'China's strengthened new order and the role of propaganda', *Journal of Contemporary China* 18(62), (2009), pp. 767–788.

18. Gunther Kress and Theo Van Leeuwen, *Multimodal Discourse—The Modes and Media of Contemporary Communication* (London: Arnold, 2001).

19. Murray Edelman, 'Language, myths and rhetoric', *Society*, (January/February 1998), p. 139.

20. Zhao, 'The mandate of heaven'.

BCE),[21] the mandate of heaven was later re-conceptualized by followers of the Confucian tradition, most notably Mencius (孟子) and Xunzi (荀子), who promoted moralistic and benevolent rule.[22]

In this early Confucian tradition, the mandate of heaven was not a religious belief in patrimonial power, as it had been during the Zhou, but was predicated on the propriety of the ruler, i.e. his willingness to govern according to the Confucian code of conduct (礼 *li*), and his ability to set a moral example for his subjects.[23] The heavenly mandate therefore ties in with the idea of a righteous sovereign (君子 *junzi*) who secures his people's acceptance through his virtue (德 *de*)—an idea that became highly popular during the Han Dynasty (206 BCE–220 AD) and remained influential throughout Chinese history. It is important to note that the ideal of a ruler's virtue was not merely an ideological construct, but required actual material benefits for the populace.[24] As Mencius famously stated, 'To pursue virtue alone does not suffice for governance'.[25] Hence, the way for rulers to secure the 'hearts of the people' (民心 *minxin*) was not only to possess 'benevolence' (仁 *ren*), but also to perform their duties well. The legitimacy of rulers was thus to a large extent performance-based.

In this early discourse on legitimate rule, heaven conferred its mandate upon the sage ruler, but this conversely also meant that the ruler could lose this mandate if he neglected his duties. Important signs that a ruler had upset the cosmological order were natural disasters. As Zhao Dingxin notes: 'Throughout Chinese history, drought, flood, earthquakes, epidemics, and so on were all treated by the rulers and rebels as messages from Heaven. They cautioned the rulers to work harder and inspired the suppressed to rebel'.[26] It is not surprising that those who opposed the ruler, especially the literati who recorded the rulers conduct, often used natural disasters to legitimate their own cause, often emphasizing natural disasters and heavenly phenomena like earthquakes, floods, eclipses or comets in their historical records. According to Fairbank and Goldman, this moral and psychological 'autosuggestion' became part of the dynastic cycles and is still alive in contemporary Chinese political discourse.[27]

As central as such competency was to pre-modern rulers, it continues to exert a hold on the imagination of Chinese political thinkers today. In Chinese academic circles, advocates of so-called contemporary Neo-Confucian Thought, such as Jiang Qing[28] or Zhao Tingyang,[29] have promoted the idea that pre-modern conceptions of

21. John K. Fairbank and Merle Goldman, *China—A New History* (Cambridge, MA and London: Belknap Press, 2006), p. 40.
22. Jacques Gernet, *A History of Chinese Civilization* (Cambridge: Cambridge University Press, 1972/2002), pp. 95–96.
23. *Ibid.*
24. Wm. Theodore De Bary, *Asian Values and Human Rights: A Confucian Communitarian Perspective* (Cambridge, MA: Harvard University Press, 1998), p. 31.
25. Cited in *Ibid.*
26. Zhao, 'The mandate of heaven', p. 420.
27. Fairbank and Goldman, *China—A New History*, p. 48.
28. Qing Jiang, *Zhengzhi ruxue—dangdai ruxue de zhuanxiang, tezhi yu fazhan* [*Political Confucianism—Changes, Characteristics, and Developments in Contemporary Confucianism*] (Beijing: Sanlian shudian, 2003).
29. Tingyang Zhao, *Huai shijie yanjiu—zuowei di yi zhexue de zhengzhixue* [*The Study of the Bad World—Political Philosophy as the Primary Philosophy*] (Beijing: Zhongguo renmin daxue chubanshe, 2009).

benevolent rule should be a model for politics in present-day China.[30] Halper acknowledges this when he argues that the CCP has adopted a performance-based model of legitimacy that has much in common with the 'role-based system of ethic' promoted by Confucian thinkers: as long as the leadership is able to demonstrate its benevolence to its citizens by assuring their welfare, the citizens are believed to be willing to play their role in the Confucian ruler–subject relation, i.e. supporting their rulers rather than rising up against them.[31]

The point we are trying to make is not that the CCP 'wields its power in a way similar to Chinese emperors of the past', as others have argued.[32] The idea of the heavenly mandate indeed matters, but not because today's leaders supposedly continue the tradition of ancient Chinese rule, or because such tradition dominates all discussions on the topic.[33] It matters because those reviving this idea 'set the agenda, and thus productively generate a powerful discourse that sets the boundaries of how people think about China's past, present and future'.[34] In other words, the 'heavenly mandate' discourse influences the ways legitimacy can be imagined and represented in today's China. In this understanding of legitimacy, properly managing natural disasters is thus fundamentally important, prompting rulers to demonstrate wisdom, virtue and caring for the welfare of their people.

III. Cultural governance and the management of disaster

For the Chinese leadership, it is thus crucial to not only manage natural disasters to reinsure that its performance-based legitimacy does not wane, but more importantly, it is also essential to manage the *meanings* that events like earthquakes and government responses to such disasters have in popular discourse. CCP propaganda today no longer consists solely of official proclamations, but is increasingly concerned with public relations efforts and soft controls of cultural products.[35] In the words of Price, the Chinese propaganda system's aim is 'the control of symbols'.[36] This control at times entails direct intervention in the form of censorship, but mostly consists of indirect strategies to manage cultural expressions in ways favorable to the

30. Cf. Daniel A. Bell, *China's New Confucianism: Politics and Everyday Life in a Changing Society* (Princeton, NJ: Princeton University Press, 2008).

31. Stefan Halper, *The Beijing Consensus: How China's Authoritarian Model will Dominate the Twenty-first Century* (New York: Basic Book, 2010), pp. 150–151.

32. Yongnian Zheng, *The Chinese Communist Party as Organizational Emperor—Culture, Reproduction and Transformation* (Oxon and New York: Routledge, 2010), p. 16.

33. As Jinghan Zeng shows in this issue, advocates of a 'Confucian revival' are largely ignored by social scientists working on legitimacy issues in China, and seem to not yet have convinced their compatriots of their arguments. See Zeng, 'The debate on regime legitimacy in China: Bridging the wide gulf between Western and Chinese Scholarship', *Journal of Contemporary China* 23(88), (2014), doi: 10.1080/10670564.2013.861141.

34. William A. Callahan, 'Chinese visions of world order: post-hegemonic or a new hegemony?', *International Studies Review* 10, (2008), p. 753.

35. Brady, 'Mass persuasion as a means of legitimation and China's popular authoritarianism'; Shambaugh, *China's Communist Party*.

36. E. Monroe Price, 'Introduction', in E. Monroe Price and Daniel Dayan, eds, *Owning the Olympics—Narratives of the New China* (Ann Arbor, MI: DigitalCultureBooks, 2008), p. 11.

leadership's political agenda. It is best understood as a process akin to what Michael Shapiro has referred to as cultural governance.[37]

Shapiro notes that cultural governance is a set of practices of cultural representation, involving diverse genres of cultural expressions, which legitimate state sovereignty.[38] These practices involve, but are not limited to, the state. Power, in this sense, is diffused throughout the diverse cultural fields of society. In his analysis, Shapiro examines how actors spend large amounts of financial and symbolic capital in attempts to create coherent identities. While state sovereignty initially relied on 'military and fiscal initiatives', Shapiro argues that these 'coercive and economic aspects of control have been supplemented by a progressively intense cultural governance, a management of the dispositions and meanings of citizen bodies, aimed at making territorial and national/cultural boundaries coextensive'.[39]

The case of disasters offers insight into how cultural governance processes play out. An event like the Wenchuan earthquake indeed poses not only a risk but also an opportunity: it is a 'discursive event' that allows actors to recalibrate discourses on a wide range of issues.[40] One need only think of cases such as the 1997 Asian financial crisis, the terrorist attacks in the USA on 11 September 2001, or the Tsunami and nuclear reactor crisis that hit Japan in 2011, to see how such moments can fundamentally shift the perspectives of entire populations on issues such as security, development or technological progress. This is why the Chinese authorities have continuously tried to frame how their citizens derive meaning from such events: Chinese cultural governance is informed by the realization that representations of disasters and hazard events not only influence future crisis management and disaster preparedness, as suggested by Webb,[41] but also shape politics at large. We have visualized this theoretical argument here in Figure 1.

The diagram shows how the cultural governance of disasters could be conceptualized, and allows claims as to how such processes might work out in a specific case like the Wenchuan earthquake. To elaborate, as a *discursive event* occurs at a particular point in time (DE_1), this event will create an *impact response* (IR_1): for example, as an earthquake hits, individuals may cower under tables. Emergency personnel will dispatch to the crisis area, and protocols of crisis management will take effect. The effectiveness of these reactions influences the next impact responses (IR_2) to future discursive events (DE_2): if it turns out that ducking under tables killed many people during the last earthquake, or that the response time of emergency personal was too slow, behavior may change—people might cower next to stable objects from now on, and emergency personnel may alter their training.

37. In this sense, we suggest that studies of legitimation do not necessarily have to take a 'top-down perspective', as Schubert maintains. While the authorities indeed play a role in 'steering' legitimation, or at least try to play such a role, there are more actors involved in shaping legitimacy discourse than state and Party institutions alone. See Schubert, 'Political legitimacy in contemporary China revisited'.

38. Michael J. Shapiro, *Methods and Nations—Cultural Governance and the Indigenous Subject* (New York and London: Routledge, 2004).

39. *Ibid.*, p. 34.

40. Cf. Siegfried Jäger, *Kritische Diskursanalyse* (Münster: Unrast Verlag, 2012).

41. Gary R. Webb, 'The popular culture of disaster: exploring a new dimension of disaster research', in Havidán Rodríguez, Enrico L. Quarantelli and Russell Dynes, eds, *Handbook of Disaster Research* (New York: Springer, 2007), p. 434.

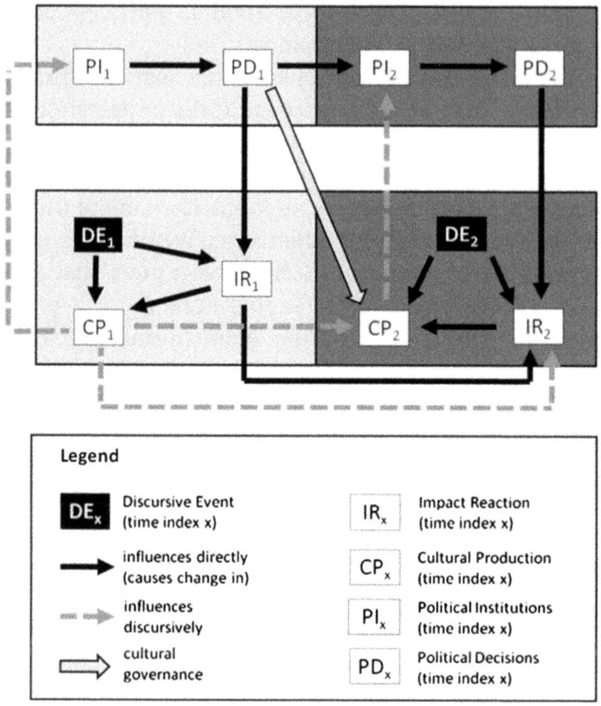

Figure 1. Discursive events in politics and culture.

What is more, the discursive events as well as the way societies deal with such events are reflected in a range of *cultural products* (CP_1). This can include anything from disaster jokes and on-site graffiti to films, songs or monuments.[42]

The sum of these products feeds back into the discourse on disasters, and thereby also influences how society will react to future events: if I have seen believable images on TV that I can survive a Tornado by hiding under a highway overpass, I may do exactly this, even though such behavior is likely going to be fatal. In our diagram, these discursive effects of cultural products are marked as dotted gray arrows. Note how our diagram goes beyond the interplay of disasters and response, and includes overarching *political institutions* (PI_1 and PI_2) and the *political decisions* (PD_1 and PD_2) that these institutions produce. Our argument is that cultural representations of discursive events influence the broader political fabric, indirectly informing and (de)legitimizing political institutions and processes that may not be related to disaster relief. Examples include the wide-ranging implications of establishing homeland security institutions in the USA after September 2001, or accelerated attempts to opt out of nuclear energy throughout Europe following the Japanese reactor melt-down in 2011. Similarly, the 2008 earthquake and its cultural meanings have an impact on institutions and their legitimacy in China.

42. Cf. *Ibid.*, p. 433.

Finally, the diagram includes another mechanism. Since actors in the political realm are well aware of the power that cultural representations of a disaster can have as tools of legitimation, they may attempt to influence such representations. This may include direct forms of political intervention, such as propaganda and censorship. It may also include softer regulatory mechanisms, such as financial incentives for the production of certain content, or convincing cultural producers to see certain content as 'unhealthy' or 'unpatriotic'. The sum of these activities is represented in the figure as the diagonal arrow from political decisions following the first event (PD_1) to the cultural products that represent future events (CP_2). The arrow represents the state's involvement in acts of cultural governance.

This theoretical representation of cultural governance processes shows how the connection between a discursive event, the cultural artifacts that lend meaning to that event, and political legitimacy can be conceptualized. The question then is: does the Chinese case provide evidence to confirm this model? Were the authorities indeed managing the meanings of the Wenchuan earthquake, and can cultural products give insight into legitimation processes in China?

IV. The official discourse of 'putting people first'

It is in this context that we first turn to the official statements that the Chinese leadership made in the aftermath of the Wenchuan earthquake. The PRC government has tried to link its disaster responses to the duties of the Party and the state to safeguard people's livelihood, thereby presenting itself as a 'humane', 'benevolent' and 'competent' ruler over China. For instance, the spokesman of the Chinese Foreign Ministry made the following remarks at a press briefing roughly two weeks after the earthquake: 'In this earthquake you can see that the Chinese government has carried out a "people-centered" relief effort ...'.[43] The political message here is that the Chinese government was dedicated to maintaining and promoting its people's right to life; a message summarized in a CCP slogan that has become a cornerstone of the disaster discourse: 'putting people first'.

The slogan is not new in CCP propaganda rhetoric. In fact, it could be said to have been part of the CCP's principle ideology for a long time. As early as 1945, Mao Zedong stressed that the Party should whole-heartedly 'serve the people' (为人民服务 *wei renmin fuwu*).[44] With this statement, Mao reiterated that the CCP should always exercise its power solely for the sake of its people and safeguard the public interest. In this context, the slogan 'putting people first' can be interpreted as a fusion of the pre-modern concepts of benevolent rule and modern Maoist notions of service to the people, which themselves arguably conjure up pre-modern ideals of virtue.

In the context of the Wenchuan earthquake, the slogan frames the legitimacy discourse of the CCP. The following is an excerpt from the Party newspaper *People's Daily* (人民日报 *Renmin ribao*), in which the author stresses the idea that people's lives stand above anything else:

43. Michael Bristow, 'Quake reveals softer side to China', *BBC News Online*, (28 May 2008), available at: http://news.bbc.co.uk/2/hi/7424262.stm (accessed 23 December 2012).

44. Mao Zedong, *On Coalition Government* (Beijing: China News Agency, 1945), pp. 123–124.

> ... life, either an individual life or the life of every Chinese citizen, is elevated to a place of paramount importance. It is essential to show the respect and solicitude for and the understanding of people, to protect them and be at their service, and to explain the connotation of the concept of 'putting people first'.[45]

Note how the right to life is established as the highest value in a country like China, which in a related statement is said to face frequent natural calamities and an acute shortage of per-capita resources.[46] The rescue and relief efforts are thus framed as an exercise in 'putting people first'. Chinese officials frequently used political mottos such as 'ensuring the safety of the people's lives' or 'saving lives is the priority' during the earthquake's aftermath. This emphasis on people's lives echoes the official discourse on human rights, with its emphasis on subsistence rather than political rights, and collapses Marxist and Mencian conceptions of welfare.[47] To give an example, an article in the *People's Daily* concludes (our emphasis):

> ... it is the governing concepts of 'putting the people first' and the national will of 'placing lives above anything else' that have turned a tragic earthquake ... into a nationwide rescue of human lives, and *only* the concrete, trying deeds during the earthquake relief can be said to be the *true* record of China's convincing human rights effort.[48]

Such statements achieve two things. On the one hand, they open up possibilities to discursively establish that an authoritarian government is as capable as, perhaps even more capable than, a liberal-democratic political system in responding to the needs and suffering of its people. This becomes clear in Chinese comparisons between the Wenchuan disaster relief effort and, for instance, the US administration's responses under George W. Bush to cyclone Katrina in 2005.[49] On the other hand, these discursive statements establish political categories that justify government action and shift responsibility away from issues of disaster preparedness to issues of disaster relief. We return to this issue below.

What is important in this context is that the discourse presents the CCP and the Chinese government as leaders of all rescue efforts and establishes state organizations,[50] especially CCP leaders such as President Hu Jintao and Premier Wen Jiabao, as model 'servants of the people'. For instance, the *China Daily* reported that Hu instantly called for an all-out effort to save people's lives, and that Wen boarded a plane bound for the disaster areas less than two hours after the quake had

45. 'Learning to experience "people coming first" concept amid quake', *People's Daily Online*, (11 June 2008), available at: http://english.peopledaily.com.cn/90001/90780/91342/6428348.html (accessed 23 December 2012).

46. 'A special lecture on China's national conditions', *People's Daily Online*, (26 May 2008), available at: http://english.peopledaily.com.cn/90001/90780/91342/6418410.html (accessed 23 December 2012).

47. Cf. Robert Weatherley, *The Discourse of Human Rights in China* (Hampshire and New York: Palgrave, 1999), p. 123.

48. 'A special lecture on China's national conditions', *People's Daily Online*.

49. Cf. Guibin Xiong and Dinghong Chai, 'Comparison of the disaster relief system between China and the USA—based on the Wenchuan earthquake and the Katrina hurricane', *Journal of East China University of Science and Technology (Social Science Edition)* 24(1), (2009), pp. 16–21.

50. Steve Tsang, 'Consultative Leninism: China's new political framework', *Journal of Contemporary China* 18 (62), (2009), pp. 873–874.

hit.[51] This discourse also had a visual component, as state news services showed pictures of Wen, the 'commander-in-chief of the anti-earthquake disaster relief headquarters', on the charter plane: Wen studying a map of Sichuan; Wen surrounded by his aids 'researching and arranging the disaster relief work'.[52] The press would later broadcast images of Wen walking through ruins and paying his respects to those who lost their lives.[53] By depicting Hu and Wen as swift, diligent and warm-hearted, the state press disseminated the CCP's legitimacy discourse, both visually and verbally.

Moreover, the press coverage in China focused heavily on the PLA as the backbone of, and indeed a strong guarantor for, citizens' safety. The official news in the aftermath of the earthquake reported that the military response to the earthquake was rapid.[54] PLA soldiers reportedly went to the disaster-stricken areas to save lives, some even dying during the rescue operations. The state discourse framed these soldiers as heroes, and the disaster as a military battle: the soldiers, so the reasoning went, fought the disaster (抗震 *kangzhen*)—an allusion to China's War of Resistance against Japan—and saved others without regard for their personal safety.

Finally, the presentations of the earthquake stress the importance of a Chinese nation united through its solidarity towards the victims.[55] As Lan Yuxin's analysis of 5,500 print-media items in the four months following the disaster shows, these tropes were also adopted by more commercial press organs.[56] Across all print-media, the top five themes during this time period were solidarity donations, public and private disaster response, reconstruction planning, the concept of 'putting people first', and social responsibility.[57] What is striking is that 'an overwhelming amount of the writing was emotional', and that the print coverage of the event repeatedly included phrases such as 'China hold on! Sichuan hold on! Wenchuan hold on!' or 'We are all Wenchuan people'.[58] The question then is how this official disaster discourse was reworked in cultural products that were commissioned by the authorities, but not necessarily designed by state or CCP actors. What role did emotional appeals to an imagined community play, for instance, at the public–private collaborative mass events of the Olympic Games, the PRC 60-Year Anniversary or the Shanghai Expo?

---

51. 'Information is power indeed', *China Daily Online*, (14 May 2008), available at: http://www.chinadaily.com.cn/opinion/2008-05/14/content_6683433.htm (accessed 23 December 2012).

52. 'Wen Jiabao dida Sichuan Chengdu, zai chuanjishang fabiao zhongyao jianghua' ['Wen Jiabao arrives in Sichuan's Chengdu and gives important speech on charter plane'], *CCTV.com*, (12 May 2008), available at: http://news.cctv.com/china/20080512/107201.shtml (accessed 23 December 2012).

53. 'Premier's hands-on approach an inspiration', *People's Daily Online*, (15 May 2008), available at: http://english.people.com.cn/90001/6410952.html (accessed 23 December 2012).

54. 'Near 20,000 soldiers arrive in quake-hit SW China, 30,000 more coming', *People's Daily Online*, (13 May 2008), available at: http://english.people.com.cn/90001/90776/90882/6409855.html (accessed 23 December 2012).

55. See: Ni Chen, 'Institutionalizing public relations: a case study of Chinese government crisis communication on the 2008 Sichuan earthquake', *Public Relations Review* 35(3), (2009), pp. 187–198; Liangen Yin and Haiyan Wang, 'People-centred myth: representation of the Wenchuan earthquake in *China Daily*', *Discourse & Communication* 4, (2010), pp. 383–398.

56. Yuxin Lan, 'Coverage of the Wenchuan earthquake: an overview', *The China Nonprofit Review* 1(2), (2009), pp. 221–245.

57. *Ibid.*, p. 225.

58. *Ibid.*, p. 242.

V. From official to collaborative discourse: Wenchuan at China's mass-media events

The various mass-media events that took place in China between 2008 and 2011 saw repeated use of recognizable, emotionally charged symbols related to the Wenchuan earthquake, which were deployed to communicate that unity and solidarity are crucial to China's developmental agenda, especially if the nation is to weather seemingly unpredictable crises such as large-scale disasters. References to the earthquake abound: for example, on 8 August 2008, only three months after the earthquake, the Beijing Olympics Opening Ceremony explicitly referenced the event on national TV. Lin Hao, a nine-year-old boy from the quake-affected Sichuan province, carried the Chinese national flag side by side with NBA star Yao Ming, as they led the Chinese delegation of 639 athletes into the National Stadium, suggesting that the athletes were united behind the boy and what he symbolized.

Another example is the 60-Year Anniversary of the PRC in 2009, which included several references to the Wenchuan disaster. During the parade, a float was dedicated to overcoming natural calamities. In addition, in a multi-media opera performance called *The Road to Revival* (复兴之路 *Fuxing zhilu*), which was staged specifically for the anniversary, one scene pays homage to the Wenchuan earthquake by enacting a stylized drama of relief workers saving a little girl. The quake is represented in Act 4, Scene 14, and is introduced by two announcers in grey suits. This is their introduction to the events:

> *Female Announcer*:
>
> On 12 May 2008, the exceptional Wenchuan earthquake shocked the world. Pairs of helping hands stretched out towards the disaster region. In this time of peril, everyone demonstrated great, boundless love.
>
> *Male Announcer*:
>
> Complete unity reigned, and in unity there is strength. [We] defied all hardship and kept fighting despite all setbacks, putting people first and respecting scientific knowledge. The stirring and inspiring anti-earthquake disaster relief proved that much distress regenerates a nation. Regardless of the difficulties and obstacles we face, the Chinese nation cannot be conquered!

The subsequent performance utilizes a large mass of actors, dressed in army fatigues and doctor's coats, who scour the ground for hints of survivors. A sole female actress sings a melancholic ballad. The performers create iconic scenes with their bodies, repeatedly emphasizing their anguish and distress with slow-motion gestures and stylized facial expressions. The scene reaches its climax as the helpers discover a little girl in a red dress, hidden under the imaginary rubble. The girl is lifted up by the actors, and is passed along a seemingly endless sea of helping hands. As the girl is finally saved, the actress sings 'I am calling out to you'.

Other examples of the disaster discourse were the Chinese-sponsored pavilions at the Shanghai Expo in 2010, where the earthquake was a recurring theme. While the content of the exhibits had to be approved by CCP censors, the creators consisted of both state organizations and private actors. For instance, the theme pavilion 'City

Being', a joint-venture between the China Central Academy of Fine Arts and the London-based design consultancy Land Design Studio, included a short film about Wenchuan Square in the city of Hanwang, which witnesses the heart-wrenching story of a young boy searching for his dead father's chess board in the rubble of the 2008 earthquake. The International Red Cross and Red Crescent Pavilion included slow-motion footage of the Wenchuan rescue effort and images of Chinese Red Cross flags in its four-minute feature film about human suffering in the wake of disasters. The pavilion of the state-owned People's Insurance Company of China (中国人保控股公司 *Zhongguo renbao konggu gongsi*) contained a miniature aerial model of the company's Wenchuan aid effort, laid into the floor of the main exhibition hall. In the Chinese provincial exhibitions hall, the Sichuan pavilion also alluded to the disaster. Aside from featuring giant panda statues, regional cultural products and the miniature model of a nuclear reactor, it included an information board on ethnic minority villages that were rebuilt after the earthquake. This is the text:

> During the Wenchuan earthquake of 12 May 2008, the Qiang villages of Beichuan and Wenchuan suffered massive destruction. With the assistance of all local governments and their provincial and municipal counterparts, a brand new Qiang village was erected. The Qiang people have their own beautiful new homeland after the disaster.

Note how the emphasis is on an ethnic minority community, and how the focus rests not with the people of that village, but with the benevolent Chinese authorities under whose guidance the village was rebuilt.

Most notably among the various Expo pavilions, the event was also showcased at China's National Pavilion, as part of the China Pavilion's eight-minute theme film *Process* (历程 *Licheng*), directed by Lu Chuan (陆川). This film integrates the earthquake into its epic story of Chinese modernization and development. *Process*, which is designed to be projected across three separate screens, includes a range of high-tech editing techniques as well as a monumental music score, all of which contribute to a highly melodramatic narrative. The narrative covers 30 years of reform-era history, depicting four generations of a Chinese family who leave their rural homes, construct urban China, and move towards a prosperous future. The break-neck urban development displayed throughout this film is only halted by one watershed moment: the Wenchuan earthquake.

In the last third of the film, one of the protagonists, the third-generation son, moves through a revolving door while a decade flies by in images and dates. The center screen displays a large clock that stops at 14:28 (the time of the earthquake). Various Chinese are shown gazing up in shock at a large digital screen that shows CCTV news footage of the event, while the sound of a ticking clock is audible in the background. The film cuts to a new location: the young protagonist finds himself standing amidst the ruins of Wenchuan, in a relief-effort scene that is frozen in time. The camera zooms past helicopters, PLA helpers and medics. The protagonist walks through this frozen scene in a daze, before spying a lone hand reaching out of the debris. He looks down into a dark hole, where a young woman is trapped. He reaches out and their hands meet. The next shot shows a scene eerily similar to iconic rescue efforts featured in official news broadcasts and other cultural representations of the event: in slow-motion, PLA soldiers and medics lift a stretcher high above the ruins. The woman on the stretcher and her savior gaze at each other across the split screens. When the scene ends, the two are gathered with friends and family in front of the Pudong skyline, where they are wed. Only now does progress continue.

Noteworthy about this short multi-media extravaganza is how it elicits strong emotional responses through technically sophisticated editing and the juxtaposition of emotionally charged signs. *Process* functions at an almost entirely non-verbal level. It does not confront the viewer with plot or character development, nor attempts to relay a rational argument. Instead, the visitor is immersed in a (semi)-surround media environment, bombarded with visual–acoustic signals, and exposed in short order to a host of emotions that are resolved at the end in the promise of a brighter tomorrow.

In terms of narrative, the eight-minute film tells a story of urban development and Chinese modernity. Within this narrative, the Wenchuan earthquake plays a pivotal role. While time moves forward in a linear way, often literally 'flying' by as dates flash across the split screen, the earthquake becomes a national moment of pause. According to Benedict Anderson, such moments of 'homogenous empty time' are one of the mechanisms that help create 'imagined communities' such as the nation.[59] By constructing the shared experience of the disaster, infusing this experience with strong emotions and tying it to continuously reproduced signs (such as stylized images of outstretched hands or PLA soldiers and relief workers struggling across debris), cultural products such as this film contribute to the Chinese discourse of a harmonious, modern society. Throughout this discourse, the disaster is framed in the language and imagery of war, and is turned into a national narrative, complete with heroes (the government, PLA and volunteer workers), villains (nature) and readily available moral statements ('in unity there is strength', 'putting people first', etc.).

Throughout the various mass events, the disaster discourse therefore achieves three things: firstly, it creates a sense of unity that makes all actors of the disaster relief (the government, the Party, civilian helpers and the average citizen) coterminous with a larger community: the Chinese nation. Secondly, it strengthens the rationale for a specific framework of political action, one that includes a strong sovereign state, collaboration with private interests and the leadership of the CCP. This framework is portrayed as the only guarantor for a modern China and, by extension, for the prosperity of the Chinese people. Thirdly, this discourse suggests that events with a negative impact, which include but may not be limited to natural disasters, are unpredictable externalities to Chinese modernization. The focus is shifted from mitigating such events, from exploring the factors that exacerbate their impact, and from the fact that 'society can plan and prepare for most natural events, even though they cannot be predicted precisely',[60] to creating a 'nation-wide system' (举国体制 *juguo tizhi*)[61] for disaster response to deal with such events once they have occurred. By extension, this implies that the authorities cannot be held responsible for natural disasters and the damage they cause. The discourse emphasizes the positive,

59. Benedict Anderson, *Imagined Communities* (London and New York: Verso, 2006), p. 204.

60. J. T. Mitchell *et al.*, 'Catastrophe in reel life versus real life: perpetuating disaster myth through Hollywood films', *International Journal of Mass Emergencies and Disasters* 18, (2000), p. 388.

61. Lan, 'Coverage of the Wenchuan earthquake', pp. 230–231.

legitimizing elements of the heavenly mandate tradition while simultaneously attempting to delete the delegitimizing elements.

VI. Wenchuan at the box office: the *Aftershock* blockbuster

While the examples so far have contained a strong element of state influence, our final case is an entirely commercial cultural product: the highly popular 2010 blockbuster *Aftershock* by director Feng Xiaogang (冯小刚). *Aftershock* is an instructive example of a popular Chinese film that is government approved, i.e. backed with state funding and accepted by the government censors, but commercially produced.[62] What is more, the film broke several box-office records, including at the time highest-grossing film in Chinese history.[63]

What is noteworthy here is how this film ties into the discourse of disaster and legitimacy, and how it draws from the iconography of the 2008 Wenchuan earthquake to sell box-office tickets. Ostensibly, the movie is not primarily about the 2008 disaster, but about the 1976 Tangshan earthquake, to which its Chinese title refers, 'The Great Tangshan Earthquake' (唐山大地震 *Tangshan dadizhen*). However, the film is closely connected to the events of 2008 in ways that make its discourse highly relevant to this analysis. The fact that filming began in 2009, a year after the events in Sichuan, suggests that the studio hoped to capitalize on the recent tragedy. In fact, the historical content should be understood in line with Croce's argument that 'all history is contemporary history'.[64]

Aftershock tells the story of a family torn asunder during the 1976 Tangshan earthquake. In the wake of the earthquake, mother Li Yuanni (李元妮) loses her husband and finds her seven-year old twin children, son Fang Da (方达) and daughter Fang Deng (方登), trapped under the rubble of their house. Li is confronted with a dilemma reminiscent of Sophie's choice: she can save only one of her children, and has to condemn the other to death. Li saves her son, who loses his arm in the process. She leaves the bodies of her husband and her daughter behind, and sets out for the nearest PLA relief camp. Unbeknownst to Li, her daughter Fang Deng is only unconscious, and awakes amidst the rubble and corpses to find herself abandoned. So begins a melodramatic Odyssey that spans the same three decades of modern Chinese history as the short-film *Process* discussed above. From their individual perspectives, the three surviving family members witness the death of Mao Zedong and the developments in reform-era China, always haunted by the 'aftershocks' of the Tangshan earthquake. While mother Li remains in Tangshan, her son Fang Da leaves for Hangzhou, where he works his way up from a rickshaw driver to become the owner of a prospering travel agency. Daughter Fang Deng, who has been adopted and raised by two PLA officers, drops out of university after an accidental pregnancy and

62. The film is a public–private co-production that involved a range of companies, most notably the private production company Huayi Bros., the Chinese state-owned film conglomerate China Film Group Corporation, and the Tangshan Broadcast and Media Company.

63. Yuankai Tang, 'Movie market booming—China on track to become world's second largest film market', *Beijing Review* 2, (13 January 2011), available at: http://www.bjreview.com.cn/print/txt/2011-01/10/content_323793.htm (accessed 23 December 2012).

64. Cf. George Allan, 'Croce and Whitehead on concrescence', *Process Studies* 2(2), (1972), pp. 95–111.

raises her daughter alone. She later marries a Canadian lawyer and moves to Vancouver. It is only in 2008, following the earthquake in Sichuan, that she returns to China to join the Tangshan volunteer relief troops. There, among the ruins, she meets her long-lost brother Fang Da, who has also joined the relief effort. The two return to Tangshan, where mother and daughter are tearfully re-united.

Aftershock sets the stage for its narrative with a four-and-a-half minute disaster impact scene that, in terms of destruction and carnage, easily compares to US blockbusters. The film is then dedicated to the personal lives of the protagonists. Mundane issues such as going to college or finding a job are juxtaposed with highly melodramatic scenes of characters dying, leaving their families, being forced to leave their children behind, returning to their families after long absences, etc. Director Feng Xiaogang maximizes the emotional impact of these scenes through tools such as close-up and low-angle shots of emotionally torn protagonists, hand-held and slow-motion camera actions, and heart-wrenching musical scores. On average, every five minutes the film presents the audience with a carefully designed tear-jerking moment. We return to the relevance of this emotional impact below.

First, we turn to the main narrative sequence that explicitly deals with the Wenchuan earthquake, which comprises a total of roughly six minutes. After the siblings witness the disaster from their respective perspectives, they each make their way to Sichuan to assist in the relief effort. The scope of the entire sequence is monumental. Squadrons of military helicopters pass over destroyed townships, while convoys of civilian and military vehicles deliver personnel and equipment. Propaganda banners along the highway read 'rise and extend a helping hand to the people in the disaster zone' and 'lend a helping hand in times of peril—the earthquake may be merciless, but people are affectionate!'.

In a sense, the sequence reiterates the relevance of state disaster relief troops, and particularly of the PLA, that is introduced earlier in the movie, when the young orphaned Fang Deng is placed in the care of two PLA officers. This narrative choice provides several opportunities to showcase both the heroic and the caring nature of PLA staff, and allows the director to place not only Maoist paraphernalia but also propaganda slogans in the background of shots. All throughout, the troops are thus associated with a humanitarian discourse that is juxtaposed with statements of self-sacrifice in the service of the people.

Connected to these portrayals of the PLA is the emphasis of civilian volunteer work. The film draws from similar discourses as the news media representations described earlier. It frames the volunteer effort as an endeavor of national solidarity and as a moral imperative for all Chinese, including those living abroad (note Fang Deng's exclamation after watching the disaster on CNN: 'I have to go back. I have to help them'). That such glorification does not correspond to the actual situation becomes clear in much of the critique voiced by Chinese commentators following the event. As Lan has argued, the flood of volunteers not only caused traffic jams and impeded rescue operations, but also posed an additional strain on the already heavily taxed region; the results were bottlenecks and inefficiencies in the overall relief effort.[65]

65. Lan, 'Coverage of the Wenchuan earthquake', p. 231.

The representations of volunteers in *Aftershock* suggest the very opposite. Volunteer Fang Da, for instance, moves across the disaster site with purpose, continuously organizing the work of his team through walky-talky commands. Other volunteers join the official PLA staff in a highly effective and well-organized manner, demonstrating their willingness to lay down their lives alongside the professionals. An example is a scene in which soldiers and relief workers find a girl trapped under the rubble. A relief worker explains to the mother that freeing her daughter would endanger the helpers, who are referred to with the same word used in official propaganda: *zhanshi* (战士, combatants).

> If we want to save your child we need to lift this board, but if we lift it, the lives of your child and of the combatants will be in danger. Rest assured, I will do everything in my power to save your child.

In this fashion, a unitary effort by military personnel and volunteers is encased in the language and imagery of war, and is presented as selfless martyrdom. Showing the collaboration between PLA professionals and lay volunteers as effective, and continuously stressing the idea of sacrifice in the name of larger community, is essential to the discourse that the film relays: the filmmakers provide the sense that all Chinese come together in unity when faced with disaster, always under the guidance of the benevolent Chinese state.

In the scene in question, this compassion of the helpers to sacrifice their lives in the end leads the mother to *reject* their offer and instead have her daughter's leg amputated. The sequence ends emotionally: much like in the scenes from other cultural products discussed above, the helpers emerge from the ruins, in slow-motion, carrying the girl on a stretcher. The mother launches herself back into the disaster zone, only barely constrained by volunteer Fang Deng. The last shots show the woman's outstretched, battered hands, reaching towards the ruins, as she cries out: 'My daughter's leg! I want my daughter's leg! Mama is sorry!'.

The overall discursive message and the emotional impact of the cinematography most strongly come together in the final scene of the film, which breaks away from the narrative to show the present. The camera tilts down from a clear blue sky to reveal the wall of the Tangshan earthquake memorial. Accompanied by solemn music, the camera slowly moves across a calm basin of water towards the wall. The half-minute shot is accompanied by the following superimposed caption:

> In 2008, the Tangshan municipal party committee and the Tangshan city government erected a memorial wall in commemoration of the 240,000 compatriots who fell victim to the great 1976 Tangshan earthquake.

The camera cuts to an elderly man staring at the wall, as the caption reads:

> Song Shoushu, 65 years old, a retired former worker at the Tangshan metal manufacturing plant, lost his wife, his younger sister, and his son in the great Tangshan earthquake ... his son Song Shuijie was only five years old when he was killed.

The camera zooms in on the man's face, who quietly says: 'I'll be back to visit you again in two days', before getting on his bicycle to slowly ride past the memorial wall. The camera follows him, sweeping past the length of stelae, and finally tilts up and zooms in on one of the wall segments, until the entire screen is filled with the names of victims. The caption reads:

> We deeply mourn the 240,000 compatriots who fell victim to the great Tangshan earthquake. This film is solemnly dedicated to a city that rose from the ashes like a phoenix—Tangshan. We sincerely thank the people from all walks of life who vigorously supported the making of this film.

Aside from reiterating the film's general focus on community, solidarity, suffering and ultimately perseverance, this last scene is arguably most important for tying these ideas together with the continuous leadership of Party and state. Although depicting a memorial for the 1976 quake, the emotional impact has to be seen in context with the previous scenes of the Wenchuan disaster, and with the fact that the cinematographic 'present' is explicitly tied to the year 2008. It is this arrangement that infuses the discourse with its overt pathos. This scene, like so many others throughout *Aftershock*, is designed to elicit a maximum emotional response from the viewer. This is achieved by framing touching human stories of loss and redemption through carefully calibrated camera dynamics, visual set-ups (such as close-ups of actors visibly struggling with their emotions) and highly emotive musical scores, while contextualizing the narrative through repeated references to the recent earthquake in Sichuan.

The potential effect of such techniques is twofold: firstly, throughout the film, the nationalist discourse of unity and solidarity, as well as the political discourse that glorifies the role of the Party and state, are tied to memorable iconic signs, such as relief workers carrying the wounded or battered hands reaching across debris. These signs can then be reproduced elsewhere as shorthand for the overall, continuous national narrative that spans over 30 years of modernization effort. Secondly, these signs are charged in a way that creates affect. This, in turn, does not simply prompt viewers to rationally *understand* that Chinese modernity can only be realized if in times of crises the authorities lead and the public stand strongly united. This technique furthermore invites them to become emotionally *invested* in these ideas.

The movie thus contributes to the overall disaster discourse, which collapsed into readily recognizable packages, or 'pathos formulae', for instance iconic visual representations of suffering victims or heroic relief workers, which are reproduced and re-deployed in a variety of contexts (Figure 2).[66] What is more, these symbols are arranged in a way that elicits strong affect, which in turn intimately links the rationale of the disaster discourse to emotions. This process invites audiences to associate themselves even more strongly with the discourse, and to invest themselves in the various parts of its logic without questioning whether that logic is itself sound.

VII. Conclusion

The Wenchuan earthquake has become part, not only of official propaganda, but also of Chinese mass cultural products in general: various actors, including Party and state

66. Cf. Edelman, 'Language, myths and rhetoric', p. 133. On 'pathos formulae', see Marion Müller and Arvid Kappas 'Visual emotions—emotional visuals. Emotions, pathos formulae, and their relevance for communication research', in Katrin Doveling, Christian von Scheve and Elly A. Konijn, eds, *The Routledge Handbook of Emotions and the Mass Media* (Abingdon, Oxfordshire: Routledge, 2011), pp. 310–331.

Figure 2. Replicable series of signs—symbols of the earthquake across different cultural products.

media outlets but also private media producers, use the disaster to depict China's mode of development as a story of Chinese unity in the face of hardship. Whether the motives are political or commercial, the various representations, and the way they rework a small set of tropes and symbols, reinforce a narrative of suffering, struggle, solidarity and ultimately victory of the Chinese nation.

The various examples we have analyzed provide an idea of how certain agents (e.g. government and Party actors) try to stake out a field of meanings in which they want their own actions to be situated. By providing both hard and soft mechanisms of cultural control, and by utilizing the logic of market mechanisms and commercial entertainment, the relevant stakeholders not only construct an official discourse on political legitimacy but also assure its proliferation across society through outlets that do not necessarily have to be part of the state system. This confirms our earlier theoretical argument that the management of disaster discourses should be understood as processes of cultural governance. However, an element missing from that discussion, and from the figure presented earlier, is the degree to which the attempt to construct state sovereignty through cultural production coincides with cues for political subjects to emotionally invest in a specific vision of Chinese identity. The finding that the disaster discourse, both in its official and its popular guise, strongly hinges on the capacity of cultural products to elicit emotional responses, offers insights into the role that feelings play in the construction of political discourse. We refer to this emotional dimension as 'emotional governance', and argue that it works in tandem with cultural governance. While the latter is a process of regulating society by managing overarching frameworks of meaning, emotional governance contributes to this process by tying these meanings to specific emotions.[67]

67. The term 'emotional governance' was originally coined by Barry Richards in *Emotional Governance: Politics, Media and Terror* (Houndmills: Palgrave, 2007). Richards argues that governments in liberal-democratic societies have a responsibility to manage the public's emotions in times of crises (p. 6). His approach might better be termed 'governing of emotion'. Our use of the term is significantly different, since we are not concerned with

However, despite the seemingly monopolistic ideological efforts of state and Party to regulate meanings and emotions, it is by no means certain that these efforts will have the desired effect. The ideological dimension of claims to Chinese legitimacy has a flip-side: it leaves the political order open to contestation; each element of this discourse can potentially be turned against the leadership, possibly providing fuel for counter-hegemonic struggle. Adopting strategies of cultural and emotional governance means opening cultural spheres up to collaboration, and consequently allowing for the possibility that discourses will shift in unintended directions, or will be deployed in ways that directly challenge the dominant interpretation of Chinese developmental politics. In the case of the Wenchuan earthquake, one example is the First Beijing Biennale of 2009, organized at the Beijing 798 arts district, which included critical (albeit arguably tasteless) reflections not only on Chinese modernity, but also on the Wenchuan earthquake, some of which were later banned.[68]

Yet it is important to note that these counter-examples all constitute what Carroll refers to as avant-garde art, rather than mass communication.[69] In the realm of mass culture, the collaborative attempts to create recognizable earthquake representations seems to have been largely successful, considering that many non-state actors readily turned to the established tropes and symbols when presenting their interpretation of the disaster in films or exhibits. While we do not assess conclusively to what extent the diffusion of this discourse generates legitimacy in the sense that Schubert discusses in this issue, our analysis does lead us to formulate a theoretical model of how cultural governance might work, and in turn leads to hypotheses that should be assessed in future research on political legitimacy.[70]

Our hypothesis with respect to disaster discourse in China is that the ubiquity of emotive symbols, allied to rhetorical arguments, indeed spreads not only beyond official propaganda (i.e. to entertainment products in the Chinese media) but also to other levels of discourse (for instance the policy-making realm, the private realm, etc.), where it informs opinions and ultimately decision making. For the case of the Wenchuan earthquake, the degree to which Chinese around the world responded positively to the disaster relief effort suggests that the governance of the disaster discourse may have had such an effect: the event prompted not only generous financial donations, but also small symbolic acts of patriotism, for instance of users changing their online status in social networks to 'I♥China'. Such outcomes should be carefully checked through reception analyses and ethnographic research for the causalities that are at play in these cases, in order to clarify whether discursive mechanisms like 'pathos formulae' indeed play a role in prompting these actions.

Footnote 67 continued

normative questions of how to govern emotions well, but instead use the term to explain how political actors manipulate what William A. Callahan, in *China—The Pessoptimist Nation* (Oxford: Oxford University Press, 2010), has called 'structures of feeling', or what Geremie R. Barmé has termed 'psycho-cultural norms', in 'CCP™ & AdCult PRC', *The China Journal* 41, (1999), p. 20.

68. Tania Branigan, 'Earthquake works banned from Beijing art show', *The Guardian Online*, (17 August 2009), available at: http://www.guardian.co.uk/world/2009/aug/17/beijing-art-biennale-sichuan-earthquake (accessed 23 December 2012).

69. Carroll, *A Philosophy of Mass Art*.

70. Cf. Schubert, 'Political legitimacy in contemporary China revisited'.

Our argument is that the practices we describe as cultural governance can be mapped for the kind of discourse they promote, and that this discourse can be empirically traced as it proliferates. In this particular case, our analysis shows how the propaganda efforts in China have established the Wenchuan earthquake of 2008 as an important and lasting theme in Chinese political discourse—a theme that aims to legitimate the current Chinese government's attempts to establish a 'harmonious society', and that various actors now reproduce as they use its series of easily recognizable signs in their own cultural productions.

Repression Backfires: tactical radicalization and protest spectacle in rural China

KEVIN J. O'BRIEN and YANHUA DENG

In spring 2005, villagers in Dongyang County, Zhejiang were unhappy. For four years they had been complaining about pollution emitted by 13 factories located in the Zhuxi Chemical Park, but nothing had been done. So they set up a tent encampment to block delivery of supplies to the factories. At first, they employed restrained tactics, including going about daily life in the tents, badgering cadres sent to demobilize them, and kowtowing. After a harsh repression produced hundreds of injuries and left dozens of damaged vehicles and other evidence of police action strewn about, the tent-sitters switched to more aggressive tactics, including denouncing local leaders, carrying out mock funerals, interrogating factory owners and ransacking the homes of 'traitors'. The authorities' ill-considered and poorly-timed repression led to tactical escalation, helped draw thousands of people to the scene, and ultimately resulted in the chemical park being closed. This episode speaks to the 'dissent–repression nexus' and suggests that repression can be counterproductive when it encourages protesters to ratchet up their tactics and a 'protest spectacle' ensues. In today's China, striking displays and theatrical performances, especially in the wake of a crackdown, can attract an audience, bring in financial support and create a carnival-like atmosphere in which popular acclaim, the breakdown of social order and the inversion of power hierarchies grants protesters leverage and induces the authorities to make concessions.

Students of contentious politics have long examined the 'dissent–repression nexus',[1] but their findings are all over the map. Some show that police suppression dampens

1. Mark I. Lichbach, 'Deterrence or escalation? The puzzle of aggregate studies of repression and dissent', *Journal of Conflict Resolution* 31(2), (1987), pp. 266–297; Christian Davenport, 'State repression and political order', *Annual Review of Political Science* 10(1), (2007), pp. 1–23.

protest,[2] while others argue it inspires dissent.[3] Still others observe a more complicated pattern, with repression leading to more or less protest, depending on circumstances and timing.[4] No matter what they find, researchers tend to agree that using force to break up a demonstration, march or sit-in is often a turning point that can shape the course contention takes.[5]

As a transformative event, repression not only affects how much protest occurs, it can also influence tactical choices.[6] Under the threat of police disruption, challengers sometimes adapt their approach and conduct underground mobilization in lieu of public action.[7] They may also opt for more confrontational tactics, especially if forceful suppression is seen to be illegitimate and people come to believe that resorting to violence is justified,[8] or if they 'come to see peaceful protest as futile'.[9] But just how and when tactics are radicalized is not well understood. Compared to a

2. Douglas A. Hibbs Jr, *Mass Political Violence: A Cross-National Causal Analysis* (New York: Wiley, 1973), pp. 82–93; Charles Tilly, *From Mobilization to Revolution* (Reading, MA: Addison-Wesley, 1978); Susan Olzak, Maya Beasley and Johan Olivier, 'The impact of state reforms on protest against apartheid in South Africa', *Mobilization* 8(1), (2002), pp. 27–50; Jean Calterone Williams, 'The politics of homelessness: Shelter Now and political protest', *Political Research Quarterly* 58(3), (2005), pp. 497–509.

3. Robert W. White, 'From peaceful protest to guerrilla war: micromobilization of the Provisional Irish Republican Army', *American Journal of Sociology* 94(6), (1989), pp. 1277–1302; Ronald A. Francisco, 'The relationship between coercion and protest', *Journal of Conflict Resolution* 39(2), (1995), pp. 263–282; Ronald A. Francisco, 'After the massacre: mobilization in the wake of harsh repression', *Mobilization* 9(2), (2004), pp. 107–126; Paul D. Almeida, 'Opportunity organizations and threat-induced contention: protest waves in authoritarian settings', *American Journal of Sociology* 109(2), (2003), pp. 345–400; David Hess and Brian Martin, 'Repression, backfire, and the theory of transformative events', *Mobilization* 11(2), (2006), pp. 249–267.

4. For an inverted-U relationship, see Edward N. Muller and Erich Weede, 'Cross-national variation in political violence: a rational action approach', *Journal of Conflict Resolution* 34(4), (1990), pp. 624–651; Karl-Dieter Opp, 'Repression and revolutionary action: East Germany in 1989', *Rationality and Society* 6(1), (1994), pp. 101–138. For a lagged positive effect, see T. David Mason and Dale A. Krane, 'The political economy of death squads: toward a theory of the impact of state-sanctioned terror', *International Studies Quarterly* 33(2), (1989), pp. 175–198; Karen Rasler, 'Concessions, repression, and political protest in the Iranian revolution', *American Sociological Review* 61(1), (1996), pp. 132–152. For the effects of different kinds of repression, see Jennifer Earl and Sarah A. Soule, 'The impacts of repression: the effect of police presence and action on subsequent protest rates', *Research in Social Movements, Conflicts and Change* 30, (2010), pp. 75–113; Ruud Koopmans, 'The dynamics of repression and mobilization: the German extreme right in the 1990s', *Mobilization* 2(2), (1997), pp. 149–165. For recent reviews, see Jennifer Earl, 'Political repression: iron fists, velvet gloves, and diffuse control', *Annual Review of Sociology* 37, (2011), pp. 261–284; Christian Davenport and Molly Inman, 'The state of state repression research since the 1990s', *Terrorism and Political Violence* 24(4), (2012), pp. 619–634.

5. Doug McAdam and William Sewell Jr, 'It's about time: temporality in the study of social movements and revolutions', in Ron Aminzade, Jack Goldstone, Doug McAdam, Elizabeth Perry, William Sewell, Sidney Tarrow and Charles Tilly, eds, *Silence and Voice in the Study of Contentious Politics* (Cambridge: Cambridge University Press, 2001), pp. 89–125; Guobin Yang, 'Emotional events and the transformation of collective action: the Chinese student movement', in Helena Flam and Debra King, eds, *Emotions and Social Movements* (London: Routledge, 2005), pp. 79–98; Hess and Martin, 'Repression, backfire, and the theory of transformative events'.

6. Doug McAdam, 'Tactical innovation and the pace of insurgency', *American Sociological Review* 48(6), (1983), pp. 735–754; Lichbach, 'Deterrence or escalation?'; Larissa Titarenko, John D. McCarthy, Clark McPhail and Boguslaw Augustyn, 'The interaction of state repression, protest form and protest sponsor strength during the transition from communism in Minsk, Belarus, 1990–1995', *Mobilization* 6(2), (2001), pp. 129–150.

7. Will H. Moore, 'Repression and dissent: substitution, context, and timing', *American Journal of Political Science* 42(3), (1998), pp. 851–873; Paul Y. Chang, 'Unintended consequences of repression: alliance formation in South Korea's democracy movement (1970–1979)', *Social Forces* 87(2), (2008), pp. 651–677.

8. On the development of a 'norm of violence,' see Karl-Dieter Opp and Wolfgang Roehl, 'Repression, micromobilization, and political protest', *Social Forces* 69(2), (1990), p. 524.

9. White, 'From peaceful protest to guerrilla war'. Also see Almeida, 'Opportunity organizations and threat-induced contention'.

number of studies that explore the effects of coercion on protest frequency, we know little about how repression can 'shift challengers from one tactic to another'.[10]

The existing literature also pays less attention than it might to how repression can sensitize the public by creating a 'protest spectacle'[11] packed with striking displays and dramatic performances. Repression enhances a spectacle in various ways. Among others, it may lead to more intense and theatrical confrontations. Police action may also leave evidence of coercion on the scene, such as tear gas shells and burned vehicles. Compelling performances with effective props on a site where an injustice occurred can sacralize a location and become an element of an ongoing show. Protest spectacle, especially in the wake of a harsh crackdown, can have great power. It may attract an audience, bring in financial support, and even create a carnival-like atmosphere,[12] in which popular acclaim and the breakdown of social order grants protesters extra leverage and induces the authorities to make concessions.

Drawing on an episode of an environmental activism in Zhejiang, we examine repression, tactical escalation and the power of spectacle. We show how restrained popular action, in this case erecting tents, first led to a measured response from the authorities that focused on persuasion. But within several weeks this changed. After people from other villages joined the tent-sitters, the encampment was broken up with overwhelming police force. The deployment of over 1,500 police officers and local cadres to suppress several dozen elderly protesters was considered excessive by the activists and the broader community, and produced additional mobilization and a noticeable radicalization of tactics. The tent-sitters ratcheted up the theatricality of their actions and demonstrated considerable skill manipulating symbols. Evocative, subtle performances moved the audience and repeatedly wrong-footed the authorities. In particular, the display of evidence that undue force had been employed contributed to the spectacle and drew in onlookers and new participants from neighboring villages and even other counties. A carnival-like atmosphere ensued and the number of tents grew. People milled about the encampment for weeks and sellers of sesame cakes and iced desserts came to serve the crowd. With the hierarchies of everyday life on the verge of being inverted,[13] county leaders felt great pressure to end the 'chaos' (*luan*), and concessions soon followed.

To trace how repression affected the tent-sitters' tactics and helped create a 'protest spectacle', the second author conducted three-and-a-half months of fieldwork in Huashui town, Zhejiang in 2007, two years after the encampment ended. She revisited the area in April 2008 to observe the first local elections after the protest. Altogether, she conducted 122 semi-structured interviews, with most arranged in a snowball fashion as one person put her in touch with the next. The interviewees ranged from

10. Davenport and Inman, 'The state of state repression research since the 1990s', p. 624. For an exception, see Titarenko *et al.*, 'The interaction of state repression, protest form and protest sponsor strength during the transition from communism in Minsk, Belarus, 1990–1995'.

11. Baz Kershaw, 'Fighting in the streets: dramaturgies of popular protest, 1968–1989', *New Theatre Quarterly* 13(51), (1997), pp. 255–276; David McNeil, 'The spectacle of protest and punishment: newspaper coverage of the Melksham weavers' riot of 1738', *Media History* 7(1), (2001), pp. 71–86.

12. On protest and carnival, see Abner Cohen, 'A polyethnic London carnival as a contested cultural performance', *Ethnic and Racial Studies* 5(1), (1982), pp. 23–41; P. Jackson, 'Street life: the politics of carnival', *Environment and Planning D: Society and Space* 6(2), (1988), pp. 213–227.

13. Mikhail Bakhtin, *Rabelais and His World* (Cambridge, MA: MIT Press, 1968).

ordinary villagers to protest leaders, village cadres, township cadres and municipal officials. Taking advantage of her affiliation with a prominent newspaper, she enjoyed exceptionally good access to both local leaders and protesters. Her quasi-official capacity also made it possible to collect nearly 1,000 pages of written materials, including petition letters, leaflets and posters penned by villagers, work diaries and reports written by local officials, official regulations, meeting records and an internal 'Daily Report' (*Meiri Yibao*) that meticulously traced what happened each day.

Restrained tactics

In early 2001 the Dongyang County government opened the Zhuxi Chemical Industrial Park in Huashui town, Zhejiang. Within a few years, the 13 chemical, pesticide, dye and pharmaceutical factories housed in the park became notorious for the water and air pollution they emitted. As crops withered or died, and a suspicious number of birth defects and miscarriages occurred, residents of nearby villages became alarmed.[14] Lawsuits and petition drives were launched and on two occasions activists traveled to Beijing to request that the chemical park be closed. On 24 March 2005, disgruntled residents of Huaxi No. 5 village, the most seriously affected site, stepped up their opposition by erecting a large tent at the entrance to the park and beginning a round-the-clock vigil. Their hope was to block the delivery of supplies and to force the factories to shut down.

The tactics used at this point were quite restrained. Rather than mounting demonstrations or marches or other confrontational acts, the tent-sitters (mostly elderly women) just went about their lives.[15] They brought beds, quilts and cooking equipment to the tent, and spent their days eating, chatting and sleeping there. This was done at the behest of the leaders of the action, one of whom told the protesters: 'the only thing you have to do is sit in the tent. Don't touch people going into the factories or their cars. Don't break into the chemical park'.[16] In these early days, contention was mainly symbolic: an attempt to create a measure of inconvenience that would demonstrate the villagers' frustration and persistence.

The first escalation occurred after the authorities dismantled the tent and the protesters rebuilt it—three times—and residents from ten other communities joined the action, with each village putting up its own tent. Over the next week, despite government efforts to remove the tents, the size of the encampment grew. The tent-sitters also altered their tactics. After the county leadership assembled a 60-member 'work team' (*gongzuo zu*) to

14. On circumstances under which pollution leads to (or does not lead to) protest, see Anna Lora-Wainwright, 'An anthropology of "cancer villages": villagers' perspectives and the politics of responsibility', *Journal of Contemporary China* 19(63), (2010), pp. 79–100.

15. On the performance of everyday life as a form of protest, see Bruce Missingham, 'The village of the poor confronts the state: a geography of protest in the assembly of the poor', *Urban Studies* 39(9), (2002), pp. 1647–1663. On the 'performance of threat' in China, see Diana Fu, 'Disguised collective action: mobilizing without the masses in authoritarian China', November 2013, unpublished paper.

16. Interview P3 with a protest leader, 11 June 2007. Choosing restrained tactics had a history. When the chemical park opened in 2001, villagers were concerned about the pollution it would produce. They sought a 'dialogue' (*duihua*) with the town party secretary, which ultimately led to the secretary being cursed, beaten and dragged to the site, where villagers made him walk a lap around the park barefoot. Windows and doors of three plants were smashed, and phones and computers in factory offices were vandalized or stolen. Following this incident, 12 villagers were tried for disturbing social order and ten spent between one and three years behind bars.

coax the protesters to leave the encampment,[17] people began to venture outside the tents to badger, pressure and challenge the 'thought workers' sent to demobilize them.

'Badgering' (*fanrao*) involved irritating work team members in any number of ways. Tent-sitters would berate them for acting against villagers' interests and insult them by calling them 'traitors' (*pantu*). When they knew team members and felt able to push back against the thought work, they would nag them to leave the tent area or urge them to do their job less diligently. The atmosphere at the park entrance became very boisterous and heckling and jostling were common. As a report issued by the town government put it:

> When county work team members and town cadres went to investigate the situation, the masses besieged them and bombarded them with 'seven mouths and eight tongues' (*qizui bashe*) [i.e. everyone talking at once]. When team members went to the encampment, they were often surrounded, with the masses pulling at their clothes and tugging on their arms. ... This made it nearly impossible for them to open their mouths, let alone to explain and propagate relevant regulations and new polices. ... Work team members even found it difficult to exit the tent area.[18]

One police officer confirmed how difficult it was to fulfill his assignments amid the badgering and the din: 'There were always a handful of people buzzing around asking us to solve the pollution problem, no matter why we went to the encampment'.[19]

Beyond pestering the work team, tent-sitters and the spectators they attracted were sometimes more aggressive. On several occasions, local leaders were pushed to the front of the crowd to speak and when the audience concluded that their remarks resembled 'a dragonfly flitting along the surface of the water' (*qingting dianshui*), protesters and onlookers insisted that they not leave until they vowed to halt the pollution and gave a date for doing so.[20] One county official whose speech the crowd found especially wanting ended up fleeing the tent area and running into nearby fields with a gaggle of older women chasing after him shouting 'wait, wait, the problem hasn't been solved'.[21]

As the authorities intensified their thought work, the tent-sitters' tactics became less restrained. When work team members entered the encampment, elderly protesters often immediately donned white mourning robes and hats, lit incense, knelt down and began kowtowing.[22] While kowtowing they would chant: 'we beg you to

17. On the local authorities' efforts to demobilize the protest, see Yanhua Deng and Kevin J. O'Brien, 'Relational repression in China: using social ties to demobilize protesters', *The China Quarterly* 215, (2013), pp. 533–552. On drawing thought workers from work units and using family ties to apply pressure on homeowners who are fighting eviction, see Kevin J. O'Brien and Yanhua Deng, 'The reach of the state: work units, family ties and "harmonious demolition"', unpublished paper, June 2014.

18. Huashui Town Government, '3 yue 24 ri yilai huashui zhen huaxi cun bufen cunmin zai zhuxi gongye gongnengqu lanlu qingkuang de chuli huibao' ['Report on handling traffic blocking by a handful of villagers around the Zhuxi Industrial Functional Area in Huaxi village, Huashui town since March 24'], (2005), unpublished document available from the second author.

19. Interview C17 with a police officer, 21 June 2007.

20. Interview V4 with a village cadre, 13 April 2007.

21. Interview C17 with a police officer, 21 June 2007.

22. For kowtowing as a protest tactic, see Michael Wines, 'Police fire tear gas at protesters in Chinese city', *New York Times*, (23 December 2011), available at: http://www.nytimes.com/2011/12/24/world/asia/china-jails-rights-activist-chen-wei-for-9-years.html?ref=china&_r = 0 (accessed 8 September 2013). On the symbolic meaning of wearing white and kneeling in supplication, also see Xi Chen, 'The power of "troublemaking": protest tactics and their efficacy in China', *Comparative Politics* 41(4), (2009), pp. 457, 459.

save us' (*qiuqiu nimen, jiujiu women*). After they finished, they often scooped up a handful of dirt, placed it on the hood of an official's car, and stuck incense in it. Sometimes they also pasted slips of white paper on government vehicles.[23]

These actions mirrored funeral rituals, but were sufficiently ambiguous[24] that the tent-sitters could claim they were merely asking for help rather than threatening the cadres sent to demobilize them.[25] But the targets of this tactic saw it otherwise. A police officer who took part in the thought work said:

> There were two meanings conveyed by their kowtowing. Superficially, they were begging you for assistance and treating you like a Buddha. However, according to Chinese culture, your 'life will be shortened' (*zheshou*) if older women kneel down and kowtow to you, since we are too young to deserve that.[26]

A town cadre who was on the work team also felt threatened. He explained: 'Though they were chanting "we beg you to save us", their real meaning was "we wish you would die". Their kowtowing had malicious intent'.[27]

Although the protesters escalated the intensity of their tactics during the first three weeks of the encampment, their actions remained within the bounds of contemporary Chinese protest. As late as early April, while the tug of war between tent-sitters and local authorities was still developing, one official report concluded that 'the protest by the masses is well organized, but their behavior is moderate and not excessive. The situation is still under control'.[28]

But this assessment would soon change. The number of spectators was mounting day by day. People from nearby villages frequently headed to the encampment, 'to walk around and have a look'.[29] Some went to see what the commotion was about and to 'join in the fun' (*cou renao*),[30] but the majority came to show support for the tent-sitters. Only a few days after the protest started, snack-sellers and kabob hawkers appeared to cater to the onlookers[31] and the area took on the feeling of a bustling, open-air market. According to an on-the-spot report filed by a government informant, crowd size surged at noon and then again in the evening after villagers finished their day's work. 'Going to the tent area' (*qu dapeng de difang*) became a leisure activity that drew hundreds from the surrounding area.[32] When the tent-sitters set off firecrackers or struck a gong, as they did whenever the work team appeared to undertake thought work, 'people came from all directions, as if they were on the way

23. Interview P15 with a villager, 24 May 2007; interview V4 with a village cadre, 13 April 2007.
24. On 'polyseminous' rituals open to many interpretations, see David I. Kertzer, *Ritual, Politics, and Power* (New Haven, CT: Yale University Press, 1988); Bronislaw Szerszynski, 'Performing politics: the dramatics of environmental protest', in Larry Ray and Andrew Sayer, eds, *Economy after the Cultural Turn* (London: Sage, 1999), pp. 211–228; Steven Pfaff and Guobin Yang, 'Double-edged rituals and the symbolic resources of collective action: political commemorations and the mobilization of protest in 1989', *Theory and Society* 30(4), (2001), pp. 539–589.
25. Interview V1 with a village cadre, 3 June 2007.
26. Interview C17 with a police officer, 21 June 2007.
27. Interview C20 with a town cadre, 20 June 2007.
28. Huashui Town Government, '3 yue 24 ri yilai huashui zhen huaxi cun bufen cunmin zai zhuxi gongye gongnengqu lanlu qingkuang de chuli huibao'.
29. Interview P8 with a villager, 27 May 2007.
30. Interview P11with a villager, 27 May 2007.
31. Interview C7 with a town cadre, 17 June 2007.
32. Interview P9 with a villager, 27 May 2007; interview P11 with a villager, 10 June 2007.

to a theatre performance'.[33] By early April, a small, but effective spectacle had been created and the standoff was the best show for miles around. In the view of the party secretary of Huashui town, the site of the protest had become an entertainment center.[34]

Repression and tactical radicalization

From 30 March to 9 April, despite the work team's efforts and the detention of several protest leaders, the size of the encampment continued to grow: by 4 April there were 15 tents; by 6 April there were 18. Town and county officials began to fall under great pressure to prevent the appearance of new tents.[35] Owing to concerns that the tent-sitters were 'replacing' (*qudai*) party leadership in some villages and that the international press might pick up the story, the county party secretary instructed that 'no more tents be built'.[36]

Despite this order, the number of tents expanded from 18 to about two dozen and onlookers continued to stream into the area. County leaders, at this point, decided to turn to a more forceful approach. At about 3am on 10 April, they sent in over 1,500 local cadres and public security personnel to put an end to the encampment. During their efforts to clear out the protesters, violence broke out and over 100 officials or police officers and more than 200 villagers were injured; 68 government vehicles were also burned or damaged.

The 'April 10th Incident' was considered excessive by many villagers for three reasons. First, the targets: it was unseemly for representatives of state power to use force on the elderly.[37] Second, word spread that over 3,000 armed police had been sent in, an outsized number to remove a couple of dozen tents and suppress a handful of older protesters. Finally, the action was launched under the cover of darkness, like 'Japanese devils [soldiers] who snuck into the village' (*riben guizi jincun*) during World War II and were beaten back by villagers.[38]

Seen by many to be overkill and underhanded, the 'April 10th Incident' significantly altered the tone of the protest. Older activists immediately gathered up evidence of the repression and used it to decorate the protest site. They adorned their tents with scraps of police uniforms, batons, helmets, shields, knives, tear gas shells and red armbands that the police had left behind when they hurried from the scene. These served as both trophies and tangible proof of state repression. Over the next few days, tent-sitters blew whistles periodically to draw spectators to the site and stirred up the audience with pep talks and slogans like 'persistence leads to victory' and 'the Center is coming down to help us'.[39] They also shifted toward more aggressive

---

33. Interview V8 with a protest leader, 17 April 2007.
34. Interview C7 with a town cadre, 17 July 2007.
35. Interview C7 with a town cadre, 17 July 2007.
36. Interview C16 with a town cadre, 20 June 2007.
37. Yanhua Deng and Kevin J. O'Brien, 'Societies of senior citizens and popular protest in rural Zhejiang', *The China Journal* 71, (2014), pp. 172–188.
38. Interview V8 with a protest leader, 17 April 2007.
39. Interview V14 with a retired town cadre, 31 May 2007.

tactics, including denouncing local leaders, carrying out mock funerals, interrogating factory owners, and ransacking the homes of those they deemed 'traitors'.

Instead of merely badgering officials, protesters started to challenge and openly vilify them. The county party secretary who had approved the repression was called a 'slaughterer of the masses' in a big-character poster. On a second poster hung in a prominent location near the encampment, he was condemned as a 'devil in power' who had mobilized several thousand policemen to repress 'grey-haired, dry-boned seniors' by shooting off tear gas shells and brandishing truncheons. Even more dramatically, the tent-sitters held a mock funeral for the county party secretary. On the morning of 5 May, an urn with his snapshot on it was set up with burning incense in front of it. This ceremony attracted more than 10,000 spectators.[40]

The county mayor was also subject to abuse. A week after the 'April 10th Incident', he went to Huashui and convened a meeting with the tent-sitters to open lines of communication and dampen the passions that the suppression had inspired. The mayor delivered a speech and knelt in front of the crowd to demonstrate his remorse about the pollution and to apologize for the government's overly forceful response to the encampment, but few paid him any attention.[41] In the midst of his talk, a villager, who had never made a public speech before, grabbed the microphone and said:

> Since the 'April 10th Incident', television and radio broadcasts have been replete with lies, confusing what is right and wrong. But the truth is that during the early morning of April 10, the police sneaked into our village to repress us ordinary people and we were forced to fight back in self-defense.

At this point, the microphone was snatched out of his hands, but he retook it and continued: 'If the police dare come back, no one will leave alive and no vehicle will be left intact'.[42] Over the following month, villagers often called work team members assigned to demobilize the protesters 'dogs' and other derogatory names.

Before the 'April 10th Incident', few actions were directed at factories besides stopping the flow of supply trucks in and out of the park. After the police action, however, tent-sitters sought to disrupt the lives of factory owners and workers. Elderly tent-sitters took and ate box lunches sent to migrant laborers who lived in the park and claimed that anyone employed by the polluting factories deserved to be starved.[43] Physical pressure was also employed. On 25 April, the owner of one factory was hustled to the encampment and burned with incense. His wife was pushed into a tent and questioned for more than five hours. Her interrogators required that she write a 'self-criticism' (*ziwo jiantao*) and admit that their factory produced toxic waste. She was also forced to promise to compensate villagers. Some older protesters pasted slips of white paper on factory gates, once again evoking funeral rituals. More than 2,000 onlookers watched the drama unfold that day.[44]

40. From a government informant's daily report, which is on file with the second author.

41. Interview C5 with a county official, 30 April 2008; interview C7 with a town cadre, 17 July 2007; interview P23 with a villager, 2 June 2007.

42. Interview P23 with a villager, 2 June 2007.

43. Interview C17 with a police officer, 21 June 2007.

44. Huashui Town Government, '"Huashui Shijian" dashiji' ['Chronicle of events during the "Huashui Incident"'], (2005), unpublished document; Huashui Town Government, 'Dongyang shi Huashui zhen "4.10 shijian"

Labeling a person a traitor is a common form of protest discipline in China. Those who cooperate with the government, fail to act with the majority or withdraw from collective action are often called traitors.[45] Before the 'April 10th Incident', traitors were generally treated mildly. After the police suppression, however, those thought to have betrayed the cause were often denounced in 'big-character posters' (*dazibao*). For example, a village party secretary who had helped clear away some of the damaged cars became a target of criticism. In a leaflet entitled 'A Letter to All Huaxi Villagers' he was called a 'dog wagging its tail to please those above him' and a 'lowbred, spineless coward'. He was said to be 'more disgusting than a traitor, since he signed an "unequal treaty" which humiliated villagers and made them lose power'.

Some collaborators were treated even more harshly. For example, on the afternoon of 30 April, two people who had been denounced as traitors in big-character posters for earning money from the factories by removing toxic waste went to the encampment and quarreled with several tent-sitters. This enraged the protesters and others present. As a result, hundreds of people set out on a 'search and confiscation' (*chaojia*) mission to find evidence that the men had benefited from their contracts with the factories.[46] The raid soon spiraled out of control, and searching turned into ransacking. At the homes of both men, furniture, appliances and windows were broken or damaged.[47]

The evidence of repression and increasingly dramatic performances drew tens of thousands to the encampment.[48] Beyond local people, spectators poured in from nearby counties, especially from 10 to 15 April, when burned-out vehicles and other signs of police action remained on the scene.[49] Huashui became a popular site for tourism and pilgrimages.[50] One taxi driver told a *Guardian* (UK) reporter who was on his way to cover the story: 'Aren't these villagers brave? They're so tough. It's unbelievable. Everybody wants to come and see this place. We really admire them'.[51] Another person the journalist spoke with, a fashionable young woman from Yiwu County, said excitedly: 'We came to take a look because many people have heard of the riot. This is really big news'.[52] So many onlookers flocked to Huashui that it

Footnote 44 continued
gongzuo jinzhan qingkuang' ['The "April 10th Incident" in Huashui Town, Dongyang City'], (2005), unpublished document. Both documents are on file with the second author.

45. Ying Xing, *Dahe Yimin Shangfang de Gushi* [*Petitioning Stories of Migrants along the Yangtze River*] (Beijing: Sanlian Press, 2001), p. 410; Yu Jianrong, 'Dangdai zhongguo nongmin de yifa kangzheng' ['Lawful resistance in contemporary rural China'], *Shehuixue Yanjiu* [*Sociological Studies*] 2, (2004), pp. 49–55; Kevin J. O'Brien and Lianjiang Li, *Rightful Resistance in Rural China* (Cambridge: Cambridge University Press, 2006), p. 105.

46. Interview P6 with a villager, 15 June 2007.

47. Huashui Town Government, '"Huashui Shijian" dashiji'.

48. On attracting onlookers through 'suicide shows', see Fu, 'Disguised collective action'. See also Xin He, Lungang Wang and Yang Su, 'Above the roof, beneath the law: perceived justice behind disruptive tactics of migrant wage claimants in China', *Law & Society Review* 47(4), (2013), p. 717.

49. Interview V12 with a villager, 27 May 2007.

50. Francis Markus, 'China riot village draws tourists', *BBC News*, (15 April 2005), available at: http://news.bbc.co.uk/2/hi/asia-pacific/4448131.stm (accessed 26 January 2010); Lu Xiangfu, 'Dongyang Huashui shijian xianchang baodao' ['Live report on the "Dongyang Huashui incident"'], (2005), available at: http://www.peacehall.com/news/gb/china/2005/04/200504151144.shtml (accessed 9 September 2013).

51. Jonathan Watts, 'A bloody revolt in a tiny village challenges the rulers of China', *The Guardian*, (15 April 2005), available at: http://www.guardian.co.uk/world/2005/apr/15/china.jonathanwatts (accessed 9 September 2013).

52. *Ibid.*

became difficult to find a spot to park a car. Traffic at times came to a standstill, but visitors were so eager to see the encampment and the residue of the repression that some walked the entire 18 km from Dongyang city to the chemical park.[53]

The power of spectacle

Vigil tents, dramatic performances and evidence of suppression gave rise to a full-fledged protest spectacle in Huashui. The power of the display was partly a product of effective, increasingly radical tactics that drew more and more people to the site. But equally important, this long-running show was fueled by a blunder made by the county government. As the party secretary of Huashui town explained:

> Our key problem was that many cars had been destroyed, which attracted too many people to visit. The incident was originally nothing, but it got 'stir-fried' (*chaozuo*). ... If they had taken my advice to clean up all the vehicles damaged on the night of April 10, no trace would have been left.[54]

Repression and the tactical escalation that followed brought newcomers to the encampment and empowered the tent-sitters in a number of ways. First, the spectacle helped people in the surrounding area learn about a protest that the state-run media was ignoring.[55] Prior to the police action of 10 April, there were no reports in the official press, even though more than 100 work team members had descended on the encampment and the number of tents had grown from one to two dozen. Even with the news blackout, word that something was happening started to get around; villagers from neighboring communities heard about the protest, passers-by saw the tent-sitters blocking the park's entrance, and shoppers wandered through on market days. That the 10 April repression occurred on a market day and an annual fair took place from 11 to 13 April only heightened the number of onlookers on hand to watch the intensifying spectacle and become part of it. The scheduling of the police action was a serious miscalculation that boosted the audience, as a number of food sellers and early shoppers witnessed the repression and many other non-locals observed its immediate aftermath.

The growing spectacle also conveyed information about the protest from the tent-sitters' perspective and offered a counter-narrative to the official one.[56] After the

53. Lu, 'Dongyang Huashui shijian xianchang baodao'.

54. Interview C7 with a town cadre, 17 July 2007.

55. On the media and dramatic protests, see Doug McAdam, 'Movement strategy and dramaturgic framing in democratic states: the case of the American Civil Rights Movement', in Simone Chambers and Anne Costain, eds, *Deliberation, Democracy and the Media* (Oxford: Rowman and Littlefield, 2000), pp. 117–134.

56. On tactics and dramatic performances serving as 'alternative media', see Benjamin Shepard, *Queer Political Performance and Protest* (New York: Routledge, 2010), p. 243; Doris Yvonne Wilkinson, 'Tactics of protest as media: the case of the black revolution', *Sociological Focus* 3(3), (1970), pp. 13–21. For protest theatre creating a space to 'bear witness' to state oppression, see Annalise Moser, 'Acts of resistance: the performance of women's grassroots protest in Peru', *Social Movement Studies* 2(2), (2003), pp. 177–190. On counter-narratives, see John Downing, Tamara Villarreal Ford, Geneve Gil and Laura Stein, *Radical Media: Rebellious Communication and Social Movements* (Thousand Oaks, CA: Sage, 2001), p. 45. On Chinese protesters in 1989 usurping rituals, capturing the public stage and creating 'political theater', see Joseph W. Esherick and Jeffrey N. Wasserstrom, 'Acting out democracy: political theater in modern China', *Journal of Asian Studies* 49(4), (1990), pp. 835–865.

'April 10th Incident', some stories appeared in the state-run media, but almost all offered a strong defense of the repression.[57] For example, on the second day after the injuries and destruction, there was a piece in the *Dongyang Daily* entitled 'Local officials were besieged by the masses when clearing illegally erected tents'.[58] Two days later, *Jinhua Daily* published a brief report headlined 'The environmental claims of the masses were exploited by a handful of people with ulterior motives, and a mass incident took place in Huashui, Dongyang'.[59]

The spectacle and the ability of onlookers to observe the effects of the repression, hear from the tent-sitters, and soak up the heady atmosphere undercut the government's account of what had transpired. For example, after looking at the dozens of burned vehicles, one person who had read that many officials were injured while 'helping' villagers solve their problems, sarcastically said: 'Seeing this, I guess everyone here understands how our government helps ordinary people: they came in the thousands, drove up in 60 to 70 vehicles, and carried knives, truncheons, and tear gas canisters'.[60] The tent-sitters recognized the power of the field of debris and tried their best to prevent the authorities from removing evidence of the repression. Three days after the police action one Huashui villager told a reporter: 'We have to protect the scene and make sure more people realize the inconsistencies between what the government is saying and doing'.[61]

The mounting spectacle also led many who flocked to the encampment to offer moral and monetary support. One observer described the scene the second day after the repression as follows: 'Onlookers were shocked by the trophies that villagers had seized. They were taking pictures, reading every slogan, and going into tents to talk with older protesters. No one wanted to leave'.[62] Spectators provided more than sympathy and praise. An elderly female protester recalled: 'One night when I kept vigil, a stranger came to our tent with candies, biscuits and money. He said to us: "You are suffering bitterness. Here is some food for you, in case you are hungry at night"'.[63] Visitors also made significant financial contributions to keep the protest going. Several donation boxes were set up in the encampment, with lit candles placed in front of them, to suggest the worthiness of making an offering. By the time the protest concluded, over 100,000 yuan (about US$16,000) had been contributed.[64]

Finally, the crowd that the residue of repression attracted protected the tent-sitters and increased the likelihood that concessions would be made. Right after the 'April 10th Incident', the protesters and villagers who supported them were worried

57. *The New York Times*, *The Guardian*, *The BBC*, *The Times (London)*, and especially *The South China Morning Post* all picked up the story, but these reports could only be read by bilingual readers and thus did little to alert the public in China.

58. Shan Changyu, 'Wo shi qingli zhuxi feifa dajian zhupeng shou qunzhong weidu' ['Local officials were besieged by the masses when clearing illegally erected tents'], *Dongyang Ribao* [*Dongyang Daily*], (11 April 2005).

59. On managing popular backlash, see Hess and Martin, 'Repression, backfire, and the theory of transformative events'.

60. Lu, 'Dongyang Huashui shijian xianchang baodao'.

61. 'Huashui ren tan guanmin maodun' ['People in Huashui talking about the conflict between the government and the people'], *Chinaelections*, (2005), available at: http://www.chinaelections.org/NewsInfo.asp?NewsID=9474 (accessed 14 February 2010).

62. Lu, 'Dongyang Huashui shijian xianchang baodao'.

63. Interview P15 with a villager, 24 May 2007.

64. Interview V4 with a village cadre, 13 April 2007.

because they had damaged over 50 vehicles and a number of cadres and police had been hurt.[65] At that time, 'the whole town was trembling'[66] and many expected more repression soon.[67] However, after they saw a flood of supporters arriving, their anxiety declined and they started to experience the joy of success. A victory celebration went on for nearly a week and the encampment and its environs took on the atmosphere of a festival. One commentator noted: 'People were coming and going, the town was bustling with noise and excitement. ... The shouts of street vendors were rising here and subsiding there. ... Everybody was marveling at the scene'.[68] According to a government report, some villagers even called the national tourism bureau to organize trips for vacationers to spend the Labor Day holiday (1–7 May) in Huashui.[69]

As hierarchies began to invert, fear of the police sank, villagers were emboldened, and the tent-sitters became local heroes. During the 'April 10th Incident', police officers fleeing the area had been forced to strip off their uniforms before they surrendered.[70] After that, police did not dare enter the encampment in uniform and had to wear plain clothes.[71] Previously timid villagers seized microphones out of the hands of officials, denounced the local government, and challenged factory owners directly. When the factory owner who was interrogated by tent-sitters went to the police to complain about her treatment, she was told an investigation was impossible because 'the villagers have great power'.[72] As for the two traitors whose homes were damaged, the deputy party secretary of Dongyang County said in a widely-disseminated speech that although the ransacking was violent and should be treated seriously, there was 'no urgency' (*buji*) for the police to look into it.[73] The party secretary of Huashui town summed up the shift in power relations that was taking place:

> The social status of those people [the elderly tent-sitters] had been very low. ... Then, suddenly they became heroes, with others providing them food and clothes. They were dancing on the [damaged] vehicles and making speeches every day. The protest was like the communist revolution, taking weak, grassroots power and turning it into a great force. During the protest, those people received support, acclaim, money and food. Their social status increased overnight.[74]

Out of fears that the situation was getting out of control, higher-level authorities decided to intervene.[75] At the insistence of tent-sitters and the crowd they had

65. *Ibid.*
66. Interview C7 with a town cadre, 17 July 2007.
67. Markus, 'China riot village draws tourists'.
68. Lu, 'Dongyang Huashui shijian xianchang baodao'.
69. Huashui Town Government, 'Dongyang shi Huashui zhen "4.10 shijian" gongzuo jinzhan qingkuang'.
70. Interview P1 with a protest leader, 8 June 2007.
71. Interview C17 with a police officer, 21 June 2007.
72. *Ibid.*
73. Deputy Party Secretary of Dongyang County, 'Zai Huashui zhen cun ganbu huiyi shang de jianghua' ['Speech at a meeting of Huashui village cadres'], radio broadcast delivered in Huashui town, 1 May 2005.
74. Interview C17 with a police officer, 21 June 2007.
75. On intervention elsewhere in China, see O'Brien and Li, *Rightful Resistance in Rural China*; Yongshun Cai, 'Disruptive collective action in the reform era', in Kevin J. O'Brien, ed., *Popular Protest in China* (Cambridge, MA: Harvard University Press, 2008); Yongshun Cai, 'Power structure and regime resilience: contentious politics in China', *British Journal of Political Science* 38(3), (2008), pp. 411–432.

drawn, and owing to pressure from superiors reaching all the way to Beijing, the Dongyang County leadership made a difficult decision. They accepted 'complete defeat' (*chedi de shibai*)[76] and announced that the chemical park would be shut down.

Conclusion

Hard repression often works. It can end an episode of contention and leave protesters feeling beaten and hopeless. But force may also be counterproductive, especially if it is thought to be excessive and information about its use is 'communicated effectively to receptive audiences that are substantial enough that authorities must take their outrage into consideration';[77] 'Repression can sometimes turn the tables on a government, exposing its brutality and undermining its legitimacy while generating public sympathy for protesters'.[78]

In Huashui, repression clearly backfired. An ill-considered and poorly-timed police action led to tactical escalation and left protesters with proof that undue force had been used. Burned-out cars, tear gas shells and dramatic performances drew thousands to the scene and generated financial support and acclaim for the tent-sitters. As protesters deployed ever-more radical tactics, officials at higher levels became concerned that social order was breaking down and power hierarchies were being upended. In response to prodding from above, county leaders acted to douse the spectacle. They decided to close the chemical park to quiet the protesters and put an end to the show.

The part that repression plays in tactical radicalization suggests that more research is needed into how tactics change over time. In Huashui, protesters initially limited themselves to restrained acts that are par for the course in contemporary China. The suppression of 10 April, however, established a 'norm of violence'[79] and more radical elements of the tactical repertoire were activated. Repression precipitated tactical change, and physical evidence of disproportionate force gave the tent-sitters striking props that made their performances more moving. This is a reminder that a tendency toward tactical escalation in China that has been associated with failure,[80] defending one's honor in the face of non-responsiveness[81] and acclaim (or pressure) from followers,[82] can also spring from policing mistakes and popular reactions that increase the dramaturgical power of a performance and draw onlookers to a spectacle that the authorities and protesters have jointly created.

Focusing on protest spectacle also tells us something about why some episodes of contention succeed and others do not. In China, it is often said that a 'big disturbance creates a big solution, a small disturbance creates a small solution, and no disturbance

76. Interview C2 with a county official, 25 June 2007.

77. Hess and Martin, 'Repression, backfire, and the theory of transformative events', p. 251.

78. Sharon Erickson Nepstad and Clifford Bob, 'When do leaders matter? Hypotheses on leadership dynamics in social movements', *Mobilization* 11(1), (2006), pp. 1–22.

79. Opp and Roehl, 'Repression, micromobilization, and political protest', p. 524.

80. O'Brien and Li, *Rightful Resistance in Rural China*, pp. 71, 80–81.

81. Xianwen Kuang and Christian Göbel, 'Sustaining collective action in urbanizing China', *The China Quarterly* 216, (2013), pp. 850–871.

82. Lianjiang Li and Kevin J. O'Brien, 'Protest leadership in rural China', *The China Quarterly* 193, (2008), pp. 1–23.

creates no solution' (*danao da jiejue, xiaonao xiao jiejue, bunao bu jiejue*). Several quantitative analyses have confirmed that the number of protesters is strongly associated with concessions.[83] This study reminds us that size and 'disturbance' are not merely a function of how many people take part (the Huashui tent-sitters seldom numbered over 100), but also how many people are watching. Spectators are as crucial as participants and dramatic tactics and ham-fisted repression are a reliable way to boost their numbers and extract concessions from leaders who are obsessed with social stability and fear a boisterous crowd viewing a show that the authorities cannot stage-manage.

In Huashui, the size of the spectacle led, in sequence, to repression and giving in. When tactics were still restrained and the number of onlookers comparatively few, forceful repression seemed a good bet to halt the protest. But when coercion failed to end the action, and then backfired as people came from far and wide to see what had transpired, a large and noisy crowd became a resource rather than a vulnerability for the protesters. A spectacle thus made suppression more likely when it was small, but made concessions more likely when it became large. The growing number of onlookers hamstrung the authorities and left them in a difficult position: use even more coercion to terminate the protest or find a way to pacify the tent-sitters. Even for a muscular authoritarian regime that could have swiftly dismantled the encampment and dispersed the crowd with devastating force, hordes of spectators cheering on the tent-sitters' caused pause. Although pollution is allowed to continue in many locations, in Huashui it was not.

83. Cai, 'Disruptive collective action in the reform era', p. 164; Yongshun Cai, *Collective Resistance in China: Why Popular Protests Succeed or Fail* (Stanford, CA: Stanford University Press, 2010); Xi Chen, *Social Protest and Contentious Authoritarianism in China* (New York: Cambridge University Press, 2012), pp. 182, 184; also Kevin J. O'Brien and Lianjiang Li, 'The politics of lodging complaints in rural China', *The China Quarterly* 143, (1995), pp. 756–783.

Patrolling Harmony: pre-emptive authoritarianism and the preservation of stability in W County

Xiaojun Yan

University of Hong Kong, Hong Kong

ABSTRACT

Today, with social protests a daily phenomenon in China, the Party-state's survival hinges upon its institutional capacity to prevent, monitor, process information on, and overcome real and potential challenges. Over the past decade, the Communist Party has consistently stressed the critical importance of 'stability preservation' (*weiwen*) as central to ensuring the longevity of the authoritarian regime. Drawing upon intensive interviews and archival research, this article looks into the stability-preservation system in W County in North China. By exploring the institutional configuration, work mechanisms, daily activities and operational principles of the stability-preservation apparatus in the county, the author seeks to gain insight into the PRC regime's mythical operations of 'system maintenance' and the ways in which the Party-state exerts control over society.

From the grand military parades in Buenos Aires when Peronism was at its peak, to the excited crowds that protested relentlessly to topple dictatorial rule during the Arab Spring, moments of high drama have long attracted students of authoritarian politics. However, despite the abundant literature on authoritarian resilience and fragility, scholars around the globe have yet to develop a clear understanding of the everyday operations of power and domination under such regimes. For example, the questions of how authoritarian rule is 'effectuated, organized and executed'[1] and how authoritarian rulers maintain their grip on power by avoiding systematic political collapse are yet to be adequately explained.

Drawing on archival research conducted in W County in North China in 2012, along with intensive interviews, in this article, the author examines an understudied but important component of the ruling apparatus of the People's Republic of China (PRC), namely, the regime's stability-preservation system (*weiwen xitong*, 维稳系统). By exploring and scrutinizing the institutional configuration, working mechanisms, daily activities and operational principles of the stability-preservation apparatus in one 'sample' county, this article seeks to gain insight into the PRC regime's mythical internal operations of 'system maintenance' at a grassroots level.

Preserving stability

With social protests now being a daily phenomenon in the PRC, the survival of the communist state hinges on its institutional capacity to prevent, monitor, interpret and overcome real and potential challenges. Over the past decade, the ruling Chinese Communist Party (CCP) has consistently stressed

[1]Oliver Schlumberger, ed., *Debating Arab Authoritarianism* (Stanford, CA: Stanford University Press, 2007).

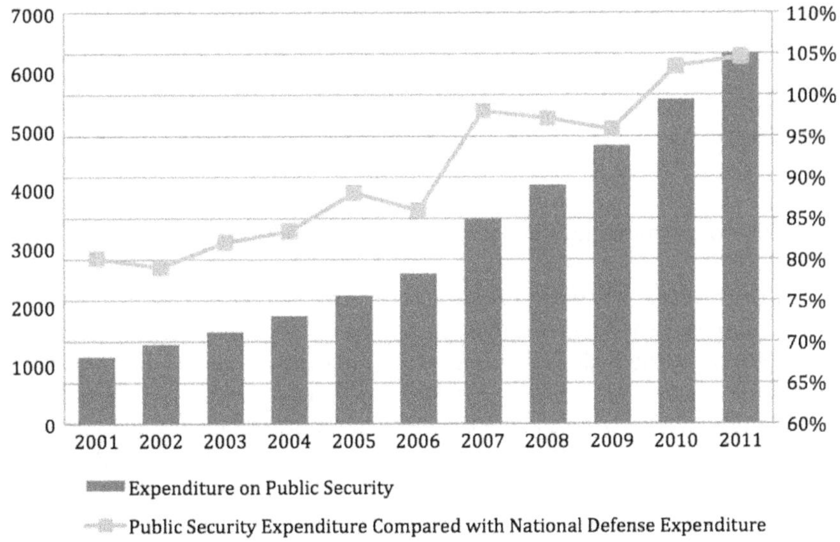

Figure 1. Ratio of national defense budget to central budgetary funding for public security per year (2001–2011). Notes: From 2001 to 2006, expenditure on public security was listed separately in national statistical documents as expenditure on law enforcement and expenditure on armed police. Since 2007, the two items have been combined into a single item entitled 'expenditure on public security'. *Sources*: Ministry of Finance of the People's Republic of China, *Zhongguo caizheng nianjian 2002* [*Finance Yearbook of China 2002*] (Beijing: Zhongguo Caizheng Zazhishe, 2002), p. 295; National Bureau of Statistics of China, *Zhongguo tongji nianjian 2003, 2004, 2005, 2006, 2007, 2008, 2009, 2010, 2011, 2012* [*China Statistical Yearbook 2003, 2004, 2005, 2006, 2007, 2008, 2009, 2010, 2011, 2012*] (Beijing: Zhongguo Tongji Chubanshe, 2003–2013), p. 292; p. 308; p. 278; p. 288; p. 286; p. 264; p. 264; p. 290; p. 280; p. 293.

the critical importance of 'stability preservation' (*weihu wending*, 维护稳定, or the shorter *weiwen*, 维稳) in constructing a 'socialist harmonious society' and ensuring the longevity of the authoritarian political regime.

The term 'stability preservation' first appeared in the *People's Daily*, the Party's mouthpiece, in 2002. The use of this 'buzzword' by the regime's top news outlet has since increased sharply, from approximately 50 instances in 2008 to 180 in 2011.[2] To cope with the growing social unrest, the CCP has significantly increased its spending on maintaining social order and preserving political stability. As a result, the expenditure on public security in China soared from RMB 113.692 billion in 2001 to RMB 630.427 billion in 2011.[3] Figure 1 compares the national defense budget and the central budget for public security from 2001 to 2011. In both 2010 and 2011, China's expenditure on public security can be seen to rival its defense budget.[4] With the regime in grave danger due to increasing political unrest at the grassroots level, *weiwen* appears to provide a lifeline for the regime's safety and survival.

Students of non-democratic politics have long offered substantially different explanations for the durability of authoritarian regimes, ranging from cultural determinism to voluntarist arguments that focus on human agency and initiative.[5] In the past two decades, however, political scientists have

[2]Gang Qian, 'Weiwen heshi chengwei changyongyu' ['When did "stability preservation" become a buzzword?'], *The New York Times*, (12 August 2013), available at: http://cn.nytimes.com/article/china/2012/09/19/cc19qiangang2/ (accessed 12 September 2015).

[3]Ministry of Finance, *Zhongguo caizheng nianjian 2002* [*Finance Yearbook of China 2002*] (Beijing: Zhongguo Tonggji Chubanshe, 2012); National Bureau of Statistics of China, *Zhongguo tongji nianjian 2012* [*China Statistical Yearbook 2012*] (Beijing: Zhongguo Tongji Chubanshe, 2012).

[4]See the note on sources beneath Figure 1.

[5]For example: for cultural theories, see Yahya Sadowski, 'The new Orientalism and the democracy debate', *Middle East Report* 183, (1993), pp. 14–21; Elie Kedourie, *Democracy and Arab Political Culture* (London: Frank Cass, 1994). For structural arguments, see Dirk Vandewalle, *Libya Since Independence: Oil and State-Building* (Ithaca, NY: Cornell University Press, 1998); Michael L. Ross, 'Does oil hinder democracy', *World Politics* 53(2), (2001), pp. 325–361; for political agency, see Lisa Wedeen, *Ambiguities of Domination* (Chicago, IL: The University of Chicago Press, 1999).

gradually come to realize the essential role of political institutions in ensuring the persistence of authoritarian systems. For example, Greene found that the fiscal strength of an authoritarian state is a vital determinant of its survival, as a fiscally strong regime can always 'politicize public resources' to its own advantage.[6] Political parties also play a crucial role in binding 'opportunistic leaders...together institutionally' and helping create credible power-sharing arrangements between dictators and their ruling coalitions.[7] The legislature under an authoritarian regime can also contribute to the regime's survival by providing a central institutional forum in which to incorporate the interests of opposing forces by revealing their demands, hammering out compromises, and addressing and publicizing agreements in a legalistic form.[8]

Recent studies on the durability of the PRC reflect this institutional emphasis.[9] Remarkably, having witnessed the Communist Party's increasing emphasis on stability preservation, China scholars have paid particular attention to the regime's various institutional arrangements and strategies for coping with the mounting social and political challenges. Keith and Lin examined the Party-state's instrumental use of politicized legal codes and legislative procedures to counter rebellious quasi-religious sects and social organizations.[10] O'Brien and Li explored the dynamic interplay between the local Party-state and its societal challengers in administrative litigation procedures. They found the PRC to constitute a 'far-flung, many-layered state' that is 'less a monolith than a hodgepodge of disparate actors, some of whom have multiple identities and conflicting interests'.[11] Their observations on the 'segmented and layered structure' of the Party-state are especially important for understanding the everyday exercise of control in the PRC.

Cai examined the suppression of popular resistance by local governments—a particular form of state response to social challenges that has had variable results.[12] Chen and Xu examined the role of the judicial system in settling collective labor disputes and demonstrated that the courts' extrajudicial intervention, and their strategy of individualizing collective disputes, can serve to 'foreclose labor movements in China'.[13] Lee and Zhang constructed a heuristic framework for analyzing the micro-foundations of authoritarianism in China, and showed that protest bargaining, legal-bureaucratic absorption and patron–clientelism are the three primary tactics used by the local Party-state to depoliticize social unrest. Together, these tactics 'constitute a lived experience of authoritarian domination as a non-zero-sum situation'.[14]

Although these groundbreaking studies provide numerous insights, little systematic archival and field research has examined the institutions that make up China's stability-preservation apparatus—a

[6]Kenneth F. Greene, 'The political economy of authoritarian single-party dominance', *Comparative Political Study* 47(7), (2009), pp. 807–834.

[7]Jason Brownlee, *Authoritarianism in an Age of Democratization* (Cambridge: Cambridge University Press, 2007).

[8]Jennifer Gandhi and Adam Przeworski, 'Cooperation, cooptation, and rebellion under dictatorships', *Economics & Politics* 18(1), (2006), p. 14.

[9]For example, Andrew J. Nathan, 'Authoritarian resilience', *Journal of Democracy* 14(1), (2003), p. 6; for Party adaption see, Bruce J. Dickson, *Wealth into Power* (New York: Cambridge University Press, 2008) and David Shambaugh, *China's Communist Party: Atrophy and Adaptation* (Berkeley, CA: University of California Press, 2008); for state and petitioning, see Xi Chen, *Social Protest and Contentious Authoritarianism in China* (New York: Cambridge University Press, 2014); for regime inclusion, see Xiaojun Yan, 'Regime inclusion and the resilience of authoritarianism: local people's political consultative conference in post-Mao Chinese politics', *The China Journal* 66, (2011), pp. 53–75; and for the coercive apparatus, see Xuezhi Guo, *China's Security State* (New York: Cambridge University Press, 2014).

[10]Ronald C. Keith and Zhiqiu Lin, 'The Falun Gong problem: politics and the struggle for the rule of law in China', *The China Quarterly* 175, (2003), pp. 623–642.

[11]Kevin J. O'Brien and Lianjiang Li, 'Suing the local state: administrative litigation in rural China', *China Journal* 51, (2004), pp. 75–96.

[12]Yongshun Cai, 'Local government and the suppression of popular resistance in China', *The China Quarterly* 193, (2008), pp. 24–41.

[13]Feng Chen and Xin Xu, 'Active judicial: judicial dismantling of workers' collective action in China', *The China Journal* 67, (2012), pp. 87–107.

[14]Ching Kwan Lee and Yonghong Zhang, 'The power of instability: unraveling the microfoundations of bargained authoritarianism in China', *American Journal of Sociology* 118(6), (2013), pp. 1475–1508.

unique institutional agency of the PRC.[15] Previous studies mostly tackle the issue of stability preservation in the PRC with reference to various forms of contentious claim making and the Party-state's handling of collective action during periods of social unrest. Thus, the existing studies have failed to address the everyday operations of the authoritarian regime, and the pre-emptive measures it implements to prevent unrest. Yet, as shown in this article, such pre-emptive actions are the backbone of the regime's overall strategy for maintaining socio-political order at the foundational level. Hence, the inadequate attention that previous studies have paid to these pre-emptive mechanisms has hampered our understanding of authoritarian stability in China. In the following sections, this article examines the institutional configuration and daily operations of the stability-preservation apparatus in W County and describes the major threats it is required to handle. Overall, the author seeks to shed some light on the everyday practice of pre-emptive authoritarian control in the PRC, and to dynamically depict the system of power that has enabled the CCP to tenaciously retain its authoritarian rule into the twenty-first century.

Chains of command

Accompanying an increased emphasis on stability and harmony over the past decade, how to keep society in order, and how to ensure compliance among the Chinese people, are the major questions and challenges faced by local governments across China. W County is no exception. A powerful and well-integrated institutional framework for maintaining social and political stability, with efficient chains of command, has been established in the county. Stability-preservation or *weiwen* mechanisms, with their crucial role in ensuring the regime's survival, operate under the strict scrutiny and control of the country's prerogative authority, the Communist Party, rather than its normative authority, county-level government.[16]

The stability-preservation system in W County is just such an interconnected structure under the direct leadership of the county's Communist Party representatives. At the top of the hierarchy is the Standing Committee of the CCP Committee of W County (*xianwei changwei*, 县委常委), which is formally considered to have final approval within the territory. However, as the 'principal cadre' accountable for the socio-political stability of the county, the Communist Party Secretary of W County shoulders the full responsibility for any decisions taken. Indeed, stability preservation is one of the most important criteria used by Party Secretaries' supervisors at the provincial and prefectural level to evaluate their subordinates' performance. Any negative record for this single criterion may disqualify a county-level Party Secretary from political awards or promotion for a couple of years. This so-called 'single-item veto' (*yipiao foujue*, 一票否决) is a powerful mechanism for holding local Party officials in China accountable for the safety of the regime, and forcing them to invest their full complement of financial and human resources in the project of preventing social upheavals from taking place. For this purpose, the CCP Committees conduct annual inspections at all levels to review the implementation of pre-emptive measures and evaluate the performance of their subordinate Party Secretaries in terms of stability preservation.[17] This strictly enforced accountability system exerts immense pressure on local Party officials, enabling higher-status Party cadres to transmit their concern for regime safety to the grassroots level of the ruling apparatus. It thus ensures a consensus as well as a united force for safeguarding the regime's survival across administrative levels.[18]

---

[15] See Appendix A, Notes On Fieldwork.

[16] In *The Dual State* (Clark, NJ: Lawbook Exchange, 2010), Ernst Franenkel proposed a 'dual-state' model for the National Socialist regime in Germany. The 'prerogative state' denotes a 'governmental system that exercises unlimited arbitrariness and violence unchecked by any legal guarantees', whereas the normative state is 'an administrative body endowed with elaborate powers for safeguarding the legal order as expressed in statutes, decisions of the courts, and activities of the administrative agencies' (see p. xiii).

[17] Other criteria treated with sufficient seriousness to warrant the 'single-item veto' include family planning and extraordinarily serious safety accidents with high casualties. See Interview 20120628-01.

[18] Interview 20120628-01.

One of the core members of the Standing Committee is held responsible for the daily management and supervision of the *weiwen* system in each county. In W County, the individual in charge is the Secretary of the Political and Legal Affairs Committee (PLAC, *zhengfa wei*, 政法委). Accordingly, the county's PLAC is assigned the second title 'Office of the Stability Preservation Leading Group' (OSPLG, *weiwen ban*, 维稳办). The OSPLG is empowered to 'supervise, co-ordinate and lead the entire law-enforcement and judicial systems' in working towards the prevention of social unrest and the maintenance of political stability. The members of the OSPLG thus include the county's People's Court, People's Procuratorate, police force, Bureau of Legal Affairs (*sifa ju*, 司法局) and Bureau of Civil Affairs (*minzheng ju*, 民政局).[19] Under the OSPLG, an 'Office of Comprehensive Management of Public Security' (*shehui zhian zonghe zhili bangongshi*, 社会治安综合治理办公室) has been established in each township. Together, these institutions constitute the local branches of the *weiwen* system. Each village government has a 'Station of Comprehensive Management of Public Security' (*shehui zhian zonghe zhili zhan*, 社会治安综合治理站) staffed by CCP cadres, a village security director and ordinary CCP members who live in the village. The operations of the Letters and Visits Bureau (*xinfang ju*, 信访局), the Party-state agency dealing with petitions, are also closely integrated with those of the stability-preservation system. At the grassroots level, the Party-state has also established quasi-official mass organizations such as the Public Security Society (*zhibaohui*, 治保会), the Dispute-Mediation Society (*tiaojiehui*, 调解会) and the local militia to support the official *weiwen* apparatus. The entire system is a giant 'interlocked pyramid of Party machinery'[20] extending from the County Secretary to grassroots village members, and boasting extensive coercive power, the capacity to respond in real time and to provide around-the-clock surveillance, plentiful resources that can be mobilized in response to emergencies, and enormous discretionary power outside the command of the normative county government.[21]

Among the major responsibilities of the stability-preservation system is the protection of political security (*zhengzhi anquan*, 政治安全), public security (*gonggong anquan*, 公共安全) and production safety (*anquan shengchan*, 安全生产). Political security denotes the safety of the political regime: the OSPLG must ensure that no anti-regime activity, political protests, anti-government demonstrations, open practice of 'evil cults' such as the *Falungong*, or mass riots occur within the territory. Provisions for public security entail the maintenance of basic social order and a crime-free environment. In particular, the OSPLG must strive to prevent major violent accidents with high casualty rates, radical social protest due to unaddressed grievances, and the collective petitioning of the provincial capital or Beijing. Production-safety practices involve the monitoring of workplace safety and the prevention of serious workplace accidents such as explosions in factories, severe traffic accidents that cause a certain number of deaths, and coal-mining accidents.[22] The *weiwen* apparatus in W County, headed by the OSPLG, appears to be a cross-agency system that systematically coordinates the maintenance of overall stability. With its responsibility for coordinating and supervising the local implementation of almost all of the government's important policy areas, it is only natural that the OSPLG and its staff have attained an increasingly important status within the Party-state hierarchy.

Threats

For an institutionalist study of the *weiwen* apparatus in the PRC, it is first essential to clarify the major threats to socio-political stability the Party-state may have to routinely deal with at the grassroots. Fortunately, the county archives provide plenty of materials that reflect the basic contour of the threats

---

[19]In neighboring counties, where the PLAC Secretary is not a Standing Committee member, the Committee creates a specific 'Stability Preservation Leading Group', headed by another member of the Standing Committee, as the county-level headquarters of the *weiwen* apparatus. See Interview 20120705-01.

[20]Andrew Walder, *Fractured Rebellion* (Cambridge, MA: Harvard University Press, 2009).

[21]Interview 20120705-01.

[22]The specific threshold for traffic-accident casualty rate at which a given accident is considered a cause of public instability is confidential government information and not available to this study. See Interview 20120713-01.

the *weiwen* system in W County has to handle on a daily basis. In the official language, the stability-preservation apparatus of W County is required to deal with a variety of 'indications of potential instability' (*buwending zhenghou*, 不稳定征候) and to handle on site any emergent incidents (*tufa shijian*, 突发事件) that might influence social or political order.

In terms of the extent of threat, timing is equally—if not more—crucial. As a local official in the OSPLG noted in an interview:

> There are sensitive periods [in a year] in terms of the threat to socio-political stability. Usually, when there is an election to change the leadership of a village government, you are more likely to see social unrest and collective protests. Also, during the weeks of 4 June [the anniversary of the 1989 Tian'anmen Movement], 5 July [the anniversary of the 2009 Uighur Riot in Xinjiang], or before and during major local festivities or traditional holidays, we are always on high alert. In addition, each year, when peasant workers from other places who work here are due for salary payment, the entire *weiwen* system is set in full motion as this is another period when mass incidents are likely to break out.[23]

At the county level, the stability-preservation system is rarely required to deal with 'high politics' or anti-regime activities directly. Such events are normally addressed by provincial Party bodies, or representatives even higher in the Party-state hierarchy, unless concrete and detailed county-level instructions are provided from above (such as the prevention of *Falungong* activities). The day-to-day threats to socio-political stability in W County come from four overlapping issue areas, namely feud warfare, competing economic interests, land disputes and unanticipated triggering events.

Feuds

Due to its location on the borders of two provinces and nine counties, the major causes of social instability or 'mass incident' in W County are historical feuds between people from neighboring territories. The situation is described in one government document as follows:

> W Lake connects W County with the neighboring jurisdictions—particularly P County and T County of Jiangsu Province. In our county, seven townships are bordered with Jiangsu Province. In some places, 'you take one step and have already crossed two provinces; you take two steps and have already crossed three counties' (*yibu kua liangsheng, liangbu kua sanxian*; 一步跨两省，两步跨三县). Since 1959, the people from these two provinces who live on the shores of W Lake have engaged in more than 400 instances of armed conflict of different scales, due to disputes over the reclamation of land from the lake, and the harvest [from these lands] … the hostility is so grave that family members have not been allowed to cremate the corpses [of a few victims of this armed combat] for more than a decade.[24]

In a document released by J City's Party Committee, which operates in a supervisory capacity at prefectural level, it was noted that '31 people were killed and more than 800 injured' in the 400 or more instances of armed combat (*xiedou*, 械斗) in this region.[25] Furthermore,

> the relatives of victims who died in these fights repeatedly blocked the entrance to the compounds of the local CCP Committee and local government, assaulted the respective township government and the local police, and even attacked members of a central investigation group dispatched by Beijing.[26]

Economic interests

With the PRC's transition to a market economy, competing economic interests have also become a major cause of social unrest. If feud is more or less peculiar to W County, disputes over economic interests

---

[23]Interview 20120625-03.

[24]Archival Document 1-7, The CCP Committee of W County and W County Government, 'Qianghua "Wulian" Cuoshi, Quanli Weihu Weishanhu Bianjie Diqu Hexie Wending' ['Enhancing the "five connections" measures and wholeheartedly maintaining the harmony and stability of the border region around W Lake'] (date of issue ca. 2005–2006), pp. 1–2.

[25]Archival Document 1-6, The CCP Committee of J City and J City Government, 'Jianli Changxiao Jizhi, Henzhua Zonghe Zhili, Quanli Weihu Lusu Bianjie W Hu Diqu Hexie Wending' ['Create long-term mechanisms, pay close attention to comprehensive social management, wholeheartedly preserve the harmony and stability of the W Lake region on the border of Jiangsu and Shandong Province'], (June 2009), pp. 1–2. See also Archival Document 3-18, The CCP Committee of W County and the W County Government, 'W Xian Huqu Bianqu Wending Gongzuo Qingkuang Huibao' ['Briefing on the stability preservation work in the lake and border region of W County'], (March 2009), p. 1.

[26]Archival Document 1-6, p. 2.

might represent a more general pattern of threats that the *weiwen* system has to face at the grassroots. In W County, it is not unusual for disputes over property rights, profit sharing, business privileges and other monetary issues to escalate into open protests, demonstrations or riots.

An example of unrest due to the infringement of local business privileges occurred in 2009, when the officials at a major coalmine in W County decided to hire fewer vehicles privately from villagers for the long-distance transportation of coal products and chose instead to use the state-owned railroad. This caused the peasants who relied on this business for a living to violently assail the compound of the mine to signal their opposition to the plan. The stability-preservation apparatus was immediately instructed to step in.[27] In the same year, another 'indication of instability' was identified when the outside wall of an explosive-materials storage building collapsed in heavy rain, which damaged the drainage channel in a nearby village. When the powerful corporation who owns the storage exhibited arrogant carelessness toward the small village community, the villagers organized and engaged in direct confrontation with the company. To prevent a major 'mass incident' capable of attracting nationwide media attention, the county's stability-preservation force was again fully mobilized to dissolve the high tension.[28]

In W County, conflict over economic interests usually arises from civil disagreements between individuals or families, or tensions between peasants and local corporations. The weaker side in the dispute may use collective action or public protest as an effective instrument to demand justice. Regardless of their particular motivations, economic conflicts constitute a huge reservoir of causes of potential social upheavals, which must be treated with great seriousness by those responsible for the country's stability preservation.

Land disputes

Land disputes in W County are a specific kind of economic conflict involving the ownership, rights, privileges, profits and/or revenue associated with farmland or residential lots. China's drastic development of her industrial and urban sectors have made disputes over land rights increasingly significant, violent and complicated over the past decade—particularly in rural areas. It is unsurprising then, that conflicts over land rights have come to constitute another grave threat to W County's socio-political stability.

In W County, most serious land disputes with the potential to cause social protest occur between members of the rural community and local corporations. For example, in 1989, the state-owned D Company claimed around 60 *mu* of farmland from D Village with a promise that 106 workers from D Village would be hired by the factory. By the end of 1993, however, only 28 villagers had been hired. When the company refused to honor its promise, the villagers launched a series of collective petitions all the way up to Beijing, and threatened to take any protest action they saw fit until the contract was enforced. The County OSPLG thus had to spend an enormous amount of time and considerable resources to deal with this 'major indication of instability'.[29] State-directed projects—when violating the land rights of the local community—are also potential causes of instability. In 2008, for instance, the government began a construction project to strengthen the dykes near B Village. However, the site was immediately besieged by villagers, and the construction machinery was seized by the angry

[27] Archival Document 2-6, 'Shou Kuangba Youzuzhi Ganrao, Meitan Baoxiao Yunshu Hetong Yanzhong Shouzu De Qingkuang Fanying' ['Briefing and petition: contract for the production and transportation of coal blocked by organized harassment'], (10 November 2009), p. 1.

[28] Archival Document 2-5, 'W Xian Chenggong Chuzhi Guanyu Kongzhuang Meikuang Zhayao Ku Weiqiang Daota De Jiufen' ['W County successfully handles dispute over the collapse of the wall of the explosive materials storage building owned by Kongzhuang Coal-mine'], *Jianshe Ping'an J Jianbao* [*Briefs on the Construction of a Peaceful J City*] no. 47, (23 July 2009).

[29] Archival Document 2-10, The Leadership Group on the Coordination of State-owned Coal-mines and the local government of W County, 'Guanyu Datun Meidian Gongsi Wei Lvxing Zhengdi Xieyi Jiejue Nongmin Didaigong Qingkuang de Diaocha Baogao' ['Investigative report on the non-compliance of D Thermal Power Company in implementing the agreement on "Employment to Substitute Land Rights"'], (18 August 2008).

crowd. The villagers' grievance was that government officials had paid insufficient compensation for the farmland claimed from the village for another project in 2000. When the local officials tried to approach the angry crowd, villagers 'beat down the principal cadre of the township government and assaulted other officials violently. More than ten government staff and two policemen were injured'.[30] W County's stability-preservation officials took over the case, hoping to foreclose a potentially larger and more radical conflict.

Unanticipated triggering events

Sensitive incidents that take place suddenly and without the state's foreknowledge can also have a serious effect on county-level stability. The likelihood of large-scale social unrest is even higher when such incidents involve casualties among members of certain social groups (such as students and ethnic minorities), overlap with politically sensitive events (such as the CCP's five-yearly National Congress) or arouse rumor and mass discontent. One of the daily tasks of W County's stability-preservation system is to prevent potential activists from assigning to triggering events 'symbolic political connotations' upon which to found and mobilize a movement.[31]

In July 2008, for example, a 21-year-old male student drowned during a trip with high-school friends after receiving a university-admission offer. The boy's family did not accept the results of the police investigation and suspected murder or at least foul play. They threatened to organize a radical protest and to post the case on the Internet. The family even planned to move the corpse to the house of one of his friends—whom they suspected to be the 'murderer'—and to make a scene there. As this incident took place only one month prior to the opening of the Beijing Olympics, and even closer to the scheduled local Olympics Torch Relay Ceremony, it was immediately classified as one of the most serious threats to the county's socio-political stability that warranted immediate government intervention.[32]

Another such event took place in 2007. In the morning of 23 August, one Muslim prisoner—who was a Hui Chinese in terms of ethnicity—was found unconscious in his cell and was immediately sent to the W County Hospital, where he died. After his family was informed of his death, a large crowd of Muslims started to gather in front of the county jailhouse. The following morning, two buses loaded with more than 100 Muslims arrived, and their occupants attempted to break into the prison, but were blocked by the police. Afterwards, the protestors attempted to smash the administrative building of the prison, and claimed that more Muslims from neighboring cities would soon arrive in support.[33] As this unanticipated incident involved a sensitive population and a sensitive place, it was immediately identified as a serious indicator of social unrest.

Unanticipated and agitating 'triggering events' usually attract large crowds of people with various potential grievances regarding the Party-state, and make it easy for potential leaders of movements to assign symbolic connotations to social unrest.[34] When casualties among sensitive social groups are involved, or the incident overlaps with important political affairs, it is especially convenient for anti-systematic forces to rally supporters around such events and construct larger social movements.

---

[30]Archival 2-7, PLAC of W County, 'Guanyu "3.26" Shijian Chuli Qingkuang de Huibao' ['Report on the handling of the "March 26 Incident"'], (29 April 2008).

[31]Hank Johnston, *States and Social Movements* (Cambridge: Polity Press, 2011).

[32]Archival Document 2-8, 'Guanyu J Shi Tuoshan Chuzhi Yi Zhongxuesheng Nishui Siwang Shijian Youxiao Huajie Yingxiang Shehuiwending Yinhuan Qingkuang de Tongbao' ['Briefing on the ways in which J City successfully handled the case of the drowning of a high-school student and effectively removed the potential threat to social stability'], (6 August 2008), p. 10.

[33]Archival Document 2-1, PLAC of J City, 'Guanyu J Jianyu J Jianqu Huizu Zuifan J Yinbin Siwang Yinfa X Xian Huimin Juji J Jianqu Shijian Chuzhi Qingkuang de Baogao' ['Report on the gathering of Muslims from X County in J prison caused by the death of prisoner J'], (29 August 2007).

[34]Archival Document 2-8, p. 8.

The net of stability

In response to various kinds of threats of social unrest, the individuals and institutions responsible for stability preservation in W County have constructed a safety-net of control mechanisms to prevent nascent social unrest from flourishing, and to deal effectively with collective political protests when they do break out. Founded upon an institutional framework that enables formal and informal information gathering, population control, conflict resolution, emergency-response tactics and political surveillance, the apparatus of stability preservation in W County has historically served as an important pre-emptive force, safeguarding the political regime and ensuring peace within the county. In the following section, the author examines the primary components of the daily operations of W County's *weiwen* system.

Cross-border institutional collaboration

As W Lake accounts for two-thirds of W County's territory, the county's CCP Committee has repeatedly emphasized that 'maintaining a socio-politically stable lake region is the most difficult and the most essential work of this county'.[35] The lake itself straddles borders, leading to considerable struggle for its natural resources and thus enormous long-term hostility between local communities. This has made the lake region famous for feud warfare and high crime rates, both of which pose major threats to the socio-political stability of W County.[36] As one document issued in 2005 noted,

> the stability-preservation work in the lake region is not only a focus of the stability-preservation work of W County, but also of the entire prefecture and province. If we have an orderly and safe lake region, we have a socio-politically stable county; if we have a safe border region, we have a safe county.[37]

The complexity of the issue lies primarily in the fact that the authorities of the neighboring counties are all invested in the competition for W Lake's natural resources, and tend to protect their own people when a feud breaks out. The lack of communication between these neighboring jurisdictions has also created a law-enforcement vacuum. When large-scale cross-border protests occur and the claims made by the protestors involve people from other counties, it is difficult for W County's *weiwen* system to effectively address people's grievances, control the crowds or solve the problem.

Accordingly, a major part of the daily work of the stability-preservation apparatus of W County is to create, maintain and enhance liaison and cooperation with governmental authorities in the neighboring counties. This emphasis is common at all levels, from village police to the county's highest-ranked Party cadre. Representatives of W County's stability-preservation system spend considerable time every year visiting and holding regular bilateral or multilateral meetings with the Party-state agencies of neighboring counties. Since 2006, a county-level working conference on stability preservation has been hosted in W County once every six months, and involves all of the neighboring counties. The principal cadres of W County have also visited its neighboring counties frequently, and signed a number of Memos of Understanding regarding collaborative law enforcement and stability preservation. Township governments in the border region have also reached out to the townships of neighboring jurisdictions to establish 'joint work forces' to screen, detect, mediate and solve cross-border social conflicts or deal with early signs of socio-political

[35]Archival Document 4-1, The CCP Committee of W County and W County Government, 'Jinjin Weirao Kexue Fazhanguan, Shenru Tuijin Huqu Bianqu Wending Gongzuo' ['Closely adhering to the Concept of Scientific Development, Deepening and Furthering the Stability Preservation Work in the Lake and Border Regions], (December 17, 2009), p. 1.

[36]Archival Document 3-18.

[37]Archival Document 3-6, The CCP Committee of W County and W County Government, 'Quanmian Jiaqiang Jiceng Jichu Gongzuo, Quanli Dazao Ping'an Huqu Bianqu' ['Comprehensively enhancing grassroots and foundational work, wholeheartedly constructing a peaceful lake and border region'], (June 2005), p. 2.

unrest.[38] In W County's official documents, this work is termed as 'four kinds of liaison' (*silian*, 四联), comprising 'friendly' liaison between county-level Party-states, liaison between the government agencies of different counties for 'development' purposes, liaison between the local police forces of neighboring counties to foster 'stability', and liaison between villages in different counties for the purpose of 'unity'. These four types of liaison, collectively *silian*, are deemed an ultimate guarantee of the success of W County's stability-preservation work.[39]

Institutions also liaise and collaborate in infrastructure investment, anti-crime campaigns, and the creation of routine communication and cooperation mechanisms to prevent mass incidents.[40] The stability-preservation authorities in W County work closely with those of neighboring counties to provide everyday surveillance and law enforcement, hoping to facilitate the county's overall work of fighting crime and to prevent serious cross-border conflicts from taking place. For instance, as disputes over summer and autumn harvests on the land reclaimed from W Lake have traditionally been a cause of feud warfare and other contentious action, W County's authorities have established a specific strategy for dealing with this problem that if a harvest is controversial and has the potential to cause feud warfare, it must be given up. For people of W County who incur any financial loss by implementing this strategy, they must be compensated in cash by the government of W County.[41]

In 2008, W County's authorities worked closely with those of the neighboring P and T Counties to solve historical cross-county enmity and thereby to remove a major cause of future collective unrest. They reached agreements with the family members of victims, and cremated the four corpses that had remained in the morgue for several years.[42] Between 2006 and 2008, W County successfully collaborated with its neighboring counties to mediate 64 cross-border disputes of various types, prevent 14 civil disputes from turning into criminal conflicts, and solve 19 cases in which the relevant parties had launched petitions to either the provincial capital city or Beijing.[43]

The institutional collaboration between W County and its neighbors also facilitated the mediation of social conflict and reduced the possibility of collective violence. For example, a W County official recalled that in March 2012, when the Z family of W County entered into very serious dispute with the Y family of the neighboring P County over the ownership of a graveyard with good *fengshui* (风水), each side recruited more than 200 male family members in preparation for armed combat. When this significant indicator of social unrest was reported, W County's authorities immediately notified the government of P County, and suggested dealing with the tension together. The police forces of the two counties also dispatched a joint force to deter the two parties from engaging in armed combat. Eventually, an agreement was reached under the supervision of the two county governments, and the plans for feud warfare were given up.[44] The successful resolution of this cross-county conflict and the prevention of major armed combat were highly praised by the supervisory Party-state cadres.[45] Indeed, the Party-state considers this kind of grassroots-level cross-border collaboration to be one of the most critical components of the preservation of socio-political stability in W County. As one document notes,

---

[38]Archival Document 3-15, The W County PLAC Secretary, 'Wanshan Huqu Bianjie Wending Jizhi, Quanmian Goujian Hexie Xin Weishan' ['Improving stability-preservation mechanisms in the lake region, comprehensively constructing a new and harmonious W County'], (September 2008), p. 3.

[39]Archival Document 3-6, p. 2.

[40]*Ibid.*, pp. 2–3.

[41]Archival Document 3-4, 'Guanyu Jiaqiang Lianxi Miqie Hezuo Gongtong Jianli Wending Xiezuo Jizhide Xieyi de Shishi Xize' ['Detailed instructions on the implementation of the agreement on the joint construction of stable mechanisms of cooperation by strengthening liaison and enhancing collaboration'], (issuing authority or date not indicated), p. 3.

[42]Archival Document 3-5, The W County PLAC, 'Huqu Bianqu Wending Gongzuo Qingkuang Huibao' ['Briefing on the Stability-Preservation Work in the Lake and Border Region'], (December 2005).

[43]Archival 3-11, 'Qianghua Wulian Cuoshi, Quanli Weihu W Hu Bianjie Diqu Hexie Wending' ['Strengthening the "five measures", wholeheartedly safeguarding harmony and stability in the W Lake border region'] (issuing authority or date not indicated), p. 7.

[44]Interview 20120705-01.

[45]Archival Document 4-4, '2005 nian Geji Lingdao de Pishi' ['Comments made by leaders at different levels in 2005'] (issuing authority or date not indicated), p. 12.

> When indications of social unrest start to emerge, we should coordinate our stability-preservation work from the grassroots level. Through real-time communication between villages and townships across county borders, people could reach an understanding and solve disputes by negotiation and discussion. At the same time (through cross-border collaboration mechanisms), we could take advantage of kinship influence, family pressure and social relationships to solve contradictions at the grassroots and ensure the peaceful co-existence … of people from different jurisdictions.[46]

Screening and detecting social disagreements

Although cross-border collaboration provides an improved institutional infrastructure for stability preservation in W County, the 'screening and detection of social disagreements' (*paicha shehui maodun*, or simply *paicha*; 排查社会矛盾) constitutes the foundational everyday work of the system. The Party-state considers the screening and detection of 'social disagreements' an important tool for removing potential threats to socio-political stability before they mature into visible social unrest. This work has thus been attributed tremendous importance. Indeed, the crucial pre-emptive measure of *paicha* has become a daily endeavor to which a substantial amount of the resources and manpower of W County's stability-preservation apparatus is assigned.[47]

These screening and detecting mechanisms are operated by the OSPLG at all levels of stability preservation in W County. A senior police officer in the county described their operation as follows:

> We have a comprehensive system for screening and detecting [social contradictions and conflicts] … In every village, this work must be conducted once a week; at the township level, it is conducted every two weeks. The results of the village government's weekly screening are reported to the township government. For this work, we have a very clear responsibility and division of labor. Each piece of information reported by the village government should be carefully scrutinized and analyzed by higher authorities [to identify any indicators of potential socio-political unrest]. And all of these procedures are documented in detail in official archives for future reference.[48]

Led by the village's Party Secretary or Director of Security (*zhibao renzhu*, 治保主任), various forms of screening and detection are carried out at the grassroots level, such as field investigation, information gathering and analysis, household visits and discussions with relevant parties. Information is transmitted efficiently through the hierarchy: when indicators of potential social unrest are detected, the OSPLG and the law-enforcement agencies under its supervision become involved at an early stage. If the problem concerns inter-village or even cross-county conflict, the handling of the case is directly reported to and overseen by the principal cadres of W County. In addition to this hierarchical information-transmission channel, the OSPLG employs more than 500 ordinary villagers as full-time or part-time 'informants' (*xinxi yuan*, 信息员) who report any serious irregularities directly to the county-level stability-preservation cadres, thereby bypassing the bureaucratic ladder. As the county's CCP Committee has boasted, W County has created an information-gathering and reporting system that 'reaches vertically down to the grassroots level and horizontally to the farthest border of the county', enabling the Party-state 'to carry out its [stability-preservation] work with clear targets and in a timely manner'.[49]

As cross-border conflicts in the W Lake region are a major source of social unrest in W County, the screening and detecting mechanisms also include a number of 'joint groups' comprised of representatives from W County and its neighboring counties along the lakeshore, who work collaboratively to identify and remove indications of cross-border socio-political unrest. The W County Party Committee released a document acknowledging that 'these joint groups, operating at the township level, greatly facilitate our timely communication and intelligence sharing with neighboring counties. The work of

[46]Archival Document 3-3, The CCP Committee of W County and the W County Government, 'Renzhen Guanche Luoshi Wuxiang Xieyi, Quanli Weihu Huqu Bian[qu] Wending' ['Seriously implementing and realizing the five agreements, wholeheartedly safeguarding stability in the lake and border region'], (16 December 2004), p. 3.

[47]Archival Document 3-22, The PLAC of J City, 'Woshi Zhaokai Lusu Bianjie W Hu Diqu Wending Gongzuo Diaoduhui' ['A conference was held in this city on the coordination of stability-preservation work in the border regions of Shandong and Jiangsu Provinces'], (26 April 2006), p. 3.

[48]Interview 20120707-01.

[49]Archival Document 3-6, p. 4. See also Interview 20120707-01.

these groups ensures that we are able to prevent disputes and contradictions from escalating [into social protest and riot]'.[50] In addition, the Communist Party's traditional 'letters and visits' system, designed to handle petitions from the people, has become another important instrument for screening and detecting early signs of political instability or social unrest. A township Party Secretary made the following observation on this process:

> [An important part of the screening mechanism is to] identify and scrutinize grievances reflected in the petitions we receive through the letters and visits system. Especially for those cases that are still being processed by the Letters and Visits Bureau, we usually pay much closer attention and seek to establish direct contact with the petitioner. The purpose is to clarify what the issue is and how to address the problem without radicalizing the relevant parties. For those cases that might lead to petitions to Beijing or the provincial government, we have to organize a special work team. Again, by doing so, our goal is that these cases should not be allowed to escalate into socio-political unrest and grievances not turn into anti-regime political sentiment.[51]

To facilitate the screening of signs of socio-political unrest, six categories of social unrest most likely to cause mass incidents in W County, and to which Party officials at all levels are thus instructed to pay particularly close attention, have been designated. First, issues that emerge during harvest seasons; second, events that coincide with important and sensitive memorial dates; third, disputes over the natural resources of W Lake; fourth, serious disagreements regarding economic transactions; fifth, serious struggles regarding marriage; and sixth, serious disputes between neighbors. The OSPLG has prepared detailed action plans for identifying, mediating and controlling potential conflict in each category, and quelling mass incidents if they do break out.[52] It is thus clear that central to the Party-state's endeavor to screen and detect social conflict is a coordinated and systematic pre-emptive framework designed to remove any threat to the county's socio-political stability at an early stage. Also,

> [u]sing the information and intelligence provided by this mechanism, the Party-state can prepare all kinds of action plans well in advance. Once social unrest or turmoil indeed breaks out, the government can handle and stop it as early as possible, as promptly as possible and as effectively as possible.[53]

Mediating social disagreements

Another essential part of the daily operations of the stability-preservation apparatus in W County involves the mediation and resolution of social disagreements (*tiaochu shehuimaodun*, 调处社会矛盾) and the removal of potential causes of political unrest or social upheaval. The CCP Committee of W County has set out the requirements for this mediation work as follows:

> We must proactively mediate and resolve social contradictions and conflict, and take this work as an important pre-emptive measure in stability preservation. The goal is to properly solve each and every social contradiction at the grassroots level and at an early stage. Once social conflict takes place, we should properly solve it based on the principle that 'you should have fewer enemies rather than more', and disagreement should be handled from the perspective of the county's general [socio-political stability] as the top priority.[54]

For this purpose, the OSPLG has re-established a People's Mediation Committee (PMC) in W County, and appointed an influential local community leader as its 'Chief Mediator'. The PMC runs eight Petition and Mediation Groups to help resolve civil disputes at the township level. Higher-ranking officials are dispatched directly from the county government to help village cadres mediate conflict in villages with a higher likelihood of unrest due to existing disputes within their communities. The cadres in each village are instructed to behave as 'servants' to their village community, 'mediators' of social conflicts, 'informants' of public opinion, 'educators' in the implementation of security measures and 'supervisors'

[50]Archival Document 3-16, The CCP Committee of W County and the W County Government, 'Huqu Bianqu Wending Gongzuo Qingkuang Huibao' ['Briefing on the stability-preservation work in the lake and border region'], (November 2008), pp. 3–4.
[51]Interview 20120707-02.
[52]Archival Document 3-21, The Policy Research Office of the CCP Committee of W County, *Diaoyan Yu Tongxun* [*Research Correspondence*] no. 1, (26 February 2006), p. 8.
[53]Archival Document 1-5, The CCP Committee of W County and the W County Government, 'W Xian Wending Gongzuo Qingkuang Huibao' ['Briefing on the conditions of W County's stability-preservation work'], (1 April 2009), p. 6.
[54]Archival Document 1-5, p. 6.

of their village's stability-preservation work.[55] One component of the stability-preservation apparatus is a monthly inspection of the subordinate townships to 'identify and solve social contradictions'. For every instance of social conflict discovered during this tour, the OSPLG requires a separate record to be created in the official database, and a cadre assigned to follow up the case, communicate with the parties in dispute, and report any new information to the OSPLG. The intention is thereby to 'solve the problem when it first emerges and minimize the scale of conflict'.[56]

In addition, all of the senior cadres in W County are required to serve by rotation in the county's Letters and Visits Bureau, to address petitioners' grievances and resolve their issues in a more direct and effective way. The Party-state has established a fund to solve the most difficult problems, 'unaccountable petition cases' (*jian huajie jijin*, 积案化解基金). Twenty percent of this funding is supplied by transfer from the central government budget, and the rest comes from the local government's revenue from land sales. This funding supplies the necessary financial resources to 'buy off' petitioners when necessary.[57] However, local cadres in W County are extremely reluctant to use this fund to 'purchase stability'. As one senior police officer observed,

> in some places, the leaders seek to buy off troublemakers by satisfying their demands. In the long run, however, this only makes the situation worse, because everyone thinks that 'the crying baby gets the milk' (*huiku de haizi younaichi*, 会哭的孩子有奶吃), which tends to encourage an endless cycle of social unrest.

In W County, this funding is considered the last resort, and is rarely used.[58]

The Party-state has set up a strict accountability system to evaluate the performance of cadres in mediating and solving social conflict at the grassroots level. In general, it requires that 'the case is closed, the issue is finished and the relevant parties are satisfied' (*anjie, shiliao, renfu*; 案结,事了,人服): the three criteria for a successful outcome proposed by the central PLAC. If social conflict escalates into political protests or riots that threaten 'the political security and national security' of the Party-state, the cadres responsible are disqualified from promotion for the next few years, and the state agency to which they belong is disqualified from competition for any award, prize or group honor during the same period.[59]

On the spot: handling collective actions

The most visible component of the daily operations of stability preservation in W County is, of course, the handling of imminent or ongoing collective unrest. Despite the provisions made for tight surveillance, coordination and mediation, social conflict of every kind still has the potential to intensify quickly, sometimes giving rise to protests in the street or other forms of public confrontation. At these critical moments, stability-preservation mechanisms must be implemented immediately at the scene of the conflict. Those responsible for stability preservation must control the crowds effectively, take suitable emergency measures and resume social order in the shortest possible time. The ultimate goal is still pre-emptive: to prevent the protest or collective action from escalating into a large social movement or violent riot that could attract media attention.

The handling of mass incidents is part of the routine training of local police; however, the OSPLG always requires the police to deal with contentious activities professionally and with the minimum level of state coercion. When the OSPLG receives notification of an imminent mass incident from informants or through other channels, its representatives inform the local police of the situation, and begin investigative work with village cadres to determine the cause of the unrest, the probable number of participants, the individuals responsible for its organization, and the planned location and schedule of any activity. The results of this investigation are reported to the chief county-level cadres responsible for stability

[56] Archival Document 3-21, p. 8. On the dispatching of higher-rank cadres to important villages, see also Archival Document 3-6, p. 4; and Interview 20120713-01.
[57] Interview 20120625-02.
[58] Interview 20120709-03.
[59] Interview 20120713-01.

preservation, who then give instructions to the police. The police do not usually make arrests or deploy state violence prior to the outburst of a mass incident, as a fierce government response in the early (and emotional) stages of a social protest runs the risk of merely fuelling its fire. While the police monitor the potential protestors and maintain basic order, the stability-preservation apparatus is mobilized in collaboration with township and village governments, with the primary purpose of engaging in direct conversation, discussion and negotiation with the leaders of the movement. This kind of persuasive work can continue until the moment before the crowd bursts onto the street.[60]

When a protest or other form of collective action does takes place, the priorities for cadres and officers on the scene remain roughly the same: to disperse the protestors, limit the scale of their action and end the protest as soon as possible without applying massive state force and attracting media attention. A district-level police inspector described the behavior of the police force at such times as follows:

> One of the basic principles set by the Ministry of Public Security is the careful deployment of police force [at the scene of a mass incident]. Although we always arrive as soon as the collective action starts, our primary job is to ensure an orderly gathering and ensure that the persuasive work carried out by Party-state officials can continue. So long as the protestors do not assault civilian officials or smash public property, we do not forcefully intervene ... In W County, we basically rely on direct communication and conversation with the leaders of protests, as well as our collective strength [*qunzhong gongzuo*, 群众工作], to solve problems.[61]

A senior police official explained the principle in more general terms:

> Even when the police are on the spot of public protests, our role is still pre-emptive. Our purpose, by taking proper measures very carefully, is to direct the crowd to be calm and to facilitate the government's work in mediating conflicts on the spot and negotiating with both sides of the conflict ... In our opinion, if we were to use violent means on the protesting masses regardless of the concrete situation, we would only make the confrontation more radical and aggressive. For stability preservation, our work on the spot of a protest is to set a boundary for the people and let them know which things they absolutely cannot do according to the law. By maintaining the basic order on the scene, we create conditions for our colleagues in the stability preservation system to do their job and to pacify the tension in a more effective way.[62]

The handling of political crises is a test of the capacity of an authoritarian state. The case of W County indicates the state's strong preference for pre-emptive measures over outright violence to preserve stability, even in the most critical moments. The entire *weiwen* apparatus appears to be founded on the constrained deployment of a police force and the importance of 'mass work' in preventing imminent social unrest from breaking out and in putting a halt to existing social upheavals.

Concluding remarks

As Jennifer Gandhi and Adam Przeworski argued, 'institutions do matter under authoritarian regimes'.[63] Recently, increasing scholarly attention has been paid to the ways in which various authoritarian institutions are used to facilitate policy compromise, coalition building, regime consolidation and national defense. However, as David Art pointed out, the early scholarship on authoritarian institutions tended to 'focus on the democratic-looking features of authoritarian regimes at the expense of, ironically, their authoritarian ones'.[64] Indeed, the institutions that supply the means for monitoring society, detecting problems, mediating conflict and preventing anti-systematic social unrest are precisely the components that define a regime as authoritarian.

To understand the endurance of the PRC's authoritarian regime, it is all the more important to place its authoritarian institutions in context, and to examine the regime's everyday practice of power through these dynamic agencies of control. In this article, the author has shown that the stability-preservation

---

[60]Interview 20120709-03.
[61]Interview 20120709-03.
[62]Interview 20120713-02.
[63]Jennifer Grandhi and Adam Przeworski, 'Authoritarian institutions and the survival of autocrats', *Comparative Political Studies* 40(11), (2007), pp. 1279–1301.
[64]David Art, 'What do we know about authoritarianism after ten years?', *Comparative Politics* 44(3), (2012), pp. 351–373.

apparatus operating in W County indicates that the Party-state in China has woven a tight and dynamic net of pre-emptive surveillance and control, which is a crucial component of the regime's overall effort to protect the body politic. These pre-emptive processes help the regime to detect and handle all kinds of potential threats to socio-political stability, and ensure that the power of the Party-state is not shaken by any outright collective defiance. This unique institutional feature of the authoritarian regime in the PRC merits considerably more attention from scholars and observers who seek to predict the future of the country.

Compared to similar autocratic regimes in other parts of the world, the stability-preservation system in W County has three distinct features. First, the entire *weiwen* apparatus in W County goes beyond the usual concept of 'law enforcement' or 'coercive' agencies under authoritarian regimes, in that it appears to be a more synthesized, better coordinated and closely supervised Party-state bureaucracy that enjoys wide intergovernmental support based on cross-agency and cross-regional collaboration. The PRC's efforts in system maintenance—at least in well-run counties—are regularized, bureaucratized, routinized and neatly integrated into the regime's daily operations and system-wide workflow. Second, although W County possesses considerable coercive force, its stability-preservation apparatus appears to be intentionally focused on everyday pre-emptive actions that aim to prevent major social turmoil from taking place, rather than preparations for heavy-handed control and repression in the event of violent social unrest. This requires the rather mundane monitoring of potential social conflict, the daily monitoring and solving of social tensions, and dealing with social problems before they escalate into hard-to-control situations or actual riots. In fact, by operating a highly organized and routinized stability-preservation apparatus that focuses on its day-to-day engagement with grassroots society, the Party-state apparatchiks in W County have successfully avoided the use of excessive state violence in maintaining public order and overall socio-political stability. Third, the stability-preservation apparatus in W County is characterized by an institutionalized division of labor that is based on the hierarchical ranks of the Party-state. While the Party-state agencies higher-up in the ranks may be more concerned about political dissent, regime challenges or underground religious activities, the W County stability-preservation apparatus—which is at the very grassroots of the incumbent regime—devotes all of its attention to detecting, locating and solving everyday social conflicts, problems and tensions. After all, the Party-state's efficient, localized and mundane efforts in extending its reach to China's grassroots society have enabled the incumbent political regime to build its strength and consolidate the durability of its socio-political basis, at least at the beginning of the twenty-first century.[55]Interview 20120713-02.

Acknowledgements

The author wishes to thank Zhou Kai and Jiang Weikang for their research assistance in conducting fieldwork. The valuable comments and suggestions offered by the anonymous reviewer and editor of *Journal of Contemporary China* are highly appreciated. The author is grateful for the generous funding support provided by the Research Grants Council of the Hong Kong Special Administrative Region (Project # 790012) and the University of Hong Kong.

Appendix A. Notes on fieldwork

W County is located in North China. In 2012, W County had a population of around 720,000, comprising 29 ethnic groups, including a significant Hui Muslim population. Although W County is small in size and remote from the major provincial centers, it has achieved relatively strong local industrial development. In terms of per capita GDP and per capita income,

W County is ranked in the middle for the Prefecture and around 50th–60th among the 173 country-level jurisdictions in the Province.

Permission to access archives and conduct field interviews was granted by the Politics and Law Committee of the supervisory prefectural municipality through a personal network, with full disclosure of the intent of the academic research. The archives the author consulted included the archives of the Public Security Bureau of W County and the Politics and Law Committee of W County (also known as the County Stability Preservation Office), and the County Archives. Documents from the early 1980s to the present were examined, including general working documents, briefings, reports, instructions and official statistics. The interviews were arranged through the County's Public Security Bureau in the form of a series of individual or group meetings. All interviews were fully recorded and transcribed, and the personal identities of the interviewees were removed. The author had relatively broad and unrestrained access to all of the above-mentioned archives, except for documents related to classified information. The author was unable to consult the archives of other relevant Party-state agencies, such as the Propaganda Department, Organization Department or the County Militia.

Index

Note: **Boldface** page number refer to figures and tables, Page number followed by n denote endnotes.

INDEX

For Product Safety Concerns and Information please contact our EU
representative GPSR@taylorandfrancis.com
Taylor & Francis Verlag GmbH, Kaufingerstraße 24, 80331 München, Germany

www.ingramcontent.com/pod-product-compliance
Ingram Content Group UK Ltd.
Pitfield, Milton Keynes, MK11 3LW, UK
UKHW052055230926
475702UK00031B/2830
* 9 7 8 0 3 6 7 1 3 9 3 1 5 *